Editor: Donna Wood
Designer: Kat Mead
Verifiers: John Sparshatt of the LDWA and Jennifer Wood
Picture Researcher: Lesley Grayson
Image retouching and internal repro: Jackie Street
Cartography provided by the Mapping Services Department of AA Publishing
Contains Ordnance Survey data © Crown copyright and database right 2011
Production: Rachel Davis

Produced by AA Publishing
© Copyright AA Media Limited 2011

ISBN: 978-0-7495-6911-2 and 978-0-7495-6923-5 (SS)

Published by AA Publishing (a trading name of AA Media Limited, whose registered office
is Fanum House, Basing View, Basingstoke RG21 4EA; registered number 06112600).

A04541

The contents of this book are believed correct at the time of printing. Nevertheless, the
publishers cannot be held responsible for any errors or omissions or for changes in the
details given in this book or for the consequences of any reliance on the information
provided by the same. This does not affect your statutory rights.

Printed and bound in China by 1010 Printing International Ltd.

theAA.com/shop

LONG DISTANCE WALKERS' ASSOCIATION

This book has been compiled with the help of the Long Distance Walkers' Association (LDWA), an organization that has pioneered the communication of information on the Long-distance Path (LDP) network in the UK since its formation in 1972. With over 150 routes developed by 1980, it published its first comprehensive directory, the *Long Distance Walkers' Handbook*, edited by one of its founders, Barbara Blatchford. The latest edition has details of over 720 long-distance routes.

The LDWA is a users' association, rather than a campaigning organization. It aims to 'further the interests of those who enjoy long-distance walking', with a particular emphasis on non-competitive walking in rural, mountainous and moorland areas. As well as covering long-distance paths, it promotes 'challenge walks'. These are cross-country walks, sometimes based on an LDP, undertaken by many walkers on the same occasion aiming to complete a route within a given time limit. Its challenge walks range up to 100 miles.

Since 1985 the LDWA has been recognized by Sport England (formerly the Sports Council) as the governing body for long-distance walking. The LDWA has over 7,000 members and 40 local groups across Britain, each with programmes of regular walks. Its members' magazine, *Strider*, is produced three times a year. It covers all aspects of long-distance walking, including path updates and features, listings and reports of challenge walks, and local groups' programmes.

Similar listings are available on its public website and non-members are welcome on most of these social walks and events. The LDWA maintains a public 'National Trails Register', open to anyone completing several National Trails, with an attractive range of certificates up to 'diamond' standard for those achieving all of the British Trails. It also maintains a 'Hillwalkers' Register' for those who have completed ascents of hills in various categories.

New members can join online at www.ldwa.org.uk or email membership@ldwa.org.uk.

WALKERS' BRITAIN

DISCOVERING 30 LONG-DISTANCE FOOTPATHS

AA

Contents

Spey Bay

29

Tomintoul

Fort William

Scotland

28

St Andrews

30

Milngavie

Inverkeithing

Kirk Yetholm

27

Carlisle

Alston

26

The North Country

Bowness

Helmsley

Filey Brigg

Ulverston

23

Gavel Gap

22

24

25

Longton

Ilkley

Hessle

Castleton

19

Matlock

Mow Cop

18

Wales &
the Marches

Abbots Bromley

Central England & East Anglia

Cromer

20

21

Great Yarmouth

Knettishall Heath

Hay-on-Wye

Chipping Campden

Dedham

Goodwick

14

Abergavenny

17

4

Ivinghoe Beacon

13

Broad Haven

Tredegar

Painswick

Bourton-on-
the-Water

Epping

15

16

Chepstow

12

Newport

Caerleon

11

Henley-on-Thames

South & South East England

Overton Hill

Inkpen Beacon

St Martha's Hill

Gravesend

Lynmouth

1

King Alfred's Tower

Witley

Dorking

Braunton

6

9

10

3

Queen Elizabeth
Country Park

8

The West Country

Ham Hill

7

Yeoford

Emsworth

Botolphs

Eastbourne

2

5

Ryde

Ivybridge

Introduction

In Britain, a long-distance path, known colloquially as an LDP, is usually defined as a route of at least 20 miles (32km) that has been given a distinctive name, and for which a guide exists. Sometimes shorter routes are also referred to as long-distance paths, especially if they provide a link between two other long-distance paths. The term 'wayfarer' is applied to a person who walks a long-distance path, as in 'Pennine wayfarer'.

It is likely that the Schwarzwaldverein (Black Forest Association), formed in Germany in 1864, was the first organization to promote and develop long-distance paths. The first of these was the 280-mile (450km) West Way from Pforzheim to Basle, opened in 1900, which was followed in 1903 by the 145-mile (233km) Middle Way (Pforzheim to Waldshut), and the 148-mile (238km) East Way (Pforzheim to Schaflhausen). Sweden established the Kungsleden in Lapland before World War I, and James Paddock Taylor founded the Green Mountain Club and began to carve out the 265-mile (426km) Long Trail, from Massachusetts to the Canadian border, in 1910.

In 1921, Benton MacKaye first proposed the establishment of the 2,113-mile (3,400km) Appalachian Trail down the eastern side of the United States from Maine to Georgia, which was completed in 1937.

In England, Tom Stephenson first publicized the idea of establishing a long-distance path along the watershed of northern England in an article in the *Daily Herald* newspaper in June 1935. This led to the formation of the Pennine Way Association, but long-distance paths were not formally established in England until the implementation of the National Parks and Access to the Countryside Act of 1949, which followed the publication of the Hobhouse Report. Scotland and Northern Ireland had to wait much longer for legislation.

Long-distance paths have been established in most European countries, as well as in other developed nations. There are now a number of European international long-distance paths (E routes) that crisscross Western Europe, and it is likely that as time goes by there will be progressively more links with the long-distance routes in Eastern Europe.

FOUR KINDS OF PATH

There are four kinds of long-distance path in the United Kingdom: National Trails, regional routes promoted and maintained by local authorities, other long-distance paths which have a valid publication, and 'open challenge' walks, listed and promoted by the LDWA, often with a certificate and badge available for a successful completion.

There is no uniform legislation governing rights of way and long-distance paths in the United Kingdom, and each constituent country has its own distinctive laws. England and Wales have many more LDPs than Scotland and Northern Ireland.

In England and Wales, National Trails were first established under the provisions of the National Parks and Access to the Countryside Act, 1949. In England, the following National Trails are the responsibility of Natural England: the Cleveland Way, the Cotswold Way, Hadrian's Wall Path, the North Downs Way, the Peddars Way and Norfolk Coast Path, the Pennine Way, the Pennine Bridleway, the Ridgeway, the South Downs Way, the South West Coast Path, the Thames Path and the Yorkshire Wolds Way.

In Wales, the Countryside Council for Wales is responsible for Offa's Dyke Path, Glyndwr's Way/Llwybr Glyndwr and the Pembrokeshire Coast Path. In Scotland, provision for the creation of long-distance paths was included in the Countryside (Scotland) Act of 1967, which also established the Countryside Commission for Scotland (now Scottish Natural Heritage). This is the body responsible for the Great Glen Way, Southern Upland Way, the Speyside Way, and the West Highland Way. Initially, the concept of LDPs was not received enthusiastically by many Scottish walkers, who feared that their existence would compromise the traditional freedom that exists in Scotland to roam in open country.

Northern Ireland currently has nine promoted Waymarked Ways. These are walking routes spread across Northern Ireland and accredited by the Northern Ireland Countryside Access and Activities Network (CAAN), an umbrella organization. The CAAN website, www.walkni.com, provides excellent information on these routes, including useful updates.

National Trails and many other long-distance paths are plotted and named on Ordnance Survey maps. However, it is always advisable to have the appropriate guide book with you when following a long-distance path.

The Long Distance Walkers Association (LDWA) is a voluntary organization that exists to further the interests of those who enjoy long-distance walking. It promotes organized challenge walks, pioneers new walking routes and receives and publishes information on all aspects of non-competitive walking. It maintains a free online database of over 1,200 long-distance paths on its website, www.ldwa.org.uk. The LDWA is recognized as the governing body for the activity of long-distance walking, and information on the various walks, including some detailed guides, can be downloaded from the LDWA website.

The Ramblers' Association (2nd Floor, Camelford House, 87-90 Albert Embankment, London SE1 7TW, telephone +44 (0)20 7339 8500; www.ramblers.org.uk), is the national organization that looks after the interests of all walkers in Britain. It aims to help everyone towards a greater love, knowledge and care of the countryside, and works hard to keep open and protect rights of way, including long-distance paths.

ENJOYING BRITAIN'S SPECTACULAR SCENERY

For such a small country, Britain is blessed with a variety of outstandingly beautiful scenery, which makes walking a delight. There are few other countries in the world where, during the course of a day's walking, you can pass from airy cliffs or sand dunes through riverside, meadow and woodlands to towering crag-bound lakes and mountains.

This collection of the best of the LDPs includes walks in some of the most attractive parts of England, Wales and Scotland. The whole British landscape has been described as a palimpsest – a living manuscript that has been written on over and over again – and with a little knowledge it can be read like a book. The first thing that a landscape historian discovers, as Professor W G Hoskins pointed out around 50 years ago, is that everything is older than you think. Those dimpled impressions in a clearing of the conifers in Norfolk's Breckland mark the neolithic flint mines, which were among the first industrial sites in Britain. That insignificant mound on a Peak District hilltop may be the last resting place of a Bronze Age prince, buried with all his riches some 4,000 years ago. And those strange corrugations that mark many Midland pastures, or the step-like lynchets on the slopes of the southern chalk downlands, show where every available piece of land had to be cultivated to counter the threat of starvation in the early medieval period.

Strategic sites are a feature of LDPs, their presence recalling a violent past. Border towns like the ancient city of Carlisle, which first developed as a Roman frontier town when Hadrian's Wall was built, went on to play a part in the Border Wars between Scotland and England for 600 years. A network of ancient tracks crosses our countryside, from the prehistoric Ridgeway over the Wessex downs to the paved packhorse routes of the Pennines. These once important arteries of commerce and industry now offer quiet highways rich in history for the observant walker.

Many other areas remain treasured havens for wildlife: the ancient beechwoods of the Cotswolds, the coastal paths of Devon and Cornwall, the marshes and fens of the Norfolk Broads; you may be surprised at the diversity that survives in Britain. The scenery of the British Isles, whether spectacular or gentle, wild or welcoming, has often inspired great human artistic achievements, and many of these walks lead you in the footsteps of great writers, thinkers, painters and poets who have been influenced by its ever-changing landscape.

TOP, LEFT TO RIGHT
Early morning mist surrounds hikers on the shore of the lake at Buttermere; Ribblehead Viaduct in the Yorkshire Dales; rowing boats moored on Derwent Water

USING THIS BOOK

This book describes in detail specially selected highlights from 30 long-distance paths in Britain. For the purposes of the book, the country is divided into six regions, as shown on the Locator Map on page 5. Each region of Britain is well covered with long-distance paths; there are four in the West Country, nine in South & South East England, four in Wales & the Marches, four in Central England & East Anglia, six in the North Country and three in Scotland. The description of each walk starts with a general introduction, describing the terrain and the history of the area, accompanied by a map of the long-distance path or, in some cases, the section of it covered in this book. The distances of the complete route covered by the long-distance path is given, as well as just the section covered in this book.

Also on these introductory pages is a Useful Information panel, giving details of Tourist Information Centres along the way and other sites that will assist in planning your trip, and the Ordnance Survey 1:25,000 Explorer maps that it is strongly recommended walkers take with them. Other long-distance paths that cross or coincide with the route are also listed, making it possible to plan further walks.

A detailed route description follows the introduction, divided into sections that may generally be walked in an average day by a person of reasonable fitness. Precise starting points are given, with grid references, and details of car parking places where possible. 'Escapes' are suggested (marked with a house symbol) for those who may wish to leave the path and return home or back to the start point using a different route or, in some cases, public transport. Grid references are given for the break-out point, but full details of these 'escape' routes are not given in the text, or on the map, and readers will need to refer to the relevant Ordnance Survey map or local guides if they wish to take advantage of them.

To help in planning the walk, whether it be an afternoon's outing or a full week's hike, the Places to Visit panel lists places of interest on or near the path. The LDWA and Ramblers' Association websites both have information on accommodation and public transport specific to the routes. The official route guidebooks often provide help, too. The Tourist Information Centres listed will provide further details of accommodation and public transport (or, in the case of buses, may refer the reader to the relevant local bus company or enquiry line). Note that, although a place may be described in this book as 'open all year', it may be closed over Christmas, and that bank holidays may affect normal opening hours. It is always advisable to check current opening times in advance by telephone or via the website to avoid disappointment.

THE MAPS

The maps show the featured section of the long-distance path, marked with a red dotted line and broken down into stages as they are covered in the text. All maps are orientated north but are shown at slightly different scales. Refer to the scale bar on each map.

GRID REFERENCES AND HOW TO USE THEM

Grid references are given in this book for specific points of interest. These may be used with Ordnance Survey and other maps which make use of the National Grid.

The National Grid divides Britain into 100km squares, each of which is identified by two capital letters, such as SO. Each 100km square is in turn divided into 10km squares, which, on the Ordnance Survey 1:50,000 Landranger and 1:25,000 Outdoor Leisure and Pathfinder walkers' maps, are further sub-divided into 1km squares. The vertical lines dividing the 1km squares are known as Eastings, while the horizontal lines dividing the 1km squares are called Northings. Each grid reference in this book has six numbers. The first two numbers refer to the Eastings vertical grid line read from left to right across the map, while the third number refers to each 10th of a kilometre (100 metres) from left to right. The fourth and fifth numbers refer to the Northings horizontal grid lines read upwards from the bottom of the map, with the sixth number referring to each 10th of a kilometre upwards. Using these numbers, draw an Eastings line up or down the map and a Northings line across; the intersection of the two lines is the point in question. The reverse procedure is used to provide the grid reference for any point. Eastings must always be quoted before the Northings.

ABBREVIATIONS USED IN THE TEXT

LDP: Long-distance path
NT: National Trust
EH: English Heritage
Cadw: Welsh Historic Monuments
TIC: Tourist Information Centre

TOP LEFT An azure sky enhances an uphill climb over farmland
TOP RIGHT Youlgeave near Bakewell in Derbyshire
MIDDLE Ross-on-Wye by the River Wye
BOTTOM Daisies growing along the wayside

MAP LEGEND

M4 Motorway with number	Transport café	Toll Road toll, steep gradient (arrows point downhill)
Toll T4 Toll motorway with toll station	BATH Primary route destination	Railway line, in tunnel
11 Motorway junction with and without number	A1123 Other A road single/dual carriageway	Railway station and level crossing
3 Restricted motorway junctions	B2070 B road single/dual carriageway	Tourist railway
S Fleet Motorway service area	Minor road more than 4 metres wide, less than 4 metres wide	Airport, heliport international freight terminal
Motorway and junction under construction	Roundabout	City, town, village or other built-up area
A3 Primary route single/dual carriageway	Interchange/junction	628 637 Lecht Summit Height in metres, mountain pass
11 Primary route junction with and without number	Narrow primary/other A/B road with passing places (Scotland)	Sandy beach
3 Restricted primary route junctions	Road under construction	National boundary
S Grantham North Primary route service area	Road tunnel	County, administrative boundary

Scenic route	Aqueduct or viaduct	Hill-fort	Ski slope (natural, artificial)
Tourist Information Centre	Garden, arboretum	Roman antiquity	National Trust property (England & Wales, Scotland)
Tourist Information Centre (seasonal)	Vineyard	Prehistoric monument	English Heritage site
Visitor or heritage centre	Country Park	Battle site with year	Historic Scotland site
Picnic site	Agricultural showground	Steam railway centre	Cadw (Welsh heritage) site
Caravan site	Theme park	Cave	Other place of interest
Camping site	Farm or animal centre	Windmill	Boxed symbols indicate attractions within urban areas
Caravan & camping site	Zoological or wildlife collection	Monument	World Heritage Site (UNESCO)
Abbey, cathedral or priory	Bird collection	Golf course	National Park and National Scenic Area (Scotland)
Ruined abbey, cathedral or priory	Aquarium	County cricket ground	Forest Park
Castle	RSPB site	Rugby Union national stadium	Heritage Coast
Historic house or building	National Nature Reserve (England, Scotland, Wales)	International athletics stadium	RYDE Start/finish point
Museum or art gallery	Local nature reserve	Horse racing, show jumping	6 Stage number
Industrial interest	Viewpoint	Air show venue, motor-racing circuit	

PLANNING A LONG-DISTANCE WALK

Planning a long-distance walk can be almost as much fun and as rewarding as the walk itself. It can involve many evenings poring over guides and maps, working out daily itineraries, accommodation and transport. When planning your walk, bear in mind the following guidelines:

BOOTS AND CLOTHING

What to wear will depend on the weather and the terrain. Over lowlands in summer, trainers and light clothing such as shorts and a T-shirt may suffice if the weather is guaranteed settled. However, 15 miles (24km) or more can be a full day's walking, and that gives the British weather plenty of time to change its mind. Much greater care needs to be taken in colder weather or when walking in the hills, where rapid changes in temperature can be brought about by the onset of mist, wind or rain. Extra clothing should be carried, to be put on or taken off in layers, which provide insulation by trapping the air between them. Two middleweight sweatshirts are better than a single heavy pullover. So for a long-distance day walk in summer, consider clothing that includes T-shirt, sweatshirts, shorts, long thick socks which can be rolled down or pulled up as required, and lightweight walking boots, or possibly trainers if the terrain allows. If there is any chance of rain, carry waterproofs. A jacket made in a brightly coloured, lightweight, breathable material is to be preferred; most of these are designed to fold up into a small bag which can conveniently be worn on a belt.

For winter, a heavier duty, fully waterproof coat and overtrousers are necessary, along with waterproof boots and gaiters to keep water out of the top of the boots. Quick-drying polycotton trousers are usually worn, with extra layers of insulation provided by pullovers over a shirt or thermal vest. Waterproof mittens provide the most effective protection for the hands, while a woolly hat prevents heat loss from the head.

A good pair of boots is vital for happy long-distance walking, although in warm weather, if the ground is dry and you are not carrying much weight, a pair of trainers with a thick sole and a good grip may prove more comfortable. Proper walking boots are essential for rough or rocky terrain, and steep downhill walking. In the old days it was considered necessary to 'walk boots in', but with a well-designed modern boot that fits properly this is no longer necessary. When buying new boots, always try

them on with thick walking socks, and check there is enough length in the boot by sliding your index finger down behind your heel and wiggling your toes. The lacing can be adjusted to hold the boot rigidly. Fully waterproof boots, with sewn-in watertight tongues, are a must for British long-distance walking.

EXTRA EQUIPMENT

A long-distance walker must compromize between what is needed, and what can comfortably be carried. For those who are not carrying camping gear, a lightweight daysack should suffice for basic necessities: waterproofs, spare sweaters, hat and gloves, map and compass, mobile phone, watch, whistle to summon help if lost or injured, pencil and notebook to keep a note of your progress, food and drink as necessary, plus emergency rations such as chocolate bars, nuts and raisins, or mint cake. Those who choose to backpack can stay in their own tent whenever possible, which is both convenient and cheap. However, it requires a long list of extra equipment, the most important item being a comfortable, waterproof nylon backpack, mounted on an internal or external frame. The weight of the pack should be no more than a quarter of the weight of the person carrying it. The heaviest items should be carried as high up and as close to the shoulders as possible. Another golden rule is last in, first out, which makes packing a backpack a thought-provoking exercise. The average kit needed for backpacking may include a tent of sufficient size, an insulated sleeping mat, a sleeping bag, a torch, extra clothing for sitting around in on a cold night, a stove, food and drink, mug, plate and cutlery, water container, basic materials for washing-up, tin opener, first aid box, complete change of clothing and personal washing gear.

HOW TO NAVIGATE WITH A COMPASS

A compass is an invaluable aid to navigation which should be carried on a lanyard round the neck at all times. Despite the fact that most long-distance paths are well signposted, when visibility is bad and no landmarks can be seen, the compass may be the only means there is of finding the way. Most modern walkers' compasses are based on the Swedish-made 'Silva' which is lightweight, tough, and easy to use. Principal components are the compass base, fitted with direction-of-travel arrow and a magnifying glass, and the rotating compass dial with orienting

TOP Looking along the River Bure to Stracey Arms Mill, near Acle
MIDDLE The 12th-century Garrison Tower at Usk Castle
BOTTOM The south transept of the largely 14th-century Tintern Abbey ruins

arrow, enclosing a red compass needle which naturally points to magnetic north. (The vertical lines, or Eastings, on an OS map point to grid north, which may be a little different from magnetic north, though by an insufficient margin to affect navigation.) The 'Silva' method of navigation combines following a compass-bearing while walking towards a landmark. First place the compass flat on the map with one of its edges aligned with the route. Turn the dial until the letter N points to north as shown on the map; then pick up the compass, and turn round until the red end of the compass needle points to N on the dial. The direction-of-travel arrow then points in the direction of the route; if possible, pick a landmark and walk towards it.

ESTIMATING TIME AND DISTANCE

The time taken to complete a section of a long-distance path depends on your own experience and level of fitness, prevailing weather conditions, and the type of terrain to be walked. For instance, on a hard track it is possible to walk at a good speed, but that speed may be halved when crossing rough moorland.

The main governing factor of speed and time taken is likely to be the number of hills encountered on the way. Naismith's Rule is a formula used by walkers to estimate how long it will take to cover a particular distance and height. It suggests you should allow 15 minutes for every kilometre covered on flat ground, plus four minutes for every 30 metres of height to be climbed. Changed into miles and feet, which were the measurements originally used by Naismith, this means you should allow one hour for every 2.5 miles over flat ground, plus one hour for every 1,500 feet to be climbed. The daily mileage covered on a long-distance walk should be less than one normal day's walk a) to take into account the extra weight carried in a backpack and b) because it is more taxing to walk apace for consecutive days.

SAFETY

Ten principal rules for safe LDP walking are:
1. Choose a route that reflects your walking experience; do not attempt the Pennine Way, for instance, if you have never walked in wild terrain. Always plan out each section of your route. Be sure to take a compass and map, and make sure you know how to use them. When walking on high ground, avoid low cloud and mist on the hills if possible. If you are not sure where you are, do not be shy about asking for help from other walkers.
2. Check what clothing and equipment you should take with you. Always carry a watch, a pen or pencil and some waterproof card to write on, and a mobile phone, although mobile phones have limited coverage in deep valleys and remote areas. Take snacks as necessary. In hot weather it is important to carry sufficient drink. Carry information about public transport and taxi services in case of emergencies.
3. Tell someone responsible where you are making for, and when you expect to arrive. When estimating how long a particular walk will take, never risk getting caught by nightfall, especially on hills or mountains. In winter, always carry a torch with spare batteries. If you are caught by nightfall, make your way slowly and carefully to the nearest road. Book accommodation in advance.
4. When walking on a road, walk towards oncoming traffic. Wear bright clothing so you are easily spotted. At night, swing a torch in your roadside hand so that drivers will be sure to see you.
5. Check the weather forecast. If high wind, heavy rain, fog or mist are forecast, do not commit yourself to a long distance. Keep an eye on the weather while walking and, if it turns bad, decide in plenty of time whether to turn back or to look for an escape route to lower, safer ground.
6. If it starts raining, put on waterproofs immediately. Do not risk getting wet and cold.
7. Keep your party together. Wait for anyone who is slow.
8. A whistle is easily carried, and useful for signaling in an emergency. The international distress signal is six long blasts, followed by a pause of one minute. The answering signal is three long blasts. The same signaling technique can be used with a handkerchief or clothing or with a torch if it is dark. If you are being rescued by a helicopter, the ground to air signal is a Y.
9. A small first aid kit should be part of your equipment. This should contain plasters, dressings, blister pads, bandages, safety pins, antiseptic cream, a small pair of scissors, and tweezers to remove splinters.
10. In the case of a serious accident, one person must stay with the injured person while a competent map-reader goes to find help. The guidelines for helping a severely injured person are: prevent further injury, make the injured comfortable without unnecessary movement, maintain breathing and circulation, control bleeding, treat for shock, get help.

TOP Winter in Keswick and Skiddaw, Lake District National Park
MIDDLE Loch Tulla near Bridge of Orchy
BOTTOM Osborne House and Garden on the Isle of Wight, beloved home of Queen Victoria

A bench with a view at Cleeve Common

The West Country

South West Coast Path

COMPLETE ROUTE MINEHEAD TO POOLE HARBOUR **630 MILES (1014KM)**
SECTION COVERED LYNMOUTH TO BRAUNTON **42 MILES (68KM)**
MAPS OS EXPLORER OL 9, 139

The South West Coast Path is the longest National Trail in Britain. It runs from Minehead in Somerset to South Haven Point at Poole Harbour in Dorset. On this path, walkers can enjoy some of the country's finest and most varied coastal landscapes, from rugged and remote clifftops to sheltered estuaries, busy harbours and resorts. Two World Heritage Sites cover sections of the coastline, adding to the interest of this exciting route. This book covers a section of 42 miles (68km) between Lynmouth and Braunton, chosen because it offers great contrasts, from the high cliffs of the Bristol Channel to the Atlantic surf and sand, and the sheltered Taw estuary. The Bristol Channel coast is relatively sheltered; it faces north and the prevailing winds are southwesterly. In the lee to the east of the headlands, woods often cloak the cliffs. These are fairly undisturbed and contain a great variety of wildlife, including rare whitebeam trees. Red deer can be found in the wooded combes and cliffs. Atlantic grey seals breed on Lundy Island and are frequent visitors to this coast.

The coastal heaths in some of the more exposed areas are a blaze of colour in late summer, with purple bell heather and bright yellow gorse. Look out for the pink-flowered parasite dodder on the gorse. Baggy Point has some Cornish heath, possibly introduced. Braunton Burrows claims over 400 species of plants. It is particularly resplendent with orchids in June and July, along with marsh helleborine and round-leaved wintergreen in the dune slacks. Seabirds nest all along the higher cliffs. Gulls and fulmars are found throughout, shags and cormorants in places, and guillemots, razorbills and kittiwakes at Martinhoe and the Valley of Rocks. Jackdaws and ravens are common, although choughs ceased to nest early last century. Peregrine falcons are making a comeback after disappearing as a breeding bird in the 1960s. The Taw estuary abounds with wintering waders.

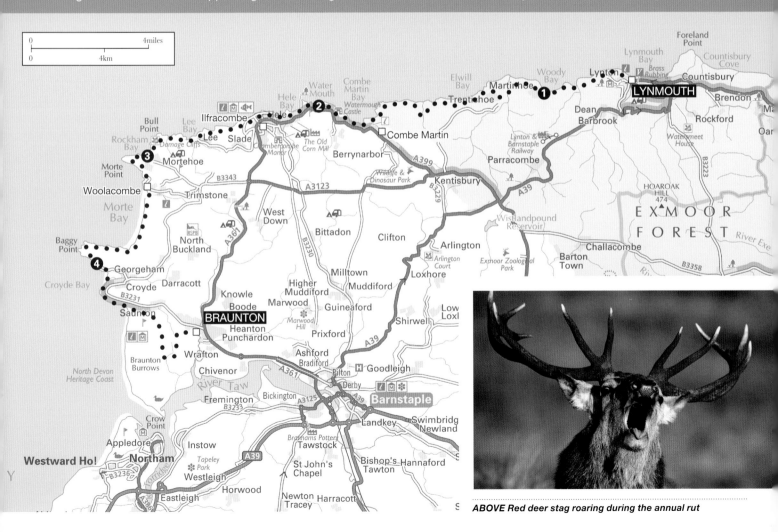

ABOVE Red deer stag roaring during the annual rut

LYNMOUTH TO ILFRACOMBE

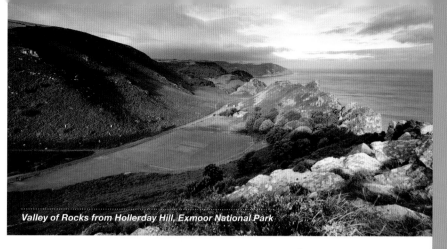

Valley of Rocks from Hollerday Hill, Exmoor National Park

STAGE 1

LYNMOUTH to COMBE MARTIN

DISTANCE 12.9 miles (20.8km)
MAP OS Explorer OL 9
START AT GRID REFERENCE SS 723 494
START POINT Lyndale Bridge at Lynmouth

Lynmouth is an attractive village at the confluence and mouth of the East and West Lyn Rivers. A disastrous flood occurred here in 1952, reminders of which are at the Glen Lyn Gorge (there is a charge for the walk along West Lyn River) and Flood Memorial Hall on The Esplanade. Lynmouth retains its Victorian character, with some older cottages above flood level on Mars Hill and around Shelley's Cottage, near where the poet lived for a while.

Walk to the Cliff Railway at the far end of The Esplanade. The path lies up some steps between the two, zig-zagging across the Cliff Railway and eventually turning right along the level North Walk to the Valley of Rocks. To save the climb, use the railway, turning left at Lee Road at the top, and then left again at the church and down to North Walk.

OPEN CLIFFS AND UFOs

The route continues along the toll road (free to walkers) past Lee Abbey, a Christian retreat near Lee Bay. Follow the narrow road upwards towards Woody Bay Hotel, near which the path drops through woods. It then ascends the Woody Bay road for a short distance and turns off to the right at a hairpin bend in the road. If you like, detour down the road to the bay, with its old cottage, limekiln and base of a pier which was demolished in 1903 after a futile attempt to develop Woody Bay as a tourist resort. Alternatively, detour uphill to the road towards Martinhoe and turn off at the next hairpin bend along a path running parallel with the main Coast Path to the Hunters Inn. This passes the site of Martinhoe Roman Signal Station, a fine viewpoint. The main path continues through oak woods and out into a dramatic section of open cliff from Hollow Brook waterfall to the Heddon valley. The path descends from Highveer Point to the River Heddon. Here, a detour can be made downstream to the pebbly beach with its limekiln, or upstream to the Hunters Inn (refreshments and toilets).

From the Heddon valley (grid ref. SS 654 489), you can return to Lynmouth on an inland route, via the Hunters Inn. A road runs steeply uphill beside the inn to Mannacott Farm. A path runs through the farm

up to the road at Martinhoe. Follow the road to Slattenslade, from where a path leads to Croscombe Barton and Lee. From Lee, a path overlooking the Valley of Rocks leads to Lynton along South Cleave.

The main path crosses the river a short distance upstream, then zig-zags up the cleave and out to Peter Rock and an exposed section of the route. It then follows the cliff along the heads of various 'guts', or gullies, to Holdstone Down. This heath-clad hill is believed by many to have mystical qualities and reports of UFO sightings here are common.

The path continues along the estate drive known as Sea View Road down into Sherrycombe and up towards Great Hangman. A detour can be made along an old miners' track to Blackstone Point, where there were iron mines in the 19th century. Return to the main path, which continues over Great Hangman to Little Hangman and descends Lester Cliff to the car park and Information Centre at Combe Martin.

From Combe Martin (grid ref. SS 577 473), return to the Hunters Inn and the Heddon valley via the main street. This passes the 18th-century Pack o' Cards inn, built like a card house, to the crossroads near the church. Continue up the street to Combe Martin Wildlife and Dinosaur Park or turn left up Comer Lane and past the old silver mine, then right along minor roads and path to Holdstone Farm, Trentishoe and the Hunters Inn.

STAGE 2

COMBE MARTIN to ILFRACOMBE

DISTANCE 5.2 miles (8.4km)
MAP OS Explorer OL 9
START AT GRID REFERENCE SS 577 473
START POINT Kiln car park, adjacent to Combe Martin Beach

Combe Martin's harbour was never fully developed, despite ambitious plans. In the 19th century, however, it was important for the export of iron and copper ores from Exmoor to South Wales, and the import from that area of limestone and coal. The lime was used for making cement and plaster, and for dressing the acid Exmoor soils during moorland reclamation. There are old silver workings in Lester Point at the far end of the beach.

The path keeps close to the edge of the bay, passing Combe Martin Visitor Centre. At the far side of the beach some rough steps cut in the rocks are said to have been made by Phoenicians coming to trade for local silver. The path climbs the lane at the back of the beach and up to the main road. After a short ascent, it diverts alongside the main road, rejoining it further up. Turn right along the old road to reach Sandy Cove Hotel. A track alongside the hotel takes the route past the steep access to Broad Sands beach, shortly after which it diverts right and down over fields to rejoin the A399 at Watermouth. The path continues alongside the road to a gateway opposite

LEFT Lynmouth's curving harbour wall

USEFUL INFORMATION

THE ROUTE
• www.southwestcoastpath.com
Excellent official site covering all aspects of the route, including information on accommodation, maps, travel updates, guided walks and a luggage service.
• www.nationaltrail.co.uk
Official website of the 15 National Trails in England and Wales.
• www.swcp.org.uk
☎ 01752 896237
The South West Coast Path Association site has useful links, from accommodation and public transport to tide times.

TOURIST INFORMATION CENTRES
• www.lynton-lynmouth-tourism.co.uk
Town Hall, Lee Road, Lynton EX35 6BT;
☎ 0845 660 3232
• www.visitcombemartin.co.uk
Cross Street, Combe Martin EX34 0AR; ☎ 01271 883319
• www.visitilfracombe.co.uk
Landmark Theatre, The Seafront, Ilfracombe EX34 9BX;
☎ 01271 863001
• www.woolacombetourism.co.uk
The Esplanade, Woolacombe EX34 7DL;
☎ 01271 870553
• www.brauntontic.co.uk
The Bakehouse Centre, Caen Street, Braunton EX33 1AA;
☎ 01271 816400

PLANNING YOUR TRIP
• www.southwestcoastalpath.co.uk
Recommends pubs, restaurants, and places to stay near the path.
• www.yha.org.uk
☎ 0800 019 1700
The Youth Hostel Association has a site south of Ilfracombe.
• www.ramblers.org.uk
☎ 020 7339 8500
The Ramblers Association website has general information about long-distance walking and specific help covering the SWCP.
• www.ldwa.org.uk
The Long Distance Walkers Association provides similar details, including local walking groups and challenge events.

OTHER PATHS
This SWCP section meets the Two Moors Way (pages 18–23) at Lynmouth and the Devon Coast to Coast at Ilfracombe, which also includes the Tarka Trail from Braunton to Meeth.

the entrance to Watermouth Castle. This leads to Watermouth harbour. The main path leads along the road and into the woods, but a diversion can be made along the beach at low tide to some steps up to the woods. Keep to the coast around Widmouth Head, with its old coastguard lookout, to Samson's Bay, Rillage Point and the coastguard cottages. Continue alongside the road to Hele, with its Old Corn Mill, to which a diversion can be made up the road towards Ilfracombe. The Corn Mill operates a tea room at weekends April-October, and during the week in July and August, so the diversion may be very welcome! The path skirts the small bay and ascends steeply to the summit of Hillsborough, with fine views of Ilfracombe.

On the way down to Ilfracombe harbour, the path passes through the double rampart which defended Hillsborough as an Iron Age promontory fort. This part of the route ends at the quayside car park at Ilfracombe.

For an inland escape route back to Combe Martin, take the road from the eastern end of Ilfracombe car park (grid ref. SS 527 477), up to the A399. Cross this road and ascend Chambercombe Road to Chambercombe Manor. A track continues past the manor, through Comyn Farm and up to Trayne. It then crosses a road and the waymarked route descends into the Sterridge Valley. From here, minor roads can be followed through Berrynarbor and back to the South West Coast Path just west of Combe Martin. By linking this route with the two 'escape' routes mentioned above, a complete return route to Lynmouth can eventually be made.

ILFRACOMBE TO BRAUNTON

STAGE 3

ILFRACOMBE to WOOLACOMBE

DISTANCE 8 miles (12.9km)

MAP OS Landranger 139

START AT GRID REFERENCE SS 523 477

START POINT Quay car park on southern edge of Ilfracombe harbour

Ilfracombe is a large, mainly Victorian resort with some Regency and Georgian terraces. The harbour, now used mainly by pleasure craft, was formerly the most important refuge on the northern coasts of Devon, Cornwall and Somerset. The ancient mariners' chapel of St Nicholas has acted as a lighthouse for centuries. There was a substantial herring fishing industry here in the 18th and 19th centuries.

Walk along the Strand to the 18th-century Royal Britannia Hotel, patronised by Admiral Nelson and novelist Henry Williamson, who lived near by. From the front of the hotel take Capstone Crescent opposite and walk round Capstone Parade to Wildersmouth beach. Follow the Parade around to Ilfracombe Museum, originally the laundry for the enormous Victorian Ilfracombe Hotel, now demolished. The path ascends through gardens behind the museum to the Granville Point apartment complex and then along the coastal road. Look down to the Tunnels beaches, with their bathing pools exposed at low tide. Access to the beaches is via tunnels cut through the cliffs by Welsh miners in 1836, when a bath house was built at the entrance and a small sea-water pool was heated.

Keep as close to the coast as possible as you proceed along the road, then take a right turn by a National Trust sign for Torrs Walk. The path leads back to the cliff, from where it zig-zags up to the highest point of the Seven Hills. This was once a private path for which walkers had to pay, and the remains of turnstiles can still be found.

FUCHSIA VALLEY

From the summit, keep on the path nearest to the coast. Cross a stile and turn inland, then right along a track wide enough for vehicles. This was the old road to Lee over Lee Downs and is easy to follow to the Blue Mushroom bungalow, where it becomes a tarmac road descending to Lee. Here it meets the road by the derelict Lee Bay Hotel, or a detour can be made up the road to the left to the 14th-century Grampus Inn, which includes the village shop, near which is the picturesque Old Maids' Cottage. Many fuchsias grow here, but once there were whole hedgerows of them, giving Lee the title of Fuchsia Valley. The route continues on the road by the derelict Lee Bay Hotel and the beach, at one end of which is an old mill and at the other, the 17th-century Smugglers' Cottage.

From the car park near the beach at Lee (grid ref. SS 479 465), return inland to Ilfracombe. A track runs up the valley to the Grampus Inn, before which a path on the right follows the Borough valley. From here, a forest track forks left to Shaftsboro Farm and continues to the B3230. Pass under the road bridge on to the former Ilfracombe-to-Barnstaple railway line, which can be followed into Ilfracombe via the Cairn Nature Reserve.

Climb the road past the cottage and fork right at the National Trust sign for Damage Hue. The path is easily followed along the coast to Bull Point. Here, the original lighthouse was replaced by an automatic one in 1975 after landslips threatened to carry it away. Hug the coast and round Morte Point, so named for the many deaths it and the infamous Morte Stone off it have caused by shipwreck. There are strong tidal currents off the Point.

It is possible to return from Mortehoe (grid ref. SS 454 448) to Lee by following the lighthouse road. Half a mile from the village, a path to the right of the road crosses a small valley to the minor road which descends to Lee from Borough Cross.

Descend towards Woolacombe and the road between Woolacombe and Mortehoe. Pass Barricane beach, renowned among Victorian shell-collectors. From here, the route follows the side of the road along the coast to the large car park on the former military road, backing on to the dunes. When the tide is low enough, it is possible to take a short cut across the beach and up one of the paths through the dunes, or to walk along the beach all the way to Putsborough.

STAGE 4

WOOLACOMBE to BRAUNTON

DISTANCE 14.7 miles (23.6km)
MAP OS Explorer 139
START AT GRID REFERENCE SS 458 433
START POINT Marine Drive car park

Woolacombe (which means 'valley of wolves') did not begin to develop until the end of the 19th century. It is now a family resort with glorious blue flag golden sands and the beach is a favoured spot for surfers. The National Trust, who own Woolacombe Warren, have struggled to help the sand dune system that is steadily being eroded back to the original cliff line.

The route runs to the end of the Marine Drive, where it becomes a bridleway following the contour above Vention to Clifton Court apartments. Vention has several buildings now, but the name refers to the old limeburners' cottage next to the kiln and is supposedly derived from the description of lime-burning as a 'new invention' in 1630 by Devon historian Tristram Risdon. The route follows the lane for about 200yds beyond the junction,

then forks right over a stile. The path continues through fields above the cliff-top to Baggy Point. There is a large cave, Baggy Hole, in the end of the point, not visible from the path, and the area is popular with climbers. The path rounds the Point and descends towards Croyde. About 300yds after the National Trust car park, turn right by a caravan site. The path follows the edge of the dunes. After crossing the stream halfway along, a detour can be made inland to Croyde village for refreshments.

THE AMERICAN ROAD

At the end of the beach the path ascends to a wartime blockhouse, rounds the end of Saunton Down and crosses the road. It then runs above the road to Saunton Sands Hotel, where it drops through the hotel grounds to the dunes. A detour can be made to the beach to examine the fossilized Ice Age dune system in the cliff and the pink granite boulder below it, brought by ice sheets travelling down the Irish Sea. The path continues inland to the road at Saunton, taking the first turning right after the entrance to the golf course.

There is a short-cut to Braunton from where the coast path joins the American Road on Braunton Burrows (grid ref. SS 463 346). Fork left here, past a car park to the road at Sandy Lane. Turn first right and after 0.5 miles (800m) take the lane to the left. Cross Braunton Great Field, a relic of the medieval open field system, and enter Braunton near Caen Street car park.

The path skirts the golf course and continues behind Braunton Burrows dunes to a dirt road known as the American Road, made by US forces in World War II when the area was used for tank training prior to the Normandy landings.

To return inland from Saunton to Woolacombe, follow the bridleway over Saunton Down, which starts opposite the entrance to the golf club (grid ref. SS 457 377). It joins the road at Forda, following it to Georgeham. Fork left by the church, along the lane through Pickwell and on to the coast path at Woolacombe Warren.

Continue along the road for a mile to a car park. Detour along the boardwalk to view the Taw/Torridge estuary. The path continues through the car park to the White House, a former ferry house, and along a flood bank to the Taw and Caen estuaries. The dyke was built in the 1850s as part of the reclamation of Braunton Marsh. The original route of the river can be seen on the inland side of Horsey Island. The new channel starts opposite the end of the main runway of Chivenor airfield. Cargo vessels used the quay until the 1950s, exporting gravel and farm produce to South Wales and importing coal and limestone for the kilns.

Beyond the quay the path joins the road at Velator Bridge. At the former level-crossing, turn left along the old railway line to Braunton Countryside Centre and car park. The disused railway line is now a cycle path along the coast path and it links with the Tarka Trail cycle path through to Barnstaple and Bideford.

 **PLACES TO VISIT**

• LYNTON AND LYNMOUTH CLIFF RAILWAY
www.cliffrailwaylynton.co.uk
☎ 01598 753908
Take a ride on the 1 in 1.75 gradient railway lift, built in 1890, which connects Lynton, at the top of the cliffs, with Lynmouth 500ft (152m) below. Environmentally-friendly, it uses no power, just large water tanks to mechanically balance the twin cars. Open daily Feb–Oct.

• WATERMOUTH CASTLE AND FAMILY THEME PARK
www.watermouthcastle.com
☎ 01271 867474
The Victorian folly and estate of Watermouth Castle lies next to the coast path, between Combe Martin and Ilfracombe. It is now a major tourist attraction, containing displays within the castle that include a Great Hall with suits of armour, the Victorian kitchen, antique pier slot machines, mechanical music machines and a model railway room. Outside, the sub-tropical gardens include an adventure playground, camera obscura, and water gardens with splashing fun and water rides, alongside many other attractions. Open most days Apr–Oct, except Saturdays.

• BRAUNTON COUNTRYSIDE CENTRE
www.brauntoncountrysidecentre. org.uk
☎ 01271 817171
Call in at the free countryside centre by the Caen Street car park in the town of Braunton. Run by volunteers, it has displays on the remarkable UNESCO Biosphere Reserve and its wildlife, including both the shifting sands of the Braunton Burrows dunes and nearby Braunton Marshes, renowned for its extensive flora and fauna. Hire a Braunton Explorer GPS system, which guides you on a variety of local tours using headphones and a small screen. Open Apr–Oct.

BELOW, LEFT TO RIGHT
Low tide at Appledore;
Yachts moored in busy
Ilfracombe Harbour; Surfing
at Saunton Sands

Two Moors Way

COMPLETE ROUTE IVYBRIDGE TO LYNMOUTH **102 MILES (164KM)**
SECTION COVERED SEQUER'S BRIDGE TO YEOFORD **43 MILES (69KM)**
MAPS OS EXPLORER OL 9, OL 20, OL 28, 113, 114, 127

The Two Moors Way tends to be a quiet path, with most walkers taking just the Exmoor or Dartmoor sections of the route. It is planned to extend the route from Ivybridge to the mouth of the Erme to make it a coast-to-coast walk, linking with the South West Coast Path at each end. At the time of writing, negotiations have not been completed, but this guide covers the area south of Ivybridge from Sequer's Bridge, where public footpaths already exist, and details a 43-mile (69km) section north from here to Yeoford. Although it is easy going in places and avoids the bleakest parts of Dartmoor, it is not generally an easy walk. The route is undulating, muddy in places and can be exposed, so proper equipment is essential. The route reaches a maximum height of 1,735ft (529m) at Hameldown Tor. In higher areas the path is generally along ridges, avoiding the boggier parts of the moors.

The fast-flowing River Erme

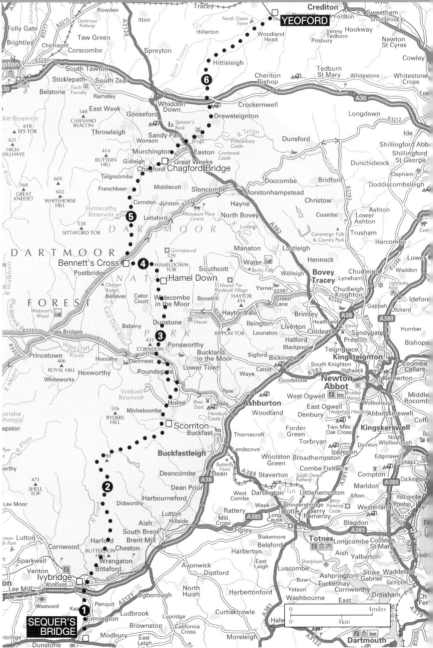

SEQUER'S BRIDGE TO SCORRITON

STAGE 1

SEQUER'S BRIDGE to IVYBRIDGE

DISTANCE 3.7 miles (5.9km)
MAPS OS Explorer OL 20, OL 28
START AT GRID REFERENCE SX 632 518
START POINT Sequer's Bridge, where the A379 crosses the River Erme

Sequer's Bridge is a lovely old bridge at the head of the Erme estuary. Cross the bridge and turn left where the footpath is signposted. Cross the field to Sexton Farm and follow the track beyond. Cross two stiles, keep to the edge of the wood and drop to the riverbank. Follow the waymarks to the left of the buildings at Fawns. Take the road opposite and walk up past Strode, with its ornate gateway. This was home to the Strode family from the 13th to 15th centuries and traces of their mansion remain at the farm. Just past the next junction, turn left through the gateway with the footpath sign. Continue downhill towards Thornham Bridge, passing a barn. Before the bridge turn right and follow the track across the fields to the road. Keep ahead, then left at the next bend to the bridge at Keaton.

Here (grid ref SX 640 545) it is possible to return to Sequer's Bridge by crossing the bridge and following the road around to the left to Ermington. Just before the village is a trout farm and Ermington Mill. Ermington Church is known for the crooked spire of its 13th-century tower. Inside is much beautiful woodwork, both old and new. The latter was carved by the daughter of a former vicar. Turn left after the church and descend to the A3121. Turn right and follow the road to Plantation House Hotel, taking the footpath opposite. Follow the path alongside the river, crossing stiles by the sewage works and returning to Sequer's Bridge.

REACHING IVYBRIDGE

To continue to Ivybridge from Keaton, do not cross the bridge, but turn right up the track with the footpath sign. Pass the weir and continue through a field and along a track to a road by a bungalow. Continue up the road and pass through the field by the South Devon Tennis Centre. Pass through two subways under roads and follow the riverbank to the car park by the Ivybridge Leisure Centre.

STAGE 2

IVYBRIDGE to SCORRITON

DISTANCE 12.3 miles (19.8km)
MAPS OS Explorer OL 20, OL 28
START AT GRID REFERENCE SX 636 561
START POINT Ivybridge, on the A38

Ivybridge was a hamlet around its 13th-century bridge until the late 19th century, when it grew with mills and the coming of the railway. Its church was built in 1882. The area still has some light industry, shops and the Watermark Centre.

From the car park join the main street to the east of the bridge. Keep upwards along Harford Road, passing the former paper mill and school. Follow the signs for Harford, crossing the railway bridge. Just before the bridge a stone marks the beginning of the Two Moors Way. The bridge crosses the former Great Western Railway of Brunel, who designed the viaduct just to the west.

Continue straight ahead for a few hundred yards and turn right along a lane signposted 'Bridleway to the moor'. A left turn takes you up a lane to reach the moor. Continue ahead through gorse to reach a cairn beside a track. The Two Moors Way follows the track northwards for several miles, although in dry weather it is easier to follow the ridgeway above. The track is the bed of a tramway used between 1910 and 1932 by the isolated Redlake china clay works, 6 miles (9.5km) further north. There are views westwards to the huge modern china clay works at Headon and Lee Moor.

Follow the track up to Spurrell's Cross on the ridge. Although it has been restored, only the head of the cross remains. Most such crosses are medieval and mark routes over the moors used by local abbeys.

From the cross (grid ref. SX 658 600) it is possible to return to Ivybridge by following the track down the valley to the left. This passes through a small car park on the edge of the moor and down a lane to Harford. The little 15th-century church has two 16th-century brasses to Thomas Williams, former Speaker of the House of Commons. Take the footpath by the farm opposite the church. This crosses a bridge and fields to the road at Broomhill. Follow the road downhill to Ivybridge, making a circular route of about 6.5 miles (10.5km).

PREHISTORIC RELICS

From Spurrell's Cross, return to the tramway and continue along it. Running alongside to the left is one of Dartmoor's longest stone rows, over 1.5 miles (2.5km) long. Hobajon's Cross is inscribed on one of its stones, although the name may refer to a former cross. The purpose of most Bronze Age stone rows is unclear. This one is extended by more recent boundary stones, dividing Ugborough from Harford Commons.

The route passes above Piles Copse in the Erme Valley. The copse of stunted oaks covered in ferns, mosses and lichens is one of three much-studied relics of Dartmoor's prehistoric forest cover. Later it passes the flooded pit of Leftlake china clay works, closed in the 1920s. Above, on Western White Barrow, is Petre's Cross, one of several erected in the 16th century to mark the boundary of Sir William Petre's property on Brent Moor.

After a sharp right-hand bend, the route leaves the tramway by some ruins and continues ahead on the Abbot's Way, down the Avon valley to Huntingdon Warren. This was a rabbit enclosure with many 'pillow mounds' in which the rabbits burrowed. The route keeps to the south of the river, fording it beyond the 16th-century Huntingdon Cross, but a diversion can be made to the medieval clapper bridge and the north bank followed to the cross.

A diversion can also be made up the Western Wella Brook to an old mine. Next to it are the remains of a blowing house (tin-processing mill) used as a chapel by the Reverend Keble Martin, the well-known flower painter. Beyond the cross, the

LEFT A Dartmoor pony mare with her foal at Haytor in Dartmoor National Park

USEFUL INFORMATION

THE ROUTE
• The Two Moors Way Association produces the official guide to this route and an accommodation list. Contact them at Coppins, The Poplars, Pinhoe, Exeter EX4 9HH.
• *www.devon.gov.uk/two_moors_way*
• Devon County Council promotes the 2MW. It gives some basic information and a leaflet at this site.

TOURIST INFORMATION CENTRES
• *www.ivybridge.gov.uk/tourism*
The Watermark, Erme Court, Leonards Road, Ivybridge PL21 0SZ;
☎ 01752 892220
• *www.dartmoor-npa.gov.uk*
The Dartmoor National Park Authority has various visitor centres, including one close to this section of the route, at Postbridge (open daily Easter–Oct). However, the High Moorland Visitor Centre at Princetown is open daily all year
☎ 01822 890414.
• *www.visit-exmoor.co.uk*
Exmoor National Park Authority has a seasonal visitor centre at Lynmouth ☎ 01598 752509, but this website gives information for planning a trip to the area if you intend to walk the full route.

PLANNING YOUR TRIP
• *www.ldwa.org.uk*
The Long Distance Walkers Association provides helpful details on the 2MW, including accommodation, luggage services and maps/publications.
• *www.ramblers.org.uk*
☎ 020 7339 8500
The Ramblers Association website has general information about long-distance walking and specific help covering the 2MW.
• *www.yha.org.uk*
☎ 0800 019 1700
The Youth Hostel Association has two sites close to Postbridge.

OTHER PATHS
The 2MW eventually meets the South West Coast Path (pages 14–17) at Lynmouth. To the south, the Erme-Plym Trail can be used to extend the 2MW to either Plymouth or Wembury, thus making it a Coast to Coast route. The Dartmoor Way, which forms a circuit around Dartmoor settlements, crosses the 2MW at Holne and Chagford.

route ascends Hickaton Hill and continues beyond Pupers Hill to cross the River Mardle by way of a footbridge at Chalk Ford. A track climbs the hillside opposite and eventually this becomes a broad lane descending to Scorriton.

From the Square at Scorriton (grid ref. SX 703 684) a return can be made to Spurrell's Cross. Take the road opposite the war memorial. At the bottom of the hill turn right for Hawson Cross, next to Stumpy Oak, an ancient oak pollard bound with iron rings. Take the next right turn after the cross. Continue over Cullaford Bridge and up a sunken lane. Turn left along the road at the top and right down the bridlepath at the next crossroads. At the ford turn left, skirting the edge of the moor. From Skerraton Gate the path is signposted over fields and down a lane to Moor Cross. Turn right down the road and over Gidley Bridge. At the top of the hill turn right along the bridlepath to the moor. Continue over Dockwell Ridge to the bridge over the Avon and down the drive to the car park at Shipley Bridge, site of a former works making naphtha (inflammable oil) from peat. Do not cross the bridge, but continue along the road for 0.25 miles (400m) and take the bridlepath to the right. At Ball Gate, continue along the moorland boundary past a Neolithic long barrow showing its collapsed burial chamber. Ford two streams and continue walking ahead up the hillside to Spurrell's Cross. This makes a circular route of approximately 20 miles (32km).

***ABOVE** Tucked among fields, Widecombe in the Moor in Dartmoor National Park*
***BELOW** Sunrise near Leigh Tor on Dartmoor, with warm morning light and mist filling the valley beyond*

SCORRITON TO BENNETT'S CROSS

STAGE 3

SCORRITON to HAMEL DOWN
DISTANCE 7.9 miles (12.7km)
MAP OS Explorer OL 28
START AT GRID REFERENCE SX 703 684
START POINT Scorriton village square

Scorriton is a small farming community with the Tradesman's Arms pub, and a chapel built in 1904. It is surrounded by the enclosed strips of medieval open fields.

From the square, turn down the road opposite the war memorial. Turn left at the bottom and cross the Holy Brook. Originally the Northbrooke, this stream joins the Dart at Buckfast Abbey and formed the boundary of part of the abbey's property. At the next bend, take the lane ahead and ascend to the road at Holne. Continue ahead through the village, passing the church and Church House Inn. Continue uphill to the road junction at Butts Cross. The Butts is an adjacent field where archery practice took place in Tudor times.

Turn left, then immediately right over a stile. Crossing further stiles, the path descends over fields with good views up an isolated part of the Dart valley, clothed in ancient oak woodland. It then passes through the National Trust's Cleave Wood and along the riverbank to New Bridge. Cross the bridge to the car park. Follow the river downstream along the path that starts under the bridge. The river here is on slates but contains some granite boulders washed down from several miles away by floods, some possibly from melt-water during the Ice Age. Leave the river where the path meets the road. Turn uphill on the road then take the path to the right, leading up through the bracken to Leigh Tor. The tor is made of attractively streaked metamorphic rocks. Turn left and cross two roads, heading for a car park in an old quarry. Turn upwards to the track above the quarry. Turn left along the track, known as Dr Blackall's Drive. Dr Blackall bought the 18th-century Spitchwick Manor in 1867 and so became lord of the manor. When his wife became unable to walk on the moor he had the track made for her pony and trap so that she could still enjoy the fine views over the Dart valley. The track continues past Aish and Mel Tors to the car

park at Bel Tor Corner. Cross the road and keep ahead over the moorland to the next road. Turn right to Lock's Gate Cross and take the road signposted to Ponsworthy. Descend the hill to the ford. The cottages by the ford include the former smithy with its double door. One can make a short diversion over the ford to the old bridge, with its datestone of 1666. Miller's House is next to the mill. The mill wheel is behind the building and can be seen from further on along the route.

Turn left by the ford, along the footpath signposted to Jordan. The path follows the West Webburn River, which is crossed by footbridge at Jordan Mill. Turn right by the mill, then left at the road. Keep uphill across the next crossroads to reach the crossroads on the edge of open moorland. Cross this, then strike ahead up the moorland ridge. After a mile (1.6km) you will come to a crossing of tracks on the crest of the ridge (grid ref. SX 707 773). For Widecombe (a mile southeast), where overnight accommodation is available, go over the ridge and down the track to the right.

> One can return from here (grid ref. SX 706 774) to New Bridge by crossing the ridge and descending the track to the right. This follows the edge of the moor and becomes a lane leading down to Widecombe in the Moor. At the village centre turn left by the Church House, opposite the old Inn. Walk down the road and over the clapper bridge across the East Webburn River. Pass the Rugglestone Inn, named after a large logan or balancing stone in a nearby field. Pass Venton and Shilstone Rocks Stud and turn uphill. At the open moor, turn right along the edge of the moor and keep ahead to the next road. Cross this to the bridlepath, which becomes Elliot's Hill road running down to the road at Buckland in the Moor. Turn left and then right after the church, down an unsigned road which leads to Buckland Bridge. Cross the bridge and follow the road alongside the river and back to New Bridge. This completes a circular route of some 9 miles (14.5km).

STAGE 4

HAMEL DOWN to BENNETT'S CROSS
DISTANCE 4 miles (6.4km)
MAP OS Explorer OL 28
START AT GRID REFERENCE SX 707 772
START POINT The crossing of tracks on Hamel Down, 1 mile (1.6km) northeast of Widecombe in the Moor

From the crossing of tracks, the route continues uphill along the crest of the ridge for 2 miles (3km) to its highest point at Hameldown Tor. It passes a number of Bronze Age barrows. Some of these were excavated in the 19th century and were found, uniquely on Dartmoor, to be of the Wessex culture. They are mainly made of earth within a ring of small stones. Underneath

is a small cairn, with cremated human remains under that. Excavations at Single Barrow revealed the bronze blade and amber pommel of a dagger. Hameldown Cross was a manorial boundary stone. Other such stones on the barrows were erected in 1854 and bear the initials of the Duke of Somerset, then lord of Natsworthy Manor.

The route descends through Grimspound, a 4-acre Bronze Age enclosure where 16 hut circles and eight other buildings once stood. The entrance is through a large, paved stone gateway. The huts were made by building a double-skinned circular stone wall with a filling of earth. The floor was dug out inside and a central pole held a conical roof of branches covered with turf. Pass straight through Grimspound and over Hookney Tor on the far side. Descend to cross a road. Keep straight ahead over the next hill to the B3212 road and Bennett's Cross car park.

> To return to Hamel Down, descend the West Webburn valley from Bennett's Cross (grid ref. SX 681 817). A number of tracks lead to the remains of Vitifer mine. Follow the broad track alongside the river and through the gate into the forest at Soussons Down. Take the bridlepath to the right, signposted to Soussons. Follow the path signs to Soussons Farm. Take the farm drive to the road. Turn left and keep ahead at the next junction. After a mile (1.6km) at a T-junction, take the gate ahead and the uphill track signposted to Widecombe. Take the gate on to the moor and continue up to the crest of the ridge.

BENNETT'S CROSS TO YEOFORD

STAGE 5

BENNETT'S CROSS to CHAGFORD BRIDGE
DISTANCE 6 miles (9.6km)
MAP OS Explorer OL 28
START AT GRID REFERENCE SX 681 817
START POINT Car park at Bennett's Cross, beside the B3212

Bennett's Cross dates from the 13th century, when it marked the route from Tavistock to Chagford. It was later used as a boundary stone for Headland Warren; hence the initials WB (Warren Bounds) carved on it.

Cross the road and head across the moorland, keeping slightly to the left to skirt the rather boggy area at the source of the North Walla Brook. After this, veer right, down the spine of Hurston Ridge. Hurston comes from the

ABOVE LEFT AND ABOVE
The walk route passes the remains of a Bronze Age settlement at Grimspound

ℹ PLACES TO VISIT
• **BUCKFAST ABBEY**
www.buckfast.org.uk
☎ 01364 645500
This remarkable abbey is found in the town of Buckfastleigh, less than 3 miles (5km) southeast of the route at Scorriton. The church of the abbey, which is intricate and medieval in style, was re-built by a team of between four and six monks in the early 20th century. The stone was dressed by the men and lifted into place with manual hoists, yet they completed the incredible task in just 32 years. The present monks are famous for their beekeeping and tonic wine, which is available to buy. There are shops and a tea room, and also small sensory and physic gardens in the pleasant grounds. Open daily all year.

• **RIVER DART COUNTRY PARK**
www.riverdart.co.uk
☎ 01364 652511
Just 2 miles (3km) east of Holne, on the Ashburton road, is this country park. It is actually a campsite and caravan park which also has a wealth of family activities available to residents and day visitors. Amongst other things there are adventure playgrounds, an assault course, a high rope course, a zip line and slides. There is also a lake with a beach, and canoes for hire. Open daily Apr–Sep, Sat–Sun Oct–Mar.

• **WIDECOMBE IN THE MOOR**
www.widecombe-in-the-moor.com
This delightful little Dartmoor village is a short walk from the 2MW. It is a favourite resting place for walkers. There are pubs and a café here, and the parish church of St Pancras (known as the Cathedral of the Moor due to its high tower). The 16th-century Church House is next door, owned by the National Trust. Part of the building, Sexton's Cottage, houses the NT shop.

a road between Teignworthy Hotel and Frenchbeer. Continue across fields to Teigncombe and turn right, leaving the Mariner's Way, which continues through Gidleigh. At a sharp right-hand bend, continue ahead down a lane to Leigh Bridge, where the South and North Teign Rivers meet. Cross the bridge and continue walking along the road towards Chagford. At the next crossroads turn left to Chagford Bridge.

It is possible to return from here (grid ref. SX 694 879) to Bennett's Cross via Chagford. At the crossroads, turn right for Chagford instead of left for the bridge. The return route forks right in the village at the next junction, but you can detour ahead to explore Chagford. After forking right, turn left at the next junction and up the hill to Meldon Common. At the top bear downhill to the right. Keep ahead at the next two junctions and return to the junction with the Mariner's Way.

Turn left here along the Mariner's Way, over fields and down the drive to Lower Shapley. Follow the signs across fields and between thatched farmhouses at Hurston. Turn left down the farm drive, then right as signposted, along fields through Lingcombe to Jurston. Look out for medieval gate posts, slotted to take removable poles instead of hinged gates.

Cross the road at Jurston and walk across the green to the clapper bridge, taking the track to Lettaford with its old longhouse, opposite which the path leads through a farmyard. Follow the Mariner's Way across fields and across the B3212 to Coombe. Here, the Mariner's Way used to pass through a house, presumably one of the rest houses which were spaced every 8 or 10 miles (15km) along the long-distance path. Turn right along the bridlepath, up the combe to join the Two Moors Way below Hookney Tor.

Continue ahead, crossing the road and hill to Bennett's Cross. This makes a circular walk of about 13 miles (21km).

STAGE 6
CHAGFORD BRIDGE to YEOFORD
DISTANCE 11.8 miles (19km)
MAPS OS Explorer OL 28, 113
START AT GRID REFERENCE SX 694 879
START POINT Chagford Bridge

Both Chagford and Rushford have narrow packhorse bridges, built in the 17th century, at the time when Chagford was a thriving woollen centre experiencing a lot of traffic. There was once a woollen mill close to Chagford Bridge. Cross the bridge and turn right on the footpath through fields along the

ABOVE North Teign River, Scorhill Down near Chagford
ABOVE RIGHT Scorhill Stone circle at sunset

Saxon hare or hoar stone, meaning a boundary stone. A large prehistoric stone once stood here, marking one of Dartmoor's most important ancient trackways and later the boundary of the Royal Forest. An impressive double stone row with tall menhirs at each end still survives on the ridge.

Keep downwards along the ridge to the road between Fernworthy and Chagford. There are views to Fernworthy with its reservoir, completed in 1942, and forest, begun in 1919, which hides many prehistoric remains. Turn right down the road and over a cattle grid. Turn left along the Mariner's Way down the drive to Yardworthy.

Follow the signposts and orange waymarks for the Mariner's Way, crossing the South Teign River by footbridge and

riverbank. At Rushford Bridge turn left along the road, then right, between buildings at Rushford Mill. Keep ahead along the riverbank to Dogmarsh Bridge. Cross the road, (not the bridge) here and continue along the riverbank. After 0.5 miles (800m), cross a small stream (grid ref. SX 721 895). Here there are alternative routes to the little village of Drewsteignton, via the Fisherman's Path along the River Teign or Hunters' Path above the Teign gorge.

The route along the Fisherman's Path follows the riverbank to Fingle Bridge, another 17th-century packhorse bridge and popular beauty spot. The Fingle Bridge Inn, originally a tea shelter for the nearby Fingle Mill, which is now in ruins, still offers refreshments to travellers. Do not cross the bridge, but turn left up the road to the parking area. Take Hunters' Path up through the woods to the left. This rises to the top of the Teign gorge and follows the edge for 0.5 miles (800m) until a right fork is made, joining the main route to the unspoilt village of Drewsteignton.

PRETTY DREWSTEIGNTON

The main route ascends a small combe from the river to join a farm drive. A short distance up the drive, double back to the right along Hunters' Path. This passes under Castle Drogo to Sharp Tor, where a detour left can be made to the house. After Sharp Tor, take the next turn to the left, signposted Drewsteignton. The road is joined by a stone commemorating the opening of the Two Moors Way. Turn right, then left for the Square. For anyone wishing to leave or join the walk at Drewsteignton, there is parking in the Square.

Drewsteignton is a pretty village with thatched cottages and the unspoilt 18th-century Drewe Arms inn, that remains much as it has always been. It was once called the Druid's Inn, after an association of Druids with Spinsters' Rock. It was renamed after the return of the Drewe family this century, one 'Drogo' or 'Dru' having been given the manor by William the Conqueror. The church has a tall 15th-century tower and a wagon roof with carved bosses, one of which has a face said to be a self-portrait of one of the builders. The Church House also dates back to the 15th century and served as a hall and ale house for members of the congregation. From the Square, pass the Post Office Stores

and turn right down the road beyond. Keep downhill past two junctions to Veet Mill. Take the track ahead at the road bend and follow it past Winscombe to a road. Turn left, cross the flyover over the A30 and turn right down Hask Lane. Turn left along a path which passes down over fields, through woodland and crosses a ford to a road by Forder Farm.

Turn right, then left over a stile by the gateway to Forder Cottage. Continue up fields to Hill Farm. Take the lane to the right of the farm and continue ahead, down to a bridge over a small stream. Continue up between some trees and, keeping Whitethorn Farm to your right, take the gateway to the farmyard. Follow the farm drive to the road and turn right. Keep ahead at Hittisleigh Cross, to the small hilltop settlement of Hittisleigh.

APPROACHING YEOFORD

The Church of St Andrew is mainly 14th-century and its granite arcaded aisle has a wagon roof with carved bosses. There is a Norman font of black marble. A sparsely populated parish, Hittisleigh provided the poorest church income in Devon.

Continue along the road for 2 miles (3km), where the Two Moors Way forks down a farm track to Newbury. Instead of making this left turn, continue down the road for 1.5 miles (2.5km) to Yeoford. Here is a railway station and the Mare and Foal pub, a traditional real ale pub which includes a small shop.

To return to Drewsteignton, walk up the road and turn left along a road just after the turning for Newbury (grid ref. SX 158 972). Turn right after the bridge, then left at the crossroads at the top of the hill. Turn right at the T-junction and after 300yds (275m) take the footpath to the left through two sets of double gates. The path passes under the A30 and along a lane past Lambert to Crockernwell. Turn right at the road, then left down the side street.

Crockernwell, now by-passed by the A30, grew on the old Exeter-to-Okehampton road. It is a hamlet in the parish of Cheriton Bishop. It was a Saxon manor and has had a chapel since 1390.

Turn right along the lane signposted as a public footpath. The lane passes Budbrooke and Narracott, and at Coombe Hall forks right up the drive to a road. Take the road nearly opposite and at the next bend take the farm drive ahead to Burrow Farm. Follow the footpath signs to the left of the farm buildings and down to a stream. Keep ahead uphill, following the yellow waymarks along the edge of fields to a lane returning to Drewsteignton. This makes a walk of about 6.5 miles (10.5km) from Newbury.

ABOVE Castle Drogo was built for the self-made millionaire Julius Drewe

ℹ️ PLACES TO VISIT

• GRIMSPOUND
The 2MW passes straight through the Bronze Age enclosure of Grimspound, between Hamel Down and Bennett's Cross. The stone remains of the low outer wall are visible, including a paved entrance corridor, and 24 stone hut circles. The site covers 4 acres (16,000 sq m), and the full circle can be seen clearly from Hookney Tor after you have examined it more closely on your way through.

• CASTLE DROGO
www.nationaltrust.org.uk
☎ 01647 433306
This National Trust property sits on the 2MW, just 1 mile (1.6km) west of Drewsteignton, and overlooks the wooded Fingle Gorge. Although a castle in name and appearance, this austere but attractive granite building was actually only completed in 1930. It was designed by Sir Edwin Lutyens for the retail tycoon, Julius Drewe, who only managed to live there for a few years before his death, just a year after the building was fully completed. There are beautiful Arts and Crafts-inspired gardens, complete with a croquet lawn for visitors to use, a rose garden and rhododendron walks. The castle was ahead of its time, having an internal telephone system and its own hydro-electric power supply. During WWII, the house was used as a home for babies made homeless by the London bombings. Open daily Mar–Dec.

Wild heather growing near Bennett's Cross

Leland Trail

COMPLETE ROUTE KING ALFRED'S TOWER TO HAM HILL **28 MILES (45KM)**

SECTION COVERED AS ABOVE

MAPS OS EXPLORER 129, 142

The Leland Trail crosses the lowlands of South Somerset, linking several villages, towns and historical sites. It uses definitive rights of way, tracks and lanes that follow in the footsteps of John Leland, who travelled on horseback through this area during the 16th century. A well-educated scholar who worked for King Henry VIII as a keeper of the royal libraries, Leland was commissioned in 1533 to produce a survey of England's antiquities and 'peruse the libraries of all cathedrals, abbeys, priories, colleges etc, and also all places wherein records, writings and secrets of antiquity were reposed'. He reached South Somerset some time between 1535 and 1543, and after visiting Bruton travelled southwest through Castle Gary, North and South Cadbury, Ilchester, Montacute and Stoke-sub-Hamdon. The modern route is marked on OS mapping.

The modern-day Leland Trail, if one opts to travel in a southwesterly direction like John Leland, starts at King Alfred's Tower (NT), which is just inside the Somerset county boundary and is close to the National Trust property of Stourhead in Wiltshire. It is not an arduous walk and although most of the trail is fairly level, there are opportunities for wonderful views of South Somerset from several vantage points along the route. At no point is the walker more than 3 miles (5km) from a town or village with refreshments and, in most cases, some form of public transport. The Leland Trail is very well waymarked, with its own logo depicting John Leland, and the route is relatively easy to follow throughout. Passing through the Montacute Estate, the trail goes to the south of the famous Elizabethan house (which is the property of the National Trust and worth a visit if time allows) to the picturesque village of Montacute itself. From the village the route is on a defined footpath, on National Trust land, to St Michael's Hill, where a short detour to the top and a climb up the folly tower will be rewarded with superb views. Following a series of footpaths through woodland, the trail eventually ends on Ham Hill, site of an Iron Age settlement, Roman fort and famous stone quarry, and now designated as a country park.

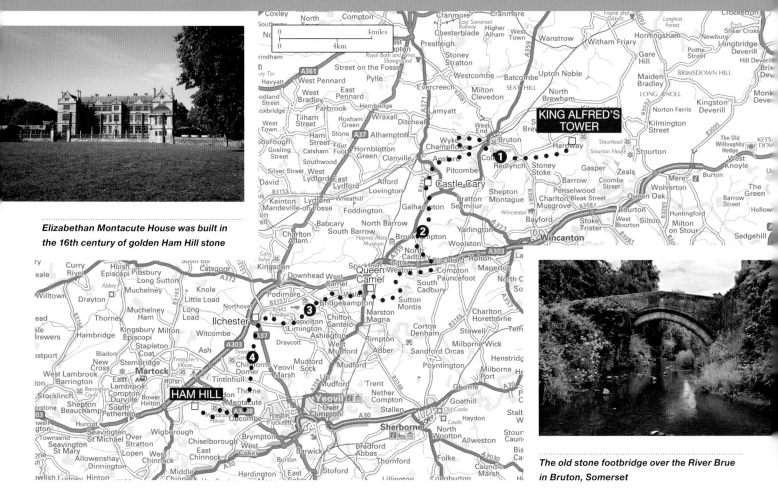

Elizabethan Montacute House was built in the 16th century of golden Ham Hill stone

The old stone footbridge over the River Brue in Bruton, Somerset

KING ALFRED'S TOWER TO QUEEN CAMEL

STAGE 1
KING ALFRED'S TOWER to CASTLE CARY

DISTANCE 3.7 miles (5.9km)
MAP OS Explorer 142
START AT GRID REFERENCE ST 745 351
START POINT King Alfred's Tower

King Alfred's Tower, on the western edge of the Stourhead Estate, stands on Kingsettle Hill on the edge of an escarpment 656ft (200m) above the Somerset Plain. It was built in 1772 to commemorate peace with France and the succession of George III two years earlier. Walk from the tower for a short distance down the adjacent metalled lane and turn left on to a track waymarked with the Leland Trail logo, to Aaron's Hill. Follow the track down through Penselwood. After 0.25 miles (400m) turn left on to a forestry track, then turn right down on to a metalled road which skirts the edge of the forest. Following the signpost to Redlynch, the route now leaves the road for a track through natural woodland, where deer can occasionally be seen, and eventually leads on to a wide path through the woods to a stile. A succession of waymarked stiles leads to a farm track. Cross this and continue through fields to Coachroad Farm. Cross the metalled road. You are now on an old coach road that eventually leads to the gates of Redlynch House on the B3081 road.

At the gates, turn right on to the B3081 and walk to the nearby crossroads, turning left down a metalled lane, past several cottages to a stile and gate signposted to Bruton. Cross over a series of stiles and fields and pass Droppinglane Farm on your right, eventually coming out at a metalled road on the outskirts of Bruton. The roofless dovecote and the church tower can be seen nestling in the valley of the River Brue. Follow the road that leads to the left of the dovecote passing an old, ivy-clad wall on the right. Bruton Dovecote (NT) is worth making a short detour to visit if time permits. Once past the dovecot, turn right into Godminster Lane over a railway bridge, then right into Silver Street and past King's School to the one-arched, 15th-century packhorse bridge over the River Brue. Cross the bridge into Patwell Street and turn left into the High Street. Bruton has much to offer the visitor and time should be allowed to explore its narrow streets. Bruton was an important Saxon town and by the 12th century an abbey for Augustinian canons had been founded. By the end of the 14th century, Somerset produced a quarter of all the wool in England and Bruton prospered as one of the main producers.

To return to King Alfred's Tower by a different route, walk along the A359 Frome road for a short distance, then take the unclassified road towards the village of North Brewham. Before the village, turn right to South Brewham. After 0.75 miles (1.25km), turn left up the hill to reach King Alfred's Tower.

FORLORN RAILWAY BRIDGES

From Bruton, the Leland Trail continues from the bottom of the High Street via Trendle Lane near the junction with Shute Lane. Walk up the sunken lane, lined with sycamores, to the top, where there are good views across Bruton to the dovecote. Follow the track through a tunnel of trees which opens out on a hill, with magnificent views. The route is downhill across waymarked stiles and fields, with the railway line visible on your left and, beyond it, apple orchards nestling beneath Ridge Hill. Emerge on to a metalled lane in the village of Wyke Champflower. Turn left on to the lane and walk past the unusual 17th-century church attached to the Manor House.

Staying on the lane, cross a disused railway bridge and then turn left into Wyke Lane, following it for about 1 mile (1.6km). The route passes under a rather forlorn railway bridge which once carried the much lamented Somerset & Dorset Joint Railway on its way from Bath to Bournemouth. Passing under a second railway bridge, which carries the main line, and crossing over the River Brue, reach the hamlet of Cole. Turn right at the road junction and walk up the lane past Cole Farm to a stile and signpost to Ridge Hill. Follow the waymarked path across a field, up through apple orchards to reach Ridge Hill, with wonderful views of the valley below. The path now follows the ridge of the hill over several stiles and down steps to a metalled lane, where a left turn followed by a right turn will bring you into a bridleway named Solomon's Lane and signposted to Ansford. Follow this shady bridleway to the A371 road at Ansford. Turn right and then turn left down Ansford Road into Castle Cary High Street.

ℹ USEFUL INFORMATION
THE ROUTE
• www.visitsouthsomerset.com
South Somerset District Council has limited information on its website, but does produce the Leland Trail Guide, which can be obtained from the Yeovil Visitor Information Centre (see below), either in person or by purchasing from them by phone.
• www.somersetramblers.co.uk
The Somerset group of the Ramblers Association has their own website, which contains a little more information.

TOURIST INFORMATION CENTRES
• www.visitsouthsomerset.com
• Castle Cary TIC: The Market House, Market Place BA7 7AH; ☎ 01963 351763 (open Tue–Fri mornings)
• Yeovil Heritage and Visitor Information Centre: Hendford BA20 1UN; ☎ 01935 845946
• Cartgate TIC: a purpose-built and award-winning centre with its own parking, at the junction of the A303/A3088, Stoke-sub-Hamdon TA14 6RA; ☎ 01935 829333 (open all year; Mon & Fri only Nov–Easter)

PLANNING YOUR TRIP
• www.ldwa.org.uk
The Long Distance Walkers Association website gives limited information on the trail itself, but good general walking advice.
• www.visitsomerset.co.uk
Accommodation can be found using this County Council website, or through the tourist information centres listed above.

OTHER PATHS
The Leland Trail connects with the Macmillan Way (which starts at Boston in Lincolnshire and continues from Castle Cary to Barnstaple) and the Liberty Trail (which stretches 28 miles (45km) from Ham Hill to Lyme Regis). The latter links the Leland Trail to the South West Coast Path (pages 14–17).

BELOW Stepping stones over the River Brue BELOW RIGHT King Alfred's Tower near Stourhead Gardens

Castle Cary, like Bruton, owed much of its prosperity in the Middle Ages to the woollen trade. However, it owes its name to a castle which was built on nearby Lodge Hill in the early 12th century and eventually stormed by King Stephen in 1138. The centre of the town is well worth exploring.

To return to Bruton, walk the short distance along the A311 to Castle Cary railway station and take a train.

STAGE 2

CASTLE CARY to QUEEN CAMEL

DISTANCE 8.6 miles (13.9km)
MAPS OS Explorer 129, 142
START AT GRID REFERENCE ST 641 324
START POINT The George Hotel, Castle Cary

From the George Hotel in Castle Cary, walk up Paddock Drain and onto a narrow footpath signposted to Lodge Hill. At the top, cross the stile into a field and walk up and over Lodge Hill, site of the former castle with earthworks of a large keep just visible from the path, to a bench on the top of the hill. From here there is an uninterrupted view over Castle Cary towards Glastonbury Tor and the Mendip Hills. Continue along the top of the hill over several waymarked stiles, passing farm buildings on the right. Follow the waymarked path across several more stiles and fields to an electricity sub-station and turn left along the A359 road for 100yds (90m) to a gate and stile, signposted to Woolston (2 miles/3km). Do not take the bridleway immediately before this. The trail now passes through several fields down a small valley, with a hedge on the right. Continue on a farm track for about 1 mile (1.6km) to a metalled lane. Walk down this lane for about 200yds (180m) to a stile and gate, signposted to Brookhampton. Crossing the stile on the right into a field, the trail now passes through tranquil and beautiful countryside. Follow the waymarked path over a succession of stiles and fields into a metalled lane in the hamlet of Brookhampton. Turn left along Sandbrook lane, past a working waterwheel and several cottages for 0.25 mile (400m) to reach a waymarked stile. The route now

BELOW *South Cadbury*
BOTTOM *Royal Navy Military Cemetery at Yeovilton*

parallels the winding River Cam before gaining the lane again. Where the lane turns sharp left, go straight ahead and continue to follow the River Cam until you reach a metalled lane leading to a main road. (A detour can be made here into North Cadbury.) Cross the main road into another lane and follow the signed route across several fields to the road at Chapel Cross. Cross the A303 by the road bridge at Chapel Cross and continue on the road to South Cadbury, beneath Cadbury Castle hill fort.

VIEWS OF GLASTONBURY TOR

A short road walk leads to the beautiful and ancient village of Compton Pauncefoot and 15th-century St Andrew's Church.

Cross the road by The Camelot pub in South Cadbury to Folly Lane, which then continues as a track. Crossing over a succession of waymarked stiles and fields, the trail skirts around the massive bulk of Cadbury Castle, with distant views to the northwest of Glastonbury Tor, and eventually leads to a metalled lane and Sutton Montis. On reaching the small 13th-century Holy Trinity Church, walk up the steps, carefully following the waymarked path across the churchyard, across a stile and into a field behind the church. The trail now crosses over a series of waymarked stiles and fields, crossing a narrow metalled lane en route, until the tall blue-lias stone tower of Queen Camel Church comes into view. Before reaching the village of Queen Camel, the Castle Cary–Weymouth railway line is crossed on the level and great caution must be taken when negotiating the track. A narrow, enclosed footpath soon reaches the village, coming out into the main street (A359) by the side of the church. Turn left along this road into the centre of the village.

To return to Castle Cary, take the series of lanes via the villages of Weston Bampfylde, South Cadbury, North Cadbury and Galhampton. Alternatively, there are several buses a day from Queen Camel back to Castle Cary (except on Sundays).

QUEEN CAMEL TO HAM HILL

STAGE 3

QUEEN CAMEL to ILCHESTER

DISTANCE 5.8 miles (9.3km)
MAP OS Explorer 129
START AT GRID REFERENCE ST 595 248
START POINT Queen Camel High Street

Queen Camel is a well-cared-for village, built of blue-lias stone and dominated by the late 14th-century tall tower of St Barnabas Church. The village flourished in the 16th century, when there was a busy market trading locally made linen and wool. The size of the church is an indication of this prosperity, but in 1639 a disastrous fire destroyed many houses, and the village never fully recovered. From the village High Street turn down England's Lane, leading into Dark Lane, and then turn right into Green Lane, signposted West Camel (1 mile/1.6km). At the end of the lane cross into a field through a gate, then go across several further fields until a kissing-gate is reached. Walk past a riding school along a track which eventually leads into a metalled lane. This ends at the crossroads, dominated by a grand old spreading horse chestnut tree, in the tiny hamlet of Wales. Walk over the crossroads, through the hamlet and at the end of the lane continue through a farmyard. There then follows a succession of waymarked stiles across fields to the village of West Camel. Keeping the early 14th-century All Saints' Church

on the right, turn right on to the main road to the village. Turn left at the thatched former village stores down Back Lane for just over 0.25 miles (400m), past Frog Lane to a stile signposted Chantry Lane. Cross the field to Chantry Lane, turning left along the lane to a road junction, then turning right and second left to a lane signposted to Chilton Cantelo and Mudford. After approximately 0.5 miles (800m) where the lane turns sharp left, cross over a waymarked stile into the field on the right.

BY THE AIRFIELD

Yeovilton Royal Naval Air Station can now be seen and the Leland Trail follows the southern perimeter of the airfield for some distance to Yeovilton village. On days when the base is operating, various aircraft can be seen (and heard) going through their paces. With the airbase radar on the left and the River Cam on the right, follow the metalled track across several fields, through a disused wartime camp. Crossing over a small bridge and still following the perimeter fence, reach the River Yeo. Yeovilton village's St Bartholomew's Church can now be seen on the right. A detour from the Leland Trail would take you to the Fleet Air Arm Museum at Yeovilton.

Reach the metalled road, turn left over a bridge, with Yeovilton Weir to the left, then turn right over a waymarked stile signposted to Limington, into a field. The path now crosses two further stiles and fields to an old mill stream, which it then follows along the east bank, crossing a sluice gate bridge on the way, to a bridge. Cross the bridge and follow the waymarked signs over a series of stiles and fields until the ancient town of Ilchester can be seen ahead. The path goes downhill over several more stiles and fields until the River Yeo is reached at Ilchester. Walk into Free Street to the B3151 main road and turn left along this road into the town. Ilchester is a good place to break for refreshment and has several hotels. It is on a bus route back to Bruton.

A return from Ilchester to Queen Camel by a different route unfortunately involves some road-walking and retracing of steps. Follow the B3151 out of Ilchester, past RNAS Yeovilton Airfield. Turn right to the village of Speckington, then retrace your steps on the Trail back to Queen Camel. The other alternative is to retrace your steps the whole way.

STAGE 4

ILCHESTER to HAM HILL

DISTANCE 6.5 miles (10.5km)
MAP OS Explorer 129
START AT GRID REFERENCE ST 522 226
START POINT Car park near the church

Ilchester was once the important Roman town of *Lendiniae*, positioned strategically on the Fosse Way (A37). In medieval times it was also a town of some importance, with walls and gates, a friary, a hospital and a county gaol, as well as a thriving market and mint. From the car park, walk south along the main street towards the roundabout with the A37 Fosse Way, crossing over this road at the traffic island to the stile in the fence opposite. From this point the waymarked Leland Trail crosses several fields and drainage ditches for about 1 mile (1.6km) to Sock Dennis Farm. Sock Dennis was named after the ancient family of Dacus and is a deserted medieval village. Some earthworks are visible in a field where the Leland Trail passes the eastern edge of the site.

Cross a stile past the farm buildings and follow the path ahead into a field. Cross a further stile into a wide, grassed lane. Follow this lane, crossing several more waymarked stiles and fields to a footbridge and two bridlegates onto a leafy enclosed

The monument at Ham Hill at sunset

footpath. A short climb leads to Cole Cross, about 1 mile (1.6km) from the village of Chilthorne Domer. From Cole Cross the route crosses the metalled road into Kissmedown Lane, signposted Windmill Lane. Walk uphill along Kissmedown Lane, a bridleway which eventually gives a good view of the approach to Montacute House and Ham Hill. The bridleway gives way to a metalled road at Windmill Farm, which is passed on the left, and shortly after this a road junction is reached. Cross straight over into a leafy enclosed lane to its end, where the busy A3088 road is crossed (with care). Follow the waymarkers across a stone millstream bridge to the grounds of Montacute House (NT). Bear left over the small hill and follow the waymarked path over a succession of stiles, with good views of Montacute House, to the main road at the southern end of Montacute village.

Walk through pretty Montacute village along the main street, past the church and the Kings Arms Inn to the village recreation grounds. Turn left through these grounds, towards St Michael's Hill. Go through a kissing-gate and follow the permissive path up the hill to the stile at the edge of the wooded hilltop. From here, the Leland Trail turns right and skirts along the lower edge of the wooded hill, but a short detour to make the steep climb to the top of St Michael's Hill is worthwhile.

The Leland Trail also affords good views towards the Blackdown and Mendip Hills in the distance. The path crosses a waymarked stile and goes down a sloping field towards a sunken path, which was once a Roman road, then uphill and right into the woods on Hedgecock Hill. The waymarked path through the woods and around the ramparts of the Iron Age hill fort on Ham Hill soon leads to the final destination.

Ham Hill was a large fortified settlement and visible for many miles around. It has been shown by archaeologists to have been in continuous occupation from the New Stone Age times, up to and beyond the Roman occupation.

On a clear day, King Alfred's Tower, the starting point of this walk, can be seen to the northeast. A fitting end to the walk would be a visit to the Prince of Wales Inn, situated on the top of Ham Hill, before descending the short distance to the village of Stoke-sub-Hamdon, which nestles beneath the Hill, just off the busy A303 trunk road.

To return to Ilchester by a different route, descend to East Stoke from the footpath from Ham Hill, then take Marsh Lane to the village of Tintinhull. From here another footpath leads back to the Leland Trail at grid ref. ST 511 195, where the route back to Ilchester can be retraced.

PLACES TO VISIT

• STOURHEAD
www.nationaltrust.org.uk or
www.stourhead.com
☎ 01747 841152
King Alfred's Tower is actually part of the 2,650-acre (1,072ha) Stourhead Estate. The main house is a magnificent Palladian mansion, which contains fine paintings and Chippendale furniture. Equally famous are the Italianate gardens, featuring a beautiful lake and various classical temples. There is also a farm shop and a restaurant, which uses local organic meat and vegetables from the estate kitchen garden. Garden, shop and restaurant open daily all year; house and tower open Fri–Tue Mar–Oct.

• FLEET AIR ARM MUSEUM
www.fleetairarm.com
☎ 01935 840565
This impressive collection lies just a short walk from the route on the B3151, between West Camel and Yeovilton. It includes all manner of aircraft, from the first manned kites to modern Sea Harriers, and including the first British-built Concorde, bi-planes and a rare Kamikaze aircraft. There is a restaurant and an outdoor playground. Open daily, except Mon & Tue Nov–Mar.

• MONTACUTE HOUSE
www.nationaltrust.org.uk
☎ 01935 823289
This National Trust property sits almost at the end of the trail. It is one of the finest Elizabethan mansions in the land and houses over 50 portraits on loan from the National Portrait Gallery in its Long Gallery (the longest of its type to survive, stretching the full length of the house). The estate also has fine formal gardens and extensive parkland, containing waymarked walks. Open daily Mar–Oct, except Tue (gardens also open Wed–Sun Nov–Feb).

Cotswold Way

COMPLETE ROUTE CHIPPING CAMPDEN TO BATH ABBEY **102 MILES (164KM)**
SECTION COVERED CHIPPING CAMPDEN TO PAINSWICK **47 MILES (76KM)**
MAPS OS EXPLORER OL 14, OL 45, 155, 167, 168, 179

The Cotswold Way is the newest of the National Trails, having gained National Trail status in May 2007. The 47-mile (76km) section described here covers the northern part of the route. The prime season for tourism in the Cotswolds is of course the summer, though the walker following the limestone ridges can rise above the parking problems and crawling traffic which besets the area. With so much on offer, the best time to walk the Cotswold Way may be in spring or autumn, when tourism is less intrusive, many of the attractions are still open to the public, and the beech woodlands that form an important part of the route are at their best. There is plenty of accommodation in the towns and villages along the way, but campsites are few and far between. With so many distractions, it is impossible specify how long the route will take to walk, and careful planning is necessary to fit in with opening times of places to visit. Generally, the going is moderate, though there may be quite a bit of mud in wet weather and a certain amount of hill-climbing in the area around Cheltenham. Walkers are frequently surprised that the height gain over the whole route is equal to three times the height of Snowdon.

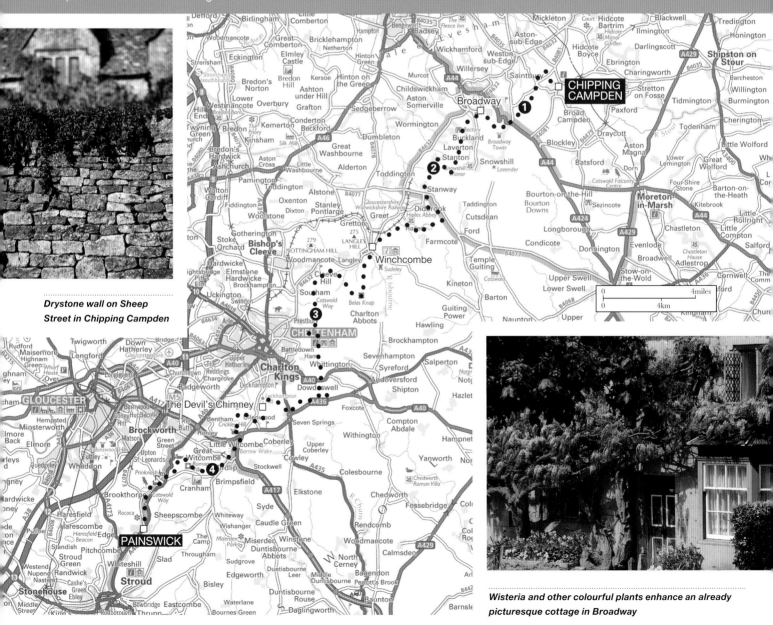

Drystone wall on Sheep Street in Chipping Campden

Wisteria and other colourful plants enhance an already picturesque cottage in Broadway

CHIPPING CAMPDEN TO WINCHCOMBE

Broadway Tower

STAGE 1

CHIPPING CAMPDEN to BROADWAY

DISTANCE 5.2 miles (8.4km)
MAP OS Explorer OL 45
START AT GRID REFERENCE SP 155 394
START POINT Market Hall

Chipping Campden has a magnificent church, built by prosperous wool merchant William Grevel in the 15th century. Next to it is the gatehouse to Campden House, built by 'mercer', or textile dealer, Sir Baptist Hicks in 1615 and burned to a shell by its retreating Royalist garrison in 1645. Sir Baptist also built almshouses for 12 poor people of Chipping Campden, which can be seen on the road leading down from the church. Beyond the almshouses, Campden High Street is splendid. Look out for Grevel House, built by William Grevel in 1380, the Market Hall, built by Sir Baptist Hicks in 1627, and the 14th-century Woolstaplers' Hall, with its museum and information centre.

Past Market Hall, the first Cotswold Way signpost points right, up a lane by the side of St Catherine's Church. The route follows Hoo Lane uphill, past a number of affluent Cotswold stone cottages, joining a track which goes straight ahead uphill. This crosses a level field, and emerges on the top of Dover's Hill, from where there are fine views, on a clear day, over the Vale of Evesham and the Malvern Hills. The hilltop area is now owned by the National Trust. It was named after Robert Dover, a 17th-century lawyer who organized a series of famous annual games which were held, on and off, until the mid-19th century. In more recent times they have been revived in a modified version.

WILLIAM MORRIS COUNTRY

Past the car park the route turns left along the road, and then right at the next crossroads, by Weston Park Farm. A short way along on the right, the Kiftsgate Stone is set just inside Weston Wood, marking the meeting point of the Saxon hundred court. The route turns off the road by the side of Campden Woods, following the Mile Drive track in an area that was landscaped in the 19th century by the Earl of Gainsborough. Crossing a road, the route leads past a small hillock surmounted by the Panorama Dial. Crossing the A44, a track leads through woodland, and then across grassy hollows and small valleys towards Broadway Tower, straight ahead. This superb folly was built in 1799 by the Earl of Coventry, and later let to two Oxford tutors who used it to introduce the delights of the area to such worthies as William Morris, the Pre-Raphaelite craftsman, artist and socialist, and Dante Gabriel Rossetti. The tower has now been renovated as part of the Broadway Tower Country Park. On the first floor there is an exhibition devoted to sheep and wool production, both old and new, while the second floor is devoted to William Morris. From the tower, a path leads steeply downhill to Broadway, emerging near the top of the High Street. This is the quintessential Cotswold village; its single street lined with impressive buildings housing antique shops, cafés, and hotels. The wide street was created to accommodate twin streams that ran down its length, with willows on either side, giving the village the name of Broadway. It prospered due to its importance as a staging post for coaches en route between Worcester and Oxford. Even when coaches were replaced by the railway, Broadway continued to prosper, having been established by William Morris and his friends as a fashionable artistic retreat.

To return to Chipping Campden (grid ref. SP 095 375), follow the footpath north to Willersey, and from there on to Saintbury Church. A footpath leads due east to the Dover's Hill car park, from where the Cotswold Way leads back down to Chipping Campden.

STAGE 2

BROADWAY to WINCHCOMBE

DISTANCE 11.8 miles (19km)
MAP OS Explorer OL 45
START AT GRID REFERENCE SP 095 375
START POINT Broadway Green

The Cotswold Way continues from Broadway near its oldest house, the Abbot's Grange, which is sited below the green. The route turns off on to a footpath opposite the church. Crossing the lane, the route climbs through the woods of Broadway Coppice, passing along the side of a field and crossing the Worcester/Gloucestershire border to go through a complicated series of gates and stiles. A long, straight track leads on above Burnhill, with views to Broadway Tower. This leads to Manor Farm, where the route follows a sometimes muddy track that doubles back to the right, before bearing left on a much firmer track by the side of woods and on along the ridge past solitary hilltop farm buildings. A short way on it passes a disused quarry on the left, and then comes to a crossroads, with the Cotswold Way signpost by a cattle grid. Here you may wish to divert to Snowshill, a quaint hamlet with an interesting manor house in the valley.

To continue along the Cotswold Way, follow the track straight on along towards Shenberrow Farm, where the hill fort at the top of the hill is sited in what must have been an impregnable position, though little remains of it today. From the farmhouse, a track leads downhill through woods. It bears left on to a narrow path and passes close by Stanton's small reservoir before entering the village. Stanton has splendid Cotswold buildings lining its main street, without the tourist trappings and massed cars that spoil Broadway and Chipping Campden. Most of its buildings were built in the 17th century and restored to their current condition by architectural enthusiast Sir Philip Stott in the early 20th century.

From Stanton the route crosses fields, before entering the fine parkland of Stanway House. It joins a lane by a most unusual thatched cricket pavilion, standing on staddle stones. The grand stately home is passed immediately on the left. It was built by Sir Paul Tracey in the early 17th century. Notice

ℹ USEFUL INFORMATION

THE ROUTE
• www.nationaltrail.co.uk
This is the most comprehensive source of information about the CW. Detailed route maps, free leaflets, transport information and maps with accommodation listings are here, alongside all the help and links you could possibly need; even GPS data.

TOURIST INFORMATION CENTRES
• www.campdenonline.org
The Old Police Station, High Street, Chipping Campden GL55 6HB ☎ 01386 841206
• www.visitcheltenham.gov.uk
77 The Promenade, Cheltenham GL50 1PJ
☎ 01242 522878
There are smaller centres at Broadway ☎ 01386 852937, Winchcombe ☎ 01242 602925 and Painswick ☎ 01452 813522.

PLANNING YOUR TRIP
There are numerous websites detailing the services along the CW. The most helpful are:
• www.ramblers.org.uk
☎ 020 7339 8500
The Ramblers Association pages provide general information about long-distance walking and specific help covering the CW.
• www.ldwa.org.uk
The Long Distance Walkers Association lists similar details.
www.cotswold-way.co.uk
☎ 0871 5200124
This link takes you to the Sherpa Van Project website, which serves a number of long-distance paths with a luggage and lodgings service. It also contains details of the route, maps and trailplanners to buy, and other useful links.

OTHER PATHS
The CW links with many other Cotswold region routes. Notable is the Cotswold Round, a 217-mile (349km) circuit devised by the Macmillan Way Association. At Chipping Campden, the CW also meets the Heart of England Way.

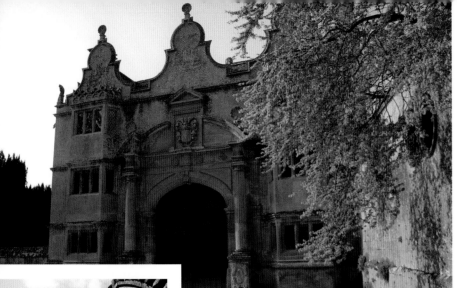

ABOVE Ruined Hailes Abbey
was founded in 1246
TOP, LEFT TO RIGHT
Gatehouse of Stanway
House; Knot Garden at
Sudeley Castle; View from
Leckhampton Hill, part of
the Edge Escarpment, with
the Devil's Chimney in the
foreground; The Cotswold
Way path at Painswick
Beacon

its magnificent south gateway in the style of Inigo Jones, just past the much-restored 12th-century church. Beyond the south gateway the route bears left on a footpath past estate cottages, going through a wooden gate with a carved duck's head.

To return to Broadway, walk east from Stanway and take the bridleway (grid ref. SP 068 320) through Lidcombe Wood towards Snowshill. From there, either follow the road due north to Broadway, or take the footpath via Great Brockhampton Farm and Buckland Wood towards Bury End.

The path leads on across the B4077, with the Cotswold Way taking an indirect route to Hailes Abbey in order to visit Beckbury Camp. At the small hamlet of Wood Stanway it bears left up the hillside above sheep pens, crossing fields, towards the imposing farmhouse at Lower Coscombe. Bear right, uphill, before the farm and then follow the contours of the hillside to the road junction at Stumps Cross. From here the route leads via a track to the imposing hill fort of Beckbury Camp. The walker should go steeply down the hill by the stone pillar, and follow the path across level ground beneath the fort's ramparts, joining a track and turning downhill towards Hailes Abbey. This is a good spot, by the church, to stop and rest awhile, before the route turns left across a field, giving fine views of the abbey ruins and crossing fields towards Winchcombe along the Pilgrims' Way. A track leads down to join Puck Pit Lane, entering Winchcombe by the A46. An optional footpath route which avoids the main road follows the east side of the River Isbourne to enter Winchcombe by Castle Street.

WINCHCOMBE TO PAINSWICK

STAGE 3
WINCHCOMBE to THE DEVIL'S CHIMNEY
DISTANCE 16.6 miles (26.7km)
MAPS OS Explorer OL 45, 179
START AT GRID REFERENCE SP 025 283
START POINT Winchcombe Town Hall

Winchcombe has grown from the Saxon settlement of 'Wincel Cumb'. Much of its early importance was due to its prosperous abbey, which played host to pilgrims paying homage to the shrine of St Kenelm, a young Saxon king murdered in mysterious circumstances in the 9th century. The abbey was dissolved in

1539, and today nothing of it remains, though its stone was used for building in the town. Unfortunately, Winchcombe missed out on the wool boom that made other parts of the Cotswolds so wealthy and, after losing its abbey, it became a poor town. Nevertheless, there are many fine buildings, notably the Jacobean King's School House, attributed to Inigo Jones. St Peter's Church, opposite, was built in the 15th century and is notable for marks of shot in its walls dating from the Civil War, an organ case attributed to Grinling Gibbons, a magnificent collection of gargoyles, and a weathercock which is one of the finest in Britain.

ROMAN REMAINS AND A VICTORIAN RESERVOIR
The route now leaves Winchcombe at the southwest end of the town, turning left down Corndean Lane and then up past riding stables and up a hill towards Belas Knap. The Wadfield Roman Villa, on a small site to the right here, has remains of Roman walls and a mosaic pavement. The route runs alongside the road, and then follows a track signposted towards Belas Knap; a massive and very well preserved Neolithic long barrow burial chamber of the Severn-Cotswold type.

From Belas Knap, paths and tracks head across a field towards Wontley Farm, turning sharp right before the farm, and heading downhill towards Breakheart Plantation. The route now goes north through the plantation and circles Cleeve Common to the north, thereby avoiding an area of sensitive calcareous grassland within the Cleeve Hill SSSI. The route passes an ancient tithe barn and Postlip Hall before climbing to Cleeve Hill Golf Club.

From here (grid ref. SO 987 269), the B4632 leads directly back to Winchcombe, less than 3 miles (5km) distant. Alternatively, it is possible to follow a bridleway towards Postlip Hall, with a footpath heading on by the River Isbourne into Winchcombe.

The golf course poses route-finding problems as the Cotswold Way dodges the bunkers, following the west side of the ridge with fine views of Cheltenham sprawled on the plain below. Cleeve Hill Camp is worth looking out for here, as is Cleeve Cloud, a large rock formation on the hillside. Beyond the prominent radio masts the route heads along the hillside, joining a lane and then heading across fields towards Colgate Farm, close by the overhead power lines which sing oddly as the path passes under them once again. A path leads downhill by the side of Dowdeswell Wood, which has a pleasant mixture of trees being grown for commercial purposes. At the bottom of the hill the path leads out by the side of Victorian Dowdeswell Reservoir.

The reservoir could be a pleasant place to stop, but is spoilt by the proximity of the A40, which must be crossed near the Reservoir Inn. A track leads uphill over what was once a part of the Great Western Railway, heading through Lineover Wood, the 'lime tree hill'. This is pleasant undulating walking through quiet woodland, a foretaste of the extensive beech woods to come nearer Painswick. Past a solitary farmhouse in a fine position, and an improbable bed-and-breakfast sign in the middle of nowhere, a narrow track leads diagonally up to the top of the steep hill, from where there are magnificent views over Dowdeswell Reservoir and towards Cheltenham. The route leaves Wistley Hill, around a field and down through Wistley Grove, to pick up a path on the field side of a hedge alongside the A436 to Seven Springs.

Seven Springs roundabout is named after the springs that are the source of the River Churn, a short way down the A436. The Cotswold Way turns off the main road here, following a lane northwards to join a ridgeway footpath along the top of Hartley Hill, above Charlton Kings Common. From here there are immense views over Cheltenham, as the route leads to the highest point at Leckhampton Hill Fort, where there is a trig point to confirm your position. It is worth walking to the cliff edge to see the Devil's Chimney, an impressive rock tower left by the quarry workings which eventually ceased here in 1925.

STAGE 4

THE DEVIL'S CHIMNEY to PAINSWICK

DISTANCE 12.8 miles (20.6km)
MAP OS Explorer 179
START AT GRID REFERENCE SO 948 184
START POINT Trig point near Devil's Chimney, on top of Leckhampton Hill

From the Devil's Chimney the route heads south, crossing a lane where there is a small car park for Leckhampton Hill, and following a bridleway downhill towards Ullenwood, which is now a training centre for young disabled people. The route crosses the B4070, following a lane past the Nissen huts of an old military camp and passing Shurdington Long Barrow to the left. At the top of Shurdington Hill the route turns on to a footpath, following the ridge with fine views over unspoilt ground to the west, looking as far as the mountains of South Wales. The path soon enters Short Wood, with mature beech trees on either side, keeping to the side of the ridge before emerging on open ground at Crickley Hill. This famous hill fort site was founded in the Neolithic period, 4000-3000BC. It became an Iron Age camp around 600BC,

suffering destruction at the hands of enemy tribes several times. From the summit of Crickley Hill the route heads downhill, entering more beech woods and emerging at the road by the Air Balloon roundabout. This is the busy intersection of the A46, A436 and A417, and can be something of a nightmare for the walker, with the route continuing on pavement up by the side of the A46, past the Air Balloon public house. Thankfully it soon bears off on a hillside path below Barrow Wake, with the fine views over to Crickley Hill marred by the din of traffic roaring up the hill. The route follows the contours just below the hilltop, entering more beech woods. From here the route leads downhill through beech woods to Birdlip Hill, crossing the road and entering Witcombe Wood, from where there is a long stretch of woodland walking. The woods here are very fine in spring and autumn, but the wide track can be muddy. The mass of tracks is also confusing, but there are Cotswold Way waymarks. With pheasants much in evidence, the route passes a sadly overgrown entrance gate to Witcombe Park, and further on a track to the right leads downhill to the Roman Witcombe Villa.

The route leaves the Witcombe estate by a small cottage in a fine hillside position. A lane continues through the hamlet of Witcombe and past the bottom of Cooper's Hill, where the famous annual cheese-rolling event takes place. The hillside is suffering from erosion and has now been fenced off, and the footpath is a diverted route which bears left up through woods to reach the top of Cooper's Hill.

From Cooper's Hill (grid ref. SO 893 147), footpaths lead via the Roman Villa to Witcombe Park, then on to Cold Slad by Crickley Hill.

The main route enters Brockworth Wood, where there are information boards and nature trails, going on to Buckholt Wood to cross the A46 to Prinknash Park and Abbey. The park is open to the public, and the Benedictine monks are famous for their pottery and their modern abbey. From here the route passes the back of a modern Cotswold mansion, joining a bridleway track across an extensive golf course all the way to the outskirts of Painswick. The walker should divert to the highest point of Painswick Beacon, off to the right. From the trig point there are magnificent views over the surrounding countryside, and the extensive ramparts and ditches of the ancient hill fort, which has now been commandeered by golfers, can also be seen. Coming to a lane, the route follows a footpath along the hillside, passing Catsbrain Quarry and rejoining a track across behind the club house. It continues by a stone wall, reaching the far end of the golf course, where the route follows the road into Painswick.

ⓘ PLACES TO VISIT

• **SNOWSHILL MANOR AND GARDEN**
www.nationaltrust.org.uk
☎ 01386 852410
A short diversion from the route, between Broadway and Stanton, takes you to Snowshill, where you will find this Cotswold stone manor house. It is remarkable for housing the collection of over 20,000 objects amassed by the Arts and Crafts collector, Charles Wade. He saw the craftsmanship in all sorts of objects, from cow bells to Samurai armour. The colourful terraced garden is a joy. Open Wed–Sun Mar–Oct.

• **HAILES ABBEY**
www.english-heritage.org.uk
☎ 01242 602398
The route passes the remains of the Cistercian Hailes Abbey, which is an ideal picnic stop. There is a museum with objects found on the site and a free audio tour. The 12th-century church opposite is also worth a visit to see fine medieval wall paintings. Open daily Apr–Oct.

• **SUDELEY CASTLE**
www.sudeleycastle.co.uk
☎ 01242 604244
The CW passes the west entrance to Sudeley Castle. Over the last 1,000 years the castle has had many royal connections, most famously with the Tudors. The church here is the resting place of Katherine Parr. There are nine delightful gardens surrounding the castle, including the formal Queens' Garden with its lovely roses. There is also an adventure playground. Open daily Apr–Oct. No dogs allowed.

• **PAINSWICK ROCOCO GARDEN**
www.rococogarden.org.uk
☎ 01452 813204
At the end of the route you will find Painswick House and its Rococo Garden. Originally laid out in the 18th century, over 20 years of restoration is ongoing and the garden is most famous for its snowdrop displays (in Feb). Open daily Jan–Oct.

Sunset over Appley Beach on the Isle of Wight

South & South East England

Isle of Wight Coastal Path

COMPLETE ROUTE RYDE TO RYDE **68 MILES (109KM)**

SECTION COVERED AS ABOVE

MAP OS EXPLORER OL 29

The Isle of Wight has been called 'England in miniature', and not without reason; the variety of terrain and panorama offered by this coastal footpath must surely make it one of the most varied and enjoyable long-distance paths in the country. The great thing about a coastal footpath on any island is that it is circular. Walk for long enough and you are bound to end up back at the starting point. 'Long enough', in this case, can be anything from three days to a week, depending on how fast you want to go and how lightly you are travelling. The path is detailed here in an anti-clockwise direction. There are advantages in walking it either way, but the anti-clockwise approach does seem to offer more appreciation of the scenery. Ryde has been chosen as the start point because this disposes of the less scenic parts of the route on the first day. The going is generally fairly easy, nothing too steep to climb or descend, and plenty of fine open cliff-walks with excellent views in all directions. Due to the island's fame as a Mecca of the British yachting fraternity, and its general appeal as a summer holiday location, a fair amount of walking towards the beginning and end of the route will be on tarmac, and in some quite densely populated areas. However, the exhilarating hikes along the cliff-tops in the south do more than make up for this.

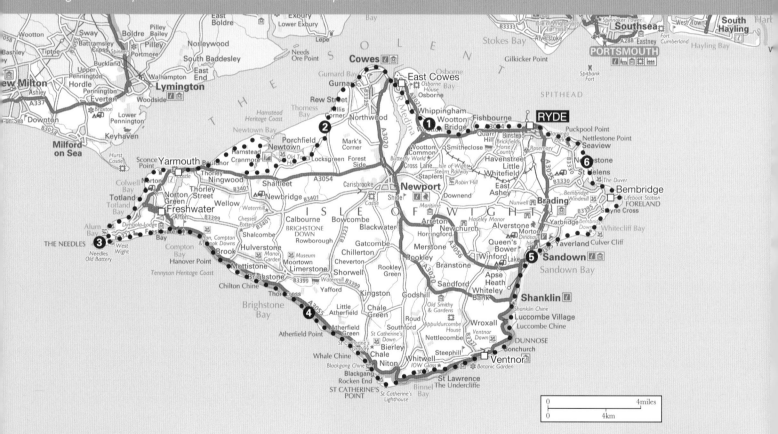

LEFT *Looking across Freshwater Bay to the hotels and Tennyson Down*
RIGHT *The Freshwater Bay viewpoint, showing the various chalk seastacks and Tennyson Down beyond*
FAR RIGHT *A small waterfall tinkling down the chine at Shanklin*

Osborne House was built in the style of an Italian villa

Looking down the length of Ryde's impressive pier

RYDE TO YARMOUTH

STAGE 1

RYDE to EAST COWES

DISTANCE 7.8 miles (12.6km)
MAP OS Explorer OL 29
START AT GRID REFERENCE SZ 594 929
START POINT Lyndale Bridge at Lynmouth

The town of Ryde is famous for its Victorian architecture; a theme throughout the island. The walk starts in St Thomas Street, and picks its way through quiet streets to Spencer Road, and thence to the footpath to 'Binstead and Quarr'.

This pleasant footpath descends gradually for about 0.5 miles (800m), bordered on both sides by the links of Ryde Golf Club, and then ascends to reach Binstead Church. The elegant and ordered appearance of this building belies its eventful history: part Norman, part Victorian, and part early 1970s (after a fire destroyed much of the old nave roof). The seat in the graveyard is well placed for the first breather of the day. The path continues westward along a bridleway and Quarr Road. Soon the towers of the new Quarr Abbey come into view.

The route to the new abbey takes the walker through the grounds of the old one; those low-lying walls to the right are all that is left of the original Abbey of Our Lady of The Quarry, founded in 1311 and built in the local Binstead limestone. The new abbey is to the right of the path and is worth a quick detour. This abbey was built early this century by a Benedictine order of monks, and is constructed of bright red bricks from Belgium. The old abbey had been dissolved by Henry VIII in 1537.

The track continues westward and, just when the walker is getting used to the peace and quiet of the countryside, emerges rather unexpectedly at Fishbourne Ferry Terminal, with all the hustle and bustle. Turn left on to the main road here, and then take the path to the right beside the telephone box, which leads to a tree-lined lane and eventually the A3054. Turn right here and descend to Wootton Bridge.

From this point (grid ref. SZ 548 919), it is a simple matter to catch the bus either back to Ryde, or ahead to East Cowes.

ON THE ROAD

The next 4 miles (6.5km) are all on-road, and there would be no shame in hopping on the next bus straight to Cowes. The official route follows through a housing estate to the top of the hill at Wootton, to join the minor road that passes through Westwood and Dallimores, heading towards Whippingham. Apart from a few views across the Solent there is little to distract walkers from their pace. Once you reach the A3021, there is a choice. Although busy with traffic, this road has a wide pavement and offers a quick march into East Cowes. Alternatively, and a much better option, take the first left to view the Church of St Mildred at Whippingham. Built in 1860 to the specifications of Prince Albert, it occupies the site of an 11th-century church and is now a popular tourist attraction, even boasting public toilets.

The road from the church continues straight into East Cowes, passing an attractive line of almshouses on the right. Make your way down to the 'Floating Bridge' ferry, resisting the temptation to stop for provisions in East Cowes. The shops and restaurants across the river are much better.

Being mainly residential, this area is not particularly well served with footpaths that might provide an alternative route back to Ryde. Bus services, however, operate regularly.

STAGE 2

COWES to YARMOUTH

DISTANCE 16.8 miles (27km)
MAP OS Explorer OL 29
START AT GRID REFERENCE SZ 500 956
START POINT West Cowes 'Floating Bridge'

The town of Cowes is steeped in marine history. From the ferry you can see the premises in which the J S White Company built and launched the first seaplane. Close by is the former home of the British Hovercraft Corporation, creators of the first hovercraft. Notwithstanding these technological achievements, Cowes is first and foremost a thriving yachting town, home of the National Sailing Centre, the Royal Yacht Squadron, Cowes Week and the Admiral's Cup. In July and early August it will be very busy.

Walking west from the ferry, head for the pedestrian precinct. Here, in summer, there is a curious mix of holidaymakers and serious yachting types; blocks and shackles rubbing shoulders with buckets and spades. Continue through the pedestrian zone until the start of the Esplanade walk. This runs for a good few miles to the city limits, passing in front of the Royal Yacht Squadron HQ and Egypt Point. It is the most northerly point on the island and site of an anti-submarine boom that, during the war, stretched right across the Solent to the mainland.

ON THE COASTAL PATH

The path eventually leaves the road, and reaches a sailing club with a slipway. Turn uphill here and take the footpath up to the right between black bollards. Follow the path into Worsley Road and then first right, downhill to Gurnard Bridge.

After the bridge turn immediately right on to a track. For the first time since leaving Ryde, the walker is now on a proper coast path. The low-lying shaley cliffs here are in stark contrast to the splendour of the chalk Needles waiting ahead. When it reaches the sandy beach in front of the Thorness Bay Holiday Park, the route turns inland to pass through the camp to the entrance

USEFUL INFORMATION

THE ROUTE
• www.islandbreaks.co.uk
☎ 01983 813813
The official website of Isle of Wight Tourism contains downloadable leaflets of the route in sections, which include a map and directions. They also produce a more detailed guide to the route and other walks, which can be ordered by post or phone.

TOURIST INFORMATION CENTRES
• www.islandbreaks.co.uk
☎ 01983 813813
• Newport TIC: The Guildhall, High Street PO30 1TY (Open daily)
• Ryde TIC: 81/83 Union Street. PO33 2LW (Open daily)
• Sandown TIC: High Street PO36 8DA (Open daily Apr–Oct; less in winter)
• Yarmouth TIC: The Quay PO41 0PQ (Open daily Apr–Oct; less in winter)
• There are also offices in Cowes and Shanklin, but they open less frequently.

PLANNING YOUR TRIP
• www.ldwa.org.uk
The Long Distance Walkers Association provides information about the coastal path and also on other routes across the island.
• www.ramblers.org.uk
☎ 020 7339 8500
The Ramblers Association page on the coast path gives links to other sites, particularly for public transport information.
• www.yha.org.uk
☎ 0800 019 1700
The Youth Hostel Association has accommodation at Brighstone and Totland Bay.
• www.wightstay.co.uk
Another possible alternative to the official tourist website for finding a place to stay.

OTHER PATHS
• www.wight-cam.co.uk is a useful website to consult for colour-coded maps of other walk routes on the island, including those which cross it and smaller circular walks from points around the coast path route.

TOP Cowes waterfront and private marinas
MIDDLE Each plank along Yarmouth Pier contains the names of sponsors who helped fund its restoration
BOTTOM Cowes Week bunting decorates Shooters Hill in the centre of Cowes

gate. From here the footpath leads across a number of fields to the village of Porchfield. The route is now well inland, avoiding the marshy tributaries of the Newtown River; a nature reserve and famous haunt for birdwatchers. Porchfield to Newtown is another 3 miles (5km) of road walk, finishing with a short cut across the fields, via a stile just after Old Vicarage Lane, picking up the route of Newtown's Nature Trail.

Newtown is well worth a few moments' pause, especially for a look at the estuary and quay, where ships of up to 500 tonnes used to dock. The walk continues up the road past the Old Town Hall, a National Trust property, and along towards Shalfleet. It branches left up a small track, over the bridge by Shalfleet Mill, and thence to the New Inn at Shalfleet, which is much acclaimed for its excellent seafood.

From Shalfleet (grid ref. SZ 414 893), it is possible to turn back to Cowes along footpaths through Parkhurst Forest, or along the road. Alternatively, catch the bus either straight ahead to Yarmouth or back to Cowes, changing at Newport.

IDYLLIC NEWTOWN ESTUARY

Turn westwards to pass the Church of St Michael the Archangel. The church tower was constructed just a few years after the Norman Conquest and, ironically, was often used as a place of refuge from French harassment in the following centuries.

Continue to the first footpath signed to the right, around a large field to a small footbridge over a muddy stream and into some dense woods. The path then joins a wider and well-signposted track. Follow signs for Lower Hamstead farm. Pause for a moment while passing Pigeon Coo Farm, to hear why it is so named. The track eventually reaches the waterside, back on to the Newtown estuary with all its wonderful birds and plants. This is a particularly popular haunt for yachtsmen, not surprising as it is an idyllic spot.

The route now skirts inland around a large tributary and then turns northeast across some low-lying fields and a long wooden bridge to reach the coast briefly again. The concrete ramp and debris here all date back to the intense activities of World War II training, defence and D-Day preparations. The track soon turns back inland, joining a lane which leads to Hamstead Farm, and then proceeding west across a couple of

fields passing Cliff Cottages, Greenacres and one or two other houses and farms. Diversions and route-changes abound here due to the movements of the cliff. Occasional views over the Solent keep the walker occupied and the first sign of approaching civilization is the sight of Yarmouth pier sticking way out into the ocean. The path does at one point reach sea level, and then climbs again past ruined Bouldnor Battery. This stretch offers an enjoyable finale along the seawall, leading straight into the High Street. Yarmouth is one of the prettier towns on the island and has its fair share of history, earning its charter in 1332. The castle by the pier was one of a number commissioned by Henry VIII to keep the French at bay, and is worth a visit.

YARMOUTH TO VENTNOR

STAGE 3
YARMOUTH to FRESHWATER
DISTANCE 9 miles (14.5km)
MAP OS Explorer OL 29
START AT GRID REFERENCE SZ 354 897
START POINT Yarmouth Pier

From the pier, walk west across the bridge, and then along the sea wall, turning left up into the woods as soon as the wall ends. The path then briefly meets a road before entering Fort Victoria Country Park. The wide and straight wooded trail is actually the site of an old military road. History students may well wish to detour here down to Fort Victoria, built in 1853 and twin sister to Hurst Castle across on the mainland.

Emerging from the park, the route passes through Brambles Chine holiday camp to the beach, and then stays by the waterside all the way to Totland. Cast a glance back over your shoulder at the fort, and across the Solent to Hurst Castle. The scenery is now improving all the time.

From Totland (grid ref. SZ 323 873), it is possible to cut the corner and short-cut straight to Freshwater Bay, removing some 4 miles (6.5km) from the route. Alternatively, there is a bus route straight back to Yarmouth or ahead to Freshwater.

LEFT *The coast and cliffs of*
The Needles
ABOVE *Tennyson's*
monument on the crest of
Tennyson Down

At the end of the sea wall the route climbs through Totland, then breaks out into open heathland as it climbs Headon Hill. Head for the Bronze Age tumulus at the summit, where you should pause to enjoy the views in all directions; this is the highest point so far, and gives a good view of the interior of the island. Walk westward along the ridge (which is draped in purple heather at the right time of year) to view The Needles and then descend to the road, and the noise and the congestion of the Needles Park. Now a busy tourist location, this was once an important scientific site. From the clifftop here, Guglielmo Marconi made his first wireless transmissions.

Beyond the car parks, a wide track leads to The Needles, the visually dramatic end to the spine of chalk that runs right across the island to Culver Down on the eastern side. Look back at the multicoloured sands of Alum Bay Cliffs and note the contrast between those pastel shades and the stark white of The Needles. For the ultimate view, you can pay to enter the Needles Battery, but there are plenty of fine clifftop views to be had without handing over your cash. A good free viewing area is at the end of the Battery by the Black Knight testing pad. From here on the walk really opens out. The path continues along the cliff-tops for the next 15 miles (24km) — open, airy walking right at the cliff-edge. From The Needles, the 500ft (152m) Tennyson Monument is the obvious next stop. Alfred Lord Tennyson lived in Freshwater for many years, hoping for peace and quiet, but suffering from his superstar status as Poet Laureate. Pause to enjoy the views before descending to Freshwater.

To return to Yarmouth from Freshwater (grid ref. SZ 347 857) take one of the footpaths straight across the neck of the peninsula, along the River Yar or up the Freshwater Way, to its west.

STAGE 4

FRESHWATER to VENTNOR

DISTANCE 17.8 miles (28.6km)
MAP OS Explorer OL 29
START AT GRID REFERENCE SZ 347 857
START POINT Freshwater Beach

This section of the route is virtually uninterrupted clifftop path, wide and very pleasant throughout, with minimal human habitation. The path is clear and simple to follow, and is never more than 0.25 miles (400m) away from the main coast road, which is regularly patrolled by buses.

From Freshwater beach, climb the wooden steps to the cliff-top, and pause to look back at The Needles and Tennyson Down. From here to Compton Chine, the path runs very close to the A3055, known as the Military Road because it served purely military purposes for almost 100 years, until it was opened to the public in 1933. The cliffs along this most exposed south-westerly section suffer constant erosion from the winter gales, which is why the footpath has in places been pushed inland.

Notice the colour change in the cliffs where the road diverges from the coast. The chalk is replaced by a darker rock, another sedimentary product known as Wealden marl, rich in paleontological artefacts. This coast is continually slumping due to the gray slipper clay. The rain permeates the top soil and when it gets to the clay, it all slips out into the sea.

DODGING THE CHINES

There is little along this stretch to distract the walker from the basic pleasures of walking beside the sea. The only thing to upset the continuity of the coastline is the occasional 'chine', originating from the Saxon 'cinan', meaning yawn or gap. Chines are deep ravines that cut into the cliff-edge, often extending some way inland. Many are completely impassable, and require a lengthy hike inland to skirt round them. Brook Chine is the first of these, necessitating a detour into the village to get past it.

Brook is a hamlet with a history. Brook Hill House was owned by Charles Seely, a wealthy Nottinghamshire coal mine owner, who made considerable improvements to it. Seely gave the island a lifeboat and libraries. It was later lived in by the Bradford-born writer, J B Priestley.

From Brook (grid ref. SZ 385 835), it is possible to return to Freshwater by walking inland towards Shalcombe and taking the Tennyson Trail along East Afton Down (a circular walk of about 8 miles (13km).

Chilton Chine is next, also requiring a detour to the Military Road. Grange Chine offers a choice; either descend within and climb the other side, or walk to the road once again. Grange is the halfway point of this stage, and the pleasant village of

PLACES TO VISIT

• **OSBORNE HOUSE**
www.english-heritage.org.uk
☎ 01983 200022
The world-famous holiday home of Queen Victoria and Prince Albert is just a short detour from the route and well worth a visit. In addition to the main house, state rooms and gardens, you can see the Swiss Cottage, where the royal children spent their days playing. You may also spot red squirrels, which remain on the island, protected by the Solent from the grey species. Open daily Apr–Oct; Wed–Sun Nov–Mar.

• **FORT VICTORIA COUNTRY PARK**
www.fortvictoria.co.uk
The coastal path passes through this country park, on the north shore of the island just beyond Yarmouth. It wraps around the remains of the fort, built to protect the Solent. There is woodland to explore but most people visit to enjoy the attractions within the park: the Island Planetarium, Model Railway, Underwater Archeology Centre and Fort Victoria Marine Aquarium. The latter is built into the fort remains and has tanks displaying creatures from the waters of the Solent, in addition to a tropical reef room. Island Planetarium open daily all year; other attractions open daily Easter–Oct.

• **THE NEEDLES PARK**
www.theneedles.co.uk
At Alum Bay you can still fill up glass bottles of all shapes with up to 20 different colours of sand from the cliffs below, although you can no longer collect it yourself. There is a chair lift down to the beach and both the Alum Bay Glass Studio and the Sweet Manufactory demonstrate their skills before enticing you into their shops. All this, and fairground rides such as the traditional carousel. Open daily Feb–Oct.

Brighstone is just 0.5 miles (800m) inland, offering refreshments and overnight accommodation. After negotiating Cowleaze Chine and Shepherd's Chine, both requiring detours inland, you reach Atherfield Point, not a popular spot with mariners. Hundreds of ships met their doom on the reef here. The cottages just inland are coastguards' cottages. Take a look over the edge at the lobster and fishing boats pulled some way up the cliff-face; not an easy way to make a living. The next chine to be encountered is Whale Chine, a classic and completely impassable fissure leaving absolutely no option but to head inland to the Military Road once again. Soon after this comes another big one; Walpen Chine. The path goes inland once again, to Chale, nestling under St Catherine's Hill. Head for Chale Church, where smugglers hid their contraband inside the tombs. The route proceeds south-east towards the more cheerful environs of Blackgang Chine theme park. Blackgang got its name from a ruthless gang of smugglers, and is still an impressively deep and dark gash in the cliff-side.

ALONG THE UNDERCLIFF

Walk through the Chine car park to the stile, and then climb the steps and path to the top of Gore Cliff. The first views from here of the area down below, known as the Undercliff, are magnificent. This lush fertile area, caused by years of landslip, is now a haven for wildlife, with some very desirable human residences too. There is also a lower cliff with its own cliff path, but for various reasons the higher route has been chosen as the official long-distance footpath route.

While rounding St Catherine's Point, look out to sea at the horrendous tidal race. Even on a flat, calm day this can be a swirling maelstrom, caused by a variety of different tidal flows and currents. The tides of the Solent and surrounding areas are the most complex in the United Kingdom.

Look inland, too, to the top of St Catherine's Hill, where there appears to be a rocket about to take off. This is called the Pepper Pot and the odd building adjacent to it is known as the Salt Cellar. Both are the remains of medieval lighthouses — the octagonal Pepper Pot dating back to 1320, while the Salt Cellar was begun in 1800 but never finished. The modern lighthouse can be seen down on the lower cliff.

The path continues onwards along the cliff-top around the southernmost point of the island, following a well-defined track.

After passing the large radio station, the route then descends into the Undercliff. Descending through St Lawrence, the walker is eventually reunited with the lower cliff path. The path then continues to seaward of the Botanic Garden and it makes an interesting diversion to walk amongst the exotic flora. The coastal path, signposted Steephill Cove, eventually leads into Ventnor, former spa town and now a busy holiday resort.

VENTNOR TO RYDE

STAGE 5

VENTNOR to BEMBRIDGE
DISTANCE 11.4 miles (18.3km)
MAP OS Explorer OL 29
START AT GRID REFERENCE SZ 563 773
START POINT Ventnor Pier

The walk starts with an easy mile along the shore to Bonchurch, following the sea wall. Above are the Winter Gardens, an attractive sight in full bloom. Bonchurch is a small waterside hamlet; a few houses, a church and a pottery. Once past the pottery, take the next path uphill, over a small stream to the church. Bonchurch Old Church is a delightful building, appearing in the Domesday Book as 'Bonecerce'. There is a strong Norman influence, but artefacts include a medieval painting on the north wall. From here the path enters the Landslip, a lush area of dense foliage once again caused by unstable ground slowly but inexorably making its way towards the sea. The route is well maintained throughout this area, with wooden duckboards and steps over the more tricky bits of path. After passing through hydrangea plantations, the path emerges on to a lane by Luccombe Chine. This part of the coast has numerous footpaths, but the coastal route is well signposted. Turn right into Popham Road, and then go through gardens down steep steps to the sea. After a short section along the beach, reach the main promenade. Here the route takes the road back up past the Chine Inn to regain the upper ground.

It is pleasant to walk beside the sea and on the actual sand when the tide is out all the way to Sandown, with fine views of Sandown Bay and Culver Cliff away in the distance. While both Shanklin and Sandown may appear little more than holiday resorts, there is history and interest to be found in both. The lift to the beach in Shanklin played a part in preparations for PLUTO, World War II's famous PipeLine Under The Ocean.

Sandown Zoo is on the site of an old fort which is why the walls are so thick; however you may hear the roar of the tigers. Dinosaur Isle is also an interesting diversion.

From the zoo it is simple to catch the bus back to Ventnor, or ahead to Bembridge. Alternatively, the Bembridge trail cuts out the stretch around Culver Cliff, to go straight to Bembridge.

ON CULVER DOWN

From Sandown pier, continue along the esplanade to the very end. The path up Culver Cliff is easy to see up ahead. This is the last bit of climbing and decent cliff on the walk, so enjoy it. The path leaves the road to begin the climb up Culver Down at Yaverland, the site of another Wealden marl outcrop, equally rich in dinosaur artefacts. The large obelisk on top of the Down is clearly visible, and the path heads towards it.

Walk right up to the obelisk, and take a moment to read the inscription. 'Raised by public subscription' to commemorate the Earl of Yarborough, it goes to some length to extol the virtues of the fine naval architect and First Commodore of the Royal Yacht Squadron. From the monument, the path leads down towards the large and unsightly caravan site at Whitecliff Bay, with views of Bembridge airfield to the left. Rejoining the cliff-edge, the route continues through another area of serious slumping and the path is continually being re-routed due to landslips. It soon emerges beside an outdoor activity centre and continues along the coast path. The occasional signpost keeps walkers roughly on the correct track, which should eventually lead down past a small golf course to the lifeboat station. If the tide is out, there is also the option of walking along the beach for some way.

From the lifeboat station the path continues along the shore, and then turns inland, if the tide is in, on a woodland path. Once again in a quiet residential district, the route proceeds along cycleways and metalled footpaths, eventually emerging at Bembridge Point, by the harbour.

STAGE 6

BEMBRIDGE to RYDE

DISTANCE 5.8 miles (9.3km)
MAP OS Explorer OL 29
START AT GRID REFERENCE SX 642 877
START POINT The entrance to Bembridge harbour by Bembridge Point

It is interesting to walk around the harbour and look at the variety of houseboats moored along the waterfront; some very plush, others in considerable decay. The road skirting the harbour is Embankment Road, built in 1878 for a quarter of a million pounds, a princely sum in those days. However, there is a pleasant path just inland, which is on RSPB land and off-road.

After crossing the (second) River Yar, turn right into Latimer road and make your way through the buildings of St Helen's Tide Mill to the Old Mill Dam Wall. The walk across the dam gives good views back across the harbour and of the old mill workings. The dam leads to The Duver, once a golf course, now a National Trust property designated a Site of Special Scientific Interest because of its population of 250 or so different, and sometimes rare, wild plants.

Walk straight across here towards the red-roofed building. The official path does not connect with the shore, but a short detour to the site of St Helen's Old Church is worthwhile. Now only the tower remains, built in the reign of Henry III (1216–72). The church began its seawards disintegration in about 1550 and was eventually bricked up in 1703, and painted white for use as a seamark.

Heading back inland from the church, the route proceeds northwest over a couple of fields to reach a road, and then turns left into the drive of the Priory Bay Hotel. It soon forks left again along the edge of a wood, to reach a sharp right-hand corner and a track leading right down to the sea. Turning left by the public toilets, the track then leads into the attractive little village of Seaview.

From the High Street it is possible to catch a direct bus either back to Bembridge or ahead to Ryde.

THE FINAL SECTION

At Nettlestone Point the sea wall can be reached from the yacht club, and from here on it is sea wall all the way into Ryde. The 0.5 mile-long (800m) pier can even be seen away in the distance. The best views now are across the Solent towards busy Portsmouth and the granite forts out in the middle of Spithead.

The last half hour of the walk passes seaward of the pleasant gardens of Puckpool Park and Appley Park. Appley House can just be seen through the trees, as can St Cecilia's Abbey, home of the Benedictine Order of Ryde Sisters. After passing the large boating lake (watch out for the 'Dotto Train', which runs up and down this section of the esplanade), it is roadside all the way to the pier from which the walk started. You have now completed the 68-mile (109km) coast path around the Isle of Wight. Ryde Pier makes a very prominent and suitable final destination.

ⓘ PLACES TO VISIT

• BLACKGANG CHINE
www.blackgangchine.com
☎ 01983 730330
The coastal path passes right by Blackgang Chine, which is the site of a major tourist attraction. For those wishing to learn more about the island, its coast and the disappearing village of Blackgang, there are interesting exhibits and a large screen cinema show. Those with children could easily fill a day at the sister theme park site, with activities ranging from a hedge maze to thrilling rides, a pirate fort and dinosaurland, not to mention the Chocolate Heaven shop. Open daily Mar–Sep; variable opening during winter.

• VENTNOR BOTANIC GARDEN
www.botanic.co.uk
☎ 01983 855397
This lush and green haven is easily accessible from the coastal path. Set in the sheltered climate of the undercliff, as you approach the town, it is able to cultivate a wide variety of plants, many of them Mediterranean and Subtropical. The garden is free to enter, and an open public space. Only the Green House and Visitor Centre (including a gift shop and newly furnished café) close. Open daily Mar–Oct; variable opening during winter.

• DINOSAUR ISLE
www.dinosaurisle.com
☎ 01983 404344
The collection of the former Museum of Isle of Wight Geology now resides in this modern exhibition space on Sandown's seafront, reminiscent of a flying Pterosaur. Inside there are life-size models of dinosaurs known to have roamed nearby, including an animatronic Neovenator (a species discovered and named by the curator), in addition to thousands of fossils that have been found on the island. Open daily all year.

BELOW LEFT The Causeway from St Helens across the Mill Ponds to The Duver
BELOW Sunrise at Appley Tower, Ryde

Wayfarer's Walk

COMPLETE ROUTE EMSWORTH TO INKPEN BEACON **70 MILES (113KM)**

SECTION COVERED AS ABOVE

MAPS OS EXPLORER 119, 120, 132, 144, 158

Hampshire's principal long-distance footpath stretches from south to north across the county. In the south it starts close to the West Sussex border, at the harbourside town of Emsworth, while in the north it finishes just over the Berkshire border at Inkpen Beacon. The route has been skilfully designed to show the best that rural Hampshire has to offer, leading through quiet farmland on little-used footpaths and bridleways, passing through occasional villages, and generally avoiding long stretches of road. The walk is easy and flat for most of its distance, until it heads steeply up towards Watership Down and a fine high-level finish.

ABOVE, TOP TO BOTTOM
Inkpen Beacon; Fulling Mill, Alresford; Ladle Hill

EMSWORTH TO KILMESTON

STAGE 1

EMSWORTH to DENMEAD

DISTANCE 13 miles (21km)

MAPS OS Explorer 119, 120

START AT GRID REFERENCE SU 755 055

START POINT Emsworth Slipper Sailing Club, Emsworth, off the A259, 0.5 miles (800m) south of the railway station

Emsworth is a small and rather charming town on the shores of Chichester Harbour, boasting an old quay and a nearby marina. It came of age in the Middle Ages, rapidly overtaking nearby Warblington and becoming an important centre for corn milling in the early 18th century. The Wayfarer's Walk starts from the Emsworth Slipper Sailing Club, housed in one of the town's old tidal mills. Just past here, look out for the bollard with the commemoration plaque to Lord Mountbatten, a past Commodore of the club. The path continues by the front of some harbourside houses, and there are fine views over the mudflats and sandbanks of the harbour as the route heads towards Hayling Island in the distance. Turning inland, it then passes through woodland before heading towards the tower of Warblington Castle; all that remains of a once-mighty 16th-century building.

The route crosses a stream, heading for St Thomas a Becket's Church at Warblington. It is worth taking time to stroll through the ancient graveyard, noticing the 600-year-old yew, and the grave-watcher's flint hut in the corner, dating from the time when corpses were stolen for medical use. From here the route crosses the modern graveyard, rejoining the shores of Langstone Harbour, where the ominous black turret of the 18th-century mill built out over the water comes into view. Beyond it is the Royal Oak pub.

JOHN KEATS WAS HERE

Past the Royal Oak the route goes straight ahead to cross the busy A3023 Hayling Island–Havant road, crossing over the quiet grassland of South Moor. Heading towards the sewage works ahead, the Wayfarer's Walk at this point separates from the Solent Way, which continues for another 60-odd miles along the coast towards Milford on Sea. Signposting for both walks is poor

in this area, and some care with the OS map is needed to find the way as it heads inland and over the A27 by the footbridge (passing over a surprising area of green fields close by the railway), and crosses the old railway bridge into Bedhampton. Now it is no more than a suburb of Portsmouth, but in its day Bedhampton was a village in its own right. At Lower Mill, now the Old Mill Bed-and-Breakfast, the Romantic poet John Keats finished his poem 'The Eve of St Agnes' in 1819, and here in 1820 he spent his last night in England, while en route for Italy where he died so tragically young.

From Bedhampton, the route crosses the A3(M) on the B2177, passing thoughtful signs provided by the Samaritans on each side of the bridge. Past a fine Strawberry Hill Gothic house on the far side, it continues due west along the top of Portsdown Hill, a chalk ridge high above the coastal plain, though you are not aware of any undue uphill walking. This ridge stretches for 6 miles (9.6km) from Bedhampton to Fareham. On a clear day there are fine views past Portsmouth to the Solent and the Isle of Wight beyond.

After a long but not unpleasant road section, the route follows a footpath round the back of the redbrick Fort Purbrook, sunk low into the hilltop, with a dry moat and keep which is preserved today. This was one of six hilltop forts built to defend Portsmouth from the French in the late 19th century, all part of a massive, unused defensive system.

To return to Emsworth from Fort Purbrook, either retrace your steps, or continue westwards along the road to Fort Widley (grid ref. SU 663 066), and then turn back to walk down the hill, following the A3 southwards to Cosham railway station, just over a mile (1.6km) distant. From here there are regular services to Emsworth.

Past Fort Purbrook, the route continues west beside the golf course before turning north on to a signposted footpath. Following the back gardens of a terrace of houses downhill, the path leads out across fields to a quiet country road at Purbrook Heath. Here it once again heads west for 0.5 miles (800m) or so, before turning north on to a track which leads into woodland on the corner where the road bends left.

The route emerges at the road by Sheepwash Farm, leading by road and footpath past Closewood Farm and Glenfield Farm to the outskirts of Denmead, a modern village which has grown from a collection of scattered farms over the last 100 years. Here a Wayfarer's Walk signpost points the way back to Emsworth for those bound north in the opposite direction.

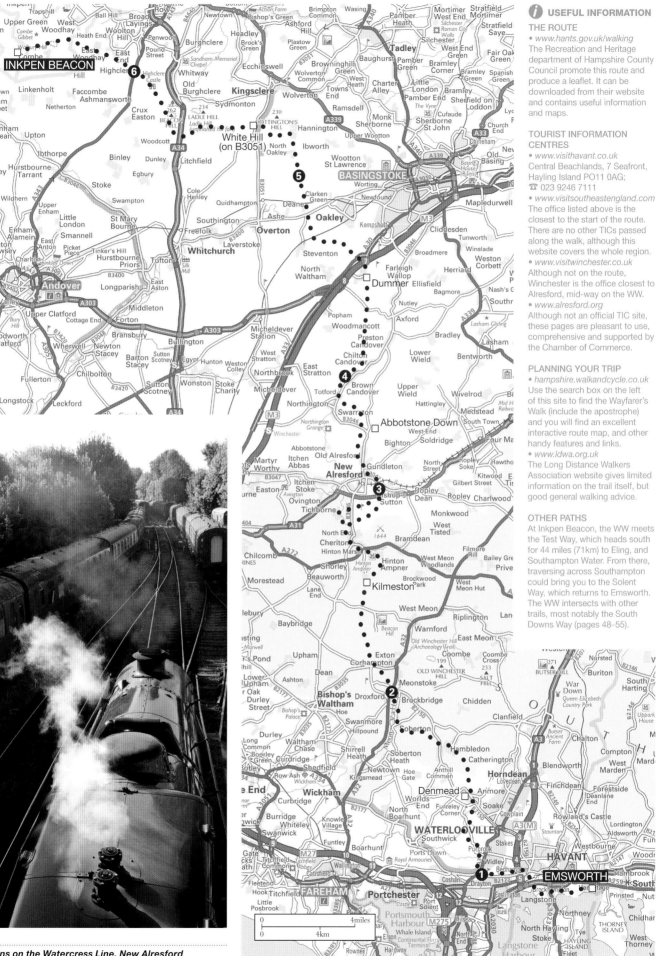

ⓘ **USEFUL INFORMATION**

THE ROUTE
• *www.hants.gov.uk/walking*
The Recreation and Heritage department of Hampshire County Council promote this route and produce a leaflet. It can be downloaded from their website and contains useful information and maps.

TOURIST INFORMATION CENTRES
• *www.visithavant.co.uk*
Central Beachlands, 7 Seafront, Hayling Island PO11 0AG;
☎ 023 9246 7111
• *www.visitsoutheastengland.com*
The office listed above is the closest to the start of the route. There are no other TICs passed along the walk, although this website covers the whole region.
• *www.visitwinchester.co.uk*
Although not on the route, Winchester is the office closest to Alresford, mid-way on the WW.
• *www.alresford.org*
Although not an official TIC site, these pages are pleasant to use, comprehensive and supported by the Chamber of Commerce.

PLANNING YOUR TRIP
• *hampshire.walkandcycle.co.uk*
Use the search box on the left of this site to find the Wayfarer's Walk (include the apostrophe) and you will find an excellent interactive route map, and other handy features and links.
• *www.ldwa.org.uk*
The Long Distance Walkers Association website gives limited information on the trail itself, but good general walking advice.

OTHER PATHS
At Inkpen Beacon, the WW meets the Test Way, which heads south for 44 miles (71km) to Eling, and Southampton Water. From there, traversing across Southampton could bring you to the Solent Way, which returns to Emsworth. The WW intersects with other trails, most notably the South Downs Way (pages 48–55).

Steam trains on the Watercress Line, New Alresford

TOP **Houses on Alresford's**
Georgian Broad Street
MIDDLE **Leafy Drove Lane,**
Alresford
BOTTOM **An engine on the**
Watercress Line pulls into
the station

STAGE 2
DENMEAD to KILMESTON
DISTANCE 14.3 miles (23km)

MAPS OS Explorer 119, 132

START AT GRID REFERENCE SU 658 122

START POINT The village green of Denmead

The most urban section of the Wayfarer's Walk now follows, as it makes its way through Denmead's modern housing estates to the cemetery. Here it once again enters peaceful countryside, following a footpath along the side of a field across Anthill Common to Rookwood Farm. Following the route onwards for another couple of miles, footpaths lead to the hangers, or wooded hillsides, above Hambledon, which is a charming Hampshire village nestling in the valley.

Hambledon is an excellent place to stop and rest a while (with a choice of pubs). It has a history as a famous cricketing village and just to the north is Hambledon Vineyard, whose dry white wines are among the most successful of English vintages. The vineyard is no longer open to the public, but its wines are on sale in the village. At the bottom, a lane leads down past some fine Georgian houses to the road.

From Hambledon (grid ref. SU 645 149), a 4-mile (6.5km) return may be made to Denmead by taking a footpath eastwards to Denmead Mill, then taking a lane leading south back to the village.

To continue the main walk, walk up towards the 11th-century Saxon church, then follow the footpath across fields to the B2150 Droxford road, with fine views back to the church. Cross the road by modern houses, and then follow the woodland path uphill and across a field, crossing a minor road near East Hoe Manor, from where there are distant views to the sea.

The route enters woodland, joining OS map 185 as it approaches the village of Soberton. Here, the White Lion pub is in an attractive setting on the corner of the village green, while on the far side of the green the route passes St Peter's Church, whose tower has some unusual carvings featuring a man's head with a key and a woman's head with a pail. The walk crosses a disused railway line, once part of the Meon Valley Line, built between Alton and Fareham in 1903 and closed with so many others in the 1960s. The route then turns right on to a footpath across fields, following the course of the River Meon in a very pleasant setting, passing a horse chestnut copse with beech trees on the hillside to the right and water meadows to the left, before entering the village of Droxford via a narrow footbridge.

This village, with its attractive Georgian houses, is where Izaak Walton, of *Compleat Angler* fame, spent much of his later life. Of the Meon Valley he wrote that it 'exceeds all England for swift, shallow, clear, pleasant brooks and store of trout'. The route continues west, passing through wooded countryside, before turning north via Steynes Farm and St Clair's Farm. Here it passes through a large clearing amid Norway spruce and Canadian pines, passing the strangely named Betty Munday's Bottom. Though there is nothing to see, the name is from the folklore story of a local lady who got up to no good, luring passing travellers to her house before murdering them and throwing their bodies down her well.

Beyond here a route skirts a tennis court at the end of a track from Preshaw, carrying on towards Lomer Farm with a view across to the site of Lomer, a medieval village which died out due to bad harvests and plague in the late 14th century. Heading west once again along the road, the route passes Wind Farm before crossing the Winchester-bound extension of the South Downs Way, at a point where there are fine views down the hillside and over the low-lying land ahead, towards New Alresford. Dropping down over Kilmeston Down, the path leads to the attractive hamlet of Kilmeston, with its imposing manor, pretty church, and one of the few obvious bed-and-breakfast signs along the route.

KILMESTON TO DUMMER

STAGE 3
KILMESTON to ABBOTSTONE DOWN
DISTANCE 11.2 miles (18km)

MAP OS Explorer 132

START AT GRID REFERENCE SU 590 258

START POINT South end of Kilmeston village

A footpath leads northwards through Kilmeston, passing by magnificent beech trees and giving fine views of Dean House over to the right. It emerges on the north side of the hamlet, where it is worth walking up the lane to the left for a look at St Andrew's Church and the 18th-century Kilmeston Manor, before carrying on along the footpath which leads over a small hill towards Hinton Ampner. This is believed to be the old Winchester–Petersfield coach road. It gives fine views of the south side of Hinton Ampner House ahead, entering parkland and heading up by the side of the ornamental gardens before emerging by the small church of All Saints.

From Hinton Ampner, which is really no more than a hamlet formed by one very large house and its collection of associated buildings, the route leads downhill past the Old Rectory, with more fine parkland to the left. If you wish to stop for a drink here, a footpath deviates diagonally across the park, leading almost directly to a pub by the side of the A272 Winchester–Petersfield road. Continuing on the main route, cross straight over the A272 by a Wayfarer's Walk signpost which points straight ahead up a track, saying there are 42 miles (67.5km) to go to Inkpen Beacon. Turn left at a bridleway crossroads, as shown by a Wayfarer's Walk waymark, and then carry on towards the village of Cheriton. The waymarking is a little vague here, so care must be taken in following the route.

Despite being described by William Cobbett as a 'hard, iron village', Cheriton is now a pretty little place with a green, a stream and a pub called the Flowerpots Inn, including a micro-brewery. To the northeast is the site of the Battle of Cheriton, where the Royalists were defeated by Cromwell's forces in 1644. From here, the route follows a footpath along water meadows by the source of the River Itchen to the west of the village, coming out on to the road by Cheriton Mill. It crosses the B3046 to join a track which runs up the side of a field, turning left at a crossing track and continuing through trees to emerge on the road once again by farm buildings opposite Tichborne Park.

A Wayfarer's Walk alternative route leads into Tichborne, and from there on to New Alresford. Tichborne is a hamlet with a church of Saxon origins and a Roman Catholic side chapel. It is known for the Tichborne Dole, a custom that originated during the reign of Henry I. Sir Roger Tichborne, who does not sound the most pleasant of men, promised his bedridden wife flour for the needy from as much land as she could crawl round! She eventually managed 20 acres, an area known as The Crawls.

For a 2.5-mile (4km) return to Kilmeston from Tichborne (grid ref. SU 572 505), a bridleway leads southwest to Gander Down (SU 556 276), swinging southeast to Lane End (SU 564 256), where a footpath and lane lead via Beauworth to Kilmeston.

The main route misses Tichborne, following a track through woodland before dropping downhill to a golf course on the

Countryside surrounding the Woolpack Inn on the Wayfarer's Walk at Totford

PLACES TO VISIT

• HINTON AMPNER
www.nationaltrust.org.uk
☎ 01962 771305
This fine neo-georgian country house is passed on the route, just beyond Kilmeston. Although a house has been here since the 16th century, the present building was largely re-built in the 1960s, after a fire gutted its predecessor. It is filled with fine furniture and *objets d'art*, but the garden is the major draw. There is an array of formal yew topiary and elegantly planted borders, a walled garden and magnificent views across acres of rolling parkland. There are free guided walks in the garden on Tuesdays. House, garden and tea room open Sat–Wed Apr–Oct; walled garden and tea room also open Sat–Sun Nov & Feb–Mar.

• WATERCRESS LINE RAILWAY
www.watercressline.co.uk
☎ 01962 733810
The Mid Hants Railway, or Watercress Line, originally ran between Alton and Winchester. It was closed in 1973 but now runs as a private steam railway from Alresford to Alton, where you can connect to the national rail network. The Mid Hants Railway has its own station buildings at the mainline station platform. The line is renowned for the steep gradient the locomotives have to haul up at Medstead & Four Marks, affectionately called 'The Alps' by the drivers. If you have time to spare you can book in advance to actually drive and fire the engine, or take the elegant *Watercress Belle* dining train on a Saturday evening (book well in advance via the website). See website for details of operating days and times. Daily Feb–Oct.

outskirts of New Alresford. Follow the sign across the golf course and on to the footbridge which crosses the A31, turning right and then left uphill, and following the road along the east side of New Alresford. Past the railway line, you come out on to the B3047 road. In the centre, turn right down the rather grand Broad Street. Because of serious fires in the 12th, 15th, 17th, and 18th centuries, the architecture is predominantly Georgian, and very pleasing too. At the bottom of Broad Street, the route bears left on a narrow lane as shown by a Wayfarer's Walk waymark. This heads along a track by the side of Alresford's complex waterworks, the creation of the 12th-century Bishop de Lucy of Winchester, who dammed up small local streams to provide enough water to make the River Itchen navigable by boat as far as Southampton.

The route passes a pretty waterside cottage by the side of the River Alre, and further on there is a stone monument with a difference: 'Here lies Hambone Jnr, faithful friend of the 47th Infantry Regt, 9th Division US Army, May 1944'. Keep on along this track leading out of Alresford, ignoring a 'Private' sign by some houses on the left, until it brings you out on to the road. Cross over at the bend, and follow the wide grassy track ahead. This occasionally has a large gypsy encampment with fine working horses tethered along the track, known as Drove Lane. In its day it was a busy route for driving sheep to Alresford's sheep market. The track crosses a road about a mile (1.6km) on, carrying on along a leafy way through quiet countryside before turning right at a bridleway crossroads, as indicated by a Wayfarer's Walk waymark. The route passes Abbotstone, a now non-existent village which once boasted a church and a 100-room mansion built in 1719. Incredibly nothing survives. It continues along a track through fields, passing a barn by a footpath/bridleway crossroads and coming to the wildlife preserve at Abbotstone Down by a noticeboard next to the car park. This 32-acre area is managed by the County Council as natural downland.

STAGE 4

ABBOTSTONE DOWN to DUMMER

DISTANCE 8.9 miles (14.3km)
MAPS OS Explorer 132, 144
START AT GRID REFERENCE SU 585 361
START POINT Car park at Abbotstone Down

From the Abbotstone Down car park, carry straight on over the road ahead, following the route as it bears left by Oliver's Battery, an Iron Age defensive settlement where the earthworks can still be seen. The route continues along a wide track known as Spybush Lane, going due north, with fine views over farmland and woodland to the east. Passing by a belt of trees it joins a hard farm track heading north downhill between fields, in open country, on the way towards Brown Candover.

However, as it reaches the farm buildings ahead, the route turns left along a track to divert towards Totford, though the more direct route to Brown Candover is to turn right and left, coming out on the road not far from the church. The track to Totford is called the Lunway, which connected Old Sarum, Stockbridge and Crawley, and is now also part of the modern road system. At Totford's Woolpack Inn, sheep were penned on their way to market. Beyond here, the route follows a bridleway which joins a lane on the outskirts of Brown Candover, coming to the B3046. This is followed as far as St Peter's Church. Set back from the road on a green, it is notable for a fine Flemish altar rail. Brown Candover is one of three Candovers, the others being Chilton and Preston, originally small valley settlements.

For an alternative return route from Brown Candover (grid ref. SU 578 392) follow the road to Preston Candover (1.5 miles/2.5km), and turn south via Down Farm to join the Ox Drove. This rejoins the Wayfarer's Walk to the south of Brown Candover, some 2 miles (3km) away.

CHALK PITS

Cross the green and join the footpath by the west side of the church. The route bears right over a stile and then left up the side of a field, coming to a large modern barn in a clearing, which is part of Church Lane Farm. Church Lane continues straight ahead, but is well hidden as it is enclosed by the thicket that runs between two fields. The Wayfarer's Walk waymark is easily missed here, and care should be taken not to continue along the main track which bears off to the right. Follow Church Lane down to a gate, going ahead by the side of Lone Barn, now converted to residential use.

Bear right here as indicated by the right of way sign, following the track by the side of the remains of Micheldever Forest across Becket's Down. This area was once full of chalk pits, a few of

which can still be seen. The Wayfarer's Walk waymarks show the way through woodland past Breach House, with its modern driveway, and Breach Farm beyond, going on to the road ahead by Breach Cottage and turning left for a short way uphill. The route then turns right down the long, straight driveway that leads past Dummer Grange Farm to Dummer Grange, bearing left to follow a track round the side of the house, which remains well hidden.

The track ahead gives good views over the surrounding countryside, eventually coming to the road on the outskirts of Dummer with just a faint hum of a reminder that the M3 is close by. Turn right and then left opposite the 12th-century All Saints' Church, which has a pretty entrance gate to the churchyard and a 14th-century pulpit, said to be one of the oldest in England. A short way on, past a fine, stone-built house on the right, the Queen Inn makes a welcome place to stop.

DUMMER TO INKPEN BEACON

STAGE 5
DUMMER to WHITE HILL
DISTANCE 11.6 miles (18.6km)
MAPS OS Explorer 144, 158
START AT GRID REFERENCE SU 587 462
START POINT The Queen Inn, Dummer

From the pub at Dummer, turn left downhill and walk on through this picturesque village. Beyond the village, the road heads up towards the M3 roundabout. Here there is a long footpath detour which follows a sweeping driveway by the side of the motorway, passing corporate-style buildings well hidden by trees before crossing the motorway by a footbridge.

On the other side, the path bears left through trees by the side of the golf course. It emerges on the roadside at the A30, which splits here and needs to be crossed twice before you can turn on to a minor road signposted to East Oakley. On the corner here there is a footpath sign in a completely overgrown tangle, so — unless it is clear — follow the road on ahead as far as the bend, where the footpath goes straight ahead over a stile, by the

side of New Cottages and next to the farm driveway. The route follows the path along by the side of South Wood towards Bull's Bushes Farm. It passes through Bull's Bushes Copse to join the road on a bend. The route bears left here, joining a track which follows the side of a field and by the side of trees to pass under the railway, emerging on the road by Cheesedown Farm.

To return to Dummer from Cheesedown Farm (grid ref. SU 548 497) is a walk of about 2.5 miles (4km). Follow a lane southwards to Steventon, and then turn southeast through North Waltham. Continue to the Sun Inn, where a lane passes under the M3 and into Dummer.

To continue on the Wayfarer's Walk, turn right past Deane Gate Farm, crossing straight over the B3400 by the Deane Gate Inn, and going up the lane ahead with lovely views of All Saints' Church, which is set in Deane House's parkland. Follow the road to the right just opposite the entrance lodge to Deane House, turning left by Deane Cottages a short way on, as directed by the Wayfarer's Walk waymark. Do not go through the gate ahead, but bear right round the back of the houses and then left up the side of a field as directed by another sign, crossing the railway and coming out on the road by Deane Down Farm. The road here is part of the Harroway, a prehistoric route connecting Pilgrim's Way in Kent to Salisbury Plain.

Past Little Deane Wood the route crosses Summer Down, passing Great Deane Wood and Frith Wood, with much of the woodland felled in the 1960s to make space for the intensive cereal farming which characterizes this area. Though the views are extensive, they are bland indeed. Past Freemantle Farm, the route emerges on the road at North Oakley by the Manor Farm. Turn left here opposite a fine black barn and, at the bend, continue straight ahead on the track past Warren Cottages, before turning right down an overgrown track as directed by the Wayfarer's Walk waymark. This track climbs up For Down with fine views behind.

The lane ahead is part of the Portway, a Roman road which connected Salisbury with Silchester, an important Roman centre to the north of Basingstoke. The Portway crosses the countryside in a straight line, and when it leaves the modern road its course can be followed by a long line of trees to the west known as Caesar's Belt, as it makes its way towards Andover. Cross over here, and go straight ahead up the side of a field to a gate, where there is a wonderful view of the route ahead, looking towards Watership Down. The track heads downhill, emerging on the B3061 by the White Hill car park. From here on, as the walk enters its final stages on OS map 174, its character changes. The intensive farmland of central Hampshire is left behind, and the chalk downland of the North Hants Ridgeway takes over, with the route following a prehistoric track which stretches from Basingstoke to the Vale of Pewsey in Wiltshire.

STAGE 6
WHITE HILL to INKPEN BEACON
DISTANCE 12.4 miles (20km)
MAPS OS Explorer 144, 158
START AT GRID REFERENCE SU 515 565
START POINT Car park at the top of White Hill on B3051

From the White Hill car park the route follows the Portway westwards, following a track uphill on chalk and grassland. The chalk drains away any rainwater, so it is never too wet for walking and is equally suitable for the racehorse gallops which are either side of the route on Cannon Horse Down.

Watership Down inspired Richard Adams' bestselling book of that name, so look out for friendly rabbits. The Downs here are also notable for ancient barrows and hillforts. Passing the trig

Inviting leafy pathways at Ladle Hill, Sydmonton

point at 777ft (237m) on the top of Watership Down, the route follows a narrow track downhill by the side of trees, crossing a lane and following a fine avenue of beech trees, before turning right across open grassland. From here it bears westwards again to reach the great hillfort on top of Ladle Hill, an Iron Age fortification which, together with the fort on nearby Beacon Hill, defended the ancient route which is now the A34.

To get back to White Hill, take the bridleway past Ladle Hill (grid ref. SU 478 568), going north to Old Burghclere. Follow the road through Sydmonton to the outskirts of Kingsclere where the B3051 leads back up to White Hill. This makes a circular walk of about 5 miles (8km).

SEVEN ANCIENT BARROWS

The route bears south downhill on a wide grassy track dividing two fields, with the A34 in the valley below and fine views of Beacon Hill on the other side. The track twists and turns and needs to be followed with care as it descends Great Litchfield Down, eventually joining a narrow, overgrown tarmac track which heads downhill to the A34, crossing under overhead powerlines. A sign here indicates a safe route to the south to cross the A34 by an underpass.

The road here divides seven ancient barrows, a number of which can be seen on the west side, as well as a memorial to the aircraft builder, Geoffrey de Havilland, who flew his model planes here as a boy. The track climbs uphill through pretty woodland along Lower Woodcott Down, coming out by the side of a field and passing a copse with good views north to Beacon Hill. From here the route swings north along the grassy hillside of Upper Woodcott Down, heading for a belt of trees and then joining a hard track coming up from the right. Along here the views to the north look out over the 6,500 acres of the Highclere Estate, with the rounded top of Sidown Hill in the foreground. The route joins a woodland track through Grotto Copse, passing

a pretty castellated gatehouse to Highclere Castle before emerging on the A343. This has to be crossed on a blind bend, so take care.

The continuing track is about 75yds (69m) to the left uphill, heavily overgrown, with fields on either side hidden by trees and hedges. Over a lane, the route continues along another overgrown and sometimes muddy track as it follows the North Hants Ridgeway, joining a lane by the side of woodland. As the route turns right, there are fine views of Highclere Castle, which shot to fame as Downton Abbey in the popular TV series.The route then bears left, on to a waymarked track, as the road starts to head downhill.

HANGING POST

At the top of Pilot Hill this track passes a trig point at 938ft (286m). A little further on, after just over 67 miles (108km) through Hampshire, the Wayfarer's Walk crosses Berkshire's border for the last 3 miles (5km). The track joins a quiet road which continues westwards along the top of the Down, coming to the car park at Westbury Hill. From here, a hard chalk track leads on by the side of Walbury Camp; a prehistoric hillfort on top of the highest chalk hill in England, marked by a trig point at 974ft (297m). It is a massive fortification, covering some 82 acres, with a mile-long (1.6km) ditch and rampart.

The track leads on to the car park on the top of Inkpen Beacon, where you are rewarded with brilliant views, and the sight of a twin signpost marking both the beginning and end of the Wayfarer's Walk and the Test Way. However, Combe Gibbet on top of Gallows Down, the official end of the route, is 0.5 miles (800m) or so further west on the chalk track that lies ahead. This is a modern replica of the hanging post first erected here in the 17th century. Despite its grim associations, on a clear evening this is the finest possible place to end the walk.

PLACES TO VISIT

• HIGHCLERE CASTLE
www.highclerecastle.co.uk
☎ 01635 253210
There are fine views of the Highclere Estate from the WW. It is worth taking a closer look at this stunning building, home to the Earl and Countess of Carnarvon, and used in ITV's popular series 'Downton Abbey'. Reminiscent of the style of the Houses of Parliament, it was designed by the same architect. Inside, the entrance hall features gothic columns and vaulting, and the double-height saloon at the centre of the house is a truly spectacular example of gothic decorative architecture. There are state rooms which contain chandeliers, fine paintings, embroideries and painted ceilings. The cellars of the castle house the Egyptology Exhibition, which displays artefacts discovered by the 5th Earl of Carnavon, who famously found the tomb of Tutankhamun in 1922. The castle grounds are extensive, including parkland landscaped by Lancelot 'Capability' Brown, a number of follies and buildings, and the more formal secret and walled gardens that are close to the house. Some of the follies can be visited as part of suggested countryside walks that are available to download from the Highclere website. The castle has tea rooms and a shop. Open daily at Easter, Mon–Tue on May bank holiday and Sun–Thu Jul–Aug.

South Downs Way

COMPLETE ROUTE WINCHESTER TO EASTBOURNE **100 MILES (161KM)**
SECTION COVERED QUEEN ELIZABETH COUNTRY PARK TO EASTBOURNE **80 MILES (129KM)**
MAPS OS EXPLORER 119, 120, 121, 122, 123, 132, 133

The South Downs Way National Trail passes along the length of the South Downs from Winchester in Hampshire to Eastbourne in Sussex (where the route divides into two to include the Seven Sisters Loop tor those who prefer to follow the coast). This route is a bridleway, with the exception of the Seven Sisters Coastal loop near Eastbourne, which is footpath. Expect to meet horses and mountain bikes, though thankfully no motorized vehicles. Since the prevailing wind is normally from the west or southwest, we have chosen to start at the western end. Eastbourne as a start or finish point is a big town that is well served by public transport, while the other end of the route is served by train and bus from Winchester or Petersfield. The South Downs Way is an undulating route, following the high chalk ridges of the Downs and dipping in and out of valleys and combes. If the weather is kind, the views are magnificent, across mainly unspoilt English countryside, with frequent glimpses of the English Channel. The first half of the route has delightful woodland sections and the prettiest villages, while the second half is more given to open grassland.

ABOVE, LEFT TO RIGHT Seven Sisters towards Beachy Head; Thatched cottage in Amberley village; Signpost on the South Downs Way

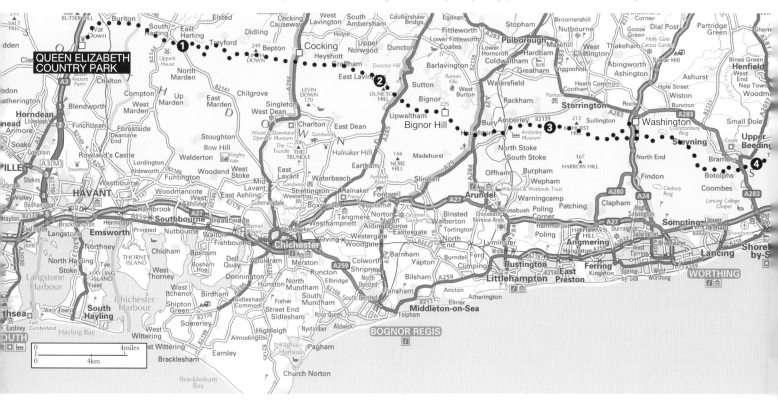

QUEEN ELIZABETH COUNTRY PARK TO BIGNOR HILL

STAGE 1
QUEEN ELIZABETH COUNTRY PARK to COCKING

DISTANCE 12.7 miles (20.4km)
MAP OS Explorer 120
START AT GRID REFERENCE SU 718 185
START POINT Queen Elizabeth Country Park on the A3

The Queen Elizabeth Country Park is a convenient place to start walking the South Downs Way, just on the Hampshire side of the county border. An alternative start point is the village of Buriton, served by buses from Petersfield and Portsmouth, and blessed with an old-fashioned pond and two pubs.

The Queen Elizabeth Country Park is en route for those extending the walk to and from Winchester. A large map on a notice board sends walkers off on the South Downs Way via dense woods until the top of the hill is reached by War Down, the first of many climbs on this route. From there, the path drops down to the south of Buriton, following both lanes and track to the east past Coulters Dean Farm. The next stage of the walk leads to Sunwood Farm, the original official beginning and end of the South Downs Way on the Hampshire–Sussex border. From here the South Downs Way acorn signs point the way along chalk tracks, with some severely muddy stretches in wet weather conditions, towards Harting Downs.

For a circular walk back to Queen Elizabeth CP, leave the South Downs Way here (grid ref. SU 772 192), heading south and then turning southwest along West Harting Down to join the Sussex Border Path. This leads to Chalton, beyond which a bridleway turns up Chalton Down towards Queen Elizabeth CP; a distance of 8 miles (13km).

The first village encountered is South Harting, notable for the church's green copper spire. It was once the home of Alexander Pope and later of Anthony Trollope, who was said to shock the village with his weekend parties. A footpath leads down the hillside to the left, and the village is about 20 minutes by foot.

Alternatively, on the south side of the Downs, make a diversion to the National Trust mansion of Uppark, built in the Wren style by William Talman in 1685–90. This gem on the South Downs, rescued after a major fire in 1989, houses an elegant Georgian interior with a famous Grand Tour collection, which includes paintings, furniture and ceramics.

A short way on you emerge by a car park at the top of Harting Downs, to experience the first of many fine views that the South Downs Way offers from here on. To the southwest the views extend uninterrupted across Chichester Harbour to the Isle of Wight. To the southeast, you look out across the city of Chichester itself, with its elegant, mainly Norman cathedral and rather more modern Festival Theatre in the foreground. Here the route follows a fine grassy trail along the top of the Downs, a popular location on fine days, for both hang gliders and model aircraft enthusiasts, who launch their craft over the flat countryside to the north.

The signpost at Cross Dykes is the next landmark, with the South Downs Way signpost giving the option of a stiff climb straight up Beacon Hill (with its ancient Iron Age hillfort, of which virtually nothing remains at the top) or the more popular gentle climb, skirting the hill to the south and east. Although clearly signposted, this is one of the few places along the Way where it is possible to wander off the route, which takes a sharp left turn before a small country estate to the right, named Telegraph House. As an alternative diversion, this track leads to The Royal Oak pub at Hooksway a mile or so on, which is a popular stopping place for walkers.

The South Downs Way drops towards Buriton Farm (far from the village of the same name) before a long climb to the top of Linch Down leads past The Devil's Jumps. These are five Bronze Age round barrows that have been excavated and are maintained by the Murray Downlands Trust. The nearest villages are Treyford and Didling. The former has two churchyards but no

ℹ USEFUL INFORMATION

THE ROUTE
• www.nationaltrail.co.uk
☎ 01243 558716
This is the most detailed source of information about the South Downs Way route. It also has an interactive map to help with your search for lodgings, or you can order a copy of the South Downs Way Accommodation Guide (alternatively, you are able to download this and other helpful publications).

TOURIST INFORMATION CENTRES
• www.visitwinchester.co.uk
The Guildhall, The Broadway, Winchester SO23 9LJ;
☎ 01962 840500
• www.enjoysussex.info
187 High Street, Lewes BN7 2DE;
☎ 01273 483448
• www.visiteastbourne.com
Cornfield Road, Eastbourne BN21 4LQ;
☎ 0871 663 0031
• www.visitsouthdowns.com
There are several other TICs listed here which cover the SDW area but are not directly on it.

PLANNING YOUR TRIP
• www.southdownssociety.co.uk
☎ 01798 875073
The society pages say little of the SDW itself, but they do produce a guide to it, available by phone.
• www.ldwa.org.uk
The Long Distance Walkers Association has good detail and links for the SDW, including details of many intersecting trails.
• www.ramblers.org.uk
☎ 020 7339 8500
The Ramblers Association website has general information about long-distance walking, and specific help covering the SDW.
• www.yha.org.uk
☎ 0800 019 1700
The Youth Hostel Association has several sites along the SDW.

OTHER PATHS
A great many paths meet the SDW. If you wish to walk both the South and North Downs Way paths, they are connected most efficiently by St Swithun's Way, linking Farnham and Winchester, and by the Downs Link (pages 58–61).

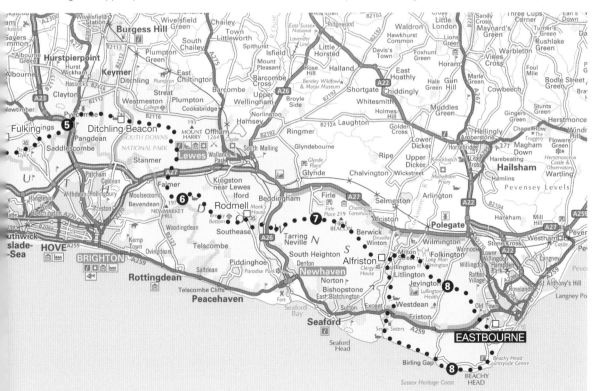

church and the latter has an isolated, 13th-century church with original pews. A short way on, the route passes through ancient woodland, bearing round the back of Monkton House. The cottage was once owned by the late Edward James, the surrealist art collector, who filled it with priceless works by such notables as Salvador Dali. Sadly his collection has been dispersed, and the house, which cannot be seen from the track, is now surrounded by a high security fence that is out of tune with its pastoral surroundings.

Linch Down is heavily wooded and here you may sometimes hear the rustling of pheasants in the undergrowth, and see the occasional rabbit hop across the path. After a couple of miles of walking through these peaceful glades, which afford excellent protection against both wind and rain, agricultural land reasserts itself once again. A magnificent view opens to the east, looking to the next great hill of Graffham Down and beyond to the twin radio masts on top of Burton Down, which dominate the surrounding country. Cocking village is about 0.5 miles (800m) to the north, complete with church, duckpond, tea rooms and pub-style restaurant (overnight accommodation available).

STAGE 2
COCKING to BIGNOR HILL
DISTANCE 7.3 miles (11.7km)
MAPS OS Explorer 120, 121
START AT GRID REFERENCE SU 878 177
START POINT From Cocking on the A286, 3 miles (5km) south of Midhurst

From the pleasant village of Cocking you can rejoin the South Downs Way via a bridleway past the church. By Hill Barn Farm is one of the few public water taps for walkers along the entire length of the route. Fill up your water bottle as the track heads steeply uphill past Manor Farm Down and Heyshott Down. To the south is Goodwood Park, while far beyond on the coast is the former RAF Hurricane and Spitfire fighter station at Tangmere. Along the top of the Down, the views are shrouded by dense woodland. You pass the village of Heyshott to the north, where 53 acres of downland are conserved and managed by the Murray Downland Trust, and a little further along the SDW a number of connected grassland reserves and woodland corridors are managed by the Graffham Downland Trust as Sites of Special Scientific Interest. Some way on you pass Graffham, also to the north and shrouded by trees; the village where the Victorian free trader Richard Cobden once lived.

For a circular 7-mile (11.25km) walk back to Cocking, turn north off the South Downs Way at grid ref. SU 927 162 to follow the bridleway track downhill to Graffham, and then follow the lanes and footpaths t due west to Heyshott and Cocking, a pleasant walk across flat country.

ALFRED LORD TENNYSON
Off to the right a little way on is the highest point of the Sussex Downs, Crown Tegleaze (836ft/255m), at the top of Littleton Down. Another long downhill stretch leads to the A285 Petworth–Chichester road by the side of Littleton Farm. Turning left, to the north, the road leads to the car park at the top of Duncton Hill. From here there are fine views towards Blackdown, the house built by Alfred Lord Tennyson, with Seaford College at the foot of the hill below.

A stark white chalk track wends its way up to the top of Burton Down, homing in towards the two radio masts. The South Downs Way passes some way to the south of them, along a narrow and sometimes muddy track, crossing National Trust land. Soon the walker comes to the car park at Bignor Hill. This part of the route is usually well used by Sunday afternoon walkers in summertime, congregating at the Bignor Post. This ancient signpost shows the way along Stane Street, built by the Romans to connect London Bridge with Chichester's East Gate in the 1st century AD.

The nearest overnight accommodation is about 2 miles (3km) away in Sutton. Good bunkhouse accommodation is also available between March and October at the National Trust's Gumber Farm, about 1 mile (1.6km) south along Stane street.

BIGNOR HILL TO FULKING

STAGE 3
BIGNOR HILL to WASHINGTON
DISTANCE 9.9 miles (15.9km)
MAP OS Explorer 121
START AT GRID REFERENCE SU 973 129
START POINT Free car park at the top of Bignor Hill

From the top of Bignor Hill, the South Downs Way follows a hard chalk track to the east, along the top of the Down, with fine views southwards over the coastal plain as far as Bognor Regis and Littlehampton. Ahead lies Chanctonbury Ring. The route zig-zags steeply downhill to old farm buildings in a spot which can frequently be muddy at the bottom of Westburton Hill, before taking the walker uphill on a narrow chalk track, passing a trig point at 584ft (178m) to the left and soon reaching the busy A29 Worthing road.

From here there is a splendid view of the route ahead, as the landscape dives down into the Arun Valley, with dramatic chalk hills beyond Amberley. Cross the A29. The bridleway that continues the route will be found a short distance to the south.

The South Downs Way carries on steeply downhill by the side of Coombe Wood on another chalk track, bringing you to a lane a short way to the north of the hamlet of Houghton. The SDW continues straight on to reach the River Arun where a modern bridge spans the River, then follow the river bank south and turn left (east) after a few hundred metres, where a narrow track and then a concrete farm track leads to the B2139. The SDW then crosses the road and follows an off-road section to meet the bottom of High Titten Lane. Alternatively, Houghton repays a visit. The George and Dragon pub is a few hundred yards uphill to the right and is well thought of, not least because Charles II is reputed to have stopped there while making his escape from near Brighton to France in the 17th century. After his time this was also an important trading place, with a long-gone wharf down by the river where barges were loaded with locally quarried chalk. The river was part of the Wey and Arun Navigation Canal system, which closed down in 1871.

On the far side of the old bridge that crosses the River Arun there is a riverside café with outdoor seating, as well as a pub, restaurant, small shop, and water trough with drinking tap. Upriver are the Amberley Wild Brooks, a scheduled nature reserve stretching as far as Greatham Bridge, to the east of Coldwaltham.

An interesting diversion follows a footpath south from Amberley (grid ref. TQ 025 118), along the banks of the River Arun. This leads to South Stoke, Offham, and on past the Swanbourne Lake nature reserve into Arundel itself, where there is plenty of accommodation. The diversion covers a distance of some 4 miles (6.5km).

To complete a circular route, footpaths can be followed northeast through Arundel Park, to the junction of the A284 and the A29 at Whiteways Lodge (where there is a large car park at the roundabout, grid ref. TQ 004 119, convenient for a pick-up by car), and on through Houghton Forest to Bignor Hill.

Turning off to the right, steeply uphill on High Titton Lane, by the side of a large Victorian house, there are fascinating glimpses of the Chalk Pits Museum below, before the route emerges on the open Downs, away from civilization. A fenced track leads steeply uphill on grass, away from Down Farm, towards Amberley Mount, and on to the top of Rackham Hill.

With few trees on the hillsides, from here on the views are mostly unobstructed all around. To the west is Amberley Castle, once a 14th-century fortified manor house belonging to the Bishops of Chichester, and now a luxury country house hotel. To the north lies Parham House, an Elizabethan mansion with wooded deer park. To the south is Arundel, an ancient town built on a hillside, with its own fine castle and Roman Catholic Cathedral of St Philip Neri.

At the top of Chantry Hill there is a car park, with a tarmac lane leading downhill to the busy village of Storrington. Nearby Sullington has a Saxon church ringed by old yew trees. The South Downs Way then divides to give two optional routes. The direct way goes eastwards and downhill, passing by a drinking tap to cross the A24 on a busy dual carriageway section. The much safer option is to divert to the northeast downhill past Rowdell House, to where a footbridge leads over the A24 and into Washington by the side of its church. Further on is the old London Road, now known as The Street, and The Frankland Arms.

STAGE 4
WASHINGTON to FULKING
DISTANCE 12.1 miles (19.5km)
MAPS OS Explorer 121, 122
START AT GRID REFERENCE TQ 123 128
START POINT Washington, on the southeast side of the intersection of the A24 and A283

The route now follows the Old London Rd to Washington car park, from where a wide chalk and flint track heads up towards Chanctonbury Ring at the top of Chanctonbury Hill. Beyond

i **PLACES TO VISIT**

• QUEEN ELIZABETH COUNTRY PARK
www.hants.gov.uk/qecp
☎ 023 9259 5040
This section of the SDW begins at the largest park in Hampshire; over 1,400 acres (565ha) of scenic downland and woodland, with 12.5 miles (20km) of trails to explore on foot, bike or horse. There are barbecue shelters to book for hire, wooden outdoor playgrounds and a visitor centre with café and shop. You can even pre-order organic meat for your barbecue. Open daily all year.

• UPPARK
www.nationaltrust.org.uk
☎ 01730 825415
This elegant Georgian mansion is close to the walk, near the village of South Harting. It has been carefully restored, following a devastating fire in 1989, and contains an impressive collection of Grand Tour art and furniture. The basement is also open to visitors, showing the servants' quarters and kitchen. The garden has been restored too, featuring peaceful woodland walks. Open Sun–Thu Mar–Oct.

• BIGNOR ROMAN VILLA
www.bignorromanvilla.co.uk
☎ 01798 869259
Just off the route, at Bignor village, are the remains of this remarkable Roman site. Struck and discovered by the farmer of the land as he was ploughing in 1811, the world-class mosaics here are still protected by the thatch-covered buildings built over them almost 200 years ago. They are of interest in their own right, but the remains themselves are both impressive and highly educational. There is a café and picnic area. Open daily Mar–Oct.

A magnificent view from the Fulking Escarpment

a dewpond, the route passes a trig point at 780ft (238m) and heads east along the top of the Downs towards Chanctonbury Ring; a mystic circle of trees which broods over the whole area. Originally an Iron Age hillfort on which the Romans built a temple in the 3rd–4th centuries, the ring was planted with trees in the late 18th century. Many of the trees were felled by the great gale of 1987, but replanting has taken place. Just over 2 miles (3km) to the south of Chanctonbury Ring lies another great ancient landmark of the Downs. The Iron Age hillfort of Cissbury Ring can be clearly seen, and is sited in an area of extensive Neolithic flint mines, with panoramic views over the English Channel.

The route turns southeast, with Wiston Park and the 16th-century Wiston House to the northeast, below. It follows a wide chalk track on a slight downhill slope, crossing open grassland with fine views ahead and the urban sprawl of Shoreham and Worthing in the distance.

Steyning comes into view at the bottom of Steyning Round Hill, where a Bronze Age burial site was excavated in 1949. By a trig point at 620ft (189m), a footpath leads steeply downhill to this small, interesting town. Close by is Bramber, which boasts the remains of an 11th-century Norman castle that are openly accessible. This was a busy port in medieval times, before the Adur estuary became too silted up for navigation.

On the top of the down above Steyning and Bramber, the South Downs Way follows an off-road route adjacent to the road for a short distance, passing by Steyning Bowl on the left. This is a magnificent natural amphitheatre cut into the hillside, and a popular launching place for hang gliders. About 0.5 miles (800m) on, the route turns left off the road, crossing a grassy field by the side of Annington Hill, with the valley of the River Adur coming into sight ahead. This is part of the South Downs Way signals the start of more open country.

PANORAMIC VIEWS

A hard track leads downhill, joining a narrow road by Annington Farm, and heads east towards St Botolph's Church, on the riverside near the site of a Saxon farmstead. A hundred yards or so before the church, a track turns left to cross the river by a footbridge; here there is a water tap to drink from.

On the east side of the River Adur, the route follows the A283 Shoreham road for a couple of hundred yards to the north, before turning right on to a track which heads up the side of Beeding Hill. This leads to a narrow road on the top of the Downs with a panoramic view of the valley behind and, far beyond to the southwest, the magnificent 19th-century chapel of Lancing College, built on a hill. The school's founder, Canon Woodward, decreed that his chapel must be seen from the sea and all around, and he indeed created a remarkable landmark.

The road leads east along the top of this bleak down, passing Truleigh Hill hostel at Tottington Barn; the only YHA youth hostel directly on the route of the South Downs Way. From here the road becomes a track, passing the radio masts and trig point at 709ft (216m) on Truleigh Hill, and crossing National Trust land by the earthwork remains of an ancient Norman motte-and-bailey on Edburton Hill. Here you can look over to Thundersbarrow Hill to the south, an important site of Roman and Iron Age settlements. Beyond the electricity pylons, as the route follows an undulating track towards Fulking Hill, a footpath leads left, down into Fulking village, where the picturesque Shepherd and Dog pub has a freshwater spring gushing from the hillside and a warm welcome for walkers.

TOP **View north over the Fulking Escarpment**
MIDDLE **Couple picnicking on top of Devil's Dyke**
BOTTOM **Mountain biker pedals towards Jack Windmill near Clayton**

From Steyning Bowl (grid ref. TQ 162 094), a track leads south and then west to Cissbury Ring, which is accessible by car and has a car park. From here, a bridleway leads due north, back to Chanctonbury

 *An early morning view of Devil's Dyke*

Ring, where the South Downs Way may be rejoined to return to Washington, a distance of about 6 miles (9.5km).

FULKING TO RODMELL

STAGE 5

FULKING to DITCHLING BEACON
DISTANCE 6.5 miles (10.5km)
MAP OS Explorer 122
START AT GRID REFERENCE TQ 248 114
START POINT Fulking, on a minor road between Upper Beeding and Pyecombe

From the Shepherd and Dog pub at Fulking, a footpath joins a bridleway which leads diagonally up the hillside to rejoin the South Downs Way. Beyond Fulking Hill, the route goes over open grassland towards the isolated Devil's Dyke pub at the top of Devil's Dyke, above the village of Poynings and its 13th-century church. The Devil's Dyke, a natural phenomenon, got its name because, according to legend, the devil dug a dyke in the hillside in order to flood the surrounding country and its churches, but was interrupted and never finished the job!

The route crosses a narrow road which connects the pub to the outside world and continues to the right of the hill fort ramparts with the dyke below to the left. A funicular railway used to bring tourists to the pub, then a hotel, and a large direction board shows the many viewpoints that can be seen on a clear day from the summit.

The SDW now follows the open grass top, staying south of the Iron Age hill fort and WWII pillbox, onto the hamlet of Saddlescombe, once the site of a Knights Templars house.

At the bottom of the hill a path leads off to the right past farm buildings, coming to a sunken track that heads up towards open downland above West Hill. The National Trust's Newtimber Hill, a popular viewpoint rich in downland flora and fauna, is about 0.5 miles (800m) to the north. Carrying on along the top of the down, the route then heads downhill on a bridleway, joining the A23 Brighton road by the Plough Inn at Pyecombe.

Having crossed the main road, the South Downs Way is signposted left, past the church, which has an unusual lead

font. Near by is the smithy, renowned for the manufacture of Pyecombe shepherds' crooks in the days when sheep rather than cereals dominated the Downs. The route turns right to cross the A273 Haywards Heath road, turning off eastwards through the entrance of Pyecombe Golf Club a short way uphill.

Past the club buildings, the route follows a fenced track along potentially muddy ground, keeping to the side of the golf course and then following the headland. Beyond New Barn Farm the twin Jack and Jill windmills come into view above Clayton village. They are one of the famous landmarks of the Downs. The white post mill 'Jill' has been fully restored and grinds flour. Jack, the black tower mill, is a private house.

The route carries on eastwards, passing the Keymer Post on the top of the Downs at 764ft (233m), then coming close by dewponds and across grassland as it climbs toward the trig point at the top of Ditchling Beacon (825ft/248m). One of the highest points of the South Downs Way, this is the site of an ancient hill fort, where fires were lit to warn of the Spanish Armada four centuries ago. From here, the North Downs can be seen on a clear day and, closer to hand, Ashdown Forest and Crowborough Beacon. A steep, narrow road connects Brighton with the village of Ditchling on the north side of the Downs. It was once a Saxon royal estate and has some interesting houses, including one known as Anne of Cleves' House, though there is no proof that she ever lived there. There is a choice of bed-and-breakfast accommodation.

For a pleasant circular walk back to Pyecombe or Clayton (from where buses run to Brighton) head south from Ditchling Beacon down Heathy Brow. Continue west to the farmstead in the valley at Lower Standean, then cross the Sussex Border Path, which divides the east and west parts of the county. A final climb up to Clayton Windmills makes a distance of around 3 miles (5km) and from here it is a short distance into Clayton, on the A273. Alternatively, turn left on the South Downs Way again to return to Pyecombe.

STAGE 6
DITCHLING BEACON to RODMELL

DISTANCE 11.2 miles (18km)
MAP OS Explorer 122
START AT GRID REFERENCE TQ 332 132
START POINT Ditchling Beacon

Cross the narrow road from the Ditchling Beacon car park with care. There is a blind bend near the top. From here, the South Downs Way continues eastwards over the grassy top of the Downs, passing a V-shaped plantation which commemorated Queen Victoria's Jubilee. Beyond lonely Streathill Farm, the view looks north across Plumpton towards the famous race course, with Plumpton church and the agricultural college close by the foot of the Downs. To the south the huge mass of Brighton, its marina jutting out into the sea, dominates this part of the coast.

Just over 2 miles (3km) from Ditchling Beacon, the South Downs Way takes a major change in direction, following the line of the Downs to the southeast. However, first it turns to the southwest, leaving the bridleway which goes straight ahead at a clearly signposted gate. This is just before the track reaches Ashcombe Bottom, the only extensive patch of woodland on this part of the Downs. Beyond is the 676ft (206m) trig point at Blackcap, and almost a mile (1.6km) further on are the electricity pylons that march across the Downs.

LOOSE BOTTOM

From here there are clear views over Lewes and its disused race course, looking out over an area where the Battle of Lewes was fought between King Henry III and Simon de Montfort in 1264. Along Balmer Down, the path crosses the site of an important Roman settlement.

The route turns down a track with wire fences on either side, before bearing left to head southeast down the edge of a field, passing beneath the overhead electricity cables. The route now turns southwest before reaching Ashcombe Plantation and drops down to Bunkers Hill Plantation, where it climbs very steeply and descends along the edge of an arable field to the A27 at Housedean Farm. Here the route turns west for 100yds (90m) and crosses the A27 via a farm bridge. There is a new drinking water tap at Housedean Farm. Once over the bridges the route runs parallel to the railway line and then ducks under the line through a short tunnel and then follows a downland bank before heading up through a small wood to come out above the Newmarket Inn.

The route continues climbing the side of the valley by Loose Bottom. At the top of the Down, the South Downs Way turns left by the Newmarket Plantation, a grove of beeches badly damaged in the 1987 gale, and left again by the side of Castle Hill, before turning right to resume its southeasterly course towards Eastbourne, above Kingston village, near Lewes.

Past a large dewpond, the route crosses Swanborough Hill, with views over Swanborough Manor below. Once the grange of Lewes Priory and later owned by Sir Philip Sidney, the manor has fine carved griffons in the driveway, a 13th-century hall and a chapel with a 15th-century dormitory.

Take the track at grid ref. TQ 391 069, down past Swanborough Manor, and cross the road for an escape by a path along the east side of the road, into Lewes (2 miles/3km).

Heading on along the top of the Downs, the route eventually comes to a concrete track that runs straight as a die along Ilford Hill and Front Hill. From here, a narrow enclosed track leads along the side of woods at Mill Hill by a large house in a fine position on the right, emerging with views towards Newhaven to the south.

An unmade road leads down to the village of Rodmell where overnight accommodation is available. The actual SDW heads down to Cricketing Bottom and then over the hill to the Telescombe village road, crossing the Newhaven road to head down into Southease village. This avoids the need to walk along the main road. Many of the older houses have an 'A' marked on

i PLACES TO VISIT

• **AMBERLEY MUSEUM**
www.amberleymuseum.co.uk
☎ 01798 831370
Close to the route at Amberley is a site which, for over 100 years, was the site of a working chalk pit. Since 1979 it has housed the Amberley Museum, which is dedicated to the preservation of many aspects of our industrial past and craftsmanship. The site currently houses over 40 buildings, many of which are exhibits in themselves (such as the 1930s village garage replica). Others contain their extensive collections of telecommunications devices, narrow guage rail artefacts, hand tools and more, including a print workshop, resident craftspeople and a vintage bus collection. There are also nature trails and picnic sites. Open Tue–Sun Feb–Oct.

• **JILL WINDMILL**
www.jillwindmill.co.uk
The famous 19th-century Jack and Jill windmills near Clayton are now privately owned, but the route passes by the Jill Windmill and if it is open, it is worth a stop for a cup of tea. Lovingly worked on by volunteers, the mill occasionally produces wholemeal flour, which can be bought if you have the means to carry it. Open most Sunday afternoons May–Sep.

• **LEWES**
www.enjoysussex.info
☎ 01273 483448
This old and interesting town is 3 miles (5km) off the route, but easily reachable by good paths and well worth the diversion if you have time. Visit the Norman castle, Cluniac priory remains, Barbican House Museum or the 15th-century timber-framed house that belonged to Anne of Cleves. The town itself is a delight to wander around, with twisting streets, individual shops and antiques centres, and some lovely cafés.

them, in homage to the Marquess of Abergavenny, who was the landowner until 1919. Beyond lies the River Ouse.

....

From Rodmell, footpaths follow close by the east side of the road via Ilford. The route north to Lewes is approximately 3 miles (5km).

RODMELL TO EASTBOURNE

STAGE 7
RODMELL to ALFRISTON
DISTANCE 8.2 miles (13.2km)
MAPS OS Explorer 122, 123
START AT GRID REFERENCE TQ 418 059
START POINT Rodmell, on the Lewes–Newhaven road

BELOW The Long Man Of Wilmington is a chalk figure cut into the South Downs BOTTOM The rooftops of Lewes seen from the castle

From Rodmell, the South Downs Way crosses the River Ouse, where Virginia Woolf drowned herself in 1941. The bridge over the Ouse is a fine example of a swing bridge that is now listed. The route follows the road south towards Newhaven, turning into Southease; a village with a green, some 17th-century cottages, and a round-towered Norman church, which has some 13th-century murals. The route passes Southease railway station and then crosses the A26 by a footbridge, to connect with the chalk track up the side of Itford Hill near to Itford Farm.

This track curves its way up the hillside to head east past Red Lion and White Lion ponds. These are dried-up dewponds, in an area where a complete Bronze Age farming settlement was discovered. The Downs here are dominated by the enormous radio mast on the top of Beddingham Hill, at 623ft (190m), while below is Beddingham itself, where a Roman villa was discovered. It would have been part of the trading routes of this region.

To the north is Mount Caburn, an Iron Age hill fort. Below it is the village of Glynde, where John Ellman, who developed the local breed of Southdown sheep, is buried. Nearby is Glynde Place, a 16th-century courtyard house. A little further north is Glyndebourne, the Elizabethan mansion which hosts the annual world-famous Glyndebourne Opera season.

Further on along the top of the down, the route meets with the road coming steeply uphill from West Firle. Firle Park is at the foot of the hill, with its house, Firle Place, built for George Gage in 1557 and rebuilt in 1730. Carrying on past the car park towards the trig point at Firle Beacon (712ft/217m), the route passes a maze of tumuli with extensive panoramic views.

....

From Firle Beacon (grid ref. TQ 485 059), an interesting 4-mile (6.5km) route can be taken to Glynde Station, on the Lewes–Eastbourne line. Follow a track down to Firle Park, a footpath east to Little Dene, then the lane and road north to Glynde.

Turning to the right to head southeast, the South Downs Way continues along the top of the Downs, passing Charleston house to the north, below. Once the home of the artists Vanessa and Quentin Bell, it is now open to the public. While heading up Bostal Hill past Bopeep Farm and Jerry's Pond, the route passes small villages of Saxon origin at the foot of the Downs. Alciston boasts a 170ft-long (52m) timber-framed barn, while Berwick Church has murals painted by the Bells and Duncan Grant.

More tumuli give an interesting variation to the landscape, before the route heads downhill on a fenced track, via Long Burgh, towards the village of Alfriston on the banks of the Cuckmere River, where there is accommodation. Here, the South Downs Way emerges in the main street by the ancient

Distant view of the white cliffs of the Seven Sisters

Star Inn. By the river is a large church known as 'the Cathedral of the South Downs'. Its handsome green is a good place to rest.

STAGE 8

ALFRISTON to EASTBOURNE

DISTANCE 9 miles (14.5km)
MAP OS Explorer 123
START AT GRID REFERENCE TQ 521 030
START POINT The church green at Alfriston

From Alfriston, the final section of the South Downs Way divides; either continuing inland over the Downs on a fairly direct route, or following the coastal path along the cliff-tops of the Seven Sisters Country Park. The first option is bridleway, and must be followed by horse-riders and mountain-bikers. The second is footpath and can only be used by walkers, who will relish the close proximity to the sea after so much inland walking.

THE INLAND ROUTE

The inland route crosses the Cuckmere River above Alfriston, heading steeply up Windover Hill on a hard, chalk track. On its northern slope the Long Man of Wilmington can be seen on the hillside, a gigantic figure cut into the turf, first recorded in the mid-18th century. At the top of the hill there is a wonderful view over the huge bowl of Tenantry Ground. Neolithic remains include tumuli and a longbarrow burial chamber, one of 12 found in Sussex. To the north lies Wilmington, with the remains of its fine Benedictine priory. From here the route crosses open grassland, with direction markers showing the way as it passes other tumuli and curves round to the south. Here it enters woodland above Jevington, descending to this peaceful hamlet, which was once favoured by smugglers, and joining the road by the Saxon church with its unusual tapsell gate.

From Jevington (grid ref. TQ 562 012), a track can be taken south-west through Friston Forest to Westdean. The alternative South Downs Way footpath can be followed back to Alfriston (approx. 5 miles/8km).

The route continues up a track by the side of the Jeavington Tea Garden, heading up the last climb of the South Downs Way for those going west to east. As the path crosses Wealdway at the top of Willingdon Hill, there is a view north over Combe Hill; a large Neolithic causeway camp. The route continues along a hard track across level ground, passing the Eastbourne golf course to the right, with Eastbourne itself at the foot of the down to the left. On reaching the A259, the track continues straight ahead, before sweeping eastwards downhill into Eastbourne and finishing on the outskirts of the town at Paradise Way. Here there is a sign marking the end of the South Downs Way.

THE COASTAL ROUTE

After crossing the bridge over the River Cuckmere at Alfriston, the footpath follows the riverbank to the village of Litlington. Continuing on past Charleston Bottom, one can glimpse Charleston Manor with its 12th-century hall. The route then enters Friston Forest, climbing a long flight of steps before heading along forest rides, and then dropping down to reach Westdean. After passing the pond, the SDW continues up another flight of wide steps to emerge at the top of the hill, with great views over the Cuckmere estuary and the Seven Sisters Country Park. The route then drops down to Exceat, the park visitor centre and the A259.

From Westdean (grid ref. TV 525 997), you can return to Alfriston by heading northeast into Friston Forest, to Snap Hill, then turning northwest through Lullington Heath Nature Reserve.

By the A259 Seaford–Eastbourne road, the route enters the Seven Sisters Country Park by the visitor centre at Exceat; a medieval village that ceased to exist in the 14th century. The Seven Sisters themselves are known as Haven Brow, Short Brow, Rough Brow, Brass Point, Flagstaff Point, Bailey's Hill and Went Hill. The route passes them on its way along the cliff-top path, across some 770 acres of National Trust land, to Birling Gap, once famous for both smugglers and wreckers. Inland, the old part of the village of East Dean has an attractive green and the 15th-century Tiger Inn, where accommodation is available.

After a diversion due to erosion of the path as the cliffs gradually slide into the sea, the route comes back to follow the cliff-top by the old lighthouse of Belle Tout, built in 1832 of Aberdeen granite and now converted to use as a bed-and-breakfast. From here, the path heads round the southernmost part of the coast at Beachy Head, where the lighthouse at the foot of the cliffs was built to replace Belle Tout in 1902.

Finally, the route turns northwards by the playing fields of Whitebread Hole, entering the holiday town of Eastbourne right on the seafront by a seasonal cafe to complete the South Downs Way.

PLACES TO VISIT

• MONK'S HOUSE
www.nationaltrust.org.uk
☎ 01323 870001
Monk's House is an 18th-century weather-boarded cottage in the village of Rodmell, which lies along the route. It is famed as the residence of Leonard and Virginia Woolf, who lived here for many years in the first half of the 20th century. The house is full of items resonant of their time in the house, where they entertained members of the artistic Bloomsbury Group. The garden room where Virginia worked on her writing is still there and contains some of Virginia's many photographs. Open Wed & Sat Apr–Oct.

• ALFRISTON CLERGY HOUSE
www.nationaltrust.org.uk
☎ 01323 870001
In the historic village of Alfriston lies this modest 14th-century 'Wealden hall house', built for a local farmer but acquired by the church. It was the first property to be bought by the National Trust and is a lovely example of a timber-framed thatched cottage, with a small and tranquil English cottage garden. Inside there is a floor made from the unusual mix of chalk and sour milk, and also an oak carved into one of the ceiling beams, which may or may not have contributed to the design of the National Trust logo. Open daily Feb–Dec, except Tue & Fri.

• SEVEN SISTERS COUNTRY PARK
www.sevensisters.org.uk
☎ 01323 870280
The Seven Sisters Country Park, named after the series of chalk hills at the coast, includes scenic chalk downland and cliffs, in addition to the estuary of the River Cuckmere. Here you can see the iconic view of the white 'sisters'. The park is an important wildlife habitat, as the visitor centre at Exceat explains with displays. Centre open daily Apr–Oct, Sat–Sun Nov–Mar.

A footpath sign points over bales of hay in a field near Newtimber towards the South Downs Way

Public Footpath

Downs Link

COMPLETE ROUTE SOUTH DOWNS WAY (ST BOTOLPH'S CHURCH, NR BRAMBER) TO NORTH DOWNS WAY (ST MARTHA'S HILL, NR GUILDFORD) **36.4 MILES (58.6KM)**

SECTION COVERED AS ABOVE

MAPS OS EXPLORER 122, 134, 145, 244, 259

The Downs Link provides a bridleway link between two trails: the South Downs Way National Trail, from the point where it passes through Botolphs, north of Shoreham-by-Sea; and the North Downs Way National Trail at St Martha's Hill, west of Guildford. If you have not yet attempted a long-distance walk, and are unsure of your abilities, the Downs Link provides an ideal choice for a first foray. The route is well waymarked, using signposts adorned with the 'two-tiered bridge' logo. There are plenty of 'escape' routes to and from well-placed parking areas, and reasonable access using public transport. You will also come across a number of pubs, conveniently spaced and within easy reach of the main route.

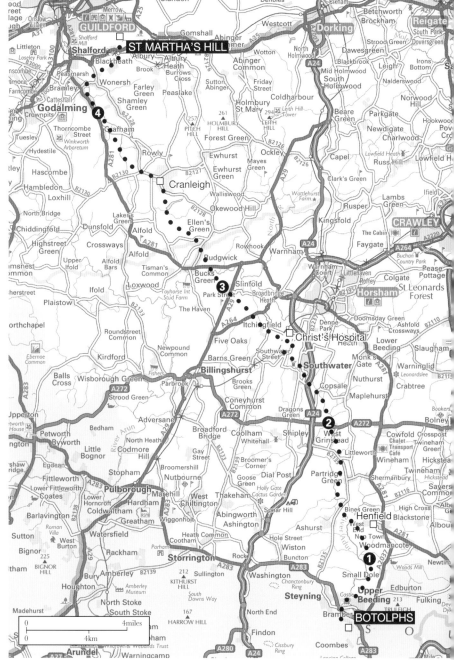

TOP *Half-timbered cottages in Church Street, Steyning*
ABOVE *The ruined gatehouse of Bramber Castle is worthy of a detour from the Downs Link path*

BOTOLPHS TO CHRIST'S HOSPITAL

STAGE 1

BOTOLPHS to HENFIELD

DISTANCE 5.4 miles (8.7km)

MAPS OS Explorer 122

START AT GRID REFERENCE TQ 193 094

START POINT The tiny hamlet of Botolphs on the narrow unclassified road running along the west side of the Adur valley, between the A27 coast road and Steyning

The Downs Link starts where the South Downs Way crosses the line of the old railway. This point is identified on the map as Botolphs, now no more than an isolated church and a handful of houses. The archaeological evidence in surrounding fields suggests that this was once a thriving community, brought down, like so many other lost villages, by a combination of the Black Death, famine and a general decline in prosperity. The tiny church retains features of its Saxon origins, including a chancel arch and a window in the south wall of the nave.

Start the Downs Link walk along the old railway track. After a little over 0.5 miles (800m), turn left along the Bramber bypass, where there is a wide grass verge. At a roundabout, follow Castle Lane, opposite.

Bramber Castle, to the right, deserves a detour. The 11th-century castle was demolished in 1641, during the Civil War. The site is now dominated by an 80ft (24m) wall fragment. In its heyday, the castle overlooked the Adur Gap, at a time when the water came right up to the foot of the castle mound.

After 500yds (460m) along Castle Lane, turn right into King's Stone Avenue. This ends at a junction with King's Barn Lane. To visit Steyning, a delightful village, turn left.

To continue the walk, turn right. After about 0.5 miles (800m), a bridge takes the track across the line of the old railway, here restored to farm use and available for walkers and riders. Shortly, go ahead along Wyckham Lane. After Wyckham Farm, the track climbs gently; the only significant incline on the Sussex section of the route.

After another 200yds (183m), turn right along a grassy path, which brings you back to the old railway. Turn left along the track bed. The next 2 miles (3km) is the most open section of the whole route, through the flat and wide Adur valley. Cross the river at Stretham Manor, near the point where the Romans, in the 1st century AD, also established a river crossing.

From here (grid ref. TQ 199 136) there is a choice of riverbank paths: either back to Botolphs along the west bank of the river, or northwards, along the east bank for 4 miles (6.5km) to Betley Bridge, where the Downs Link crosses the river.

DEEP CUTTING

On approaching Henfield, the old railway crosses a track and enters a deep cutting. For a short distance the line of the railway is occupied by a housing estate, appropriately called 'Beechings'. Use Lower Station Road, a few yards to the east, to reach the Cat and Canary restaurant and bar. A right turn here takes you into the centre of Henfield. It is a small but bustling community, with food shops, accommodation and a bus service to Brighton or Horsham.

STAGE 2

HENFIELD to CHRIST'S HOSPITAL

DISTANCE 9.9 miles (15.9km)

MAPS OS Explorer 122, 134

START AT GRID REFERENCE TQ 206 161

START POINT There is a small parking area for Downs Link users to the west of the Cat and Canary pub

From the car park, head north along the line of the railway. After a mile, beyond the northern river crossing at Betley Bridge, a bridle gate leads into a field, where the line of the railway is less clearly defined. After a second bridle gate, the track is again enclosed between two hedges.

After another 0.75 miles (1.25km), turn left on a crossing track. At the B2135, turn right and walk towards Partridge Green (where buses connect with Brighton and Horsham). Just short of the bridge over the railway, fork left on a narrow path down to rejoin the railway track bed.

After a mile (1.6km) or so, the Downs Link crosses the B2135 and shortly enters a pleasant wooded cutting. It then passes under the A272. To the north of the road, you will come to the former platforms at West Grinstead Station.

Shipley Mill can be found about 2.5 miles (4km) to the west of here. It can be reached by road or on footpaths from the Downs Link at grid ref. TQ 183 214, past West Grinstead Church and through Knepp Park. The mill was built in 1879 and is the last working smock mill in West Sussex. It was once owned by the writer Hilaire Belloc, an early long-distance walker who described a journey on foot across the country.

To the north of the A272, the Downs Link enters a more varied landscape; an attractive patchwork of small woods and fields, perhaps the most appealing countryside on the whole of the Sussex section of the path. The footpath network to the east of the old railway is well marked and provides excellent opportunities for return circuits linking West Grinstead, Southwater and Copsale.

Another 1.75 miles (2.75km) on, the track bed brings you to Copsale, where the Downs Link crosses the road next to the Bridge House Inn, a welcome refreshment stop with a garden alongside the old railway. On the south side of the road there is a car park for Downs Link users.

For an escape from here (grid ref. TQ 171 249) back to West Grinstead, start east along the road and then head south.

SOUTHWATER COUNTRY PARK

After another 0.5 miles (800m), the route burrows under the Southwater bypass and continues along a lane, parallel with and to the right of the line of the railway. After crossing another road, the Southwater Country Park is to your left and there is another large car park. At the turn of the century, the 54-acre site of

ABOVE LEFT A well hidden path cuts a swathe through fields in the Adur Valley
ABOVE Shipley Windmill

SOUTH & SOUTH EAST ENGLAND • DOWNS LINK

the park was occupied by the brickyards of the grandly named Southwater Brick, Tile, Terracotta Pipe and Clay Company. By 1981, after 1,000 million bricks had been produced, the clay ran out and the works closed. In 1985, following extensive landscaping, conversion to the Southwater Country Park was complete. After Southwater Country Park, go half-left into Andrews Lane, to cross a road into Church Lane.

From Southwater (grid ref. TQ 162 259), a reasonably direct series of field paths takes you east to Nuthurst where there is a welcome pub. From here, more paths allow you to head generally southwards to join the old railway at several points to the north of West Grinstead.

BLUECOAT SCHOOL

After 0.25 miles (800m) on Church Lane turn right on a track and then left to rejoin the old railway track. The Downs Link now approaches Christ's Hospital, alongside the main Horsham–Portsmouth railway, with the playing fields of Christ's Hospital School over to your right.

The school was founded in 1552, during the reign of Edward VI. It is familiarly known as the 'Bluecoat School'; a name derived from the traditional costume still worn by the boys, consisting of blue gowns, yellow stockings and knee breeches.

Join a metalled drive and follow it out on to a road, where you should turn left and, shortly, turn left again over the railway. If you are finishing the day's walk at Christ's Hospital Station, go ahead at this point instead of crossing the main line. After 200yds (183m), fork left. The station is no more than a few minutes' walk away.

CHRIST'S HOSPITAL TO ST MARTHA'S HILL

STAGE 3

CHRIST'S HOSPITAL to CRANLEIGH
DISTANCE 9.7 miles (15.6km)
MAP OS Explorer 134
START AT GRID REFERENCE TQ 147 292
START POINT Christ's Hospital Station

Walk along the station access road. Ignore a left fork and, shortly, join another road and go ahead. After 200yds (183m), bear right over the railway, now on the Downs Link. The route has to resort to quiet roads for the next mile (1.6km) as the track bed from Christ's Hospital Station is unavailable. At a road junction after 0.5 miles (800m), turn right.

For a short diversion, take the field path ahead for 0.25 miles (400m) to the interesting church at Itchingfield. It is notable for an oak-framed belfry dating back to the 15th century. In the churchyard you will find a medieval timber-framed building, known as the Priest's House, built for visiting monks.

Back on the main route, after another 0.5 miles (800m), where the lane bends to the left, turn right along the drive to Baystone House. Cross the old railway and double back to the left down on to the track bed.

Towards Slinfold, the Downs Link crosses the A264, where a faded advertisement on the brick wall of a house (now providing bed-and-breakfast) was clearly designed for train passengers. The village is 0.5 miles (800m) to the right here, where accommodation and refreshment is available. For anyone attempting to complete the Downs Link in two days, this is a good stop-over point, with just about half the journey (18 miles/29km) completed.

WILDLIFE CORRIDOR

The site of Slinfold Station, 0.25 miles (400m) further on, has been converted to a caravan site with a car park beside the line. From here, a nature trail has been laid out through woodland typical of the Sussex Weald, a mixture mainly of oak and ash.

From this point northwards to Bramley, the land alongside the line, all in public ownership, has been carefully 'managed' in order to conserve a wide variety of wildlife. When the railway closed, the embankments reverted to dense scrub and woodland and many plants and animals declined or disappeared. Now a valuable 'wildlife corridor' has been restored.

After another 1.5 miles (2.5km), you will come to the two-tier bridge over the River Arun which features on the Downs Link logo. The building of one bridge on top of the other was necessitated by the 19th-century railway inspector's requirement that the steep gradient up to Rudgwick should be eased.

Cross the busy A281 road with care as the traffic is fast. A few more minutes' walking brings you to the site of Rudgwick Station, where there is a small car park and easy access to the village street and shop.

A short distance beyond the next over-bridge, at grid ref. TQ 082 341, a signed field path, up three steps and over a stile on the right, leads directly to the King's Head pub, crossing a lane en route. From here a pleasant footpath may be followed back to Slinfold, via Hyes and Dedisham.

BAYNARDS TUNNEL

Very shortly you will come to the barricaded entrance to Baynards tunnel. The Downs Link climbs a ramped path on the

left. At the top, you have a choice of routes. Pedestrians may go to the right, over the top of the tunnel. Equestrians and cyclists must turn left. For a short distance the Downs Link coincides with the Sussex Border Path. For several miles, both eastward and westward, this follows the low ridge that forms the county boundary. After a few yards, turn right into Surrey and walk through woods to a road.

Turn right, cross a bridge and double back to the right, down on to the old railway. At Baynards Station, the Downs Link skirts to the left of buildings in private ownership, which have been carefully restored to their former glory. Beyond the station, there is a small picnic area for Downs Link users, and the former Thurlow Arms pub is beside the track. In 2.75 miles (4.5km), the Downs Link reaches Cranleigh, with easy access to the town.

STAGE 4

CRANLEIGH to ST MARTHA'S HILL

DISTANCE 9.5 miles (15.2km)

MAPS OS Explorer 134, 145

START AT GRID REFERENCE TQ 056 389

START POINT Knowle Lane, about 100 yds (90m) south of its junction with the B2128

The path, narrow at first but still on the line of the old railway, is well segregated from an industrial area on the right. Once clear of the town, the Downs Link runs on an embankment, with the disused Wey and Arun Canal (here no more than an overgrown ditch) to the left. A low brick wall marks the point where the canal passed under the railway. The third over-bridge north from here carries the Greensand Way across the Downs Link.

The 4-mile (6.5km) section of the Greensand Way westwards from here (grid ref. TQ 024 427), to Hascombe, provides a varied and attractive walk with a good pub at the end of it and various possibilities for circuits back to Cranleigh.

DOUBLE BRIDGE

Further on, approaching Bramley, the canal appears again, now on the right, partially restored and full of water. At Bramley, the Downs Link crosses the B2128. The village, with shops, pubs, and a good bus service into Guildford, is to the left. The walk goes ahead along the platform of the former Bramley and Wonersh Station, where the old station sign is still intact. After a short detour to the right, where a bridge has been demolished, resume your way along the track bed with a stream near by to your left.

Shortly, you will come to a double bridge. The lower arch across the Wey and Arun Canal has been incorporated into a newer bridge across the railway. The scene provides a graphic symbol of the eclipse of the canal by the railway.

Turn right in front of the bridge, cross the lower arch and walk parallel to a lane on your left. Join the lane and shortly, at a road junction, go ahead on a roughly metalled drive which soon dwindles to a bridleway. After 0.5 miles (800m) a path to the right leads up to the top of Chinthurst Hill, worth a visit if time permits. The Downs Link continues past a car park and out to the B2128. Cross the road and follow a woodland path, opposite. At a drive, turn left. At Great Tangley Manor Farm, go ahead on a soft sandy track which soon narrows and climbs between high banks. After a little over 0.5 mile (800m), go straight over an oblique crossing track and follow the Downs Link waymarks carefully across Blackheath, crossing a lane at grid ref. TQ 032 464. (For the Villagers Inn turn right, then left at a crossroads.)

About 30yds (27m) beyond the lane, fork right. Your next landmark is an isolated stone war memorial, on raised ground to the right of the track. From the memorial, you can just see St Martha's Church, over the trees. A few yards past the memorial, go ahead over a crossing track, where the Downs Link waymark is a little ambiguous. Shortly, cross the end of a drive and follow a narrow path to the right of the gateway to Lingwood House.

GLORIOUS VIEWS

Descend into a valley, heading north. Cross the railway and A248 road, and go ahead along a drive, with St Martha's Church now in clear view, perched high on the hill ahead. Beyond a footbridge, a detour along a narrow woodland path to the left leads to the ruins of Chilworth gunpowder mills; the only remaining signs of a once thriving local industry.

Shortly, cross the main Tilling Bourne stream and, after 300yds (275m), turn right for the last ascent on to St Martha's Hill. Towards the top, a Downs Link logo, with the date 1984, set in stone, marks the end of the path at the point where it joins the North Downs Way. For the summit, a few minutes' walk away, turn sharp left. St Martha's Church, almost entirely rebuilt in 1848, stands on the site of a much older church, dating back to 1087. It has, for centuries, provided a place of sanctuary and worship for travellers on a much older long-distance route, the Pilgrim's Way from Winchester to Canterbury. It is a fitting place to end the walk, with glorious views back across the Weald and along the Surrey Hills.

From here, the surest way to link with public transport is to follow the North Downs Way into Guildford, 3 miles (5km) west. Infrequent trains stop at Chilworth, 1.5 miles (2.5km) south, and there is a bus service from Albury, 2 miles (3km) east.

ℹ PLACES TO VISIT

• ST MARY'S HOUSE AND GARDENS

www.stmarysbramber.co.uk

☎ 01903 816205

This charming 15th-century half-timbered house lies in the equally picturesque village of Bramber. It has acres of tranquil gardens, which include a Victorian 'secret' garden and some amusing topiary. The house itself has both royal and literary connections, and features sumptuous wall panelling, trompe l'oeil painting and some fine stained glass. Group visits can be booked daily Apr–Sep, or public access is Thu, Sun & bank holiday afternoons May–Sep.

• SOUTHWATER COUNTRY PARK

www.horshamdistrictcountryside. org ☎ 01403 731218

The Downs Link enters this country park, passing close to the visitor centre and café. There are three lakes here: one for non-motorized water sports, such as kayaking and dinghy sailing; one for day-ticket fishing, and a final one reserved strictly for the abundant wildlife. There is also a skate park and an outdoor play area for the younger visitors. Park open daily all year; visitor centre open most weekends.

• WONERSH

The route skirts around the pretty village of Wonersh, which is well worth a detour if you are in need of a refreshment stop. There is a small 'pepperpot' shelter in the centre of the village, close to the attractive half-timbered inn. The church here is said to date back to Saxon times.

• SHALFORD MILL

www.nationaltrust.org.uk

☎ 01483 561389

A little way off the route, on the southern edge of Guildford, stands this 18th-century timber-framed watermill. It ceased operating in 1914 and the waterwheel no longer turns, but the building remains almost unaltered. Open Wed & Sun Apr–Oct.

Greensand Way

COMPLETE ROUTE HASLEMERE TO HAM STREET **105 MILES (169KM)**
SECTION COVERED WITLEY TO DORKING **23 MILES (37KM)**
MAPS OS EXPLORER 125, 133, 134, 136, 137, 145, 146, 147, 148

The Greensand Way is named after the sandstone ridge crossing Hampshire, Surrey and Kent, one of a series of ridges running west to east across southeast England. Here, we cover the 23-mile (37km) section from Witley Station, which is under 10 miles (16km) from the official start of the route at Haslemere, to Dorking. For walkers wishing to add the very attractive first section of the route to the journey described here, there is a direct railway link between Witley and Haslemere, and they will be rewarded by the exceptional landscape of Hindhead Common, Gibbet Hill and the Devil's Punchbowl.

From Witley, the Greensand Way crosses Hambledon Common to Hambledon village. It then climbs gently across open heathland before dropping steeply to Hascombe, delightfully situated in a fold of the Surrey Hills. The path now heads north-eastwards through gently undulating, well-wooded countryside.

On level ground, the Greensand Way then crosses, in quick succession, the A281 Guildford–Horsham road, the Downs Link path on the old Guildford–Horsham railway, and the disused Wey and Arun Canal, to reach Shamley Green.

A gentle climb on to Winterfold Heath marks the start of the finest section of the walk. Over the next 6 miles (9.5km) or so, the walker can enjoy a succession of spectacular summits, as the Greensand Way picks a route along the main ridge. Reynard's Hill (800ft/244m), Pitch Hill (843ft/257m) and Holmbury Hill (857ft/261m) follow in quick succession. After the descent to Holmbury St Mary, Leith Hill provides a final challenge. At 965ft (294m) above sea level, this is the highest point in southeast England.

From here, a lone and easy walk northwards through woodland, and along the Tillingbourne valley, leads to Westcott and a last climb over the Nower to Dorking.

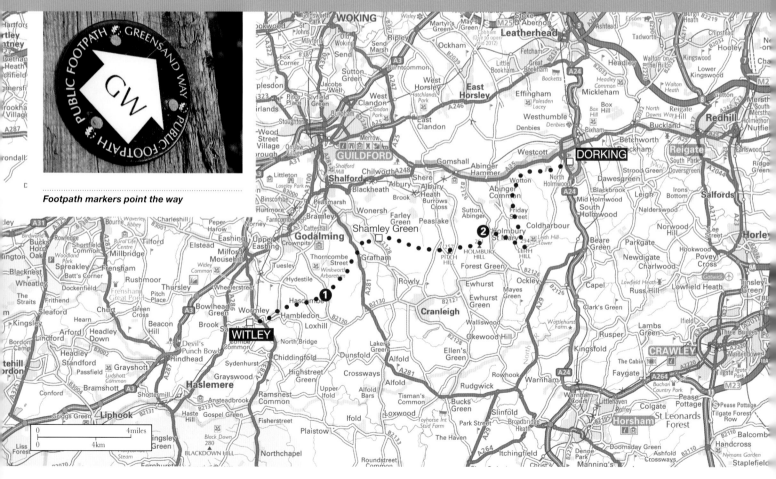

Footpath markers point the way

The 17th-century tile-hung farmhouse and 18th-century granary at Court Farm

WITLEY TO DORKING

STAGE 1

WITLEY STATION to SHAMLEY GREEN

DISTANCE 8.3 miles (13.3km)

MAPS OS Explorer 133, 134, 145

START AT GRID REFERENCE SU 948 379

START POINT Witley Station on the Guildford–Portsmouth main line

Turn left along the station approach road. An enclosed path starts beside a road junction. At the A283, turn left. After a few yards, go right and follow waymarks, embossed with the GW logo, soon crossing Hambledon Common, the first of a number of areas of open heathland which are a major feature of the greensand belt.

Descend to the road at Hambledon, which is a pleasant but rather scattered village. At a road junction, go ahead, signposted to Godalming. Shortly, beside the entrance to Rockhill House, fork right up steps and cross two fields to join a lane. Turn left, passing Hambledon Church.

St Peter's Church and the nearby Court Farm form an attractive group. The church contains a 14th-century chancel arch. In the churchyard stand two magnificent yew trees, the larger being 30ft (9m) in circumference.

Beyond the church, fork right and, at a T-junction, turn right again. After a few yards, a narrow path forks left along the top of a hanger before dropping down through the wood. After a short section, parallel to a lane, the route follows the foot of the hanger,

with wide views to the south. At Marwick Lane turn left and, after 50yds (45m), go right up a sunken track to cross the wood and heathland of The Hurtwood, ignoring all side tracks. After 0.75 miles (1.25km) go right and left, then drop down steeply between banks. Look out for a narrow, steep, descending path on the left, which can be slippery after rain. A field path leads out to the road at Hascombe, opposite the White Horse pub.

🏠 *From Hascombe (grid ref. TQ 002 395), a visit can be made to Winkworth Arboretum and from there a well-linked series of paths leads along the Juniper Valley and over Hydon's Ball, back to Hambledon.*

WELL-MARKED TRACKS

From Hascombe, an attractive village surrounded by wooded hills, a diversion is possible, to the 645ft (196m) summit of Hascombe Hill. Jutting out southwards into the Weald, it is covered with fine beech trees and crowned by earthworks marking the site of an Iron Age fort.

The Greensand Way continues along Church Road, beside the pub, passing the beautifully kept village pond and the gothic-style church, rebuilt in 1864. Where the road ends, go ahead through a gateway and, shortly, enter an ascending sunken track.

A series of woodland tracks, well marked with the GW logo at all junctions, brings you to a lane. Turn right and, after a few yards, turn left along a waymarked path, beside a fence, through woods and across pasture beside another fence. In a dip fork left, uphill, beside a high fence. Cross a track and walk down across a field. In the bottom right corner, join a track,

TOP LEFT Holmbury St Mary
church in early summer
TOP MIDDLE Walkers
descending Leith Hill, with a
hazy view of the surrounding
countryside in Friday Street
beyond
TOP RIGHT The Leith Hill
range of hills encompass the
highest point in southeast
England
ABOVE An 18th-century
Gothic tower at Friday Street

passing to the left of a barn and a wood. Turn left along the drive from Gatestreet Farm. Beyond a house called 'Keepers', the drive loses its metalled surface. Fork right at a junction and, subsequently, turn left along a lane. Where the lane bears left, go forward across a cattle grid. A field path now leads to the A281. Turn left. After 150yds, turn right through Rooks Hill Farm. The Greensand Way now crosses the Downs Link, which follows the old Horsham–Guildford railway line and is described on pages 58–61.

The Downs Link (grid ref. TQ 024 428) provides convenient access either south to Cranleigh or north to Bramley and Guildford.

OVERGROWN DITCH

The path soon crosses the former Wey and Arun Canal, which is no more than an overgrown ditch at this point. A waymarked bridleway continues to the B2128, south of Shamley Green. Turn left along the road to find pub refreshment and a bus to Guildford.

STAGE 2

SHAMLEY GREEN to DORKING

DISTANCE 14.4 miles (23.2km)
MAPS OS Explorer 145, 146
START AT GRID REFERENCE TQ 033 433
START POINT Shamley Green on the B2128 Bramley–Cranleigh road

From the village green, walk southwards along the B2128. Just past the church on the left, turn left along an enclosed path. Join a drive and, after 250yds (225m), turn right along another drive to 'Little Cuckrells'. Where the drive ends, a good path continues to a lane by Strouds Farm.

Turn right on Stroud Lane and, shortly, left along the drive to 'Franklins'. By the house entrance, keep walking ahead along a grassy path. Very shortly, fork left, uphill through woodland. Climb across an open area, passing a large pond. Re-enter woodlands and join a track. Where this track veers right, downhill, go ahead. Walk round the shoulder of the hill to a meeting of six

ways, where you should go ahead on a level track. Cross a lane and climb steps, opposite. The Greensand Way, waymarked at intervals, follows a path along the scarp of Winterfold Hill, with a series of wonderful views, glimpsed through the trees, out across the Weald.

The path eventually turns away from the edge to join a road at the top of a deep and dramatic gully. After a few yards along the road, the Greensand Way diverges to the right on a path, parallel to the road at first.

SUMMIT VIEWPOINTS

At a crossing track, turn right. Another contour path follows the top of the scarp slope to a viewpoint on the top of Reynard's Hill, the first of a series of summit viewpoints which are the main feature of the next few miles. This is the westernmost height of the Leith Hill range of hills and offers a wide view to the south and west. The bluff of Hascombe Hill stands out, with Hindhead and Blackdown beyond and to the left. On a clear day the South Downs are visible on the southern skyline.

A path continues to rejoin the road, once again for a few yards only. At a T-junction, go ahead, soon passing Ewhurst windmill. This brick post-mill was built in about 1820 and has been converted to a private residence. Drop down beside a fence to cross a road. In a few yards, turn right and climb steadily to the top of Pitch Hill, also known as Coneyhurst Hill. At 843ft (257m) above sea level, this is another magnificent summit. The village of Ewhurst is in the foreground.

From the summit of Pitch Hill (grid ref. TQ 083 423), an escape can be made by a choice of bridleways and footpaths leading north, to Peaslake, and then by quiet country lanes and footpaths to Gomshall Station, on the Guildford–Dorking line.

HOLMBURY HILL

Carry on round the edge of the hill, with views all the way. Your next challenge, the summit of Holmbury Hill, is prominent to the east. About 60yds (55m) past a metal seat, fork right down past the Duke of Kent School and out to a road. A narrow path, opposite, crosses the valley and climbs to the summit of Holmbury Hill. The way is clear throughout. This third viewpoint,

ⓘ PLACES TO VISIT

• **WINKWORTH ARBORETUM**
www.nationaltrust.org.uk
☎ 01483 208477
A footpath from Hambledon can take you to this fine collection of rare shrubs and trees. Planted along steep lakeside banks, it is especially attractive in the spring (when there are displays of English bluebells) and autumn (when the tree foliage is varied) It is a lovely spot for a picnic, although there is also a small tea room. Open daily all year; tea room open Wed–Sun Mar–Nov, Sat–Sun Dec–Feb.

• **LEITH HILL TOWER**
www.nationaltrust.org.uk
☎ 01306 712711
The highest point in southeast England is passed on the GW and capped by this 18th-century tower, giving impressive 360 degree views. There are also trails in the nearby rhododendron wood, which is stunning in May and June. Tower open Sat–Sun and bank holidays all year, plus Wed and Fri Apr–Oct.

• **DORKING**
www.visitdorking.com
The attractive and historic town of Dorking is the end point of this section of the GW. It has long been a popular staging post for travellers between the south coast and London, and has some fine old inns as a result. The Dorking Museum and Heritage Centre tells more of the town's history, and displays artefacts ranging from fossils to toys (www.dorkingmuseum.co.uk ☎ 01306 876591; see website for opening times). There are two heritage trails around the town, leaflets of which can be picked up from the Dorking Halls complex, or downloaded from the tourist website listed on page 63.

at 857ft (261m), is perhaps the best of all. You can look back across the successive ridges of Pitch Hill and Hascombe Hill as well as forward to the wooded heights of Leith Hill, which is our final and highest summit. An interesting and extremely large early Iron Age fort, with a double rampart and ditch, covers a wide expanse of the summit area.

From the elaborate seat on the top, follow the hill edge. Beyond a cricket pitch on the left, fork right down to the village of Holmbury St Mary. At the road, turn left, shortly ignoring a left fork. Walk down past the post office to a junction with the B2126. The route turns right here but the village is about 0.25 miles (400m) along the road to the left.

LEITH HILL SUMMIT

After a few yards to the right along the B2126, the Greensand Way turns left along Pasture Wood Road. After another 300yds (275m), turn right into woodland on a clear track. Beyond High Ashes Farm, go right at a T-junction and after nearly 0.25 miles (400m) turn left up to a road. The track opposite takes you on for another 0.75 miles (1.25km) up to the summit of Leith Hill, which at 965ft

(294m) is the highest point in the south-eastern counties. From here, go ahead, past the tower and then turn steeply downhill. At a National Trust notice, 'Duke's Warren', turn left on a crossing track. Now descend for 1.5 miles (2.5km) down a long valley. On reaching a road, turn right and immediately fork right again. Continue along the valley with the Tillingbourne stream nearby on your left.

At the point where the track meets a lane, the Greensand Way turns right on a path parallel with, and to the left of, a track. Cross another track and drop down through woodland. Join, in turn, a track and then an access drive that leads out to the A25 road. A few yards short of the main road, turn right up a sunken path. Cross Westcott Heath and join a path behind the houses of Westcott.

Cross a footbridge, turn left along a road and, shortly, turn right up on to the Nower. Follow waymarks up to 'The Temple', on the highest point. Maintain direction, finally bearing left down across grass to join Hampstead Lane. Turn right and then left into Dorking. The bus station is near by, but the two railway stations are nearly a mile (1.6km) further on.

BELOW Evening sunlight brightens the view south from Holmbury Hill

Wealdway

COMPLETE ROUTE GRAVESEND TO EASTBOURNE **82 MILES (132KM)**

SECTION COVERED AS ABOVE

MAPS OS EXPLORER 123, 135, 136, 147, 148, 162, 163

This route through three AONBs connects the Thames Estuary with the English Channel, through the Weald of Kent and Sussex. It spans chalk downlands, river valleys and wooded farmland in often remote country, including a full traverse of Ashdown Forest. It links the North Downs Way National Trail at Trottiscliffe with the South Downs Way National Trail, near to Eastbourne. The Wealdway crosses the centre of the overcrowded south-eastern corner of England, but the chosen route manages, for almost its entire length, to avoid main centres of population. Much of the walk is quiet and remote, with only the occasional tiny village to interrupt a varied succession of woodland, arable field, river bank, heath, orchard and downland pasture.

GRAVESEND (TOWN PIER) TO TONBRIDGE

STAGE 1

GRAVESEND (TOWN PIER) to WROTHAM HEATH

DISTANCE 13.4 miles (21.6km)

MAPS OS Explorer 148, 162, 163

START AT GRID REFERENCE TQ 747 744

START POINT Town Pier Gravesend

Follow the A227 just over 2 miles (3km) south out of Gravesend, to the Tollgate junction. Going to the left of the Tollgate Hotel buildings, find the footbridges to cross the A2 and the high speed rail link. Continue heading south on a track, passing Ifield Court on the left, and under some power lines. From Nash Street to Sole Street, the route is well waymarked and straightforward. Sole Street Station provides a useful alternative starting point for Wealdway walkers, omitting the rather dull first 3 miles (5km) of the route and the road walk out of Gravesend. There is a good train service from London.

If time allows, the delightful village of Cobham, about a mile (1.6km) across the fields from Sole Street, is well worth a diversion. The church dates back to the 13th century, and the half-timbered Leather Bottle inn features in Charles Dickens' *Pickwick Papers*. Cobham Hall, a mile (1.6km) outside the village, is an exceptional Elizabethan mansion.

From Sole Street, the Wealdway continues past the Railway Inn. After 200yds (183m), turn left on a rough track (not through the gate into Camer Park). The track leads up on to Henley Down, the first of the chalk hills of the North Downs, where, beyond a copse, there is a sudden broad view over the Luddesdown valley. The Wealdway is now well waymarked down to the hamlet of Luddesdown, which is a tiny but delightful group of buildings. Luddesdown Court (not, alas, open to the public) dates back, at least, to the 13th century and is said to be one of the oldest continuously lived-in houses in the country.

Beyond the church, walk between farm buildings and turn left on a good path for over a mile (1.6km) along the valley known as the Bowling Alley. At a road, turn right, immediately forking right again to pass Great Buckland Farm. A fork left here, off-route and another 0.25 miles (400m) along the valley, leads to the tiny church at Dode (now privately owned), parts of which are Norman.

TOP A hot air balloon floats gently over Ashdown Forest
ABOVE The village of Cobham in Kent

For walkers looking for a circuit back towards Sole Street, a choice of paths to the west link Great Buckland (grid ref. TQ 670 642) with Priestwood and Meopham Green, then lead to the railway stations at Meopham or Sole Street.

NORTH DOWNS ESCARPMENT

From Great Buckland, the Wealdway climbs steadily, overgrown in places, soon to run beside and then through Luxon Wood. After a short stretch of muddy bridleway, the route crosses a paddock to a road. Turn left and, where the road veers right, go ahead over a stile and shortly left over a second stile. Turn right to walk through two meadows and between barns to White Horse Road.

Turn right a few yards before going left through Whitehorse Wood. After 0.75 miles (1.25km), the path veers right and drops steeply down the North Downs escarpment. The spectacular view from the edge is partly obscured by foliage, but there are several good vantage points beside the path, providing tantalizing glimpses of a spectacular Wealden panorama.

At the bottom of the hill, for a few yards, the Wealdway shares a track with both the North Downs Way and the much more ancient Pilgrim's Way, running between the important religious cities of Winchester and Canterbury.

Heading eastwards from here (grid ref. TQ 652 613), the North Downs Way provides part of another convenient circuit back to Luddesdown. In the other direction, the North Downs Way climbs to the top of the escarpment and passes through Trosley Country Park. The Wealdway can then be rejoined via the village of Trottiscliffe.

SKELETONS FOUND

The direct route of the Wealdway heads south into the Weald, with more good views along the way. After 600yds (545m), you will pass Coldrum Long Barrow, the remains of a Neolithic tomb. When it was opened in 1910, 22 skeletons were found, dating from about 3,000BC.

Continue southwards on a concrete drive, forking left into Ryarsh Wood and on across fields to a road. Turn right and after 350yds, go left beside a sand quarry and under the M20 road. Immediately beyond the road tunnel, turn sharply right up a bank and along a path, beside the motorway fence at first.

At Westfields Farm, turn left along a drive and, shortly, right on an unmarked path. At the next lane, turn right. After 0.5 miles (800m), just beyond a large house on the right, turn right on a clear path, cross a minor road and continue ahead to reach the A20 at Wrotham Heath.

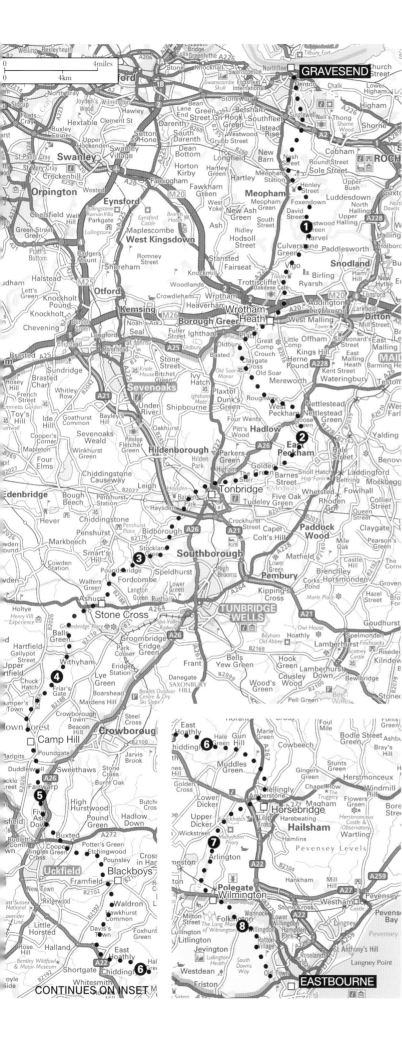

ABOVE The ancient Norman church at Dode, Great Buckland

i USEFUL INFORMATION

THE ROUTE
• The Kent County Council
website has little on the
Wealdway, and the East Sussex
County Council pages give
even less, but they do have a
comprehensive guidebook, 'Along
and Around the Wealdway', for
sale by phone. Contact them on
☎ 01273 481654.

**TOURIST INFORMATION
CENTRES**
• *www.towncentric.co.uk*
18a St George's Square,
Gravesend DA11 0TB;
☎ 01474 337600
• *www.visiteartofkent.com*
Tonbridge Castle, Castle Street,
Tonbridge TN9 1BG;
☎ 01732 770929
• *www.visiteastbourne.com*
Cornfield Road, Eastbourne BN21
4QA; ☎ 0871 663 0031
• Off the route, but also useful, is:
www.visitkent.co.uk
The Old Fish Market, The
Pantiles, Tunbridge Wells TN2
5TN; ☎ 01892 515675

PLANNING YOUR TRIP
• *www.highweald.org*
Between Tonbridge and Uckfield,
the Wealdway crosses the higher
ground of the High Weald AONB.
These pages give details of the
area, including accommodation
and wildlife spotting guides.
• *www.ldwa.org.uk*
The Long Distance Walkers
Association gives information on
the Wealdway, including a map.
• *www.ramblers.org.uk*
☎ 020 7339 8500
The Ramblers Association provide
general information about long-
distance walking and specific
help covering the Wealdway.
• *www.yha.org.uk*
☎ 0800 019 1700
The Youth Hostel Association has
three sites close to the southern
part of the route.

*TOP The Coldrum Stones, a Neolithic
long barrow at Trottiscliffe
MIDDLE View over Ashdown Forest
BOTTOM Beachy Head*

OTHER PATHS
The WW links with and is crossed
by many paths: the North and
South Downs Way paths, and the
Greensand and Vanguard Ways.

TOP *A leisurely boat trip down the River Medway*
ABOVE *Old Soar Manor*

STAGE 2

WROTHAM HEATH to TONBRIDGE

DISTANCE 13.7 miles (22km)
MAPS OS Explorer 136, 147, 148
START AT GRID REFERENCE TQ 633 580
START POINT The junction of the A20 and A25 roads, at Wrotham Heath

Start the walk along a drive to the right of the Royal Oak pub. It narrows to a path and passes under the railway. Ignore a left fork and, at the next lane, bear left. After 300yds (275m), fork right on a narrow fenced path between rhododendrons. Ignore the many side and crossing tracks in this woodland.

At the road on the edge of the village of Platt, turn right and, shortly, left into Potash Lane. For amenities in the centre of the village, a few minutes away, go straight on from this point. Otherwise, follow Potash Lane over a crossroads and on to join a wider road. At another crossroads, go ahead between high hedges.

After 250yds (225m), fork right. For the next 2 miles (3km), the Wealdway heads south through Mereworth Woods; predominantly coppiced hazel, with a scattering of silver birch. Ignore all side and crossing tracks to reach a road at Gover Hill, a small National Trust area, with broad views southwards over the valley of the Medway.

Cross a road and continue the walk along a track beside a white-walled cottage. After 0.5 miles (800m) turn left, as waymarked. For the next mile (1.6km), the Wealdway is also part of the Greensand Way, and is the continuation, in Kent, of the route described on pages 62–65. At a lane, turn left and, very shortly, fork right. A few minutes' walk brings you to West Peckham, where the church and the Swan on the Green pub are delightfully set beside the village green.

RIVERSIDE WALKING

Follow the road between pub and church. At a road junction, turn right on a path, enclosed at first. For the next 5 miles (8km), south to the Medway, the Wealdway follows a series of field paths, subject to cultivation. Most of the paths are waymarked but there are one or two gaps. Care, plus a good 1:25,000 scale map, will ensure successful navigation.

On the first path, veer right in the third field. Cross the A26. The start of the next path, a few yards to the right, is not obvious. Cross the verge bank and go ahead on a roughly metalled track. After 0.5 miles (800m), turn right on a track which crosses two streams and continues to Peckham Place Farm. Follow the farm drive out to a lane and turn left.

The next path follows a straight southerly line through an orchard and across a field to a lane. Turn right. At Kent House Farm, a massive converted oasthouse, turn left along Pierce Mill Lane. After 0.5 miles (800m), beyond an attractive house and garden on the right, turn right along the north bank of the River Bourne. Cross the river at the first opportunity, go ahead over a field to a second footbridge, and bear left across the corner of the field beyond to a third footbridge. Continue beside a field

out to the road at Barnes Street, opposite a picturesque half-timbered house. Turn right and, very shortly, go left along a track. Walk through an orchard, bearing slightly left, to find a wide grassy track leading onwards to the River Medway. Cross the river and turn right along the towpath. At East Lock, cross back over the Medway and follow the north bank for 4 miles (6.5km) into Tonbridge. It is quite a busy waterway and you are likely to encounter pleasure boats working through one of the four locks on this lovely stretch of the river.

On the outskirts of Tonbridge, cross the Medway once again, using the Cannon Road bridge. Continue beside the river, passing Town Lock, to reach Tonbridge High Street.

TONBRIDGE TO CAMP HILL

STAGE 3

TONBRIDGE to STONE CROSS

DISTANCE 9.2 miles (14.8km)
MAPS OS Explorer 135, 136, 147
START AT GRID REFERENCE TQ 590 465
START POINT The entrance to the grounds of Tonbridge Castle

The Wealdway continues through the castle grounds beside the River Medway with the high castle wall to the right. The Norman castle was built on a prominent artificial mound, strategically placed to guard a ford over the river. It was constructed from local sandstone, but dismantled, like so many English castles, during the Civil War. The solid 13th-century gatehouse is still reasonably intact.

After 250yds (225m), turn left over a footbridge, signposted as the Eden Valley Walk, and then right past a miniature railway and a car park, a useful alternative starting point for walkers arriving by car (grid ref. TQ 588 468). The Eden Valley Walk, distinctively waymarked, runs beside the Medway and its tributary, the Eden, for 15 miles (24km) between Tonbridge and Edenbridge, and for Wealdway walkers it is a useful means of visiting Penshurst Place.

The two long-distance routes remain together for 2 miles (3km), past playing fields, under the railway, left over two footbridges and on beside the Medway for 0.5 miles (800m).

Cross the river by the second bridge and bear right and left past a wood. Beyond the railway, bear left and left again, out to a road. Go ahead through Haysden. At Manor Farm, the Wealdway is waymarked across a field, under the A21, left for a few yards, and then right beside a hedge to a lane.

VIEWS ACROSS THE VALLEY

The path opposite marks the start of a gentle but steady climb out of the Medway Valley. Cross a field to join a track. After another 0.5 mile, a steeper climb through woodland brings you to the B2176. A bus service along this road links Tunbridge Wells and Penshurst.

The Wealdway now follows the road for 0.5 miles (800m), with magnificent views northward across the Medway valley to the greensand ridge and the North Downs beyond. Look out for a narrow path on the left, signposted to Bidborough Church. (For the Hare and Hounds pub, carry on along the road.)

The small sandstone church at Bidborough occupies a superb site on high ground with views towards Speldhurst, the next objective. The Wealdway passes through the churchyard and descends a flight of steps to the lych gate.

Turn sharply back to the left, down Spring Lane and onwards through a quiet and secluded valley. After a steep climb, a woodland path cuts through a sandstone outcrop, a characteristic feature of the area, and then crosses high ground before dropping down into another quiet valley.

The route now bears right along the edge of Southborough Common, an area of heath, criss-crossed by paths.

STAINED GLASS WINDOWS

If time permits, the spa town of Tunbridge Wells deserves a detour. The resort was developed and became fashionable after the discovery of a chalybeate (iron-bearing) stream in the 17th century. The Pantiles, a colonnade of shops and houses built beside the springs in about 1690, remains an elegant and carefully preserved pedestrian precinct.

At the bottom of the hill, the Wealdway joins a lane and climbs steeply. After 0.5 miles (800m), an inconspicuous kissing-gate on the left marks the start of a field path, which soon bears right in front of a garden and rejoins the lane 0.5 mile further on. The next path starts a few yards to the right, through the gateway to Forge House, and drops down steeply across pasture.

Walk past a disused mill, where the rusting water wheel is still in place. Shortly turn right and climb the hill to Speldhurst. The Wealdway, as it did at Bidborough, picks a route through the churchyard. The church, although rebuilt twice after the original structure was destroyed by lightning in 1791, is not without interest. Dating from 1870, it contains some exceptional stained-glass windows by the Pre-Raphaelites, Edward Burne-Jones and William Morris. The George and Dragon, nearby, is a fine old pub that has been carefully restored.

From Speldhurst (grid ref. TQ 553 415), there is a bus service, as well as several footpath routes, into Tunbridge Wells, which is still within comfortable walking distance.

PICNIC SPOT

The Wealdway follows the Penshurst road. A wrought-iron gate on the left marks the start of a path through to Bullingstone Lane at grid ref. TQ 545 411. The next path, a few yards to the right along the lane, starts beside two picturesque 15th-century cottages and descends, forking right, into Avery's Wood. The stream crossing within the wood is a delectable spot, perfect for a picnic.

A clear path leads to a road and on for 0.75 miles (1.25km) into the village of Fordcombe, all on the tarmac except for one short linking field path. Fordcombe is a pleasant village with a shop, a pub serving real ales, and a village green. The Wealdway continues beside the cricket ground and along a headland path across high ground for 0.75 miles (1.25km) to the A264 at Stone Cross.

From here (grid ref. TQ 522 390) Ashurst Station is just over a mile (1.6km) to the right along the main road. For a footpath alternative, carry on along the Wealdway and then follow the Sussex Border Path which goes directly to Ashurst Station.

STAGE 4
STONE CROSS to CAMP HILL
DISTANCE 8.5 miles (13.7km)
MAPS OS Explorer 135, 147
START AT GRID REFERENCE TQ 522 390
START POINT Stone Cross, on the A264 East Grinstead–Tunbridge Wells road

From Stone Cross, the Wealdway is narrow and enclosed for a short distance. It then follows one of the finest sections of the walk, along a sloping, grassy hillside. Over the next 0.5 miles (800m), the view ahead into Sussex steadily widens, with the heights of Ashdown Forest now clearly visible across the valley.

For the second time, the route descends into a valley carved by the River Medway. For 0.5 miles (800m), the Wealdway and the Sussex Border Path coincide, marked by two solid wayposts. Over the stream on the Kent–Sussex boundary, a bridge, designed and built by local ramblers, stands in memory of one of their colleagues. The Medway, crossed near Hale Farm is, in these higher reaches, little more than a modest stream. For the next mile (1.6km), to the road at Summerford Farm, the Wealdway is never far away from the river. Beyond the farm, the way is clear and obvious at first, along a cart track. After 0.25 mile (400m), watch carefully for a narrow, unmarked path which drops down left.

Shortly, cross the old railway, now the Forest Way; a 15-mile (24km) route linking East Grinstead with Groombridge.

PLACES TO VISIT
• **OLD SOAR MANOR**
www.nationaltrust.org.uk
☎ 01732 810378 ext. 100
Approximately 0.5 miles (800m) west from the route, outside Mereworth Woods, is this rare example of a knight's home. Built in the 13th century, it still contains features such as a chapel and garderobe, but there are no visitor facilities here. Open Sat–Thu Apr–Sep.

• **TONBRIDGE**
www.tmbc.gov.uk
☎ 01732 770929
The route passes through this small market town. There are the remains of a Norman castle to wander around (the TIC within the castle grounds supply audio guides), with its fine restored gatehouse, and also a delightful park beside the River Medway. This makes an ideal spot for a picnic, particularly with young children as there is a large play area. If you have a whole day, the Hidden Heritage bus runs between May and September, exploring the villages of the area and allowing you to hop on and off the three tours a day that leave from Tonbridge station. For those who prefer to walk, the TIC have leaflets and details of local walking groups and guided tours.

• **PENSHURST PLACE**
www.penshurstplace.com
☎ 01892 870307
The impressive medieval manor that is Penshurst Place sits around 3 miles (5km) west along the B2176 from the WW route and can be approached on foot via the Eden Valley Way, just north of Haysden on the edge of Tonbridge. There is much to see, including state rooms, a Long Gallery lined with portraits, weapons and armour, and the room where Queen Elizabeth I held audience. The gardens are extensive, ranging from formal garden 'rooms' to woodland. There is also a toy museum and adventure playground within the estate. Open Sat–Sun Mar, daily Apr–Oct.

BELOW Norman Tonbridge Castle BELOW RIGHT Medieval Penshurst Place, surrounded by extensive gardens

Groombridge is 2.5 miles (4km) to the east from here (grid ref. TQ 491 363) and the track bed provides convenient access for Wealdway walkers. A footpath route continues via High Rocks into Tunbridge Wells. A mile (1.6km) in the other direction along the Forest Way brings you to the attractive village of Hartfield; a good place to break the journey, with two pubs and overnight accommodation.

The tall shingled spire of Hartfield Church is a prominent landmark and the lychgate into the churchyard has been fashioned beneath a half-timbered house dating from 1520. Continue through fields to the B2110 near Withyham, where you will find a shop, a pub and an occasional weekday bus to Tunbridge Wells. The church, on high ground beside the Wealdway, replaced an older building, destroyed by lightning in 1663. It contains various monuments to the Sackville family, many of whom are buried in a vault beneath the church. The Wealdway bypasses the village to follow the access drive to Fisher's Gate for over a mile (1.6km). Then begins a long climb through Five Hundred Acre Wood on Ashdown Forest.

This is the countryside immortalized by A A Milne in *Winnie-the-Pooh* and *The House at Pooh Corner.* The wood is but a shadow of its former glory, destroyed by the 1987 storm, but the Wealdway, at one time difficult to follow, is now on a clear open track, marked by special wooden wayposts.

After 2 miles (3km), the Wealdway reaches its highest point, at Greenwood Gate Clump. At 720ft (219m) above sea level, this is also the highest point in Ashdown Forest. From here to Camp Hill is a fine open walk with superb views.

There is a good track, eastwards from the road near Greenwood Gate Clump (grid ref. TQ 476 309), for 3 miles into Crowborough. Here you can catch a bus to Tunbridge Wells or Uckfield.

CAMP HILL TO HORSEBRIDGE

STAGE 5
CAMP HILL to BLACKBOYS
DISTANCE 8.5 miles (13.7km)
MAPS OS Explorer 123, 135
START AT GRID REFERENCE TQ 469 289
START POINT Camp Hill; the nearest forest car park, labelled 'The Hollies', is beside the Camp Hill–Nutley road at grid ref. TQ 463 287, about 0.5 miles (800m) to the west

Walk up to Camp Hill, passing to the right of the clump and to the left of a trig. point to reach the B2188 road. Follow the road, signposted to Crowborough, opposite. After a short but awkward section of road, the Wealdway bears right across open heathland to Crest Farm, where there is a sensational view southwards to the distant South Downs.

From here to Oldlands Corner, route-finding requires some care and concentration. Waymarks and wooden posts indicate the line of the Wealdway but tend to be hidden by bracken,

before crossing a large field, once part of the wood, but clear-felled some years ago. After a stile in the far field corner, the path traverses a patch of heath beside the busy A26, before crossing the main road at the start of the new bypass road at Five Ash Down. There is a pub and post office down the road to the right, but the Wealdway continues beside a garage forecourt. A field path leads through to the A272 Maresfield–Buxted road. After 0.25 miles (400m) along this road, the Wealdway heads south through Buxted Park, passing the church and Buxted Park Hotel. Bear left across pasture down to the edge of the River Uck, and go ahead beside the stream to reach Hempstead Mill and Hempstead Lane. Uckfield is 0.75 miles (1.25km) along the lane to the right at this point (grid ref. TQ 483 217) and is a useful centre with all services, including a railway station and a good bus service.

The Wealdway turns its back on the town, crossing the River Uck. From the bridge there is an excellent view of Hempstead Mill. After a few more yards, a stile on the left provides access to a field path, which climbs out of the valley, crosses the railway in a deep cutting and continues to a lane near Highlands Pond.

The next path, from the lane at grid ref. TQ 498 217, follows a stream along a remote and peaceful valley for over a mile (1.6km) to Tickerage Mill, crossing two minor roads, where a remarkable and quite unnecessary proliferation of notices discourages trespass from the track up towards Blackboys. It is an attractive spot, tempting the walker to linger and admire, in spite of written exhortations to keep moving.

For a short distance, the route of the Wealdway coincides with that of the Vanguard Way, a roughly parallel long-distance path across the Weald.

From the point where the route reaches the B2102 at grid ref. TQ 517 206, Blackboys is 0.25 miles (400m) to the left. There is a shop, the 14th-century Blackboys Inn and, north of the village, the youth hostel at grid ref. TQ 521 215.

From Blackboys (grid ref. TQ 521 205), the Vanguard Way provides a convenient return route via Buxted and High Hurstwood to the top of Ashdown Forest, where it crosses the Wealdway again at grid ref. TQ 411 306.

STAGE 6
BLACKBOYS to HORSEBRIDGE

DISTANCE 10.25 miles (16.5km)
MAPS OS Explorer 123, 135
START AT GRID REFERENCE TQ 511 206
START POINT The B2102 road, 0.25 miles (400m) west of Blackboys. Bus service from Uckfield. Parking is possible on wide verge near the start

The Wealdway uses the B2102 road for a few yards only before cutting through to the next lane. From the start of the path at grid ref. TQ 516 204, the South Downs come into view for the first time since the Wealdway descended the southern slopes of Ashdown Forest.

The route soon passes through the elaborately landscaped area surrounding New Place. Here, in sharp contrast to Tickerage, the track is open and unfenced and there are no unfriendly notices. From a large pond, a stream drops down a series of artificial cascades. It is a delightful sight, particularly in the spring when the surrounding area is a mass of daffodils. The next 3 miles (5km) to East Hoathly are well waymarked and present few problems apart from the possibility of obstruction by growing crops. Access to the footbridge in a wooded dip at grid ref. TQ 523 183 is not obvious and, in the field beyond, the Wealdway makes a curious dog-leg turn beside a solitary tree

PLACES TO VISIT
• **GROOMBRIDGE PLACE GARDENS AND ENCHANTED FOREST**
www.groombridge.co.uk
☎ 01892 861444
To the west of Tunbridge Wells, a small detour along the Forest Way will take you to the village of Groombridge, home to this major tourist attraction. It would be easy to spend a full day here, whatever your age or interests. There are formal gardens, such as the Knot Garden and Oriental Garden, or you can delve into the world of the Enchanted Forest. Here there are all kinds of diversions, including the vineyard, canal cruises between the forest and the kitchen garden, or the Raptor Centre, which is the largest conservation centre for birds of prey in the southeast. For fun, there are giant swings hanging from the trees, fantasy gardens (such as the Mystic Pool, the Serpent's Lair or the Village of the Groms) and a wooden raised adventure boardwalk. Most recently, a whole television stage set has been rebuilt in the woods to create the island home of Robinson Crusoe, complete with treetop houses and original props. Open daily Apr–Oct.

• **SPA VALLEY RAILWAY**
www.spavalleyrailway.co.uk
☎ 01892 537715
Also at the village of Groombridge is a station for the Spa Valley Railway, which runs steam engines to Tunbridge Wells along 3.5 miles (5.5km) of track. The journey itself is a pleasure, but there is also much to see in the Georgian spa town. Learn more at www.visittunbridgewells.com. In addition to a few weekday openings, trains run Sat–Sun Apr–Oct; usually five trains per day.

• **HARRISON'S ROCKS**
www.thebmc.co.uk/bmccrag
☎ 01892 863659
Just south of Groombridge are Harrison's Rocks. This is a spectacular sandstone outcrop, which is regularly festooned with rock climbers, particularly at weekends.

---

particularly in late summer. After a short distance along a track, go left over two stiles, join another track for a few yards and then drop down across another heathy area. Skirt to the left of a cottage at grid ref. TQ 474 280, and go ahead on a narrow path down through woodland to a stream crossing by Brown's Brook Cottage. Follow the access drive from the cottage, keeping a lookout for a path to the right which crosses another area of open forest for 0.5 miles (800m) or so, to reach the road opposite the entrance to Oldlands Hall.

A short distance along the road, the path breaks away to the left through the bracken. The village of Fairwarp is 0.25 miles (400m) ahead along the road from this point and has a pub as well as bed-and-breakfast accommodation.

WEALDEN IRON INDUSTRY

The Wealdway crosses a field and a stream before climbing through Furnace Wood. The brown colour of the water in the stream and the name of the wood are a reminder that this area was once at the centre of the Wealden iron industry. From Buxted, near by, came the first cannon to be produced in England, cast in 1543. Continue through this Forestry Commission area, where a slippery scramble up one steep slope has been much improved by the provision of a flight of rough steps.

Beyond the wood, skirt to the left of a cottage and to the right of Hendall Manor Farm, who provide accommodation in a converted barn. The Way now drops down across fields and climbs more steeply through the remains of Hendall Wood,

The Wealdway bears right across a meadow to Horselunges Manor. It is possible to obtain a reasonably close look at this magnificent 16th-century timber house, complete with its impressive moat and drawbridge.

Beyond the manor, skirt to the left of a row of garages. Another 0.75 miles (1.25km) brings you out to the A271 through the entrance to Horsebridge Mill.

From Hellingly (grid ref. TQ 581 112), it is possible to pick out a fairly direct footpath route back to Chiddingly, a distance of under 4 miles (6km) via Perryland Farm, Thunder's Hill and Muddles Green. You will need a good map as the paths are not all well defined.

HORSEBRIDGE TO EASTBOURNE

STAGE 7

HORSEBRIDGE to WILMINGTON

DISTANCE 7 miles (11.3km)
MAP OS Explorer 123
START AT GRID REFERENCE TQ 418 059
START POINT The entrance to Horsebridge Mill, on the A271 road to the north of Hailsham

From the imposing entrance to Horsebridge Mill, turn right along the A271 road. After about 100yds, turn left on to a rough track and, very shortly, go left again along an estate road. Look out for a narrow fenced footpath to the right, running along between the houses.

A field path now heads south through fields to pass Welbury Farm and then reaches the A22. Beyond the A22 dual carriageway, a rather devious headland path makes its way between cultivated fields. There are waymarks and stiles at regular intervals but it is easy to miss the way. Beyond a footbridge at grid ref. TQ 567 098, the route crosses a large field with no clear sight line to guide the walker.

After another 0.5 miles (800m), the Wealdway crosses the Cuckmere once more, using a solid brick bridge. After a second bridge, across the feeder stream for the moat surrounding Michelham Priory, a field path continues to reach the road beside the Village Stop and Cafe at Upper Dicker. To visit Michelham Priory, use a short footpath which leaves the Wealdway at grid ref. TQ 557 095. At the road, turn left.

After about 0.25 miles (400m) along the road, the next path starts almost opposite the Plough Inn. After a low summit, the Wealdway converges on the Cuckmere and joins a bridleway to cross the river at Sessingham Bridge (grid ref. TQ 544 082). After a few yards along this enclosed track, a stile on the right and a rising path across pasture leads on towards Arlington's church spire.

The tiny flint church at Arlington has Saxon origins but incorporates Roman fragments and later additions, none more recent than the 15th century. Near by, the Yew Tree pub provides a convenient refreshment stop, and there is a small car park. The bumps in the field beyond the church remind us that a much larger village once stood on this site.

The Wealdway keeps forging straight ahead across rough ground and on via an access drive to the road near Chilver Bridge. The path to the right leads over a footbridge to Arlington reservoir, where there is another car park and a pleasant perimeter path.

The road over Chilver Bridge (grid ref. TQ 537 069) provides access via another field path to Berwick Station, a useful staging point for

before climbing across a large field. This was once part of Great Wood but it was clear-felled a few years ago, except for the very top. At the other side of the wood, a wide downland panorama suddenly opens up ahead, now encouragingly nearer. The Wealdway arrives at East Hoathly through the churchyard, within a few yards of two pubs and a bus stop for buses back to Uckfield, or on to Horsebridge. (Check times in advance.) Between East Hoathly and Chiddingly, another 2 miles (3km) on, the route, for the most part, follows a designated bridleway and is therefore gated rather than stiled. It is clear and well marked, but may be muddy underfoot in places as this is an area of thick and sticky Wealden clay.

Chiddingly is a quiet and charming spot. On the way into the village, look out for the remains of Chiddingly Place, now incorporated into a farm building, to the right of the lane. Beyond the Six Bells pub, there is a small car park.

This is also another meeting point with the Vanguard Way (grid ref. TQ 544 142), providing a return route to Blackboys.

The fine 130ft (118m) stone spire of Chiddingly Church is a conspicuous landmark for miles around. The church contains an Elizabethan monument to Sir John Jefferay, who lived at Chiddingly Place.

From Chiddingly to the A267, the Wealdway is, once again, well waymarked. It heads generally eastwards across a gently undulating landscape, with frequent glimpses of the South Downs escarpment. From the point where the route crosses the road at Gun Hill, the Gun Inn is a few minutes' walk to the north along the lane.

Approaching the A267, the route descends through a lovely patch of woodland and climbs between high banks. After another dip, the path is a bit vague as it crosses an area of rough ground and the stile and steps giving access to the loop of old road at Lealands are well hidden.

A quiet lane leads to Hellingly, where the Wealdway passes diagonally through the churchyard, attractively lined by a row of tile-hung cottages. Follow the road over the Cuckmere River.

ABOVE *The dramatic and magnificent view out to sea from the famous white cliffs of Beachy Head*

walkers using public transport and also another linkpoint with the *Vanguard Way and a return route to Chiddingly.*

Beyond the road, the Wealdway continues beside the Cuckmere, with the first clear view ahead to the chalk figure of the Long Man of Wilmington, 2 miles (3km) away as the crow flies, on the steep slope of Windover Hill. A bridleway heads south, crossing the railway and then the A27, where you should follow the road, opposite, signposted to Milton Street. A well-trodden path on the left takes the Wealdway through to Wilmington village street.

For the Giant's Rest pub, or a bus into Eastbourne, turn left out to the A27. The village car park is at the southern end of the village, beyond the church and priory.

STAGE 8

WILMINGTON to EASTBOURNE

DISTANCE 10.5 miles (16.9km)

MAP OS Explorer 123

START AT GRID REFERENCE TQ 541 048

START POINT Wilmington crossroads on the A27 Lewes–Eastbourne road

Walk along the village street, lined by a variety of charming cottages. The church, much restored, has an attractive weather-boarded tower. Inside, hidden in a side chapel, it is worth seeking out the unusual Butterfly Window, dating from the 15th century. In the churchyard a massive, ancient yew, much propped up, still stands (just!) after an estimated life of almost 1,000 years. Beyond the ruins of Wilmington Priory, the path to the Long Man starts opposite the entrance to the car park.

The Benedictine Priory at Wilmington was founded in the 11th century as a possession of the abbey of Grestain in Normandy. It was seized by the Crown during the wars with France and came into the hands of the Dean and Chapter of Chichester. After a period as vicarage and farmhouse, it was given to the Sussex Archaeological Trust in 1926.

The Long Man of Wilmington, standing 226ft (69m) high, is the largest hill figure in the country but very little is known of his origins. It is possible that he is a representation of Balder, the Norse god of spring. In 1874, the outline of the figure was carefully lined in white bricks and he is now, like the priory, in the good care of the Sussex Archaeological Trust.

From the foot of the Long Man, the Wealdway follows a fine, terraced path along the side of the Downs escarpment,

high enough above the Weald to command a panoramic view, with the waters of Arlington reservoir clearly visible. After a mile (1.6km), you will reach Folkington, home of yet another tiny church, surrounded by trees, tucked under the Downs at the end of a quiet cul-de-sac.

EXHILARATING HIGH LEVELS

A clear track, once an old coach road, follows an undulating route, still hugging the downland foothills, for another 2 miles (3km) to Jevington. The Wealdway follows the lane into the village as far as the Eight Bells pub, but, if time permits, it is well worth extending the walk to visit interesting Jevington Church. Carry on along the lane and, very shortly, fork right on a narrow footpath, entering the churchyard through an interesting tapsell gate. The church, with its rare Saxon tower, luxuriates in another idyllic downland setting.

The Wealdway continues up a flight of steps opposite the Eight Bells and climbs steadily along a ridge to reach the summit of Combe Hill, at 630ft (192m), where the low banks indicate the site of a Neolithic camp, dating from about 2,500BC. The banks, laid out in concentric banks and ditches, indicate that this was a 'causewayed camp'. It is one of only four in the country, all of which are in Sussex. For the next 2 miles (3km), the Wealdway follows an exhilarating high-level route, with views across the Weald, back over Jevington to the woods of Friston Forest and, to the left across the built up areas of Polegate, Willingdon and Eastbourne. Beyond Combe Hill a clear track sweeps round to the right, past the car parking area at Butts Brow and up on to Willingdon Hill (659ft/200m). By the trig. point on the summit (grid ref. TQ 577 009), the Wealdway bears left and continues with the scrub-covered slopes dropping away left.

After another 0.75 miles (1.25km), a choice is necessary. At the start of a golf course, go ahead beside the golf course, using the South Downs Way. Cross the A259, near the club house. After another 0.25 miles (400m), where the South Downs Way bears right, go ahead, passing a trig point and a dewpond.

Shortly, take the fork left along the upper edge of some scrubland and cross a road beside a junction at grid ref. TV 590 975. Now climb across open sloping downland, with superb views across to Eastbourne and eastwards along the coastline towards Hastings. At a track junction (TV 593 568) turn left down the hill to join the road into Eastbourne and continue ahead for 1.5 miles (2.5km) to the pier.

PLACES TO VISIT

• MICHELHAM PRIORY AND GARDENS
www.sussexpast.co.uk
☎ 01323 844224
The Wealdway passes Michelham Priory, just beyond Horsebridge. This historic house is a former Augustinian priory, founded in 1229, which has since been a working farm and still features a working watermill. The mill dates back to at least the early 15th century and is now staffed by volunteers, who will give you a tour around the restored building. There are also exhibits and artefacts to be seen in the house itself, a moat, Iron Age centre, forge, café and beautiful gardens to be enjoyed. Among these are a physic garden, kitchen garden and cloister garden. On Saturday afternoons, the Michelham Bowmen practice with their longbows on the South Lawn in full medieval costume. Open Tue–Sun Mar–Oct.

• DRUSILLAS PARK
www.drusillas.co.uk
☎ 01323 874100
Just across the Cuckmere River from Wilmington is one of the top tourist attractions in the country. Drusillas is a fun park centred around its zoo of small and exotic animals. In addition to the lemurs, penguins, raccoons and other animals, there are various soft play and adventure areas for different ages. Thomas the Tank Engine is on hand to provide train rides from Tidmouth Hault station and there is an interactive maze to explore and hunt the treasure within. There are numerous other activities such as mini-golf, face painting, panning for gold and various educational opportunities along the way. Open daily all year.

• BEACHY HEAD
www.beachyhead.org.uk/ centreInfo ☎ 01323 737273
Just beyond the end of Wealdway is the Beachy Head white cliff, lighthouse and countryside centre; the latter being run by volunteers. Open daily Apr–Oct; Sat–Sun Nov–Mar.

The Ridgeway

COMPLETE ROUTE OVERTON HILL TO IVINGHOE BEACON **87 MILES (140KM)**

SECTION COVERED AS ABOVE

MAPS OS EXPLORER 157, 169, 170, 171, 181

For much of its route, The Ridgeway National Trail follows part of an ancient track, the Great Ridgeway, which once ran from Dorset to Norfolk and which has been dubbed 'the oldest road' in Britain. It is impossible to walk the track without feeling that the division between past and present has been worn thin by the tramp of countless feet over the thousands of years of its use. Perhaps the most remarkable thing about The Ridgeway is the mere fact of its survival as a green track. It winds its way through some of the most intensively farmed parts of England and yet is enormously wide. Even 100 years ago, so Richard Jefferies tells us, The Ridgeway was feeling the pressure of encroaching agriculture: 'It is not a farm track: you may walk for twenty miles along it over the hills; neither is it the King's highway... Plough and harrow press hard on the ancient track, and yet dare not encroach upon it. With varying width, from twenty to fifty yards, it runs like a green ribbon...' The route of the trail initially follows the northern edge of the North Wessex Downs and finishes on paths through the rolling and wooded Chiltern AONB. These two contrasting landscapes are divided by the River Thames, which cuts through the chalk hills at Goring, and the differences are further emphasized by the route following the banks of the river for some miles before climbing back into the hills.

ABOVE Deer in Ashridge Park RIGHT The Swan pub seen from the bridge over the River Thames towards Goring

ABOVE Waymarks on wooden posts guide walkers along the pleasant paths through Ashridge Park

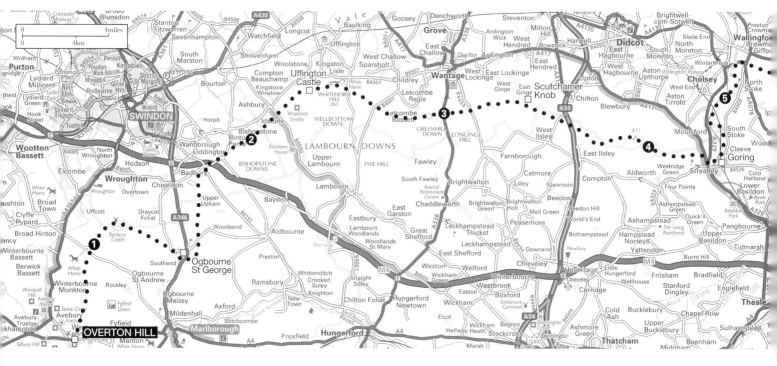

OVERTON HILL TO UFFINGTON

STAGE 1

OVERTON HILL to OGBOURNE ST GEORGE

DISTANCE 9.8 miles (15.8km)

MAPS OS Explorer 157, 169

START AT GRID REFERENCE SU 119 681

START POINT The north side of the A4 Beckhampton–Marlborough road, on Overton Hill

The start of The Ridgeway is distinctly low-key; an unpretentious track running north from the busy A4 on Overton Hill, marked with a signpost carrying the National Trail acorn symbol, the first of many to be seen along the route. In fact, for those wishing for a more romantic starting point, it is quite possible to start the walk within the great stone circle at Avebury and then join The Ridgeway some 2 miles (3km) further on by means of an equally ancient track known as Herepath or Green Street.

If, however, the official start point has been chosen, then before setting out for Ivinghoe Beacon cross the A4 to inspect the site of the Sanctuary, a double stone circle dating from 2,000BC and destroyed in 1724, but which provides a good viewpoint for some of the Avebury monuments.

From the car park, The Ridgeway begins a steady ascent to the crest of the Downs, to meet with Green Street as it climbs up from Avebury. A right turn here will lead you to Fyfield Down, a remarkable remnant of ancient downland which has been described as the 'best preserved accessible large tract of ancient landscape in Wessex'.

To cut short the walk at this point (grid ref. SU 125 708), descend Green Street to Avebury. From there follow the footpath south to Silbury Hill before returning to Overton Hill by way of West Kennet Long Barrow and the Sanctuary. This pleasant 6-mile (9.5km) circular walk is one of the greatest archaeological adventures in Britain.

KINGDOM OF WESSEX

The Ridgeway itself continues northwards to meet the first crossing of a metalled road above the Hackpen White Horse, which tradition maintains was cut in 1838 by the parish clerk and a local publican to celebrate Queen Victoria's coronation.

The Trail begins to swing eastwards at this point and before long the ramparts of Barbury Castle, a hill fort with a long and violent history, rear up ahead. Probably built around the first century BC but later abandoned, the castle appears to have been refortified to face the threat of the advancing Anglo-Saxons. A great battle is reputed to have taken place here in AD556, in which the Anglo-Saxons crushed the remaining Romano-British resistance in the area and won a period of relative stability. This allowed the foundations to be laid for the kingdom of Wessex.

Just to the west of the hill fort The Ridgeway parts company for a while with the route of the prehistoric trackway and, preferring higher ground and less tarmac, goes over Barbury Castle before swinging south towards Ogbourne St George. Ahead lies one of the most dramatic sections of the whole route, where the track undulates along the narrow back of Smeathe's Ridge, giving

ⓘ USEFUL INFORMATION

THE ROUTE
• www.nationaltrail.co.uk
☎ 01865 810224
This is the most comprehensive source of information about The Ridgeway. Everything is here, from detail on the route itself to activities for children along the way, a great accommodation map, and many helpful links. There are also official maps and guides to order by post.

TOURIST INFORMATION CENTRES
• www.visitwiltshire.co.uk
Avebury Chapel Centre, Green Street, Avebury SN8 1RE;
☎ 01672 539179
• www.visitbuckinghamshire.org
Tower Court, Horns Lane, Princes Risborough HP27 0AJ;
☎ 01844 274795
• www.tring.gov.uk
99 Akeman Street, Tring HP23 6AA;
☎ 01442 823347
• www.visitswindon.co.uk
37 Regent Street, Swindon SN1 1JL;
☎ 01793 530328
Although a little off the route, the Swindon office may be useful.
• www.visitsouthoxfordshire.co.uk
This website covers the area crossed by the central section of the trail.

PLANNING YOUR TRIP
• www.ridgewayfriends.org.uk
Although much of the information on this site is also on the official National Trail pages, the viewpoint on these pages is local and personal.
• www.ramblers.org.uk
☎ 020 7339 8500 and
www.ldwa.org.uk
The Ramblers Association and the Long Distance Walkers Association both provide general information about long-distance walking and specific help on The Ridgeway.

OTHER PATHS
To walk the ancient route of the Greater Ridgeway in full, complete the Wessex Ridgeway from Lyme Regis to begin this route at Overton, then continue along Icknield Way and Peddars Way (pages 134–143), to reach Hunstanton. Near Watlington, The Ridgeway is crossed by the Oxfordshire Way (pages 84–89).

ABOVE Signs point the way along the 'oldest road in Britain'

a feeling of unexpected airiness. The views to both sides are extensive; Liddington Castle, another Iron Age fort, to the north and the Downs stretching away into haziness to the south. Too soon a metalled road is reached, where a right turn leads down to Ogbourne St George.

STAGE 2
OGBOURNE ST GEORGE to UFFINGTON CASTLE
DISTANCE 13 miles (21km)
MAPS OS Explorer 157, 170
START AT GRID REFERENCE SU 203 743
START POINT Park in Ogbourne St George

Since Ogbourne St George is not actually on the course of The Ridgeway, it is necessary to make a short diversion to get back on to the official route. Turn right on to the old Roman road just under the bridge which carries the A346 bypass, and at the 'No through road' signpost turn left uphill on a track to the Old Lime Works. This soon becomes a green lane, which goes on to fork beside the entrance to a field. Take the left-hand branch that climbs to the northeast to join The Ridgeway at grid ref. SU 214 743.

It is also possible to walk southwards along the main street of Ogbourne St George to join the A345. After some 200yds (183m), alongside the main road, The Ridgeway is signposted off to the left along a sunken track which climbs up on to the ridge of the Round Hill Downs.

In common with many sections of the route, the next few miles of track have been subject to work to remove the worst of the ruts and improve surface drainage. The path is still climbing, crossing the minor road from Ogbourne to Aldbourne, but this is easy to forget as the views westwards open out, and it is possible to trace the course of the route from Barbury Castle.

If a shorter walk is required, turn left at the cross-tracks on Whitefield Hill (grid ref. SU 213 765) and leave The Ridgeway to follow a broad green lane towards a prominent mast. The track becomes metalled and spectacular views towards Barbury Castle can be enjoyed on the descent to the A345. At the road, turn right and left after 100yds. When the course of the old Midland and South-West Junction Railway is reached, climb the ramp on to the old track bed. Turn left to return to Ogbourne St George. The entire round trip is about 5 miles (8km) in length.

About a mile (1.6km) away down the right-hand track on Whitefield Hill lie the remains of the village of Snap, a settlement which is known to have been well established in 1377 but which steadily declined and was finally abandoned in the early part of the 20th century.

The Ridgeway itself does not deviate to visit Snap but continues ahead towards Liddington Castle. This Iron Age hill fort was beloved of Richard Jefferies, who was born at nearby Coate, and at 911ft (278m) it is the highest point on the trail. Liddington may be reached by a permissive path from The Ridgeway. From Liddington Castle it is only 2 miles (3km)

by minor roads across the Wanborough Plain and over the M4, to Fox Hill. There is room for parking at the bottom of Fox Hill, where The Ridgeway shrugs off its coat of tarmacadam and strikes off with single-mindedness north-eastwards. Below this section of the ridge is the pretty village of Bishopstone, with its thatched cottages gathered around a large pond. The scarp between The Ridgeway and the village carries a fine series of strip lynchets — contouring terraces formed over a long period of time by regular ploughing around the steep downland slopes. Just beyond Bishopstone a track runs off south towards the National Trust property of Ashdown House standing in the grounds of Ashdown Park.

This section of the route lies slightly behind the northern edge of the Downs which, together with the almost continuous hedges, give an enclosed feeling to the walking. Thus, despite signposts to the ancient monument, it is almost possible to walk past Wayland's Smithy without noticing the presence of the barrow in a hanger of beeches some 50yds (45m) off the track. The first long barrow, constructed about 3,700BC, was rebuilt some centuries later to make a larger, sarsen-faced chambered tomb. In folklore the cave-like tomb was to become the home of Wayland, the crippled smith-god of the Anglo-Saxons and legend says that if you leave your horse tethered here overnight with suitable payment, it will be reshod on your return the following day.

Beyond the Smithy lies one of the most familiar parts of The Ridgeway, as it ascends on a track towards the ramparts of Uffington Castle. Some 600yds (545m) before reaching the castle, a track leads off left towards the car park on Woolstone Hill, but before finishing this section of the route, carry on up to the fort for spectacular views out over the Vale of White Horse.

UFFINGTON TO GORING

STAGE 3
UFFINGTON to SCUTCHAMER KNOB
DISTANCE 11.4 miles (18.3km)
MAP OS Explorer 170
START AT GRID REFERENCE SU 293 866
START POINT Uffington Castle car park, signposted from the B4507, 7 miles (11.25km) west of Wantage

Before setting out on this section of The Ridgeway, take the opportunity to explore Uffington Castle and the famous White Horse (visible from the road below The Ridgeway but not on The Ridgeway itself). Uffington was never a castle in the medieval sense of the word, but is a hill fort of eight acres encircled by a single bank and ditch. The figure has been shown to date back some 3,000 years, to the Bronze Age, by means of optically stimulated luminescence dating carried out following archaeological investigations in 1994. The Castle and White Horse Hill are in the ownership of the National Trust and offer extensive views northwards over the romantically named Vale of White Horse, studded with small villages. Among these is Great Coxwell, with its medieval barn.

Just outside the hill fort lie two oval mounds, one of which proved to be a Roman barrow containing 46 burials. Some of the bodies had been placed in position with coins in their mouths; the fee charged by Charon the ferryman for their passage across the River Styx. The Ridgeway itself shuns the hill fort, as if to make it clear that it is the greater antiquity, and continues its journey eastwards.

TOP **The entrance chamber to Waylands Smithy**
ABOVE **Leafy glades around Waylands Smithy**
BELOW **Defensive ditch section at the top of Uffington Castle**

ABOVE *View northwards over countryside from Uffington White Horse* ABOVE RIGHT *Goring Lock on the River Thames*

SCUTCHAMER KNOB

From the B4001 crossing, The Ridgeway continues eastwards, with the natural amphitheatre of the Devil's Punchbowl immediately below the edge of the scarp. The village at its base is Letcombe Bassett, the 'Cresscombe' of Thomas Hardy's bleak novel *Jude the Obscure*. Hardy wrote the book while staying in the area and a number of the places passed on this section of The Ridgeway appear there with no greater disguise than a change of name. In fact, a short way ahead, the junction with the A338 marks the site of Jude's ill-fated vision of the spires of Oxford. A left turn along the A338 leads to the Court Hill Centre and Hostel on Court Hill. Beyond here, the section of trail is well-used by farm traffic and has been surfaced accordingly,   but the familiar grassy and slightly rutted surface of the track is not long in returning. This leads on towards the next crossing of a metalled road, on Lattin Down. Ahead rises the monument to Robert Loyd-Lindsay, Baron Wantage, who was a holder of the Victoria Cross and died in 1901. The inscription reads 'I will lift up mine eyes to the hills from whence cometh my help'.

The Ridgeway descends from the monument and continues ahead to a group of trees where you will find Scutchamer Knob, a mutilated round barrow. It would probably pass unnoticed were it not for its curious name, which has aroused considerable speculation as to its origin. Old maps refer to it as 'Scutchamfly Barrow' or 'Scotchman's Hob'. One argument is that the name derives from the 'scutcher', who beat out the fibres from flax which had previously been softened by soaking. A second school of thought suggests that the name is a corruption of the Saxon 'Cwicchelmshlaew'; the burial place of a Saxon King Cwicchelm, who died in AD593. At the end of the trees, just beyond Scutchamer Knob, is the head of the metalled road which climbs up from the A417 at East Hendred and marks the end of this section of the walk.

STAGE 4

SCUTCHAMER KNOB to GORING

DISTANCE 10.3 miles (16.6km)
MAPS OS Explorer 170, 171
START AT GRID REFERENCE SU 458 850
START POINT Car park to the east of Scutchamer Knob

The Ridgeway sets off eastwards alongside racehorse training gallops. Just to the north of this section of the trail, at the base of the scarp, runs Grim's Ditch, one of three linear earthworks with this name which are passed during the course of the trail. This particular Grim's Ditch stretches off and on for 8 miles (13km) but does not appear ever to have been continuous. Those sections where the ground was either too steep or wooded were left. Its date is uncertain but it has been suggested that it may represent the boundary between two Iron Age estates.

The views from this length of the track are dominated by the presence, to the north, of the great cooling towers of Didcot Power Station. To the east of the power station lies the town of Didcot, with its station and railway centre. Before long, the route meets a minor road on Bury Down, where there is car parking, and then presses on towards the roar of traffic on the A34. Fortunately, the walker is spared having to attempt to cross this road, as The Ridgeway dodges underneath by means of a tunnel, and continues to climb up on to Several Down.

The Ridgeway itself descends from Several Down and then bends sharply to the left, where a concrete track continues straight on towards Compton and the field station of the Agricultural Research Council's Institute for Animal Health. The descent continues quite steeply on a wide track, until the course of the dismantled railway. The next summit on the rollercoaster is Roden Down. To the left is the steep spur of Lowbury Hill, which, according to the Ordnance Survey map, is the site of a Roman temple. In fact, excavations at the site failed to establish the exact purpose of the rectangular, banked enclosure and it is as likely to have been a farm as a temple. One grisly find from beneath the foundations of one of the walls was the skeleton of a middle-aged woman, in a position that suggests a dedicatory burial.

LONG DESCENT

The great traverse of the Downs is coming to an end and there is a sense of finality as The Ridgeway begins the long descent beside Streatley Warren towards the Goring Gap, where the River Thames cuts through the chalk hills. The Gap itself is, in geological terms, a relatively recent feature and prior to its formation the Thames used to run northwards to join the sea near the Wash.

Just to the south of this part of the route lies the village of Aldworth, whose church is home to the Aldworth giants; nine huge effigies (dated 1300–1350) which represent members of the de la Beche family. Sir William de la Beche was tutor to

SOUTH & SOUTH EAST ENGLAND • THE RIDGEWAY

ⓘ PLACES TO VISIT

• AVEBURY
www.nationaltrust.org.uk
☎ 01672 539250
The walk begins very close to the village and prehistoric site of Avebury; co-listed with Stonehenge as a UNESCO World Heritage Site. There is much to be seen here, including barrow mounds and, of course, the famous stone circles. The outer circle, which encompasses the village, was originally made up of 98 sarsen stones, weighing up to 40 tonnes and thought to be over 2,000 years old. There are now less than 30, but these are nonetheless an impressive sight. The National Trust runs the Alexander Keiller Museum, which houses artefacts unearthed by the archeologist in the 1930s, during the process of re-erecting some of the stones. The collection is mostly neolithic and includes a full human skeleton of a child, found in a ditch at Windmill Hill. There are also interactive displays and activities for children (open daily all year). Close to the museum is the fine church of St James, which dates back to Saxon times and has some interesting features. If you work up a thirst, the Red Lion Inn in the village is said to be haunted.

• ASHDOWN HOUSE
www.nationaltrust.org.uk
☎ 01494 755569
Located on the B4000, 2 miles (3km) from the route, this 17th-century house is set in extensive woodland. It is said to have been built as a refuge from the plague by the 1st Earl of Craven. It is grand and almost cube-shaped, and often compared to a dolls' house. There are no facilities here and access to the large central staircase is by guided tour only, but the climb up to the roof is rewarded with an impressive view. The lease of the house was bought by Pete Townshend of the band The Who in 2010. Open Wed & Sat afternoons Apr–Oct.

the Black Prince. At Warren Farm, the track becomes metalled. Before long the A417 is joined and followed into Streatley, where a left turn at traffic lights just before the youth hostel leads across the Thames into Berkshire and Goring.

GORING TO CHINNOR

STAGE 5
GORING to NUFFIELD
DISTANCE 9.9 miles (15.9km)
MAPS OS Explorer 170, 171
START AT GRID REFERENCE SU 600 805
START POINT The car park in Goring

After the waterless expanse of the Downs, it is something of a surprise to follow the course of the River Thames. Note the distinctive swan's head and horseshoe waymarkers for the Swan's Way, a long-distance bridleway route from Goring to Salcey Forest, which shares the route of The Ridgeway on a number of occasions.

The trail runs close to the railway line along this section and it is difficult not to contrast the various merits of different types of travel as the Intercity trains scream past and leave the walker to enjoy the leisurely route towards South Stoke.

At South Stoke, the path draws away from the river to run through the village, at the north end turning left to return to the riverside path. The route then carries on through fields, passing under the railway, to North Stoke, where a visit to the early 13th-century church is well worth while. The ironwork on the door dates from the building of the church and inside are a number

of 14th-century wall paintings. There is a curious sundial in the south wall. The Ridgeway leaves the village past the rushing race of the old mill and along a pleasant tree-lined track, giving way to a golf course on the approach to Mongewell Park.

Just beyond the buildings of Carmel College, the path turns abruptly on to the line of another Grim's Ditch. If you were to carry straight on at this junction, a path would lead in less than a mile (1.6km) to the pleasant town of Wallingford. The walk along Grim's Ditch (also known as Devil's Dyke) gets into its swing once the A4074 has been crossed. For the most part the path follows the top of the bank which runs to the north of the dyke, a position one would have expected to be exposed. In this case, however, the whole line of the ditch is well wooded, so that the walk has an enclosed feel to it. There are occasional glimpses out at the surrounding countryside and, in the distance, the chalk-cut shape of the Watlington White Mark.

Further on, the ditch disappears into farmland and The Ridgeway turns north once more, across a carpet of beech nuts, to meet with the road close to the 14th-century Nuffield Church, with its squat, square tower. Of interest to Ridgewayfarers will be the water tap on the outside of the tower. In the churchyard is the unpretentious grave of the industrialist and philanthropist William Richard Morris, Viscount Nuffield, who founded Morris Motors in 1919.

The Trail goes on to cross the golf course on Nuffield Common, with the route clearly marked by a series of white posts, and emerges on to the A423.

STAGE 6
NUFFIELD to CHINNOR
DISTANCE 11 miles (17.7km)

PLACES TO VISIT

• **COURT HILL CENTRE**
www.courthill.org.uk
☎ 01235 760253
Set alongside The Ridgeway,
directly south of Wantage, is this
complex of five renovated barns
arranged around a courtyard.
Mostly given over to bunkhouse
and dormitory accommodation,
there is also a campsite and
picnic area. The Barn tea rooms
provide a warm welcome, light
lunches and refreshments. The
centre is both the start and finish
point for two cycle trails, whose
routes can be downloaded free
of charge from the National Trails
website (www.nationaltrail.co.uk).
Open daily all year.

• **BASILDON PARK**
www.nationaltrust.org.uk
☎ 0118 984 3040
Just over 2 miles (3km) south of
the delightful village of Streatley,
on the A329, is this historic
Palladian mansion. Between
several periods of abandonment
during the early 20th century, it
was requisitioned as a military
hospital, a barracks and a
prisoner of war camp. Its return to
grace came later in the century,
however, when Lord and Lady
Iliffe restored it over a period of
25 years. Their success was such
that it was used as a film set in
2005 during the making of *Pride
and Prejudice*. The house is now
full of an elegant collection of
fine paintings and furnishings,
salvaged from across the country.
Ground floor shop, tea room
and grounds open Wed–Sun
Feb–Dec; main house show
rooms open Wed–Sun afternoons
Mar–Oct.

• **ASTON ROWANT NATURE
RESERVE**
www.naturalengland.org.uk
There are a number of
waymarked trails through this
protected area of chalk grassland,
just to the right of The Ridgeway
after the tunnel under the M40
motorway. It is one of the best
sites in the country for seeing
Red Kites, and is particularly filled
with wildflowers and butterflies in
the summer months. Download a
leaflet from the website.

MAPS OS Explorer 171, 181

START AT GRID REFERENCE SU 675 877

START POINT Beside the A423, at the top of Gangsdown Hill

The Ridgeway leaves the main road through a gate and descends through woodland. This section of the walk is marked by the passing of two large houses, Ewelme Park and Swyncombe House. Ewelme Park is an interesting example of a 20th-century Arts and Crafts house occupying high ground, its walls rendered throughout. A couple of miles off the route to the west lies the village of Ewelme itself, which contains some gems of 15th-century architecture. The path goes on to descend into the dry valley of Colliers Bottom.

A bridleway at grid ref. SU 679 899 gives the opportunity to cut this section short. A left turn here takes you on to join the Swan's Way. From here, another bridleway may be followed close to Potter's Farm to join the green road which runs parallel to, and appears to be an older course of, the A423. A left turn along this track brings you up to join the main road near the start point. It is a round walk of 5 miles (8km).

WATLINGTON WHITE MARK

The Ridgeway itself turns right at the junction with the bridleway and follows this upwards through the Swyncombe estate to St Botolph's Church, a pleasant little building dating back to the 11th century. Above the church, the trail crosses a minor road and begins the descent towards the route of the Icknield Way, an ancient track running across southern England from the Chilterns to Norfolk. Britwell House is visible in the distance.

You cannot help but feel a thrill to be stepping back on to the line of the ancient highway. At this point it is a flint-surfaced track, whose hedges have grown up to form a tunnel. In places the track is sunken below the surface of the adjacent fields, to produce a holloway. In this enclosed environment the miles speed by, and soon after the crossing of the B480 beside Icknield House, a minor road is met where a left turn would lead down to the small town of Watlington, with its fine central town hall, built by Thomas Stonor in 1664. Cut into the hillside immediately above this junction is the 270ft-high (82m) obelisk of the Watlington White Mark, carved by Edward Home in 1674 and said, when viewed from the vale, to look like a spire added on to the top of the tower of Watlington Church. There is a camp site at White Mark Farm, just off the road into Watlington.

The Ridgeway presses on between its hedges and over the next 3 miles (5km) it passes below some of the finest chalk downland in the Chilterns. These north-facing slopes form part of the Aston Rowant Nature Reserve, which can be visited from The Ridgeway by turning right just beyond the tunnel underneath the M40.

While there is no doubt that the motorway is an intrusion into this beautiful piece of countryside, as far as The Ridgeway is concerned, its impact is minimized by crossing at right angles and the sound of the traffic soon recedes into the background. Indeed, it has been said that the Icknield Way itself was the motorway of prehistoric England, but it is interesting to contrast the modern route, with its cuttings and embankments gouging its way between the vast conurbations that it serves, and the natural lines of the ancient route; always so conscious of the terrain it is crossing, exploiting every easy slope and running with the grain of the landscape.

Route-finding along this part of the path could not be easier. The track varies in width, sometimes approaching in appearance the great grass swathe which ran over the Downs west of Goring,

TOP Looking northwest up
to Ivinghoe Beacon
ABOVE Berries growing
along the pathway

but always it is bounded by hedges and bears steadfastly northeast. It is something of a shock to realize after a few miles that the fields on the other side of the hedges have been replaced by water-filled abandoned workings and that you are following a causeway through a former cement works. Presently the path descends towards the Crowell Hill–Chinnor road, where there is some parking on the edges of the track. Chinnor lies about a mile (1.6km) away to the left, down the road. However, a bridleway some 300yds (275m) further on gives safer access to Chinnor and its facilities.

CHINNOR TO IVINGHOE

STAGE 7

CHINNOR to WENDOVER

DISTANCE 12.1 miles (19.5km)
MAPS OS Explorer 171, 181
START AT GRID REFERENCE SP 760 002
START POINT About 0.5 miles (800m) from the centre of Chinnor

Leaving the road, The Ridgeway begins to ascend gradually beneath the wooded slopes of Wain Hill, at the same time

taking the opportunity to show its cunning by contouring around the heads of the steep-sided combes which cut into the northern slopes.

For the last 10 miles (16km) the path has followed the course of the Upper Icknield Way, but at the edge of Thickthorne Wood there is a parting of the ways as the ancient route plunges straight across the valley towards Princes Risborough, leaving The Ridgeway to seek out a more interesting line across fields and to climb the grassy slopes of Lodge Hill. The view from the summit of the hill is far-reaching; on a clear day it is possible to make out the white triangle of Whiteleaf Cross in the distance. Nearer at hand is Lacey Green with its 17th-century windmill, which is believed to be the oldest surviving smock mill in Britain. The ridge from Lacey Green continues southwards towards Hughenden Manor and High Wycombe.

If you wish to leave The Ridgeway at this point and return to Chinnor, turn right through a gap in the prominent hedge on the descent of Lodge Hill (grid ref. SP 797 001). A bridleway runs southwest and climbs to Rout's Green, where a right turn allows the Bledlow Ridge road to be followed back to Chinnor. This gives a round walk of 6 miles (9.5km).

WHITELEAF CROSS

The Ridgeway itself swings northwards to cross the High Wycombe–Princes Risborough railway line and join the Upper Icknield Way once more. The route then follows the A4010 northwards for 0.5 miles (800m) to reach a track on the right. Despite its size, Princes Risborough is passed by almost unnoticed on this track, before The Ridgeway bears right, away from the Icknield Way, to begin the ascent to Whiteleaf Cross through Brush Hill Nature Reserve. This is one of the steepest climbs on the route but the effort of the climb is well rewarded by the wonderful view from the grassy clearing above the cross. Looking out westwards, it is possible to trace your route across the valley all the way from Chinnor, while in the distance the white towers of Didcot Power Station are clearly visible, with the line of the North Wessex Downs behind.

Directly below where you stand are the deeply carved arms of Whiteleaf Cross itself. First recorded in 1742, the cross may have been the work of monks in the 15th or 16th centuries. It is the oldest of the Chiltern hill figures but its purpose is uncertain. One can speculate whether it was scoured as a landmark for travellers or perhaps to obscure a more obviously pagan figure which may previously have occupied the site.

Leaving the cross, the path now descends steeply to The Plough public house at Lower Cadsden (which offers accommodation), before entering the nature reserve of Grangelands and Pulpit Hill, which contains fine areas of chalk grassland. The Ridgeway leaves the reserve by climbing up steps over Chequers Knap and enters the grounds of Chequers, where it goes on to cross the drive of the house. Chequers dates from the 16th century and was given to the nation in 1917 by Lord Lee of Fareham, as a country home for the Prime Minister.

There are good views of Chequers from the path, and in the background rises Coombe Hill, with its golden-topped monument, which The Ridgeway goes on to climb, through an area of attractive beech woodland. The open grassland around the monument is popular with local residents and The Ridgeway then follows a footpath down Bacombe Hill to the attractive little town of Wendover.

STAGE 8

WENDOVER to IVINGHOE BEACON

DISTANCE 10.6 miles (17km)
MAP OS Explorer 181
START AT GRID REFERENCE SP 868 078
START POINT Car park adjacent to the library in Wendover

Turn right out of the car park in Wendover, then turn right again by the clock-tower to follow Heron Path alongside the stream and out of the town, passing the 14th-century flint Church of St Mary the Virgin. The church contains a fine brass of 1537 to William Bradschawe, his wife and 32 children and grandchildren. The Ridgeway then climbs by means of Hogtrough Lane into Barn Wood and runs more or less level along the side of Cock's Hill.

After a while, a road is reached at grid ref. SP 989 074. A left turn will lead back to Wendover, cutting the section short. A second, slightly longer way back is possible by following the road for about 0.5 miles (800m). Take a footpath north into Wendover woods, crossing over the spur of Boddington Hill, with its Iron Age fort, and so back to Wendover. The longer of these two routes gives a 4.5-mile (7.25km) round trip.

MEMORIES OF THE IRON AGE

The Ridgeway plunges back into the woods and makes progress beside a typical Chiltern holloway, sunken 6ft (2m) below the level of the surrounding ground and muddy in the driest of weather. There is a brief interlude over fields towards a radio mast and then more woodland before a minor road is followed to Hastoe Cross. Turn left here and follow the signs through Tring Park, a wooded area, soon passing to the north of Wigginton. After crossing two roads, which lead into Wigginton, drop down to the A41.

From the outskirts of Wigginton you can see Ivinghoe Beacon clearly and, although it still seems a long way off, there is a feeling as you descend the path towards the valley – where the road, canal and railway rub shoulders as they squeeze through the gap to Berkhamsted – that the end of the walk is fast approaching. The busy A41 is crossed by a footbridge and then the A4251 is crossed, which follows the line of the Roman Akeman Street.

With Akeman Street behind you, it is not far to the Grand Union Canal and shortly after Tring Station. The Ridgeway intends to finish in style and begins the climb away from the narrow Bulbourne valley, back into the hills.

After 0.5 miles (800m) the path enters a nature reserve on Aldbury Nowers. The reserve protects an important area of chalk downland, rich in wild flowers and butterflies. It then goes on to meet an earthwork with the by-now-familiar name of Grim's Ditch, although it is unlikely that this ditch is linked in any way other than by name to the ones followed earlier in Oxfordshire and Berkshire. The ditch lies to the south of the rampart, often on the uphill side, which suggests that it marks a boundary rather than having a directly defensive purpose. The structure is generally accepted to be of Iron Age date.

The path emerges from woodland on Pitstone Hill and enjoys magnificent views to the west and north for almost all the remainder of the walk. Ivinghoe is clearly visible, with Pitstone windmill standing in isolation in a nearby field, while to the east the Whipsnade White Lion, cut into the hillside in 1933 as an advertisement for the nearby zoo, stands out well on a clear day. It is not long before you reach Ivinghoe Beacon. Arrival at the cairn indicates the end of your journey.

While contemplating the 87 miles (140km) of the ancient Ridgeway path, spare a thought for those who raised the barrows visible on the hilltop and for their Iron Age descendants, who fortified the hill in 700BC. Much of the route just followed would have been familiar to them, and it is the remains of their temples, graves and fortresses that help to make the walk so memorable for modern-day long-distance walkers.

PLACES TO VISIT

• **CHINNOR AND PRINCES RISBOROUGH RAILWAY**
www.chinnorrailway.co.uk
☎ 01844 353535
Less than 0.5 miles (800m) west of The Ridgeway, at Chinnor, lies the terminus of this former section of the Great Western Railway branch line. Steam and diesel engines haul trains to Thame Junction (a round trip of 7 miles (11km), principally at weekends). Some even have a cream tea served on board. In any event, the replica of the original station at Chinnor houses a station buffet and gift shop. See website for timetable.

• **ASHRIDGE ESTATE**
www.nationaltrust.org.uk
☎ 01442 851227/01494 755557
Just beyond Tring station it is easy to detour to the Bridgewater Monument in the Ashridge Estate. Search for the Ashridge Drovers Walk, www.chilternsaonb.org, to download a leaflet which shows the linking path. You can then continue through the estate and rejoin The Ridgeway across Clipper Down. Within the estate there are lovely bluebell woods and many more paths to explore. Visitor centre and café open daily all year; monument open Sat–Sun Apr–Oct.

• **PITSTONE WINDMILL**
www.nationatrust.org.uk
☎ 01442 851227
This is a rare example of a post mill, located close to the end of the route. However, it is only open to the public on Sunday afternoons Jun–Aug and has no facilities.

ZSL WHIPSNADE ZOO
www.zsl.org
☎ 01582 872171
If you have time to spare after you have completed The Ridgeway, this sizeable zoo is approximately 4 miles (6.5km) away. There are all manner of animals here, from elephants and zebra to giraffes and tigers. The children will love to watch feeding time for the penguins or sealions, visit the children's farm or ride on the Jumbo Express steam train. If the sun is out, watching the lemurs sunbathe is fun, and there is an adventure playground that makes a good picnic spot. Open daily all year.

LEFT Pitstone Windmill

The weir near Goring, on the River Thames

Oxfordshire Way

COMPLETE ROUTE BOURTON-ON-THE-WATER TO HENLEY-ON-THAMES **65 MILES (104KM)**

SECTION COVERED AS ABOVE

MAPS OS EXPLORER OL 45, 171, 180, 191

The Oxfordshire Way runs across the heart of England, along ancient rights of way, all of which existed long before they were thus joined together, passing through historic settlements and crossing the grain of the country. The old trucks and field paths have been used for centuries. Some are prehistoric, some are Roman, many were first trodden in Saxon times. They link villages and hamlets mentioned in the Domesday Book of 1086. The inns of these places usually provide food and accommodation, bed-and-breakfast can be found on or close to the route, and there are some campsites. Village shops survive in surprising numbers.

ABOVE The River Windrush at Bourton-on-the-Water TOP Inside Rycote Chapel BOTTOM An impressive view of Blenheim Palace across the lake

BOURTON-ON-THE-WATER TO WOOTTON DOOR

STAGE 1

BOURTON-ON-THE-WATER to ASCOTT-UNDER-WYCHWOOD

DISTANCE 11.8 miles (19km)

MAPS OS Explorer OL 45, 180

START AT GRID REFERENCE SP 168 205

START POINT Bourton-on-the-Water

The Oxfordshire Way begins in the Gloucestershire Cotswolds at Bourton-on-the-Water, a bustling centre on the grassy banks of the River Windrush. This town was founded on the wealth obtained from Cotswold wool, and in days gone by the land around echoed with the bleating of sheep. The walk passes along Moor Lane, where it is well signed through a gate to the rough grass and massive earthworks of pre-Roman Salmonsbury Camp. Immediately, the razzmatazz of Bourton is left behind and the real countryside takes over, the 1.5 miles (2.5km) to Wyck Rissington passing through water meadows and over little streams, Eye and Dickler, which flow to the Windrush.

Wyck Rissington snuggles into the Dickler Valley. The houses, mellow beneath their stone roofs, are idly clumped about a wide green of rough grasses. There is no hostelry or shop, but there is a village pond and a well, and beyond them the squat and solid Norman tower of the church. Gustav Holst had his first professional appointment here. He was organist in 1892–3, aged 17.

Passing through the churchyard, begin the ascent of Wyck Beacon. Throwing a glance back on the way up, there

are magnificent views over the Windrush valley and across the Cotswold upland. You pass over 812ft (247m) Wyck Beacon, an exposed upland for all the veneer of verdure, where the trees lean away from the winds, bitten back by their keenness. Beyond the A424 you descend along the private road to Gawcombe, past huge parkland trees and ornamental lakes. Gawcombe is no more than a cluster of stone buildings about the main house, and once beyond them the way is open and exposed.

Some 0.75 miles (1.25km) further on, the Oxfordshire Way crosses a bridle-bridge to saunter along the green banks of Westcote Brook, before striking across fields into Bledington. Bledington Church has a porch that is 700 years old, and there is a tiny chantry chapel separated from the chancel by an arch. The mottled stone houses and the King's Head Inn, which provides accommodation as well as meals, are grouped about a peaceful green.

You can leave the Oxfordshire Way here (grid ref. SP 249 223) and return to Bourton by turning left along the B4450 for about 0.25 miles (400m) and then left along a footpath via Pebbly Hill Farm to Icomb. Follow the road round and then turn right to Hill Farm and the A424. Cross the road and follow the bridleway over the hill to Wyck Rissington and the Oxfordshire Way back to Bourton. Alternatively, turn right along the B4450 for a mile (1.6km), to Kingham Station.

WHITSUNTIDE REVELS

The Oxfordshire Way enters the county after which it is named after leaving Bledington at the road bridge over Westcote Brook, and then crawls shyly along the Evenlode valley to Bruern Abbey. Of this Cistercian religious house, founded around 1137, nothing remains. Here, on its site, is a yellowing grey stone mansion built for the Cope family in about 1720.

The River Evenlode is rarely visible, but its presence can be felt as you pass into Bruern Wood, and then out into the fields again to Shipton-under-Wychwood. Shipton formerly lay on the edge of the Wychwood Forest, and Shipton Down, to the south of the village, was the scene of the Whitsuntide Revels, when local townsfolk had the right to hunt the king's deer. Today Shipton is a peaceful village of honey-coloured stone, with a shop and a choice of three hostelries. The Shaven Crown, a 15th-century building, is traditionally claimed as a guesthouse of Bruern Abbey.

The centre of Shipton is not actually on the Oxfordshire Way, therefore you need to turn right at the road in order to reach it. The Oxfordshire Way turns left here to cross the River

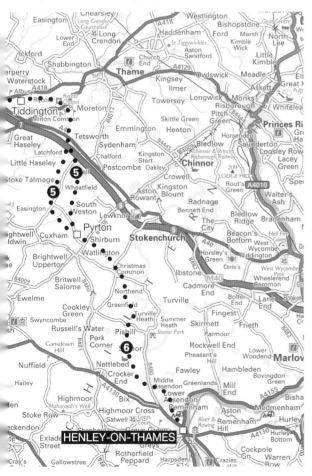

ⓘ USEFUL INFORMATION

THE ROUTE
• www.oxfordshire.gov.uk
☎ 01865 810226
The OW is promoted by the County Council, although a search on their website does not give much detail. There is, however, an official guide available for purchase by post and an accommodation and refreshment listing that can be downloaded.

TOURIST INFORMATION CENTRES
• www.cotswolds.com
Victoria Street, Bourton-on-the-Water GL54 2BU;
☎ 01451 820211
• www.oxfordshirecotswolds.org
The Oxfordshire Museum, Park Street, Woodstock OX20 1SN;
☎ 01993 813276
• www.visitsouthoxfordshire.co.uk
Henley Town Hall, Henley-on-Thames RG9 2AQ;
☎ 01491 578034
• www.visitoxfordandoxfordshire.com
15–16 Broad Street, Oxford OX1 3AS;
☎ 01865 252200
Although a little off the route, this Oxford office may be useful.

PLANNING YOUR TRIP
• www.ldwa.org.uk
The Long Distance Walkers Association web pages include the OW, and an interactive map of the route and other linking paths.
• www.ramblers.org.uk
☎ 020 7339 8500
The Ramblers Association provide general information about long-distance walking and specific help on the OW, such as public transport and nearby B&B accommodation.

OTHER PATHS
The Oxfordshire Way crosses the Ridgeway National Trail (pages 74–81) near Watlington. It joins another national trail, the Thames Path, at Henley. From there it is possible to continue either to the Thames Barrier in London or to the source of the river in Gloucestershire, near Kemble. There are details for both the Thames Path and the Ridgeway at www.nationaltrail.co.uk

View across the Cotswolds towards Bourton-on-the-Water from Wyck Beacon

TOP Blenheim Palace seen
from across the lake
ABOVE A closer view of
Blenheim Palace's elegant
golden facade

FAIR ROSAMUND

From Charlbury on to Stonesfield, famed for its 'slates', slabs of limestone split along the bedding planes to make a roofing material so splendid and so heavy that roofs had to be specially constructed to take the weight. The Romans quarried 'slates' here, and 'slates' continued to be cut until 1909. Interestingly, the 'slate beds' are full of fossils, from oyster shells to dinosaurs.

Take the route going down to the ford on the Evenlode and then turn left and up across Stonesfield Common. This passes the deserted 'slate' quarries, now a series of hollows and low green mounds, and also provides the opportunity of visiting the Roman villa at North Leigh, just off the Oxfordshire Way.

At Stonesfield Common you join Akeman Street, the Roman road from Bath to Bicester, where it rises over the last long spur of the Cotswolds. Just beyond the Combe–Stonesfield road it passes the site of a Roman villa, the first to be discovered and recorded in this country. Little now remains to show that it ever existed, but it is worth a visit.

Akeman Street enters Blenheim Park and crosses the Iron Age earthwork, Grim's Ditch. Here, on the edge of Woodstock, Henry I enclosed a deer park and built himself a hunting lodge. Henry II enlarged it, building a palace, and legend has it that he came here not just to hunt the deer but to visit his 'fair Rosamund'. He is said to have hidden her in a kind of pleasure garden in the midst of a maze, where no-one save himself could reach her. Alas, the secret was discovered and Rosamund was poisoned by jealous Queen Eleanor.

The Palace of Woodstock was severely damaged during the Civil War, and the manor was granted to the Duke of Marlborough during the reign of Queen Anne. He built Blenheim Palace on the site. From the Oxfordshire Way there is a splendid vista down the north walk to Blenheim Palace, and then all the majesty is left behind as the path passes out through Wootton Door, an actual door in the wall of the park, and leaves you standing on the verge of the busy A44. On the far side of this road, the Oxfordshire Way continues along Akeman Street, now a modern lane but very sure of its Roman origins.

Breaking the journey here (grid ref. SP 435 185), you can turn left along the A44 for 0.75 miles (1.25km) to catch a bus to Oxford or Stratford. A right turn leads to Woodstock, while a left turn down the minor road opposite takes you to Wootton on the steep banks of the River Glyme, where there is a shop and the former King's Head pub, which is now a bed-and-breakfast.

WOOTTON DOOR TO TIDDINGTON

STAGE 3

WOOTTON DOOR to ISLIP
DISTANCE 10.7 miles (17.2km)
MAP OS Explorer 180
START AT GRID REFERENCE SP 435 185
START POINT Just off A44 opposite Wootton Door

From the A44 the Oxfordshire Way continues along Akeman Street, initially along a lane. It crosses the River Glyme, whose dammed waters make the majestic lakes of Blenheim before flowing to the Thames. Over the T-junction, Akeman Street follows a raised cart track which rises up to give superb views. Glancing back, look across the Glyme valley to Blenheim, and across the clay vale to Didcot Power Station. Ahead, the panorama encompasses all the ground between this last spur of Cotswold, the Oxford Heights, where the television

---

Evenlode and the railway line near Shipton Station, with its huge old warehouse, built in the prosperous days of the Cotswold wool trade.

It then turns right to Ascott-under-Wychwood, a mellow stone village with a community-run village shop, a farm shop and one pub, the Swan, which serves food.

Ascott Station (grid ref. SP 301 188) has morning and evening commuter services, but you can return to Bledington on foot by crossing the railway and river and following the bridleway on the left to the T-junction on the hilltop. Go straight along the road to Lyneham. Turn left and then right to follow the path via Lyneham golf course back across both the railway and river to Bledington.

STAGE 2

ASCOTT-UNDER-WYCHWOOD to WOOTTON DOOR
DISTANCE 11.1 miles (17.9km)
MAPS OS Explorer 180, 191
START AT GRID REFERENCE SP 301 188
START POINT Ascott-under-Wychwood

From Ascott-under-Wychwood to Charlbury, where a vestige of the medieval forest remains, the Oxfordshire Way is strongly aware of this former haunt of beasts of the chase. The route goes to the north of, and follows, the River Evenlode through to Charlbury. It passes the grassy remains of Ascott D'Oyley Castle, just outside Ascott-under-Wychwood, and is partly coincident with the Wychwood Way.

Charlbury, which climbs up the hillside on a crook of the Evenlode, was at the centre of the glove-making industry in the days when Cotswold wool reigned supreme. Additionally, it has the distinction of being the birthplace of the first woman to preach publicly in London. Her name was Anne Downer, and she was born in 1624. Charlbury has shops, a museum and four hostelries.

It is easy to break the journey at Charlbury, as most InterCity trains stop at the station (grid ref. SP 353 194), and there is a bus service. You can walk back to Ascott-under-Wychwood by using the alternative route of the Oxfordshire Way.

ABOVE *Stunning purple blooms of wisteria and allium adorn a wall at Waterperry Gardens*

transmission mast at Beckley acts as a good location marker, and Brill in Buckinghamshire.

Akeman Street reaches the A4260 next to Sturdy's Castle, now an inn offering accommodation, and beyond this descends into the Cherwell valley. Eventually it crosses a plank bridge over a stream. Here you bid farewell to Akeman Street and turn right to a lane where the old stone house, Field Cottage, guards the humps and hollows of the now-vanished village of Old Whitehill.

You can break the walk by turning left at the plank bridge (grid ref. SP 484 198) and heading into Tackley, where there are two pubs. Tackley Station is on the Oxford–Birmingham line.

MONKEY ROOM

The Oxfordshire Way turns left at the lane, goes under the railway bridge and then turns right to cross two branches of the River Cherwell at Flight's Mill, and reach the Oxford Canal at Pigeons Lock. It continues across the canal head along Mill Lane, reaching Kirtlington at a wide triangular green. This was a busy place in Saxon times. It lay on the frontier of Mercia, where Akeman Street crossed the Port Way and Aves Ditch, all important routes. Kirtlington still has an air of prosperity and the Oxford Arms serves food. Go past a village pond and a shop before turning left at the entrance to Kirtlington Park; the mansion built between 1742 and 1746 for local worthy, Sir James Dashwood. It is not open to the public but is important for its 'monkey room', one of only two such singeries surviving in England, decorated in 1745 by the French artist J F Clermont. Monkeys are depicted disporting themselves in the landscape as elegant huntsmen.

Go across the park and through fields to Weston-on-the-Green. Here, down in the vale, are thatched cottages, a village shop and three hostelries. St Mary's Church was rebuilt in 1743 and gives the impression of being larger than it is. Inside, it is full of a sense of light. On the wall by the pulpit is a curious iron cross with an open centre. This is a strange relic indeed, a masthead cross from a galleon of the Spanish Armada. Weston's manor house, now a hotel, is on a site once belonging to Osney Abbey. The present facade dates from 1820, but hides medieval and 16th-century work. Lord Williams of Thame acquired Weston Manor in 1540, and made the 16th-century alterations. This is the first of three houses on the Oxfordshire Way which are associated with Lord Williams. He was the trusted servant of four of the five Tudor monarchs, astutely keeping abreast of political and religious changes.

EDWARD THE CONFESSOR

Leaving Weston opposite the church, pass along a lane and through fields to the B430. Cross to the road opposite and then over the busy A34. Pick up the route again on the south side of the A34, where it strikes south across fields and over the railway to Islip, one of the 'Seven Towns' of Ot Moor.

You enter Islip past green mounds and hollows. This is all that is left of the palace where Edward the Confessor was born in 1004. The palace was built by the saintly king's father, Ethelred the Unready, in the days when Islip was a town and Oxford only a village. The Confessor gave Islip to the monks at Westminster when he began building the famous Abbey, and to Westminster the living of Islip still belongs.

Famous men of Islip include Simon, who became Archbishop of Canterbury in 1348 and John, Prior of Westminster in 1500, who built the Henry VII Chapel there. Two rectors spring to mind: Dr Robert South, who came here in 1678 and built the rectory, and Dr William Buckland, Dean of Westminster and a famous geologist, who became an outspoken supporter of the glacial theory in opposition to many other churchmen of his time. Dean Buckland, who died in 1856, was an eccentric and kept a menagerie. His son, Frank, was cast in the same mould, keeping a bear which wandered at will around Islip.

A left turn into Islip leads to the Red Lion and the Swan, both former coaching inns on the Worcester road, and Islip Bridge, scene of a Civil War skirmish in which Cromwell fought off a band of Royalists. The bridge, rebuilt in 1878, spans the formerly flood-prone River Ray.

You can break the journey at Islip (grid ref. SP 527 142), either by catching a train to Oxford or Bicester, or by walking back along Bletchington Road (B4027) for a mile (1.6km) to the A34 to catch a bus.

ℹ PLACES TO VISIT

• BOURTON-ON-THE-WATER
www.bourtoninfo.com
☎ 01451 820211
Allow some time to enjoy this pretty Cotswold village, with the River Windrush and wide grassy verges at its heart. The warm Cotswold stone buildings are filled with pubs, cafés and an interesting selection of small shops but there is more to see: a model replica of the village itself (built and carved from local stone), the Cotswold Motor Museum, the Dragonfly Maze and the largest attraction of all, Birdland. Here there are over 50 aviaries and 500 birds, including penguins, parrots and falcons (open daily all year).

• NORTH LEIGH ROMAN VILLA
Just a short walk from the route, across Stonesfield Common, lie the exposed foundations of North Leigh Roman Villa. The site is open and free to visit. The remains show a building which would have had over 60 rooms. Protected by a building over it is a near complete mosaic floor, visible through the viewing windows.

• BLENHEIM PALACE
www.blenheimpalace.com
☎ 0800 849 6500
Probably most famous as the birthplace of Sir Winston Churchill, Blenheim Palace is a magnificent English Baroque mansion. It is listed as a UNESCO World Heritage Site and has become a world-renowned attraction. Make the short walk from the OW down Grand Avenue, to pass the Column of Victory and cross the Grand Bridge over the lake to the palace itself. The house boasts grandeur, in both size and opulence, on a scale that is hard to describe. The 'Untold Story' exhibit features talking portraits to bring the palace to life. Outside there are formal gardens, an adventure playground and the Marlborough Hedge Maze, all reached by a miniature train. Palace and gardens open daily Feb–Oct, Wed–Sun Nov–Dec.

ABOVE Two scenes of colourful planting in the herbacious borders at Waterperry Gardens

STAGE 4
ISLIP to TIDDINGTON
DISTANCE 13.3 miles (21.4km)
MAP OS Explorer 180
START AT GRID REFERENCE SP 527 139
START POINT Islip Bridge

Cross Islip Bridge and go uphill to take the path on the left. At last there is a glimpse of expansive Otmoor, guarded by the church towers of its ring of 'towns'. Follow an old wake path into Noke; small, secluded and seemingly lost on the edge of the fen. Noke has no shop, and the Plough, a Grade II Listed Building, is now a private residence. Next, you head on to the flat floor of Otmoor, which still retains something of its wild character. Beyond Noke Wood the route climbs the moor's southern rim to Beckley, on the Oxford Heights. Today, Beckley makes its presence known by that symbol of modernity, its television transmission mast, but it is an ancient place, dating at least from Saxon times. In 1227 a palace was built here, of which only the moat is recognizable today.

When the firing range is not in use you can return to Islip by heading out on to Otmoor along the Roman road (grid ref. SP 566 113) for about 2 miles (3km). Then turn left along the bridleway to Oddington and follow the road back into Islip.

The Oxfordshire Way leaves Beckley on the lane at the eastern end of the village, and descends back on to Otmoor. On the left is a moated mansion, Beckley Park, built in 1540 by Lord Williams of Thame, probably as a hunting lodge. The site once belonged to King Alfred, who excavated the moats.

At the bottom of the hill, cross the drive to Beckley Park and follow the waymarks across meadowland to the road between Horton-cum-Studley and Woodperry (SP 589 118), where it is possible to break the walk and catch a bus from Horton-cum-Studley to Oxford. The Oxfordshire Way crosses the road and continues via Danesbrook Farm and Menmarsh Guide Post to the second shrunken medieval forest on this walk, the royal forest of Bernwood. Medieval kings hunted Bernwood from a hilltop palace at nearby Brill in Buckinghamshire. Pass its depleted remains at gloriously named Polecat End and Drunkard's Corner, to arrive at Park Farm. Turn right here and cross a field to the road at Ledell Cottage, by the M40.

Cross the bridge over the motorway and continue along the lane, lined with tall horse chestnut trees, to the crossroads and the little village of Waterperry. From here it is through the meadows, alongside the church and Waterperry Gardens, on to a well-used path to Bow Bridge over the River Thame.

Pass Mill House, and turn left into Waterstock. Just beyond the church, turn right over a stile to go over the undulating fields to the A418. On the other side of the A-road, about 100yds (90m) to the left at the far end of the lay-by, the route turns right, crossing the disused railway line and going diagonally uphill before dropping to the village street at Tiddington. This village sits at a crossroads on the A418, where the Fox Inn serves food. It is a good place to break the walk, served by buses.

TIDDINGTON TO HENLEY-ON-THAMES

STAGE 5
TIDDINGTON to PYRTON
DISTANCE 9.2 miles (14.8km)
MAPS OS Explorer 171, 180

START AT GRID REFERENCE SU 648 052
START POINT Lay-by on the A418, near the Fox Inn, Tiddington

From Tiddington village street, south of the A418, the Oxfordshire Way follows the footpath to Albury Church, which dates from 1830 and serves both settlements. It has a Norman font, re-cut at the top but with an original lower band of zig-zag and roll moulding. The route turns right on to a broad track before descending to Rycote.

CHARLES I WAS HERE
Rycote was originally a manor of the Quatremains family, and they built the chapel of 1445 which still stands. When Lord Williams came here in 1539 he set about building on a grand scale, in the same plum-coloured brick that he used at Beckley Park. Of his great mansion nothing remains save a turret and a lonely farm among the parkland trees above an ornamental lake. Rycote was a splendid palace. Queen Elizabeth stayed here frequently, so did James I; Charles I visited Rycote in 1625 when the plague was raging in London and Parliament sat at Oxford. He came again in 1643, wearied by the Civil War, his fortunes in decline. By 1745 the property was the home of the Earls of Abingdon, and in November of that year it burned down.

From Rycote, the Oxfordshire Way heads to the A320 opposite a golf course. Cross the road, and continue across the golf course, bearing right to meet the access road by the club house. From here you can see down to the M40 snaking across the land. Then it is on to Tetsworth, emerging at the large village green fronting the A40, the old Oxford, Gloucester and Milford Haven Road.

Tetsworth, which grew fat and self-important during the coaching era, suffered dearly with the coming of the railways in 1840. Now it has succumbed to the ultimate indignity of rubbing shoulders with the M40, bypassed by the modern world. The Swan, that gracious old coaching inn dating from Elizabethan times, is now an antiques centre and restaurant. Tetsworth has a pub, the Old Red Lion, that serves food, and a collection of shops. You can break the walk here (grid ref. SP 686 018) and catch a bus to Oxford or High Wycombe.

The Oxfordshire Way goes up Back Street to Parkers Hill, crosses two fields and passes under the motorway to Harlesford Lane, which it crosses and rambles over meadowland to Adwell. A right turn along the road leads to Wheatfield, a lonely church and converted stable-block set amid magnificent parkland trees. The church was renovated in the early 18th century at the same time as Wheatfield House which, until its destruction by fire in 1814, stood between the church and the stable-block. In the church is an eastern window by Morris and Co., while the altar table has been ascribed to Chippendale. The walk skirts past the clump of beeches where Charles I breakfasted after a skirmish in the valley, and follows footpaths downhill towards the great Chiltern scarp, close to ancient Shirburn whose moated castle is hidden behind the trees. Then it turns right on to a bridleroad and so into Pyrton.

The village has a peaceful atmosphere and a cluster of houses of brick and flint, some of them picturesquely thatched. In the little flint church on Midsummer Day 1619, John Hampden, that most fearless and fair-minded of Parliamentarians, married Elizabeth Symeon, a daughter of the manor house that stands half hidden among the trees.

For a circular walk of approximately 9.5 miles (15.25km), leave the Oxfordshire Way here (grid. ref. SP 687 962) and return to Tetsworth by the other route of the Oxfordshire Way. Or, turn left at the B4009 to catch a bus to Thame.

ABOVE *The Angel seen from across the Thames at Henley*
RIGHT *Flowering gorse gives splashes of gold on Watlington Hill, with its famous viewpoint*

STAGE 6

PYRTON to HENLEY-ON-THAMES

DISTANCE 10.8 miles (17.4km)
MAP OS Explorer 171
START AT GRID REFERENCE SU 694 952
START POINT Pyrton, at the B4009

The Oxfordshire Way crosses the B4009 and heads along a bridleway under the gaze of the Chiltern Hills. This track is a medieval droveway which soon crosses ancient Icknield Way, one of the oldest trading routes in Britain, and here used by the Ridgeway Path. Beyond this you mount the steep Chiltern scarp on to Pyrton Hill. Watlington Hill, with its famous viewpoint, is on the right. The track skirts a great beech hanger and, as it gains height, the whole clay vale is spread out below, with Oxford itself hovering in the distance.

At the minor road, turn right past the Fox and Hounds into Christmas Common. This place came by its name during the Civil War. Christmas 1643 found Royalist soldiers camping here and the local Roundhead force garrisoned at Watlington. They declared an unofficial truce, in true Christmas spirit, and celebrated the day together on the common.

Christmas Common is on the summit of the Chilterns, about 780ft (238m) above sea level, and the Oxfordshire Way has climbed about 375ft (114m) since crossing Icknield Way. From here it goes downhill to enter the Chiltern Forest, not a former royal forest but an ancient woodland, and winds along the valley floor for about a mile (1.6km), through beech woods.

THE SWORD AND THE GOSPEL

Leaving the bridleroad and turning right up a path, emerge into the open and arrive at Hollandridge Farm. Cross the farm track to the path opposite and head obliquely downhill through College Wood. Then it is out of the wood and along the bottom of the steep-sided valley into Pishill. In this little hamlet, you can get food at the Crown Inn. The flint and stone church, rebuilt in

1854, has a modern southwest window (1967), by John Piper, representing the sword and the gospel.

From Pishill, the Oxfordshire Way goes through another beech wood to Maidensgrove. Stonor, with its great house and deer park lies down the road on the left. Cross the road and head uphill past Lodge Farm, where the line of sight extends across the Chiltern woodlands. Then it is downhill again, passing through the edge of the Warburg Nature Reserve, into Bix Bottom.

The Oxfordshire Way sweeps along the valley to cross the B480 at Middle Assensdon and continues uphill along a grassy path heading for a noble line of Scots pines. It crosses the road and enters Henley Park along a lane, continuing into Henley. Scene of the world-famous regatta, Henley looks to the Thames. It developed in the 12th century and later thrived as a port, supplying goods downstream to London. During the coaching era it grew further and when the railway arrived in 1857 Henley's expansion as a commuter town was assured.

The Oxfordshire Way ends at the bridge over the River Thames at Henley, and what a noble bridge this is! Rebuilt in 1786, its graceful arches skim across the river, while on the keystones are two masks carved in stone by Anne Seymour Darner, an eccentric sculptor of animal portraits. They show Father Thames looking downstream, his hair and beard matted, while Isis looks upstream, a picture of youth.

i **PLACES TO VISIT**

• **WATERPERRY GARDENS**
www.waterperrygardens.co.uk
☎ 01844 339254
The OW passes this large estate. Between 1932 and 1971, Waterperry was famous as Beatrix Havergal's School of Horticulture for Ladies. Gardening courses are still taught here, but the main focus for visitors is now on the gardens themselves, which are both a pleasure to explore and a valuable learning resource. There are formal gardens, herbaceous borders, a gravel garden, a rose garden and a waterlilly canal. The estate also has a Rural Life Museum, Saxon church, plant centre, gift shops and café. Open daily all year.

• **RYCOTE CHAPEL**
www.english-heritage.org.uk
☎ 01844 210210
Built in 1445 for the Quatremains family of nearby Rycote Manor, this large chapel is well worth a quick stop and peek. It contains a wealth of impressive Jacobean woodwork, not least of which are the large and finely carved family pews to either side of a rood screen. The pews are roofed; one with a ceiling painted as the night sky, the other topped with a musicians gallery.

• **STONOR HOUSE AND GARDENS**
www.stonor.com
☎ 01491 638587
A short walk from the OW at Pishill will bring you to Stonor, home to the Stonor family for over 800 years. An impressive manor house with a Tudor E-shape and Georgian windows, it hides older buildings to the rear. The main house contains fine paintings, bronzes, tapestries and ceramics. There is a medieval Roman Catholic chapel here, where mass is still open to the public every Sunday. There are also two walled gardens, and the lush parkland is home to fallow deer, red kites and buzzards. There is a small stone circle close to the house. Open Sun & bank holiday afternoons Apr–Sep, also Wed afternoons Jul–Aug.

Essex Way

COMPLETE ROUTE EPPING TO HARWICH **81 MILES (130KM)**
SECTION COVERED EPPING TO DEDHAM **63 MILES (101KM)**
MAPS OS EXPLORER 174, 183, 184, 195, 196, 197

Starting on the outskirts of London beside a far outpost of the London Underground network, the Essex Way winds through peaceful rural scenery in a northeasterly direction, connecting briefly with civilization at the market towns of Ongar and Coggeshall before arriving at Dedham Vale and Dedham in the very heart of Constable country. The route then continues to reach the coast at Harwich, adding another 20 miles (32km) to the stretch covered here. While Essex has for many the reputation of being a land of commuters and slightly seedy seaside towns, the route of the Essex Way sees nothing of this, being almost completely confined to idyllic rural English countryside, with views that probably have not changed too significantly in the last 100 or so years.

The Essex Way is a walk very much about history, and it is the townships and buildings on the route which provide most of the interest along the path. While plenty of evidence of the Roman occupation of England remains in Essex, the route of the walk does not coincide with too much of this. There are some hints of medieval times — the wooden nave walls of Greensted Church date back to about 835 — but the history which can be seen today really starts with the Norman conquest of England in the 11th century. William of Normandy rewarded his faithful French barons with tracts of land, many of them in Essex, and the route passes right through a couple of well-preserved motte-and-bailey castle sites.

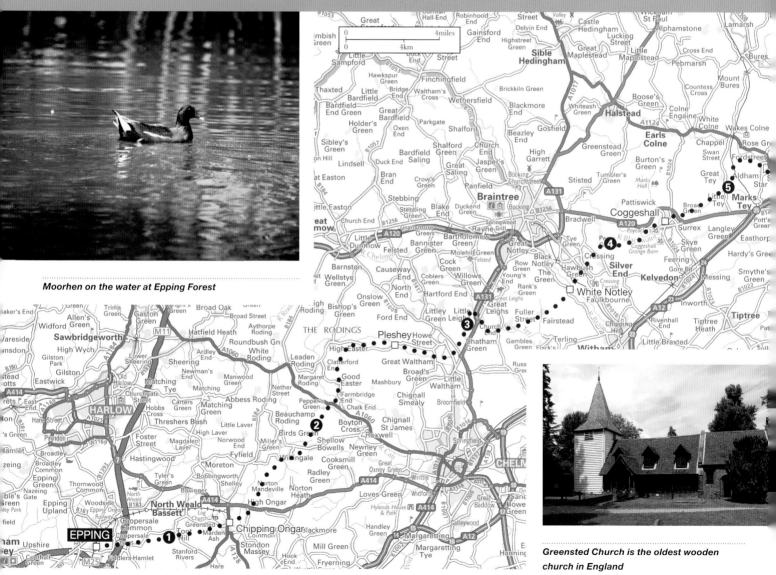

Moorhen on the water at Epping Forest

Greensted Church is the oldest wooden church in England

View along High Beach path in Epping Forest

EPPING TO PLESHEY

STAGE 1

EPPING to CHIPPING ONGAR

DISTANCE 7.5 miles (12.1km)

MAPS OS Explorer 174, 183

START AT GRID REFERENCE TL 462 015

START POINT Epping Underground Station

Once an important roadside town on the old coach route from London to Norwich, Epping had no less than 26 inns in its heyday, and many tales abound regarding the rogues and characters who frequented them. From the underground station exit, take the footbridge to the eastern side of the track and proceed down the residential street to a main road. Cross to Bower Court, and follow the footpath to the side of this development. The path leads to open fields, and continues through these to a road. Turn left and then left again back on to a bridleway. After about 0.5 miles (800m) this leads to another road and the Theydon Oak pub. Here, the walker should turn right and then take the path on the left just before the bend in the road. This stretch of the route is dominated by the M11.

Up ahead is a large chunk of Epping Forest. Its 6,000 acres were declared a public open space in 1878, and have since served to educate many generations of children in the sights and sounds of the countryside. The path skirts around the southeast edge of this part of the forest, past a school, and then follows a wide track through the trees to a footbridge over the motorway. The route then proceeds via a straight track to the edge of the forest, through pleasant countryside, and up to the village of Toot Hill.

Following the road north through the village, the path regains the countryside when the road bears sharp left, and it continues straight ahead into the field. The track follows the hedge to the right and continues east for another 0.75 miles (1.25km). It then turns to the north and crosses four stiles in quick succession, each clearly marked. The path then winds around some buildings, with good signposting at this point. The official route continues north until reaching the road.

At this road the path turns sharply east once again, and continues along the side of a small wood to Greensted and its famous church. St Andrew's is the oldest wooden church in England and quite possibly the world, and has long been a place of pilgrimage. The nave is built of oak logs split vertically in half, some dating back to the mid-7th century. Tradition has it that the body of St Edmund rested here in 1013 on its way to Bury St Edmunds, Edmund having led the Angles in their fight against the Danes in the 9th century.

From Greensted, the path continues due east across a couple more fields to Chipping Ongar, noted for its fine Norman motte-and-bailey castle. While the fortress was demolished long ago, the earthworks survive. Ongar was once the stronghold of Count Eustace of Boulogne, one of William the Conqueror's most prominent supporters at the Battle of Hastings, who later became the greatest lay baron in both Essex and Hertfordshire.

STAGE 2

CHIPPING ONGAR to PLESHEY

DISTANCE 13.8 miles (22.2km)

MAP OS Explorer 183

A stile covered with footpath waymarkers points walkers along the Essex Way

TOP Stone carving on St Martin's Church
MIDDLE St Andrew's Church at Good Easter
BOTTOM Pretty pink cottage at Pleshey

START AT GRID REFERENCE TL 553 029
START POINT Chipping Ongar Church

For those with a passion for ecclesiastical history, the Norman Church of St Martin of Tours is well worth a visit. From the church, the path proceeds by the earthworks of the motte-and-bailey, the moat now providing a very pleasant border for a row of houses. The wide grass track then zig-zags north, past playing fields and a school, to the main A414 Chelmsford–Harlow road. It is possible to walk through the culvert at the bottom of the field as an alternative to crossing this busy road. The culvert holds the water of the River Roding, with which the walker now becomes fairly well acquainted for the next few miles. About as far removed from civilization as the Essex Way gets, there is plenty of wildlife to enjoy here; moorhens in the river, rabbits, hares and squirrels on the riverbanks, and even the occasional deer. The route crosses the second bridge over the river, then follows a sunken and very overgrown track up the hill towards Cannon's Green.

Towards the top of the hill, take the left fork, leading along a field and eventually to the road at Cannon's Green. The route follows the road for a few hundred yards north, and then proceeds straight across a couple of huge fields. If these have been recently ploughed there will be no sign of a path anywhere, but it is a right of way, so fix on Willingale Church tower up ahead and march. Turn left at the road, and continue straight until reaching a farm track to the right, leading downhill. This leads all the way to the twin churches of Willingale; two churches in the same churchyard, one slightly more recent than the other. The story goes that these were built by two sisters who fell out and refused to worship together under the same roof.

From Willingale (grid ref. TL 596 074), there are regular buses back to Chipping Ongar.

From the churchyard the path crosses straight over the main street, past the sports field, and then turns north, heading towards the white house in the distance. The next few miles follow well-marked tracks through low-lying, fertile agricultural land to reach civilization at the small hamlet of Pepper's Green, and a track leading to the main A1060 road.

Crossing this, the route follows a pleasant track leading northeast and descending to Farmbridge End; an attractive hamlet on the banks of the River Can. On the other side of the small valley, the path climbs gently through a large field to the church of Good Easter, with its 13th-century nave and chancel.

A few yards of road-walking is now necessary, to the main crossroads by the former Star public house, now converted to a private residence. Turning north, the route then regains the footpath behind the left-hand row of cottages, and continues along this path to a minor road, which it leaves again a few hundred yards further on at the hard right corner. This byway leads downhill into trees and presently bears sharp left. At this bend turn right through a gate into a long field, and follow the bridleway. This continues for over a mile (1.6km), passing a variety of horse jumps and obstacles, to reach the small hamlet of Stagden Cross. Turn right here.

The route from Stagden to Pleshey is well signposted, following a long farm track to Pleshey Grange, and then another clearly marked path past the ramparts of Pleshey Castle to reach Pleshey itself. Pleshey and the surrounding 12,000 acres were given to Geoffrey de Mandeville for his services to William the Conqueror after the Battle of Hastings. The town had an eventful history from then on, including one particularly black spot on Christmas Eve 1215, when King John's forces sacked the castle and surrounding lands.

The village is somewhat quieter nowadays, but the castle is still an impressive remnant. The outer rampart encloses the entire village, some 40 acres in size — not easy to defend!

PLESHEY TO COGGESHALL

STAGE 3

PLESHEY to WHITE NOTLEY

DISTANCE 13.6 miles (21.9km)

MAP OS Explorer 183

START AT GRID REFERENCE TL 664 144

START POINT Pleshey Church, about 6 miles northwest of Chelmsford

The route takes the walker through the very picturesque village of Pleshey, to the eastern side just before Walthambury Brook. From here, the path heads due east across a number of low-lying fields beside a small stream, past a couple of small reservoirs, to the village of Great Waltham.

This pleasant settlement on the banks of the River Chelmer may be a good place to pick up provisions, as it is the only place for some time with any shops. For those with an interest in historical inns, the 14th-century Green Man in Howe Street may be a place to visit. There is a long history of imbibing in Great Waltham; it was the site of a vineyard in Norman times.

There are buses from Great Waltham (grid ref. TL 696 134) back to Pleshey.

FRIESIAN COWS

The path crosses the main road just north of the village, and then proceeds through the grounds of Langleys Park and Chatham Hall. Langleys is a large, brick mansion, still incorporating some of the original 17th-century building and standing in spacious grounds that run down to the river. Pause to read some of the inscriptions on the tombstones in the pets' graveyard by the main

building. This part of the path is well signposted, and continues northeast over pleasant fields to Chatham Green, up the road to Liberty Hall and then over more fields to Little Leighs. All the way, it is more or less parallel to the busy A131, which runs along the course of an old Roman road. The church at Little Leighs is worthy of a visit, principally to admire the early 14th-century carved oak figure of a priest in cope, scarf and alb.

From the church, the route follows the road around the block to avoid walking any distance alongside the A131, and then crosses this main road to pick up the River Ter. It then follows the banks of the river southeast over more fields to Lyons Hall. Here, the route leaves the riverside and proceeds in a north-easterly direction, along a track and then through open fields, to the village of Fuller Street.

The route turns south, then east past Sandy Wood to the small village of Terling, famous for its associations with the ubiquitous Friesian cow. The prefix Terling occurs frequently in the pedigrees of individuals of this breed, as a reminder and tribute to the work of Edward Strutt of Terling, pioneer of modern milk production and, in the opinion of many of his contemporaries, the greatest agriculturalist of his day. (Strutt's brother, incidentally, was the 3rd Lord Rayleigh; the mathematician famous for his work on wave motion and vibrating systems.)

Before entering Terling the route zig-zags north to Fairstead, whose church spire can be seen from some way off. Turn right at the church and then proceed uphill to the T-junction and southeast on the Terling road. About 300yds (275m) down this road, a farm track on the left passes Troys Hall and continues for about a mile (1.6km), eventually reaching Maltings Farm, just south of White Notley. While it may be quicker to go straight up the road to the village, it is more pleasant to continue northeast along what looks like a private drive, then over a field to the River Brain. The path follows the river northeast into White Notley, emerging at the road just below the railway station.

PLACES TO VISIT

• EPPING ONGAR RAILWAY
www.eorailway.co.uk
☎ 01277 365200
This restored branch line of the Great Eastern Railway has been a labour of love for local volunteers. They aim to open the line between Ongar and Epping. The service is due to expand but currently there are steam and diesel services between North Weald station and Chipping Ongar. A combined ticket from Epping main line station provides a shuttle to North Weald on a heritage bus, so a one-way ticket on this line could mean that you actually start walking the Essex Way when you alight at Ongar. Check online; services usually Sat–Sun all year.

• CRESSING TEMPLE
www.cressingtemple.org.uk
☎ 01376 584903
Named in reference to the Knights Templar who founded the two large 13th-century wooden barns here, this historic estate has more to see. There is a formal garden lovingly cared for within the original Tudor wall, and a farmhouse and granary dating back to the 17th century. The tea room and shop add to the visit, as do the regular themed events. Open Sun–Fri Mar–Oct.

• COGGESHALL
www.nationaltrust.org.uk
Coggeshall is located on the long Roman road, Stane Street, and has a great history. It still holds a weekly market and has over 300 listed buildings. The National Trust own two of the finest: the EW passes the 13th-century Coggeshall Grange Barn (www.coggeshall-barn.org.uk ☎ 01376 562226; open afternoons only Thu–Sun Apr–Oct), and Paycocke's is within walking distance, on the north side of the river (☎ 01376 561305; open Wed–Sun Apr–Oct). Paycocke's was built by a wealthy clothier in the early 16th century. Its elaborate panelling was clearly meant to impress. It has a pretty garden, too.

ABOVE LEFT The church at Little Leighs is worth a visit
ABOVE The windmill at Terling

STAGE 4

WHITE NOTLEY to COGGESHALL

DISTANCE 7.4 miles (11.9km)
MAPS OS Explorer 183, 197
START AT GRID REFERENCE TL 787 185
START POINT White Notley, just downhill from the railway station

While apparently out in the middle of nowhere, the proximity of the route to the railway makes a good start and/or finishing point for this section of the Essex Way.

Just downhill from the railway station is a track leading off to the northeast, which takes the walker through the farmstead of Fambridge Hall, where the ancient timber barns are worthy of a few minutes' contemplation. Beyond this farm, the track turns right and passes under the railway track, through a delightful old egg-shaped and echoing tunnel, and then continues to the Braintree–Witham road. A few hundred yards up this road, the route regains the fields and leads to Cressing Church.

Although now a sleepy hamlet, Cressing has an interesting history. It was the earliest English settlement of the military order of Knights Templar, who were given the Manor of Cressing in 1135. On their suppression by Pope Clement V, the military order of Knights of the Hospital of St John at Jerusalem replaced them in 1312. The Templar knights included farming among their activities, and the only surviving remnants of this era are two extraordinary wooden barns, one for wheat and one for barley, to be found about a mile (1.6km) to the south of the route in Cressing Temple. These 40ft (12m) high, aisled barns are nowadays the site of activities such as book fairs. They are certainly worth a visit.

From Cressing, follow the route as it zig-zags over very flat land through a number of fields. The route can be difficult to follow along this stretch, but you should emerge at a small road, within sight and sound of large gravel workings up ahead. The path proceeds down the left-hand side of a lake to join the entrance track to these gravel workings, which leads to another road east of Bradwell Hall.

TOP The wooden beams of Cressing Temple's restored medieval barley barn
MIDDLE A smiling carved figure on the portal at Paycocke's, in Coggeshall
BOTTOM The church of St Barnabus, c1150 AD

🚆 *Upon emerging from the gravel works (grid ref TL 820 222), continue north on a track for 650yds (590m) to the A120 Braintree–Coggeshall road, where there are regular buses either way.*

After following this road to the east for a few hundred yards, the path is signposted off to the left, descending to the tree-lined banks of the River Blackwater. Then follows a pleasant stretch along the side of the river for 0.5 miles (800m), to more gravel workings. After skirting these, the route climbs back up again out of the slight valley towards Curd Hall Farm, where it joins the

farm drive and proceeds once again parallel with the river for almost a mile (1.6km), eventually emerging by Grange Farm.

Grange Barn is the oldest surviving timber-framed barn in Europe and dates to the mid-12th century. It was originally part of the Cistercian Monastery of Coggeshall, and was restored to its present glory in the 1980s. It is now a National Trust property.

From here, about 0.25 miles (400m) south of Coggeshall, the walker has a number of options. It is possible to skirt the town centre and rejoin the footpath on the easternmost side of town. Alternatively, continue eastwards across the road from the barn to the remains of the abbey itself, founded by King Stephen and given over to the Cistercian order in 1148. The abbey is of particular architectural interest because of the widespread use of brick in the 12th and early 13th centuries. Continue east across the river and then take the footpath north, eventually reaching Coggeshall town church.

COGGESHALL TO DEDHAM

STAGE 5

COGGESHALL to WEST BERGHOLT

DISTANCE 9.7 miles (15.6km)
MAPS OS Explorer 184, 195
START AT GRID REFERENCE TL 854 230
START POINT Coggeshall Church, in Church Street.

The impressive Church of St Peter ad Vincula was built all to one plan in the 15th century, and its large size and memorials to various clothier families reflect the prosperous medieval cloth trade. The church suffered severe bomb damage in 1940, the repairs to which can be clearly seen from the outside.

From the church the route proceeds east and then south for a few hundred yards, into areas of rather less architectural interest. A footpath soon leaves the road to the left and then leads the walker into a field and soon to the Coggeshall bypass, which should be crossed with care.

The path makes its way eastward from the road, to run parallel with Stane Street (ancient Roman Road) through a number of flax fields, and passes to the south of the unusual buildings at Houchin's Farm. After passing in front of two small reservoirs, the path turns northeast to cross a small road at East Gores. Do note the angle of the chimney on the house to your left. From East Gores, the track turns more northwards to cross a number of fields and pass a small conifer plantation, running alongside a brook for some of the way. Keep heading approximately north and the great Norman crossing tower of St Barnabas Church in Great Tey should eventually come into view. Upon reaching Great Tey, turn left up the main street.

🚆 *For those wishing to leave or join the walk via public transport, the railway station of Chappel and Wakes Colne is only a mile (1.6km) north of this point (grid ref. TL 895 290).*

The route turns right off Great Tey main street and then meanders before the path continues northeastwards to cross the railway line, and then descends through Bacon's Farm to the banks of the River Colne. While walking downhill through these pleasant meadows, look away to your left to the elegant viaduct crossing the Colne Valley to Chappel Station, now also the home of a museum of railway artefacts. From here, almost all the way to West Bergholt, the path is never far from the River Colne. Although in many places the official footpath is more direct than the riverbanks, out of consideration for the farmers' crops the path has, over the years, ended up following the line of the river until Fordstreet, where it passes along the riverward side of a large nursery, eventually emerging by the A1124 Colchester–Halstead road.

After crossing to the north side of the river, the riverbank trail continues from the gardens of the Shoulder of Mutton pub. From Fordstreet, the path once again hugs the river fairly closely. After about 0.5 miles (800m) the route crosses Mill Road, but then meets with no interruption for the next mile (1.6km). It turns into a farm track just after passing a ruined barn. This track leads uphill through Cook's Hall Farm, turns north and continues uphill to West Bergholt Church.

From there a path leads eastward across a field and into a housing estate on the outskirts of West Bergholt. New Church Road leads into the village centre.

STAGE 6

WEST BERGHOLT to DEDHAM

DISTANCE 10.9 miles (17.5km)
MAPS OS Explorer 184, 196
START AT GRID REFERENCE TL 965 277
START POINT The junction between the B1508 and Armoury Road in the centre of West Bergholt

A great deal of this last section is on either roads or metalled pathways, but some fine views over the Vale of Dedham make up for this at the end. The route leaves town along the drive to Armoury Farm, and then goes into open fields. Due to the mildly undulating nature of the land in this vicinity, navigation across these fields can be somewhat tricky as the route heads northeast towards Horkesley Heath. Just to the west are the ramparts of Pitchbury Castle, defensive earthworks dating back to the Iron Age. Continue into Horkesley Heath and turn left on the A134 Colchester-to-Sudbury. The route turns right along Ivy Lodge Road, and follows this for about 0.25 mile (400m). At the

bottom of the hill, a footpath on the left leads northwards along a grassy meadow to a couple of small cottages. From there the path becomes a proper track, and continues past two small reservoirs on the left.

After a right and then a left turn, this track reaches a road by some cottages. The countryside along this stretch is rather flat and featureless, offering no hint of the beautiful views into Dedham Vale waiting only a mile (1.6km) or so up the road. Turn left along Boxted Lane and then right along Holly Lodge Lane; the route eventually passes a farm of the same name. The path goes through the farm buildings, and then turns right to follow a line of telegraph poles towards an orchard. This section of the route may well be across a ploughed field, making it rather difficult to know where to proceed. There is a track along the front of the orchard leading to a road on the right, which should be reached one way or the other.

A few hundred yards east along this road, a path leads north past Carter's Farm, with its shop and cafe, to arrive at another road. Directly opposite is a driveway leading to Boxted Hall. The route goes along the north side of the Hall and across a field to St Peter's Church at Boxted, which is noted for the reddish 'puddingstone' in the Norman tower.

Both Great Horkesley and Boxted have a regular bus service into Colchester, from where it is possible to return to West Bergholt or to go on to Dedham.

CONSTABLE COUNTRY

Passing the old school on the northern side of the church, the route then joins a small road running through trees and past some pleasant houses. Suddenly, the Vale of Dedham comes into view to the north, and one can immediately see why John Constable was so inspired to paint his pictures.

Where the road begins to descend, a track leads off right into the trees on the left, which takes the walker into a lush valley with a large expanse of water on the left. The track then ascends to the fine estate of Rivers Hall, where some considerable effort has gone into routing the walker around its far reaches. From the top of the drive there is another 0.25 miles (400m) of road-walking, and then the route turns eastwards across the middle of some mighty fields. For a short while the Essex Way follows the driveway of Plumbs Farm, then there are more fields to cross as it descends very slowly into the Vale.

After following the base of an area of woodland, the track turns sharp right to climb to Langham Hall and thence to Langham Church, once one of John Constable's favourite haunts. It was from here that he painted 'Dedham Vale', which hangs in the National Gallery in London.

From the church, a pleasant tree-lined drive leads to a road, which crosses over the A12 main road to Ipswich. Shortly after crossing this busy trunk road, a left turn into the driveway of Milsoms Hotel leads to a footpath that descends to the banks of the River Stour. Although little more than a stream at this point, in just a few miles it opens out into a large estuary.

The final mile (1.6km), along the riverside, leads straight into Dedham itself; another old wool town considered to be the heart of 'Constable Country'. Aficionados may recognize the Church of St Mary. The magnificent flint and stone tower, which appears in a number of the artist's paintings, was built on the wealth of the clothier families in the 15th and 16th centuries.The old grammar school at the side of the churchyard square, built in 1732, was attended by John Constable, who had been very unhappy at school in Lavenham.

LEFT Rowing boats moored along the River Stour in Dedham

PLACES TO VISIT

• **COLNE VALLEY RAILWAY**
www.colnevalleyrailway.co.uk
☎ 01787 461174
This heritage railway is just a short detour from the route. It features a line of just over 1 mile (1.6km), which you can enjoy aboard a steam train. There are regular theme days, such as ones with Thomas the Tank Engine, and the site also runs a garden railway and miniature railway. See website for details of operating days and times.

• **DEDHAM**
www.dedhamvalestourvalley.org
The area around Dedham village is often referred to as 'Constable Country', and the arts certainly abound here, though Constable is not the only focus. Certainly, it is worth the quick detour from Dedham to visit the hamlet of Flatford, just across the river and county boundary. There you can visit Bridge Cottage, the famous thatched cottage seen in many of Constable's paintings, which now houses an exhibition on his life and work: (www.nationaltrust.org.uk ☎ 01206 298260; open daily Apr–Oct, opening varies Nov–Mar).
There are many guided walks in this area by various organizations, or leaflets available at Flatford Visitor Centre if you wish to guide yourself (Flatford Lane, Flatford; ☎ 01206 299460; open daily Mar–Oct, Sat–Sun Nov–Mar).
Within Dedham itself there is the Dedham Art and Craft Centre, which showcases and sells all types of crafts, from paintings to ceramics, soap, furniture and soft toys (www.dedhamartandcraftcentre.co.uk ☎ 01206 322666; open daily all year). To the south of the village is the Sir Alfred Munnings Museum, set in his own house, which also has a pretty garden and the artist's studio (www.siralfredmunnings.co.uk ☎ 01206 322127; open afternoons only Wed & Sun Apr–Oct, also Thu & Sat May, Jul & Sep). Munnings had 230 paintings hung at the Royal Academy in the first half of the 20th century, and showed great diversity of painting in his style and subjects.

Wales & the Marches

Pembrokeshire Coast Path

COMPLETE ROUTE AMROTH TO ST DOGMAELS **186 MILES (299KM)**
SECTION COVERED BROAD HAVEN TO GOODWICK **52 MILES (84KM)**
MAPS OS EXPLORER OL 35, OL 36

The Pembrokeshire Coast Path is a national trail following the Pembrokeshire coast through the Pembrokeshire Coast National Park, from Amroth in the south to St Dogmaels, near Cardigan, in the north. The official distance is 186 miles (299km), but there are so many ups and downs and ins and outs that the real distance is impossible to measure and it is probably something closer to 200 miles (322km). This 52-mile (84km) section offers three days' good walking, along some of the most spectacular scenery that the coast can offer. However, there are a few parts of the walk where intransigent landowners have forced the route inland or on to the road. This is the case in the southwestern section between Freshwater West and Stack Rocks, where the fine limestone cliffs of the coast are out of bounds due to military occupation, however, there is now a multi-user trail following the inland boundary of the range, set up by agreement with the National Park Authority and the MoD. The walker also suffers, in other ways, from the presence of the massive oil refineries and terminals around Milford Haven/Pembroke. The distances to be covered may seem modest for a day's walking. However, the coast path should never be underestimated.

TOP Horseriding on the sands at Druidston
ABOVE The village of Solva has a busy little harbour

The beach at Newgale with the coast path on high ground

BROAD HAVEN TO ST DAVID'S

STAGE 1
BROAD HAVEN to SOLVA

DISTANCE 11 miles (17.7km)
MAPS OS Explorer 35, 36
START AT GRID REFERENCE SM 861 138
START POINT The beach at Broad Haven

Most guidebooks assume the walker will walk this route from north to south, but on this stretch of coastline it seems preferable to go from south to north. Firstly, the prevailing wind is more likely to be behind; and secondly, this way the coastal scenery, after a comparatively tame start along St Brides Bay, becomes more and more magnificent and challenging.

Broad Haven is a sprawling village in a fine location, with a long sandy beach and all the usual amenities, including a youth hostel. It is easily accessible from Haverfordwest, with a regular bus service. The coast path starts at the north end of the beach, where it is clearly signposted up a track leading to the cliff-tops above Sleek Stone. It takes an easy route across grassy headlands as it follows a new path towards Druidston Haven, named after the Norman knight Drue, who invaded Ireland in the 12th century. This part of the path is along one of many specially negotiated rights of way, but sadly it is forced to divert a short distance inland and join the road on the outskirts of Druidston, passing above the back of the hotel which, presumably, barred its passage. The beach at Druidston is one of several encountered along this part of the walk, as the path rejoins the coast above Druidston Haven. Nolton Haven is a pretty little place, set in a valley, with the Mariners Inn and a pleasant small beach, all of which make it a fine place to stop. From here the path heads steeply up along the side of the cliffs, passing above the unusual outcrop of Rickets Head, and then on down past a solitary chimney; a relic of the days when the Trefrane Cliff colliery operated here.

NEWGALE SANDS
At the top of the next rise, Newgale Beach comes into sight. This magnificent 2-mile (3km) stretch of sand faces west and, not surprisingly, it is a favourite spot for surfers and windsurfers. It is also popular for family summer holidays. Facilities include cafes at either end, and a pub. Rejoining the road, the path leads down to the beach and along Newgale Sands, which is good firm walking, with shingle piled up by the unobtrusive road on the right. This is one of the few stretches of the coast path where fast progress can be made.

Join the road at the northern end of the beach by the last buildings, going a short way uphill before turning off on the coast path, which follows the cliffs to the left. Alternatively, if the tide is out and you do not mind risking getting your feet wet, it is possible to continue along the beach to Cwm Mawr. This is the more interesting end of Newgale Sands, where there are rock pools and caves to explore. On the hillside above there is a half demolished small, cream-coloured building, and a track leads up past it to rejoin the path.

To return to Broad Haven, follow the network of minor roads south from Newgale (grid ref. SM 847 223). To return by public transport, take a bus from Newgale to Haverfordwest, and then another to Broad Haven.

Here the coast path begins to bear westwards, with extensive gorse and heather on the hillside below, making towards the headland of Dinas Fach. Coastal walker buses deliver walkers to the beach at Porthmynawyd. This is perhaps the most beautiful, secluded beach along the whole Pembrokeshire coastline, and accessible from the road only by footpath from Pointz Castle. A hillock is all that remains of the 12th-century castle.

You soon discover on the coast path that what goes down must also go up, and there is a comparatively steep climb on the other side to rejoin the cliff-top above Ogof y Cae, heading towards the splendid headland of Dinas Fawr. The site of a promontory fort which can now be reached by a solitary footpath, in good weather this is a wonderful spot for a picnic. The next beach is at Aber-west, which can be reached only by boat, and then the path passes near the site of a Neolithic burial chamber before heading down a steep staircase to reach the valley beneath the Gribin; the ridge that leads to Solva.

Here the path crosses a stream by a hidden beach, before heading steeply up the side of the Gribin. This leads to a famous viewpoint above the Solva estuary, before following the ridge eastwards, high above the estuary, until it begins to head gently downhill into Solva. Near the bottom it passes old limekilns. Limestone was once brought here by sea from West Williamston, but the trade died out when artificial fertilizers became more economical.

The path emerges by the side of the River Solva, crossing in front of the Harbour Inn. This small village is now a popular tourist spot and, though somewhat dominated by its car park, is worth a good look round. There is hotel and bed-and-breakfast accommodation. The estuary is particularly charming, being

USEFUL INFORMATION
THE ROUTE
• *www.visitpembrokeshire.com*
Click on the 'Coast Path' tab on this website to access excellent information on the PCP route, which includes a distance chart, stage descriptions and a link to the coastal bus service website.
• *www.nationaltrail.co.uk*
☎ 0845 345 7275
Since the PCP is a national trail, the official website is also a great source of information. It supplies GPS data, gives useful links to related services, lists guides for sale and offers ten leaflets covering stages of the route. It also has an interactive map for each of 15 stages, with locations of, and links to, accommodation sites.

TOURIST INFORMATION CENTRES
• *www.visitpembrokeshire.com*
Fishguard Harbour TIC: Ocean Lab, Goodwick SA64 0DE;
☎ 01348 874737
Fishguard Town TIC: The Town Hall, Market Square SA65 9HE;
☎ 01437 776636
• *www.orielyparc.co.uk*
St David's National Park Visitor Centre, Oriel y Parc, The Grove, St David's SA62 6NW;
☎ 01437 720392

PLANNING YOUR TRIP
• *www.pcnpa.org.uk*
☎ 0845 345 7275
The Pembrokeshire Coast National Park Authority has good links to help with your research, and an accommodation list specific to the coast path vicinity. There are also details of over 200 circular walks within the park.
• *www.ramblers.org.uk*
☎ 020 7339 8500 and
www.ldwa.org.uk
The Ramblers Association and the Long Distance Walkers Association both provide general information about long-distance walking and detail on the PCP.

OTHER PATHS
The Ceredigion Coast Path continues for 62 miles (100km), from Cardigan to the Dyfi estuary.

completely sheltered from all quarters and drying out almost totally at low tide, leaving all its moored boats stranded. At this time of day you can walk along the sand to the head of the estuary, but take care not to get caught by the incoming tide.

STAGE 2

SOLVA to ST DAVID'S

DISTANCE 5.5 miles (8.9km)
MAP OS Explorer OL 35
START AT GRID REFERENCE SM 805 242
START POINT The west bank of the river, in the village of Solva

The path heads up the west side of the estuary, passing a terrace of houses in a fine position before joining an ivy-covered pathway which leads once more to the cliff-tops. The walking here is both easy and spectacular, with dramatic cliffs ahead and quiet farmland inland. There is a view over the whole massive area of St Brides Bay, from Ramsey Island in the north to Skomer Island in the south, both noted as nature reserves. The cliffs themselves are quite forbidding, and evidence of their unforgiving nature can be seen in the rusting remains of a ship at Aber-long; one of three Greek tugs wrecked here while en route from Liverpool.

Passing through National Trust land, the path goes by the concentric ditches of the massive Ogof Castell hill fort, before dropping down to Porth-y-Rhaw, which was once a busy place with a woollen mill and factory that ceased production in 1915. Inland is Morfa Common; an area of heathland maintained by the National Trust. The path then leads to Caer Bwdy Bay, where you can see the purple sandstone that was used over many centuries to build St David's Cathedral. The most recent quarry was reopened here in 1996. On the headland is Castell Penpleidiau, another Iron Age fort, in a most impregnable position. Then you come to Caerfai, where the caravan and camp site intrudes upon the solitude of the cliffs, though there is a good beach in a dramatic setting and easily reached by a track down the side of the cliff. The Cambrian rocks here are dated at around 500 million years old, making them some of the oldest in Britain.

Round the next headland, at the head of St Non's Bay, is St Non's Chapel. The ruins are sited in front of a rather austere-looking, solitary grey building that is now the home of a religious retreat. From here, the road leads to the cathedral city of St David's, less than a mile (1.6km) inland.

ST DAVID'S TO TREFIN

TOP Wooden signposts point the way along the coast
MIDDLE Rugged scenery at St Non's, near St David's
BOTTOM Part of the Bishops Palace at St David's

STAGE 3

ST DAVID'S to WHITESANDS BAY

DISTANCE 8.1 miles (13km)
MAP OS Explorer OL 35
START AT GRID REFERENCE SM 753 252
START POINT St David's, City Cross

In season, St David's can become very crowded due to the attraction of its cathedral and Bishop's Palace. The limited number of car parks soon fill up, and it is advisable to find a space early. From the City Cross, follow the road downhill and then fork left along a road signposted to the Warpool Court Hotel. The nearby Carn Warpool is a gorse-fringed, rocky outcrop, which

gives views forward towards Ramsey Island and back towards the tower of St David's Cathedral. It also looks over Clegyr Boia, or Boia's Rock, to the west, and to Carn Llidi in the north; the highest point of the peninsula at 600ft (183m).

At the end of the road, a footpath leads down past the ruins of St Non's to rejoin the coast path, following the spectacular rocky coastline westwards. Visible here is the wide colour range in the lichen-covered Cambrian rock structure which has been upended by volcanic activity. As you round the headland known as Trwyn Cynddeiriog (which can aptly be translated as the 'Furious Point'), small hollows alongside the path show where farmers quarried stone to build their field boundaries. As it winds its way along the coastline, the path affords wonderful views of the near-vertical cliffs.

Past the next bay the path turns inland above Porth Clais Harbour. This picturesque inlet is a haven for a small fleet of fishing boats, the only habitation being two small cottages. A modern sea wall has been built on the remains of an old wall at the entrance, and at the head of the inlet a bridge crosses the River Alun, which flows into the sea here on its way from St David's. Porth Clais was the principal harbour for St David's from the 14th century, receiving building timber imported from Ireland as well as produce such as corn, malt and wool from as far afield as Barnstaple, Bristol and Merioneth. Coal was brought to the harbour by boats well into the 20th century, but that trade has now completely disappeared. By the side of the river the restored limekilns can be seen, but the cottages that once housed the lime-burners who looked after them are now ruins, and the pub that once stood on the quay wall has now also disappeared.

THE BITCHES

Past Porth Clais, the St David's peninsula is flat and windswept, and the path moves away from the cliff edge. Passing National Trust land, it drops downhill to cross behind the twin rocky beaches of Porthlysgi Bay. The bay is named after the Irish raider Lysgi, who killed the Celtic chieftain Boia at Clegyr Boia, a mile (1.6km) inland. For a time it looks as if you have to walk round the end of Ramsey Island, but Ramsey Sound, which separates the island from the mainland, soon comes into view. This is a fearsome stretch of water where the tidal race evocatively called The Bitches can run at up to 7 knots. The island itself is about 2 miles (3km) long by 1 mile (1.6km) wide, covering an area of around 600 acres. The Breton St Justinian built a cell on Ramsey in about AD500.

Round the headland, the path once again follows the cliff edge closely, passing ruined buildings as it heads northwards, and later the site of St Justinian's Chapel at Porthstinian. Apparently, the luckless saint was beheaded and then walked, headless, across Ramsey Sound to place his head on the spot where the chapel was built some 1,000 years later. A short way on, the lifeboat station at St Justinian dominates the coastline. It is in an important position, servicing a large area

From here a daily boat service connects Ramsey Island to the mainland, and visitors may make day trips to the RSPB Nature Reserve, where seals, whales and dolphins have been spotted basking in the waters, or simply tour around the island by boat. The island plays host to large numbers of deer, and at the southern end its cliffs and offshore stacks are nesting grounds for kittiwake, guillemot and razorbill, best viewed from the seaward side by boat.

Minor roads and tracks lead directly back to St David's from Maen Bachan, which is 2.5 miles (4km) from grid ref. SM 721 241, and from St Justinian, which is 2 miles (3km) from grid ref. SM 722 251.

POPULAR BEACH

The path past St Justinian runs perilously close to the cliff edge, and has been moved inland in places due to erosion and cliff-falls. Round Point St John, the path drops down to the delightful small beach of Porthselau, which serves the reasonably well-hidden caravan park on the hillside above. It then goes on to Whitesands Bay, which, after Newgale, is the largest beach along this stretch of the coastal path. With a huge expanse of sand backed by cliffs at either end, it faces westwards and is connected to St David's by the B4583, which makes it popular in summer, but not over-commercialized, nonetheless. Dogs are not allowed on to the beach in the main summer season. Just to the northeast of Whitesands, there is a small youth hostel at Llaethdy.

🔘 *Footpaths and minor roads run east and south from Llaethdy (grid ref. SM 739 271) back to St David's.*

STAGE 4

WHITESANDS BAY to TREFIN

DISTANCE 12 miles (19.3km)
MAP OS Explorer OL 35
START AT GRID REFERENCE SM 733 271
START POINT Whitesands Bay car park

From the Whitesands car park, the coast path continues northwards, gaining height and passing the beach at Porthmelgan, close to St David's Head. This is the last beach that is accessible from the land until Abereiddy Bay. Inland, the heather-covered headland is dominated by Carn Llidi; one of the Ordovician volcanic peaks of this wild area, which is mainly populated by seabirds, wild flowers, and other walkers. St David's Head sticks out to the west here, described by the ancient geographer Ptolemy as the Promontory of Eight Perils, because of its fatal attraction for early sail-powered ships, driven on to this unforgiving shore by relentless westerly winds. Here it is worth diverting off the coast path to follow a track on to the headland, where there is a stone barrier known as the Warrior's Dyke. The eight stone hut circles are among many prehistoric remains in this part of Pembrokeshire.

The route continues eastwards, following the cliff-tops all the way, with fine views along the coastline ahead. The path is a good way from the road here, with few connecting footpaths and little habitation apart from the occasional inland farm. Past the banks of the three Iron Age forts at Caerau, the path drops to sea level once again at west-facing Abereiddy Bay, popular with the more adventurous holidaymaker who is willing to go further afield. Back on the cliffs, on the north side of the beach, pass the remains of a slate quarry that was operational until 1901, with ruins of the quarrymen's row, engine house and dressing sheds. Most impressive is the flooded quarry, cut deep into the cliff-face of the headland. It is now known as The Blue Lagoon, with a deep entrance wide enough for a single boat. The stone tower above may have been built to aid navigation in the 18th century, and is a useful landmark for walkers today.

The next beach is Traeth Llyfn, accessible via a steep path. The coast path follows the cliff-tops until it descends steeply to Porthgain; an inlet with a fascinating small harbour, once busily engaged in the export of slates brought by tramway from Abereiddy. After 100 years or so, this trade ceased in 1931 and all that is left are the massive old brickworks and bins for the crushed stone. With a few fishing boats, a pub, an award-winning small restaurant and a green with picnic tables, Porthgain has a welcoming air today.

ⓘ **PLACES TO VISIT**

● ST DAVID'S
www.orielyparc.co.uk
☎ 01437 720392
The village-sized settlement of St David's is granted city status by way of its cathedral. It is named for the patron saint of Wales, St David, who founded a monastic order here in the 6th century. The city is a charming place to explore, and can be covered on foot in a couple of hours. The centre is marked by the 14th-century city cross, but the real landmark is the beautiful and imposing cathedral (www.stdavidscathedral.org.uk ☎ 01437 720202). The present cathedral dates back to the 12th century, though there is ongoing restoration. The relics of St David are to be found in the Holy Trinity Chapel. In medieval times, pilgrimages to St David's were of such importance that two such journeys were equivalent to one pilgrimage to Rome. Adjacent to the cathedral are the impressive remains of the Bishop's Palace (www.cadw.wales.gov.uk ☎ 01437 720517; open daily all year). The surviving sections date back to the 13th century and include a fine arcaded parapet. There is an on-site exhibition which explains the history of the wealthy and powerful medieval bishops, and the progression of the buildings.

● RAMSEY ISLAND
www.rspb.org.uk
☎ 07836 535733
This large island, just off the coast to the west of St David's, is an RSPB reserve. It is only accessible by boat between Easter and October, exclusively through Thousand Islands Expeditions (www.thousandislands.co.uk ☎ 01437 721721), who leave the St Justinians lifeboat station every day at 10am and 12noon. The cliffs around the island, at up to 396ft (120m), are home to guillemots, shags, buzzards and peregrines, to name a few. In autumn, grey seals breed on the beaches.

*TOP St Justinian near St David's, with Ramsey Island in the background
BOTTOM Wonderful scenery around Traeth Llyfn*

On the far side of the harbour, the coast path continues up past an old navigational tower, dropping to sea level once again at Aber Draw, where the path joins the road. Here the walker can continue downhill and uphill along the road into Trefin, or better, turn off to the left to rejoin the coast path by a rather untidy small bay, passing a row of painted cottages to reach the next headland. From here, a footpath heads inland to join a farm track which leads into Trefin. The path is fenced on both sides, but care needs to be taken to find it. If you go beyond the headland and start turning in towards the next bay at Pwll Olfa, you have gone too far. Trefin is an unexciting place to finish, but it has a pub, a camp site, and a hostel where you can break the journey. Alternatively, some walkers may prefer to stop at Porthgain or push on to equally picturesque Abercastle.

TREFIN TO GOODWICK

STAGE 5

TREFIN to PWLL DERI

DISTANCE 8.7 miles (14km)
MAP OS Explorer OL 35
START AT GRID REFERENCE SM 840 325
START POINT Trefin, on the coast road

To rejoin the coast path from Trefin, walk past the modern houses on the north side of the village, joining a fenced track that heads towards the cliffs. The route continues along a permitted path on the cliff-side with farmland inland, passing above the rocky bay of Pwll Llong, which can be reached by a steep path. It continues round the headland, where the fine peninsula of Pen Castell-coch is connected to the mainland, with views opening out all the way to Strumble Head.

Turning inland, the path joins steep steps, heading down the side of the inlet which leads to the small port of Abercastle. Just past the gate near the bottom, a signpost points to the Carreg Sampson cromlech, a short distance to the west. Dated at around 5,000 years old, it is considered one of the finest Neolithic burial chambers in Pembrokeshire, with a 16ft (5m) long capstone and six upright rocks. Abercastle is reminiscent of Porthgain, though it has neither pub nor restaurant. It was once a small port trading with Bristol and Liverpool, but now

the only trade there is that of a few fishing boats and fishing folk who congregate, as always, near the quay. Before you leave Abercastle, look out for the old cannons acting as bollards and the limekiln.

The path continues up the other side of the inlet behind an attractive cottage, passing a dangerously ruinous granary in a fine position, with a sign saying 'Keep Out!'. Going along a permitted path with fields inland, the route winds its way slowly above the inaccessible bays below, sometimes passing very close to the cliff edge. At Pwllstrodur it drops downhill to cross a stream by a small rocky cove, heading steeply uphill on the other side to continue round the next headland, past the Iron Age promontory fort of Castell-coch.

The path starts to head downhill towards Aber Mawr. Parts of the path were once so dangerous at this point that it had to be realigned, in the interests of public safety. The beach at Aber Mawr comes into sight, perhaps the most scenic of this walk, with perfect sets of waves rolling in from the northwest if there has been any wind. As they break, they polish the beautiful stones of the shorelines to rounded perfection; the flattest ones at the top of the pile providing a pleasant walking surface. Inland there is an unspoilt reed valley with woods beyond, which makes a pleasant change from the monotony of farmland and affords an excellent windbreak for a picnic. The beach itself is connected to the outside world via a dead-end road, but is sufficiently isolated to remain totally unspoilt. It is also considered the most important Ice Age site in Pembrokeshire, with the remains of a submerged coastal forest that can sometimes be seen beneath the sand at low tides.

🔲 *To return to Trefin, a walk of 3 miles (5km) from Aber Mawr, follow the bridleway at grid ref. SM 878 344, turning westwards inland of Mynydd Morfa, passing the farmstead at Carnachen-lwyd, and emerging on the road above Abercastle. The road then leads uphill to Trefin.*

At the far end of the beach the path joins the road, near a small white building which was the transatlantic submarine cable terminus. Either follow the coast round Pen Deudraeth, or continue along the road to a coastal path signpost pointing left. From here, the path continues above the storm beach of Aber Bach and on past the rock and sand bay at Pwllcrochan, which is inaccessible. This part of the coastline is very wild and lonely, and is therefore one of the best stretches to spot grey seals.

Keep dogs well away and never approach a seal yourself. Once a human has been close to a seal pup its mother may reject it. Seal Watch signs give emergency telephone numbers and explain what to do if a seal appears to be in difficulty. The cliffs have numerous seabird colonies, with guillemots and razorbills much in evidence.

As the path rounds Penbwchdy headland, the surroundings become rocky and wild. There is a convenient walled circular shelter here, although in westerly winds it is better to find a place on the leeward side of the rocks, beyond which there is a grandstand view over the inland plain. The coast path here is magnificently wild, with hard volcanic cliffs over 450ft (137m) high. A bench provides a convenient viewpoint for those who walk up the road from Pwll Deri.

The path joins the lonely road at Pwll Deri, and comes to the back of a youth hostel high up on a windswept hillside, with a view southwards that must rate as one of the finest in Britain. Despite the usual Spartan accommodation, this is an enviable place to stay. There is a memorial just near by to the Welsh poet Dewi Emrys, and behind the youth hostel is the dominating bulk of Garn Fawr, a most impressive hillfort.

STAGE 6

PWLL DERI to GOODWICK

DISTANCE 9.3 miles (15km)
MAP OS Explorer OL 35
START AT GRID REFERENCE SM 898 388
START POINT Pwll Deri, on a minor road 4 miles (6.5km) west of Goodwick

By the side of the youth hostel, the coast path goes downhill, passing the rocky outcrop of the fort Dinas Mawr, yet more evidence of the ancient Celts' extensive defence system. It can be reached by its own narrow track. The coast path continues through gorse and heather, winding high above Porth Maenmelyn and climbing on a crumbling path past a large, improbably sited house in the lee of the hillside to the right.

On the far headland there are the brick remains of ugly MoD buildings, which may have some use to walkers as shelter in wet weather, and then the path heads down and up through rounded hillocks of volcanic rock, passing the small, sheltered valley of Pwll Arian, or 'Silver Pool', on the way. The lighthouse at Strumble Head is in view along this stretch of the path, a handsome building in traditional, turn-of-the-century lighthouse style, with its piercing light flashing by day and night. It was built in 1908 on Ynys Meicel, one of a series of islets stretching westwards from Strumble Head. The path here joins the road, passing by a restored MoD building which is now mainly used by birdwatchers. Strumble Head is a breeding ground for herring gull and fulmar, though the principal interests are the the sighting of porpoises and the passage of seabirds from breeding sites such as Ramsey Island en route to Cardigan Bay to feed. During the breeding season, flocks of Manx shearwater can be seen going to and from these feeding areas.

REMOTE STRETCH

The final 6 miles (9.5km) from Strumble Head to Goodwick are along a remote stretch offering excellent walking, with the view ahead looking all the way to Cemaes Head; the final headland before the coast path ends at St Dogmaels. The ferry may sometimes be seen making its daily crossing between Goodwick and Rosslare in the Republic of Ireland, as the path passes above the bay of Porthsychan. At Penrhyn there is a tiny holiday cottage in an enviably remote situation, and then the path winds in and out along the cliff-tops, towards the extraordinary memorial stone above Carregwastad Point. This was erected in 1897, 100 years after the French invasion of 22 February 1797, when over 1,000 men came ashore here under the command of an American named Tate, bent on the destruction of far-off Liverpool! They surrendered without resistance on nearby Goodwick Sands, two days after landing.

Just past here the path dives down into a hidden wooded valley at Cwm Felin and then continues on to the headland of Pen Anglas, eventually joining a minor road leading into Goodwick. The hillside descent offers a fine view over the long Goodwick breakwater, with Fishguard beyond and the great mass of Dinas Head directly to the east, showing the route of the coast path continuing.

After the magnificent wildness of the coast path, arrival at Goodwick is something of a come-down. However, the town does have good public transport connections, and for those with the time and energy there are another 28 miles (45km) of mainly very wild coastal path before reaching its official terminus at St Dogmaels, near Cardigan.

ⓘ PLACES TO VISIT

• MELIN TREGWYNT
www.melintregwynt.co.uk
☎ 01348 891288
There has been a wool mill here for centuries, just a short walk from the coast path. In years gone by, farmers would bring their fleeces here to be washed in the stream and then processed by the mill that was powered by the same water. The water wheel is still turning and the mill is still working, though only weaving now (view the weaving Mon–Fri). The mill shop sells beautiful cushions, blankets and handbags created from the distinctive Tregwynt fabric. There is also a coffee shop, which serves home made snacks and light lunches made with local produce. Open daily all year.

• STRUMBLE HEAD
This headland is rounded by the coast path, so you are unlikely to miss it or the awesome views that are to be seen here. There is a whitewashed lighthouse on the small island of Ynys Meicel, just off the mainland and connected by a footbridge, but this is now unmanned and not open to the public. There is a small shelter here, converted from an old war building, where you may find one of the park ornithologists at work and wish to stay for a while to catch sight of the vast array of sea birds, or even a porpoise or seal.

• OCEAN LAB
www.ocean-lab.co.uk
☎ 01348 874737
At the end of this section of the route, the information centre in Goodwick Harbour gives children a place to let off some steam and adults a warm haven to relax with a drink. There is a soft play area, cyber café and hands-on displays and quizzes. There is also an exhibition by the Pembrokeshire National Park. Open daily all year.

ABOVE LEFT Penbwchdy at dusk
ABOVE Strumble Head lighthouse on the rocky cliff edge

Sirhowy Valley Walk

COMPLETE ROUTE NEWPORT TO TREDEGAR **26 MILES (42KM)**

SECTION COVERED AS ABOVE

MAPS OS EXPLORER OL 13, 152, 166, OS LANDRANGER 171

The Sirhowy Valley Walk is a walk of contrasts, leaving the built-up fringes of Newport to follow the Sirhowy Valley northwards towards the Brecon Beacons. There are many reminders of South Wales' mining communities and of its importance during the Industrial Revolution. Some parts of the route are extremely beautiful; others have been destroyed by man. A keen walker could cover the route in a taxing day, or it can be spread over two days to make a pleasant weekend's rambling. Some of the route follows high ground, and the normal precautions for hill-walking should be followed. Plan the route carefully, use the OS maps with a compass, and carry wet-weather gear. If the rain and mist come down it can be difficult to find the way off the hills.

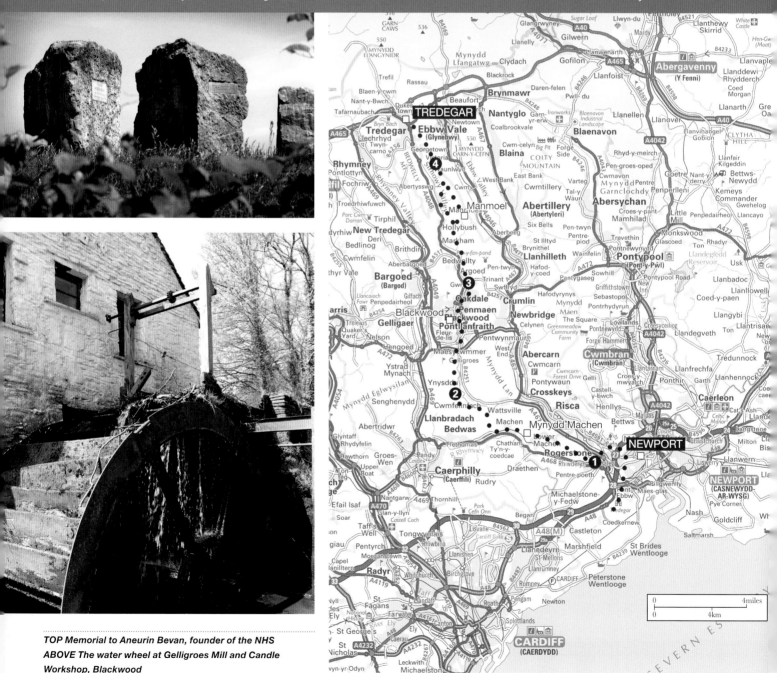

TOP *Memorial to Aneurin Bevan, founder of the NHS*
ABOVE *The water wheel at Gelligroes Mill and Candle Workshop, Blackwood*

ABOVE *Tredegar House is set in beautiful parkland* ABOVE RIGHT *Fourteen Locks Canal Centre*

NEWPORT TO TREDEGAR

STAGE 1
NEWPORT to MYNYDD MACHEN

DISTANCE 9.4 miles (15.1km)
MAPS OS Explorer 152, OS Landranger 171
START AT GRID REFERENCE ST 290 849
START POINT Tredegar House Country Park

Tredegar House is on the southwestern outskirts of Newport. If you have time, it is worth exploring the house and its grounds before beginning the walk. The start of the walk is signalled by an information board in the car park.

Signposting through the urban fringes of Newport is good. Despite the built-up nature of the surroundings, there are plenty of points of interest. The route crosses the Ebbw River on an old bridge by the early 19th-century Mill House, passing under the A48. A short way on it makes its way uphill through a large housing estate, where it is easy to miss the left turn that brings you to a gate, and a Sirhowy Valley signpost that leads on to open ground beneath the impressive Gaer Hill Iron Age fort. From the top there is a fine view, on a clear day, over Newport, Cardiff and the Severn Estuary on one side, and the mountains of the north on the other. A path leads steeply downhill towards the M4. At the bottom the route leads through the Coed Melyn Park, close to the motorway. It is easy to stray off course here and end up in a maze of suburban side roads. Going upwards through the park, the route leads to the top of the ridge aptly known as the Ridgeway, and at last, after at least an hour's walking, the built-up townscape is left behind and there is a fine view ahead over the area known locally as Little Switzerland.

The route continues downhill over farmland, crossing the Monmouth and Brecon Canal by an old bridge, and passing along the canalside through a tunnel which leads under the M4. As the motorway is at last left behind, the route follows the canal towpath to the northwest and becomes much more peaceful, passing the lock-keeper's house and going up by the side of an extraordinary series of 14 locks. A short way on is the Fourteen Locks Canal Centre.

TRULY RURAL

The route continues along the canal towpath, but then turns off to the southwest. It passes through Rogerstone by the Tredegar Arms public house, crosses the A467, and enters Ty Du Park, where the local cricket team plays on summer weekends. Three tall poplars lead the way to a metal bridge that crosses the River Ebbw, which is an impressive sight here when in full spate.

Truly rural from now on, the route heads uphill and skirts the village of Rhiwderin, going up across Fox Hill and into woods for a mile (1.6km) or so of easy walking through Coed Mawr. Coming out of these woods, the route joins a lane which turns into a track, leading uphill towards the radio mast on the top of Mynydd Machen. On the opposite side of the valley, the hillside town is Risca, originally a Roman settlement, which shot to prominence in the Industrial Revolution. Most of its industries are now dead.

Passing a small farmstead at Upper Ochrwyth, the track leads to a car park at the foot of Mynydd Machen, with fine crops of whinberries all around in the summer, which are picked by locals to make a deliciously sharp tart. It is a steep climb, indeed the hardest climb of the whole walk, to the trig point at 1,188ft (362m). From here there are fine views over a peaceful landscape, over the Severn Estuary towards England and north towards the Brecon Beacons.

🏠 *For an extensive circular walk of approximately 14 miles (22.5km), returning to Tredegar House from Mynydd Machen (grid ref. ST 223 900), footpaths lead downhill into Machen. From there, continue along the Rhymney Valley, where a footpath leads southeast across the river, through Park Wood and via Pye Corner. From there, a footpath leads directly back to Tredegar House.*

STAGE 2
MYNYDD MACHEN to BLACKWOOD

DISTANCE 7 miles (11.3km)
MAPS OS Explorer 152, 166
START AT GRID REFERENCE ST 232 898
START POINT Car park below Mynydd Machen

From the top of Mynydd Machen a track leads downhill to the northwest skirting a wide band of woodland. The route continues along a springy grass track, following the Rhymney Valley

ℹ️ **USEFUL INFORMATION**

THE ROUTE
• *www.caerphilly.gov.uk/ countryside*
☎ 01495 235219
Caerphilly County Borough Council promotes this route via the Countryside and Landscape Service. Click on the 'Walking' and 'Trails' tabs at this address to download leaflets of the route in five sections. Each contains a brief route description and an extract from the relevant OS mapping. This is also the website for Sirhowy Valley Country Park.

TOURIST INFORMATION CENTRES
• *www.newport.gov.uk*
John Frost Square, Newport NP20 1PA;
☎ 01633 842962
• *www.visitcaerphilly.com*
Visit Caerphilly Centre, The Twyn, Caerphilly CF83 1JL;
☎ 029 2088 0011
Although not on the route, this office covers the Sirhowy Valley.

PLANNING YOUR TRIP
• *www.ldwa.org.uk*
The Long Distance Walkers Association provides some detail on the SVW, and general advice on long-distance walking and other walks in the area.

OTHER PATHS
The long and mountainous Cambrian Way crosses the SVW on the Mynydd Machen ridge. From there it continues all the way to Conwy on the north coast. On the other side of Newport from Tredegar, at Caerleon, is the Usk Valley Walk (pages 108–111), which follows the river to Brecon. The Ebbw Valley Walk and Raven Walk are shorter local trails.

TOP Resting place of Welsh poet, Bard Islwyn, at Babel Chapel, Cwmfelinfach
ABOVE Gorgeous rural countryside at Cefn Manmoel

Ridgeway along the top of the hill. Close by to the left there is an enormous spoil tip from the Risca colliery, rapidly being covered by grass and undergrowth, and looking for all the world like a giant's burial mound.

By Pen-heol-Machen, the route leaves the track ahead and bears up the hill on a narrow path. Be careful to follow the yellow Sirhowy Valley waymarks here. For a time, the walk continues along the footpath (which eventually leads to Pontllanfraith), but then it bears off to the right and begins to zig-zag down the Graig Goch wooded hillside above the 1,000-acre Sirhowy Valley Country Park, where it joins a level forestry track. Here it heads downhill again to the Ynys Hywel Countryside Centre, passing a camping barn.

The centre is a welcoming place for a Sirhowy Valley walker, and the camping barn, magnificently positioned on the hillside, is used for residential courses, which must be booked in advance. A visit to the Islwyn Memorial Chapel, on the other side of the river in Cwmfelinfach, is recommended; built as a Calvinist Methodist Chapel in 1827, it is now a memorial to the 19th-century Welsh poet 'Islwyn', the Reverend William Thomas.

RADIO HAM

The route continues along a narrow track a short way down the hillside from the countryside centre, going steeply downhill to join a disused railway line. Originally built as the Sirhowy tramroad in 1805 to carry iron ore from Tredegar to Newport, it was soon replaced by the railway. The last train ran in 1960. The Sirhowy Valley route leaves the old railway line and heads

quite steeply uphill on an overgrown path. At the top of the hill the route goes in and out of woodland and across bracken-covered trails. The waymarking is not all it might be here, leading to navigation problems, which may be compounded by mist on the hills. The route eventually leads down the hillside to join a track by a secluded house on the outskirts of Wyllie. The route next crosses an old railway bridge, which was the scene of a famous incident in 1935: during the 'Stay Down' strike at nearby Nine Mile Point colliery, angry workers dropped a parapet stone on to a tram passing underneath.

The route follows a path by the side of the River Sirhowy, leading to the 16th-century watermill at Gelligroes. This was once owned by radio ham Arthur Moore, who picked up distress signals from the doomed ocean liner *Titanic* on 14 April 1912. Sadly, no one believed him, convinced the brand-new vessel was unsinkable.

For a return to Mynydd Machen, take the country lanes leading eastwards from Gelligroes (grid ref. ST 177 947), to the village of Mynyddislwyn, where a footpath leads east and south along the side of Mynydd y Lan towards Newtown and back to Mynydd Machen, a circular walk of around 13 miles (21km).

THE OLD TRAMROAD

From here the Sirhowy Valley Walk leaves the river to follow the lane which was once the Penllwyn tramroad. Never replaced by rail, it functioned until the 1870s. It continues by the side of the South Wales Switchgear factory, passing the old Greyhound pub on the outskirts of Blackwood; a meeting place for the Chartist political movement in the 1830s. The walk then rejoins the river as it passes through Blackwood.

STAGE 3
BLACKWOOD to MANMOEL
DISTANCE 5.6 miles (9km)

MAP OS Explorer 166

START AT GRID REFERENCE ST 178 960

START POINT The car park at the Islwyn Civic Centre in Blackwood

The route continues along a tarmac path by the side of the River Sirhowy, avoiding the town and leaving it by a park where it passes the Rock and Fountain Inn at a road crossing. This was originally the counting house for the Penllwyn tramroad. It continues along the line of the old tramroad but at the next road junction crosses the bridge in the valley and climbs uphill to the A4048. Opposite the Rock Country Inn it continues along another disused railway line. It served all the collieries in this part of the valley, the last of which closed in 1957.

Just by the overhead power cables a path leads downhill towards the river. Follow the path down to cross the river below the hamlet of Gwrhay, heading away from the riverside and joining a lane which heads uphill into open country, passing Pen Deri Farm on the right. A short way on, the road bends right, and the Sirhowy Valley Walk goes straight ahead down a rough track, passing the extensive disused mine-working of Llanover Colliery. At the bottom of the track there is an old railway line with sleepers and track still in place, passing close by some ruined buildings.

The route leads round the back of these buildings and away from the line, but it is easier and more pleasant to walk on the sleepers and follow the line straight ahead. It passes under and over a bridge, rejoining the official route, which then turns away from the line on a rough track that winds uphill with extensive forestry over to the right. Eventually it joins a tarmac lane, passing the farmstead of Twyn Gwyn on the left and then coming to a footpath on the right which leads across fields to Manmoel. Heading towards a solitary white cottage, it emerges at the road on a bend. The pub is down the lane straight ahead, opposite the tiny graveyard and chapel, but is often closed.

STAGE 4

MANMOEL to TREDEGAR

DISTANCE 6.1 miles (9.8km)

MAPS OS Explorer OL 13, 166

START AT GRID REFERENCE SO 179 033

START POINT The Manmoel Inn, in the village of Manmoel

Here there is a choice of two routes to take you to the finishing line. A 'short-cut' route covers just over 5 miles (8km) and keeps along the high ground. The longer route is 6 miles (9.5km) and involves a longish downhill stretch followed by a longish uphill one, but neither is very taxing and the latter seems much the better option.

The route divides at a crossroads on the western outskirts of Manmoel. Here the short route follows a lane northwards, linking with the longer route after a mile (1.6km) or so for the ridge walk along the top of Cefn Manmoel. The longer route joins a track which leads alongside the woodlands of Coed y Llanerch, before heading steeply downhill through the woodland, with fine views opening out of the valley to the left.

Near the bottom of the hill, the track bears left towards the farmstead at Pont Gwaithyrhaearn, in an area which was the site of much activity during the Industrial Revolution, though no sign of this remains today. Just before reaching the farm, the route turns uphill, crossing a stream and climbing on a track by the side of stone walls. It should come out on to common land near the top, but the route guide is hazy here and it is easy to stray too far to the east and start heading down into the neighbouring valley. The route joins the single lane road which runs along the top of Cefn Manmoel.

A return can be made to Manmoel via this road (which is the short-cut route), a distance of some 4 miles (6.5km), grid ref. SO 170 055.

NYE BEVAN REMEMBERED

Further on, the road deteriorates into a rough track as it heads north towards the Brecon Beacons. There are fine views over Tredegar to the northwest; a town which expanded rapidly when the Sirhowy Ironworks were established in 1778 to exploit the local coal and ironstone.

The route continues past the radio masts, above the forest on the left which surrounds Scotch Peter's Reservoir. It then runs along a lane towards Sirhowy, on the eastern outskirts of Tredegar. At the A4047 the end of the walk is marked on the other side of the road by the three immense Aneurin Bevan Memorial Stones. Aneurin ('Nye') Bevan represented the three principal towns of Ebbw Vale as a Member of Parliament for 30 years. He was born in Tredegar in 1897, and was one of the pioneers of the National Health Service.

i PLACES TO VISIT

• TREDEGAR HOUSE
www.newport.gov.uk/
tredegarhouse
☎ 01633 815880
This 17th-century mansion is set in beautiful parkland and is the home of the Morgan family. Tours of the house include both the state rooms and servants' quarters, such as the butler's pantry and the great kitchen. There were over 50 servants working at the house and in the gardens, so there are stories to hear, such as that of the annual Servant's Ball. There are walled gardens close to the house, in addition to tea rooms and some crafts workshops. The parkland includes woodland walks, a lake, and a playground. House open Wed–Sun Easter–Sep; park open daily all year.

• FOURTEEN LOCKS CANAL CENTRE
www.fourteenlocks.co.uk
☎ 01633 892167
The route passes close to this museum and visitor centre on the Monmouthshire and Brecon canal towpath. It has information on the building of the canal and the steep and long run of the nearby Cefn Flight of 14 locks, completed in 1799. It has small exhibitions of local artists' work, and a tea room. At 10am on the first Saturday of each month there is a guided walk starting at the centre. Open daily all year.

LEFT Memorial to 'Nye' Bevan, son of Tredegar

Usk Valley Walk

COMPLETE ROUTE BRECON TO CAERLEON **50 MILES (80KM)**

SECTION COVERED ABERGAVENNY TO CAERLEON **25 MILES (40KM)**

MAPS OS EXPLORER OL 12, OL 13, 152

The Usk Valley Walk originally linked Caerleon, on the eastern fringes of Newport, with Abergavenny, on the southern side of the Brecon Beacons. It was extended northwest to link with Brecon, in the heart of the Brecon Beacons National Park, following the route of the Monmouthshire and Brecon Canal and making the walk a full 50 miles (80km). The southern section is described here, as it follows the meanderings of the River Usk, which is not so well known as the neighbouring River Wye but no less beautiful. Like the Sirhowy Valley Walk (pages 104–107), the walk could be covered in a single day of around 12 hours' walking. Taken at a more relaxed pace over a couple of days, there would be time to look round Abergavenny, Usk and Caerleon.

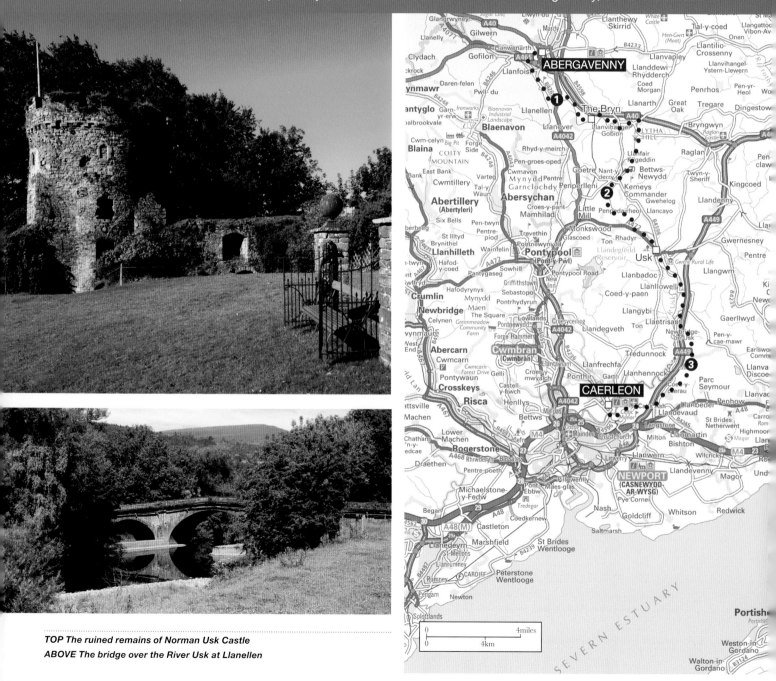

TOP *The ruined remains of Norman Usk Castle*

ABOVE *The bridge over the River Usk at Llanellen*

ABERGAVENNY TO CAERLEON

STAGE 1

ABERGAVENNY to THE BRYN

DISTANCE 6.3 miles (10.1km)

MAP OS Explorer OL 13

START AT GRID REFERENCE SO 291 139

START POINT Usk Bridge on the southwestern outskirts of Abergavenny

This section of the Usk Valley Walk appropriately starts from the fine road bridge that crosses the River Usk, looking back across meadows towards Abergavenny and its 14th-century castle. At first the route heads westwards on a track on the south side of the river, past a cemetery. It heads left, passing under the A465 Heads of the Valley Road, and skirting the village of Llanfoist. It then follows a track that leads uphill to the Monmouthshire and Brecon Canal.

The canal was originally built between 1797 and 1812, in order to connect the industrial southern parts of Gwent and the docklands of Newport with the farming country in the north. In more recent times, 33 miles (53km) of its length have been restored to make it one of Britain's most attractive cruising waterways. The towpath can be followed as a footpath along most of its length. However, while the northern part of the Usk Valley Walk keeps to the canal almost all the way to Brecon, the southern part follows it for only a couple of miles (3km) before leaving it to join the River Usk.

The turn-off from the canal towpath is not well signposted, but is marked by a bridge and a gate. The footpath heads downhill across a field towards the village of Llanellen, and the route then passes through a modern housing estate towards the conspicuous church spire. Passing by the side of the churchyard, it joins the main A4042 road close by the Llanellen Bridge over the Usk. The bridge needs to be crossed with care as there is no pavement, and then the route heads over fields, through a kissing gate. This cuts a corner of the Usk before coming close to the bank once again by a fine house known as Great Hardwick.

ALONG THE RIVERBANK

From here the route follows a path in a pretty riverside setting, though some of the path can be severely overgrown and is uneven underfoot. Further on, past a small area of woodland, it passes the farmstead of Glan-Usk on the opposite bank,

ABOVE A gate beside the charming River Usk, near the start of the walk at Abergavenny

crossing open pastureland close by Castle Arnold; a mound on the hillside that is all that remains of the fortified home of the Welsh kings of Over Gwent. It was burnt to the ground by William de Braose on Christmas Day 1177.

Notwithstanding its grim past, the river here is very lovely, being tranquil, wide and at the same time obviously very powerful. Sadly, the effect is to some extent spoilt by the noise of the nearby A40 dual carriageway. The route continues to follow the riverbank with open fields on both sides, passing a small settlement on a river bend at Llanover, close by Cwrt Porth-hir, with a characterful church and private footbridge. It then passes beneath the railway near the small village known as The Bryn, where St Cadoc's Church boasts a Norman tower, nave and chancel. Two hundred years ago the river flowed right past this church, but its meanderings have now taken it some distance away.

From The Bryn (grid ref. SO 332 099), there are two optional return routes to Abergavenny. You can follow footpaths northwards towards the conical-shaped hill known as Ysgyryd Fach or Little Skirrid (grid ref. SO 316 137). Unfortunately, tree-cover rules out all hope of fine views from the summit. From here, waymarked paths lead down to the centre of Abergavenny, a circular walk of approximately 8 miles (13km).

STAGE 2

THE BRYN to USK

DISTANCE 9.8 miles (15.8km)

MAPS OS Explorer OL 13, 152

START AT GRID REFERENCE SO 332 099

START POINT The Bryn, on the A40, 3 miles (5km) south of Abergavenny

From The Bryn, the River Usk wiggles its way through quiet countryside, with the route pursuing a straighter course across fields towards the Pant-y-Goitre bridge. The waymarks need to

LEFT The Norman tower of St Cadoc's Church at the tiny village of The Bryn

ⓘ USEFUL INFORMATION

THE ROUTE
• www.uskvalleywalk.org.uk
Although promoted by the Usk Valley Partnership (the Brecon Beacons National Park, British Waterways and Monmouthshire CC), this website is the primary portal for the UVW. It gives information on the valley itself, the path, and walker-friendly accommodation. The Usk Valley Walk Official Route Guide can be bought at tourist information centres and local bookshops.

TOURIST INFORMATION CENTRES
• www.breconbeacons.org
Abergavenny TIC and National Park Centre, Swan Meadow, Monmouth Road, Abergavenny NP7 5HL; ☎ 01873 853254
• www.newport.gov.uk
5 High Street, Caerleon NP18 1AE; ☎ 01633 422656

PLANNING YOUR TRIP
• www.ldwa.org.uk
The Long Distance Walkers Association has some detail and links for the UVW, including the interactive map of linking trails.
• www.ramblers.org.uk
☎ 020 7339 8500
The Ramblers Association website has general information about long-distance walking and some help covering the UVW, such as public transport details.

OTHER PATHS
The Cambrian Way goes through Abergavenny on its long route from Cardiff to Conwy, on the north coast. Following the CW in places, but easier in some sections, is the Beacon's Way, which traverses the Black Mountains, Brecon Beacons and Black Mountain, from Abergavenny to Llangadog. From the UVW terminus at Brecon, the Taff Trail crosses the Brecon Beacons to Merthyr Tydfil and follows the Taff valley to Cardiff.

be followed carefully here as the river goes out of sight by trees, with the route passing a modern barn conversion to the left, near Manor House Farm. The fine-looking mansion of Pant-y-Goitre House now comes into view. This neo-classical, 18th-century building is on the opposite riverbank.

The footpath comes to the splendid Pant-y-Goitre bridge, turning left crossing the B4598 and following an indistinct path along the side of a field towards a farmhouse. From here the route follows a quiet road for about 0.5 miles (800m), coming close to the noisy A40 for the last time before bearing right on to an overgrown track beside a bus shelter. This joins a path which follows the River Usk south.

Along this stretch the river is frequently obscured by trees and bushes. On the left side is Clytha Park (occasionally open to the public); an early 19th-century, neo-classical mansion faced in mellow Bath stone. Further on, hidden in the wooded hillsides above, is Clytha Castle. This building is actually a romantic crenellated folly that was built by William Jones, owner of Clytha Park, in memory of his wife in 1790. The route here follows the edge of fields, before the path climbs high above the river, passing through a delightful farmyard by Trostrey Lodge. Near by are the remains of a medieval forge on the hillside below. It once made use of local charcoal supplies and harnessed the power of the River Usk, which swirls down through rapids at this point.

Dropping down towards the river once again, the walk route continues across parkland in front of an imposing 1920s house. A mile (1.6km) or so to the east is the Iron Age hill fort of Coed-y-Bwnydd, dated to around 400BC and accessible from the riverside via a series of footpaths. For a time, the path becomes slightly hard-going along the side of a hill between woods and a field, and then it plunges into the woods to join a lane to the west of Bettws Newydd, dropping down to cross the river by the old Chain Bridge. Here, it turns left on to a minor road and continuing on the west side of the river.

To return to The Bryn, leave the UVW at the Chain Bridge (grid ref. SO 347 056) and continue west along the lane towards Nant-y-Derry. Turn off on to a bridleway/footpath that leads northwards to Highmead, joining the road by Pant-y-Goitre, and then following a footpath eastwards from the Pant-y-Goitre bridge along the south side of the Usk. Finally, cross at the railway bridge to return to The Bryn.

THE OLDEST ROCKS IN GWENT

The route turns left by the side of the first house up this minor road, leading along a grassy gated track and passing a modern farmhouse. This emerges at a magnificent sweeping field, with the wooded hillside of Craig yr Harris on the right and the river to the left.

The route leads through the trees, and on to high ground with fine views across the plain, looking over the strangely named Kemeys Commander. Dropping downhill on to an overgrown trail, it passes a well-hidden pumping station. This is said to stand on the oldest rocks in Gwent, some 430 million years old. Just past here the route crosses a track, turning right on to an indistinct path with a waymark that is easily missed. This heads out across open fields as the river winds away to the east, going up and downhill to join a quiet lane a short way from Estavarney Farm. The land here was worked by Cistercian monks between the 13th and 15th centuries. A short way on, look out for a pair of fine ornamental iron gates.

Just past here the lane bears right downhill, and the route joins a track going straight ahead uphill on the left side. Crossing fields, it passes by the side of a thick belt of trees with the River Usk far below on the left side, while on the right an enormous field slopes down to the distant A472 in the valley, with Usk College of Agriculture coming into sight ahead. Keeping by the side of the woods, the footpath emerges on to a lane by an electricity sub-station. Here the route turns left towards the river, passing by a small estate of houses and coming to Prioress Mill. This was originally the site of a 16th-century watermill used for grinding corn, but it is now used for residential purposes, and the route as has annoyingly been diverted away from the river. Instead it crosses fields, eventually rejoining the river by the Berthin Brook.

From here it is a pleasant riverside walk towards the town of Usk, passing through a preserved wildlife area and on into recreational parkland known as the 'Island' picnic site. Ahead

ABOVE The walk makes use of glorious woodland paths
RIGHT The imposing gateway to Clytha Park

you will see the road bridge that leads visitors into this attractive and historic small town, with the river flowing cleanly below on its southbound way.

STAGE 3
USK to CAERLEON

DISTANCE 10.6 miles (17km)
MAP OS Explorer 152
START AT GRID REFERENCE SO 374 007
START POINT The Usk Bridge, Usk

Usk is a small town with a castle and a museum, well worth exploring. Sadly, from here on the footpath seldom comes right alongside the river until it reaches the finish at Caerleon.

Leave Usk by New Market Street and Mill Street Industrial Estate, then join a path across fields, with the River Usk on your right. There is then a long 1.5-mile (2.5km) stretch along a country lane going southwards, which comes to the outskirts of the hamlet of Llanllowell. The road bends left to cross a bridge over a tributary of the Usk, then the route follows a footpath on to a wooded track which bears right downhill. This leads on across peaceful meadows, hemmed in by trees on the east side and with the river itself close by to the right. Passing to the left of a large public works building, the path bears left to cross a stream and joins the road at Llantrisant, where the church nestles in a very attractive setting.

Go through the village, passing under the A449, and then follow the path onto Cefn Hill, turning south and then descending to Llwynau Farm. The route then passes under the A449, turns left and left again, back under the dual carriageway.

To return to Usk from here (grid ref. ST 390 949), turn off across the fields to the village of Newbridge on Usk. Cross the river here, and then follow footpaths and lanes northwards via Llangybi, to Llanbadoc and Usk.

CHARMING RUIN

After passing under the A449 for the second time, turn right on a lane running parallel to the A449 and after 0.5 miles (800m) a great surprise is in store, as the route heads steeply up the hillside to pass Bertholey House. This is a wonderful ruin in a magnificent position. The views to the north are tremendous, looking over the Usk as far as Abergavenny with the Brecon Beacons beyond. The house itself was built around 1830 and burnt down by an accidental fire in 1905, becoming a charming and tragic ruin.

From here the path continues upwards, heading diagonally up an extremely steep field beneath the forestry of Bertholey Craig. The views from here are the best of the whole walk, making this a magnificent place to stop for a well-earned break. The route then heads on into the woods, breaking into the open on a hard forestry track running between uniform lines of plantation trees.

The woodland walk which follows via Kemeys Craig bound for Caerleon is something over 2 miles (3km), heading south-west. It starts well enough, but after a time the main forestry track disappears and the route continues along a path likely to be well laced with nettles and brambles in summer, and very muddy after rainfall. Worse, the A449 seems to become positively deafening, though one can never really see it. The only consolation comes from finding the occasional wild raspberry plant fruiting in July, until at last the path comes out of the woods on a narrow lane above Cat's Ash.

A short way along the road here, a narrow, stony and sometimes muddy track leads down to the hamlet of Cat's Ash. From there the route crosses the A449, going on for a mile (1.6km) or so along Chepstow Hill which, despite being on a road, offers relatively quiet walking. The final section of the route leads across fields via Cock-y-North Farm and downhill to the river, along the Bulmore Road. The finish is by the Ship Inn on the banks of the Usk. By this stage the river has lost much of its charm and your best bet is to cross the bridge and explore the old town of Caerleon or hop on a bus for Newport.

PLACES TO VISIT
• CAERLEON
The town of Caerleon is the site of the legendary Roman fortress of Isca, home to a Roman legion in around AD75. It was one of only three permanent fortresses in Britain. On the western edge of town are the separate and open sites of the remains of a barracks and an amphitheatre. Cadw also runs the Fortress Baths building, which allows the visitor to view the remains of the baths from an elevated walkway, and describes the original buildings and rituals (www.cadw.wales.gov.uk ☎ 01633 422518; open daily all year). Also near by is the National Roman Legion Museum, which is free to enter (www.museumwales.ac.uk ☎ 01633 423134; open daily all year). In addition to many Roman artefacts and replicas of armour, there is a reconstructed barracks room and a beautiful Roman garden. A Heritage Trail through the town can either be purchased at the Caerleon TIC, close to the two museums, or downloaded free of charge from www.caerleon.net

• USK RURAL LIFE MUSEUM
www.uskmuseum.org.uk ☎ 01291 673777
Within the historic town of Usk you will not only find the pretty remains of a medieval castle, but also this interesting museum. It displays all manner of artefacts from agricultural life, from tools and tractors to a life-size milkable cow. There is also a reconstructed farm kitchen and dairy, and an interactive model railway. Open daily Apr–Oct.

TOP Perfect walking country
LEFT AND ABOVE Aspects
of 12th-century Usk Castle

Ross-on-Wye seen across the river at dusk, with the spire of St Mary's Church jutting into the skyline

Wye Valley Walk

COMPLETE ROUTE CHEPSTOW TO RHYD-Y-BENWCH, POWYS **138 MILES (222KM)**

SECTION COVERED CHEPSTOW TO HAY-ON-WYE **75 MILES (121KM)**

MAPS OS EXPLORER OL 13, OL 14, 188, 189, 200, 201, 202, 203, 214

The southern section of the Wye Valley Walk traverses mainly English soil, passing through the heart of the Wye Valley Area of Outstanding Natural Beauty. The lower Wye Valley, between Chepstow and Monmouth, is perhaps the better-known section of the route, as it parallels the most southerly part of the Offa's Dyke Path on the opposite side of the valley. The middle and upper sections, while less well frequented, are, however, equally charming and offer a splendid introduction to old Herefordshire. While the Wye Valley Walk can, of course, be walked in either direction, there is a stronger feeling of adventure and prospect when walking the route northwards, from Chepstow to the river's source.

CHEPSTOW TO MONMOUTH

ABOVE The River Wye flows through a steeply wooded valley at Symonds Yat, along the England/Wales border area known as the Marches

STAGE 1

CHEPSTOW to TINTERN
DISTANCE 6.2 miles (10km)
MAP OS Explorer OL 14
START AT GRID REFERENCE ST 534 941
START POINT Chepstow Castle

The riverside town of Chepstow (or in Welsh, Cas-Gwent) owes its existence primarily to its role as an early market town at a crossing-point on the tidal River Wye. It was the power-seeking Norman Marcher lords who brought military significance to the settlement when they set about building a castle of enormous proportions on the Welsh banks of the river, and a wall around the town. In later centuries, Chepstow flourished as the town became known as an importer of wines and yew, and an exporter of wood products. Trade waned during the last century and in recent decades Chepstow has settled into the ways of a dormitory town, although it still retains considerable character and spirit of independence.

The Wye Valley Walk starts from Chepstow Castle, climbing through a delightful dell into Welsh Street. There is a tedious ten-minute walk up to a school and leisure centre, where the path is coralled and littered, to Alcove wood. The walk leads through the old Piercefield estate woodland, laid out for leisure purposes by Valentine Morris in the 18th century before his money ran out. The path keeps close to Chepstow racecourse, well-known for its National Hunt and flat racing meetings, as it continues to curve left above Piercefield cliffs and beyond to Giant's Cave. The name of the cave has given rise to all manner of yarns, mostly spurious. Judging by the dimensions of the cavern, the giant must have been very cramped. The route proceeds to Lover's Leap and other such locations befitting the romantic walks devised for visitors 200 years or so ago. There are also views, between the tree cover, across a large loop in the Wye, to the ancient church at Lancaut.

The path climbs up to picnic tables between tall beech trees by the A466. Cross here with extreme caution and proceed up an access track to another car park in what was an old limestone working; one of many such small workings in this area. The way is marked either to the left, for those who seek the easiest ascent of Wyndcliff, or to the right, up the 365 steps. This is far more of an adventure, even if negotiated at a steady pace. The path narrows and swerves left, soon to climb the stone steps originally built in 1828 and restored by army recruits in the early 1970s. The woodland is a remnant of a forest neither planted nor much-husbanded by humans through the centuries, despite its becoming a tourist attraction in the 19th century.

INSPIRATIONAL TINTERN

Climb to a viewpoint known as The Eagle's Nest and pause for breath. The ascent is something in the order of 700ft (213m). Here there are exceptional views down the Wye to cliffs named Wintour's Leap, after Sir John Wintour, a Royalist who escaped capture by the Parliamentarians by scrambling down the cliffs.

The going is easier, however, to Tintern. The path progresses through the appropriately named Minepit and Black Cliff woods, eventually emerging into a field which links the walk to Limekiln wood, where an old packhorse way, beautifully cool in summer, leads into Tintern opposite Tintern Abbey. It was in these environs that William Wordsworth, in 1788, wrote some of his loveliest lines. His contemporary, JMW Turner, captured the romantic dream of the abbey in a painting which is now in the Victoria and Albert Museum. The scene is almost the same today, and a visit to the abbey is obligatory.

Some walkers may want to catch the local bus back into Chepstow from this point (grid ref. SO 533 001), or make their way back along the other side of the valley using Offa's Dyke Path. This is a walk of approximately 7 miles (11.3km). From the abbey, walk into the village and, by an imaginatively restored abbey quay and mill, bear right across the old railway bridge (grid ref. SO 528 003). The path leads up the gorge to meet the national trail, where the walker bears right for Chepstow.

STAGE 2

TINTERN to MONMOUTH
DISTANCE 11.6 miles (18.7km)
MAPS OS Explorer OL 14, 167
START AT GRID REFERENCE SO 532 001
START POINT Tintern Abbey

The walk bears right from the abbey, through the village and between inns, guesthouses and shops, to cut off right, opposite

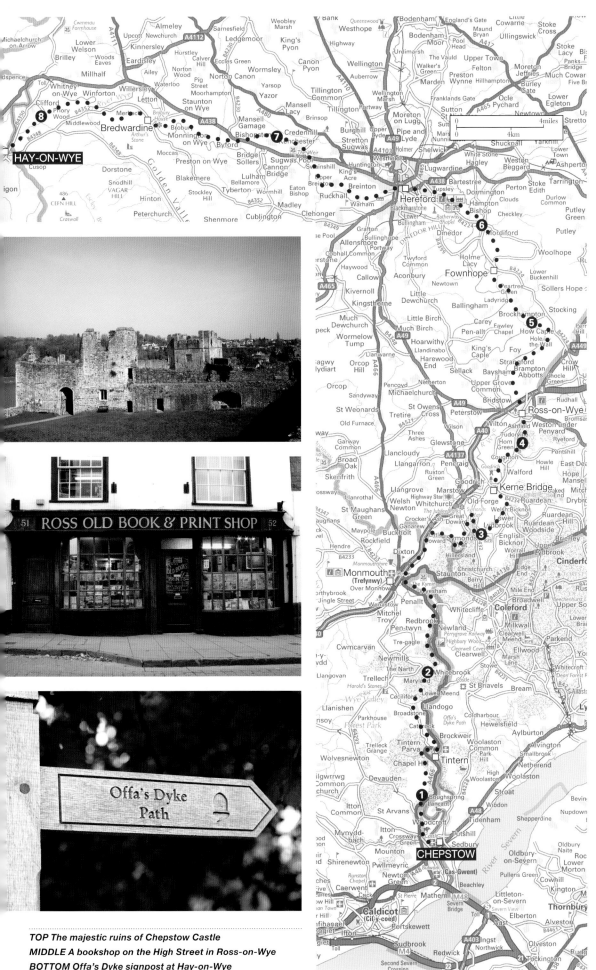

USEFUL INFORMATION

THE ROUTE
• www.wyevalleywalk.org
The Wye Valley Walk Partnership promotes this route and provides all the information you could possibly need via this website. There is also an official guide, which is available to purchase by post, and a scheme of passport stamps to collect along the way.

TOURIST INFORMATION CENTRES
• www.visitwyevalley.com
Chepstow TIC: Castle Car Park, Bridge Street NP16 5EY;
☎ 01291 623772
Monmouth TIC: Market Hall, Priory Street NP25 3XA;
☎ 01600 713899
• www.visitherefordshire.com
Ross-on-Wye TIC: Edde Cross Street HR9 7BZ;
☎ 01989 562768
Hereford TIC: 1 King Street HR4 9BW;
☎ 01432 268430
Hay-on-Wye TIC: Oxford Road HR3 5DG;
☎ 01497 820144

PLANNING YOUR TRIP
• www.wyevalleyaonb.org.uk
Here you will find all manner of information on the Wye Valley Area of Outstanding Natural Beauty, which the WVW runs through for half of this section.
• www.ldwa.org.uk
The Long Distance Walkers Association has some detail and links for the WVW, including the interactive map of linking trails.
• www.ramblers.org.uk
☎ 020 7339 8500
The Ramblers Association website has general information about long-distance walking and specific help covering the WVW, such as transport details and guide books.
• www.yha.org.uk
☎ 0800 019 1700
The Youth Hostel Association has a few sites close to the WVW.

OTHER PATHS
The Offa's Dyke Path, one of three national trails in Wales, also starts near Chepstow but takes the opposite side of the river (the east bank) to Monmouth. It crosses the WVW again at Hay-on-Wye.

TOP The majestic ruins of Chepstow Castle
MIDDLE A bookshop on the High Street in Ross-on-Wye
BOTTOM Offa's Dyke signpost at Hay-on-Wye

The Wye Valley Hotel. It passes between houses and to Tintern Church before following the river for a short stretch to the old trackbed of the Monmouth–Chepstow railway. It was built in 1876 with great expectations on the part of the shareholders but survived less than 100 years. It is hard to imagine that Tintern was at one time the centre of a 16th-century iron-working business, some remains still being visible in the Angiddy Brook area. It was also the first place in Britain to mould brass objects.

The path leads to the restored Victorian Tintern railway station and onwards to the village of Brockweir, where the path climbs up an embankment to the bridge. It is worth stepping across the bridge to Brockweir, at one time an ancient ferry point. It was also one of the main transhipment points for goods brought upstream on the tide by cargo vessels known as trows, to be transferred at the old quay to much smaller, flat-bottomed boats heading upstream or to carts for overland journeys. The quayside, pottery, glassworks and Brockweir Country Inn are all worthy of exploration.

The route crosses the A466 and enters woodland once again, up a steep zig-zag path to Coed Beddick plantation and on to Botany Bay, another reflection of the maritime influence of the Wye on these parts. The path exits on to a metalled road by a large house, only to leave it almost immediately by a camping ground and activity centre; one of many which have grown up in these parts in recent years. The path descends to another road and then climbs up to the Whitestone picnic area, where there are toilets, children's play amenities and picnic tables provided by the Forestry Commission. The path continues through commercial woodland of mainly larch and spruce, above Cleddon Shoots nature reserve and the village of Llandogo below. The walk then rises up through the woods to cross a lane by Orchard Cottage.

A long detour can be made by turning left here to the village of Trellech, to see the three standing stones known as the Harold Stones. There can be no plausible connection with King Harold. They may be Bronze Age

marker stones, indicating an important overland route. The village also has a long standing well, Virtuous Well, which draws from several chalybeate springs. The church dates mainly from medieval times or possibly earlier.

The Wye Valley Walk can be regained by following Greenway Lane out of the village, then a bridleway through the wooded Trelleck Common, going ahead at the road and then right, down the Whitebrook valley.

There are buses back from Trellech to Monmouth or Chepstow, Monday to Saturday.

WORKING MILLS

The main route continues onwards at Orchard Cottage, as signposted, to Pen-y-fan. This next section is particularly pleasant in spring, when bluebells and primroses are out and maybe even the rare Tintern spurge may be spotted.

Once through Cuckoo Wood, the path emerges on to a narrow lane. Be careful to follow the waymarks through the isolated hamlet of Pen-y-fan, threaded as it is with lanes. The descent to Whitebrook, where there were once several working mills, brings the path back to a metalled road, where a right turn is made for the short ramble down to the dismantled railway track on the left. Follow this along a narrow and pretty part of the lower Wye valley up to Redbrook, to go by the friendly Boat Inn and then over the footbridge to the village. This was once a nucleus of industrial activity with a brewery, several mills and a foundry. At the main road turn left, passing the garage and café/restaurant before rejoining the riverbank once again for the final 2.5 miles (4km) to the Wye Bridge at Monmouth. Monmouth is the birthplace of Henry V and was home to such famous and disparate characters as the valiant Lord Nelson and the industrious Charles Rolls, co-founder of the Rolls-Royce corporation. Standing at the confluence of the Wye and Monnow Rivers, the town dates back to Roman times but gained its strategic position in early medieval days, when a castle and other fortifications were built (including the impressive Monnow Gateway, which can be seen at the far end of Monnow Street).

Monmouth is not quite the market town it used to be, but it has a lively atmosphere on Fridays and Saturdays, when the market stalls are set out in Agincourt Square, which is very much the heart of the town.

ABOVE A sure sign of spring, bluebells are prevalent in the woods towards Pen-y-fan
RIGHT The Monnow bridge is a fortified Norman bridge spanning the River Monnow

The imposing ruins of 11th-century Goodrich Castle

MONMOUTH TO ROSS-ON-WYE

STAGE 3
MONMOUTH to KERNE BRIDGE

DISTANCE 12.9 miles (20.8km)
MAP OS Explorer OL 14
START AT GRID REFERENCE SO 511 127
START POINT The Wye Bridge

At Monmouth the walker rejoins the Wye at the Wye Bridge, dropping down to the left by a boathouse and towards Dixton Church. The walk then passes through a succession of riverside meadows, sandwiched between the main A40 road and the river itself. Care should be taken, as in places the riverbank has been heavily eroded.

After 2 miles (3km) the road rises and diverts to the left while the river bends eastwards into a deep and ancient landscape. Here, the River Wye has cut a channel between the high hills of Little and Great Doward on the one side and The Slaughter on the other.

The area contains many reminders of early cave dwellers who inhabited the higher reaches of these hillsides. King Arthur's and Merlin's caves, for example, are estimated to date from Bronze Age times and bones of long-extinct wild animals have been found during early excavations of the latter. These are now preserved in the City Museum in Hereford. The cave names derive, so local folklore has it, from the prolific writings of 12th-century chronicler Geoffrey of Monmouth, who is said to have assembled the King Arthur legends when at Monmouth Priory. It has even been suggested that the Arthurian treasure is buried in these parts.

Pass Wyastone Leys House, in the near distance on the left, and then join a wooded section beneath Seven Sisters Rocks. Continue through to meadows leading to The Biblins, where there is a suspension bridge built by the Forestry Commission. Cross the river to the Forest of Dean side of the Wye.

Those seeking a circular route of approx 7.5 miles (12km) to and from Monmouth, can leave the walk at The Biblins (grid ref. SO 549 144). Return by way of Lady Park Wood, beneath Far Hearkening rocks to Hadnock, and by metalled road to the Wye Bridge at Monmouth.

PEREGRINE FALCONS

The Wye Valley Walk rejoins the old track of the railway from Monmouth to Ross-on-Wye beneath The Slaughter. The name is the subject of some speculation, not in that it suggests a battle in previous times, but as to which battle. Some antiquarians suggest it was Caractacus's last stand against the Romans, others that it was the scene of a bloody battle between the Saxons and the Danes.

The path enters Symonds Yat East near the Saracen's Head public house, where a rare river chain ferry can be hailed to Symonds Yat West for a short diversion to other inns, shops and attractions. In fact, Symonds Yat is the most commercialized tourist location on the route. There is a very steep path leading up from Symonds Yat East to Yat Rock, which is a well-known and often extremely busy viewpoint. The views over Herefordshire are exceptional. There are also toilets and refreshments.

Follow the Wye Valley Walk along the riverbank to reach the upper ferry, which serves Ye Old Ferrie Inn at Symonds Yat West. The path dovetails back to a metalled road and soon begins to skirt the lower wooded slopes of Huntsham Hill. It then passes beneath Coldwell Rocks. Peregrine falcons nest here every year, and they may also be seen over Coppet Hill, in the near distance. Once again, the path joins the old railway route near the river and then moves closer to the riverbank, heading for the old works at Lydbrook before crossing the river by way of the disused railway bridge. Bearing right, the route passes below the youth hostel at Welsh Bicknor, which was once a rectory to the isolated church near by.

A good circular walk of approx 2.5 miles (4km) from Symonds Yat follows the Wye Valley Walk to Welsh Bicknor (grid ref. SO 587 177) and returns along the opposite bank to Huntisham Bridge, beneath Coppet Hill. The path passes near to a sad family monument to a boy drowned hereabouts in 1804. Bear left over Huntisham Bridge to walk along a fairly busy road for a mile (1.6km) back to Symonds Yat.

WALES & THE MARCHES • WYE VALLEY WALK

TOP Walkers on the path to Goodrich Castle
MIDDLE LEFT Ross-on-Wye
MIDDLE RIGHT Kerne Bridge
ABOVE LEFT St Mary's Churchyard at Fownhope
ABOVE RIGHT Market Hall with clock tower in Ross-on-Wye

DISTANCE 5 miles (8km)
MAPS OS Explorer OL 14, 189
START AT GRID REFERENCE SO 582 188
START POINT Car park at Kerne Bridge

The walk out of Kerne Bridge is a steep one and the way is easily missed. From the car park, cross the B4234 road to the left of Lumleys Guest House. Turn right into the steep lane and then immediately left up a driveway between cottages. The track continues to wind its way up Leys Hill, crossing others, until it eventually bears left into woodland and descends towards Walford. Before it reaches the village it climbs away again up to Bull's Hill, on to a metalled road. This goes left and soon right by houses, along a path leading up to the road at Howie Hill. Look for a track that climbs the edge of the hill, although the walk itself shortly bears left, to descend to farm buildings in Coughton.

Coughton is situated in a deep valley which at one time would have been a large loop of the Wye, but is now drained by a small tributary brook. The walk leaves farm buildings to climb through fields to Chase Hill and wood, where the overgrown ramparts of an Iron Age hill fort remain. It passes by Hill Farm and then sweeps down from Penyard Hill to pass Alton Court, now the home of a major activity holiday company, to Penyard Lane. Look carefully for the yellow arrows guiding the walker through the back of Ross-on-Wye to the main car park by Wilton Bridge, a 16th-century structure that (with some restoration) has weathered many a flood.

Many walkers will want to bear right, however, at Prospect Walk, laid out by 17th-century philanthropist John Kyrle, who gave so much to the town and became known as 'The Man of Ross'. This leads to the commanding Ross Church, with its plague cross near by, and to the town centre, nestled around the 17th-century Market House.

ROSS-ON-WYE TO HEREFORD

STAGE 5
ROSS-ON-WYE to FOWNHOPE
DISTANCE 11.3 miles (18.2km)
MAPS OS Explorer OL 14, 189
START AT GRID REFERENCE SO 592 239
START POINT The main car park before the Wilton Bridge, on the B4260

The route leaves the car park by way of a short underpass to join the riverside, a popular spot for canoeists, fishermen and strollers. The walk soon leaves town to pass beneath the 20th-century portals of the A40 main road, shortly joining the old track bed of the Hereford–Gloucester railway line; a much-loved rural railway which failed to survive the Beeching closures in the 1960s. The landscape is flatter here, with large fields of cereal crops, potatoes or oil seed rape. A little further on, the walk pulls away to the right, to skirt a loop of the river at Backney Common where, evidently, the commoners still have the right to remove gravel from the riverbank. The route then follows a contour line above the flood plain to join a metalled road. Here, the walker bears left towards the hamlet of Hole-in-the-Wall, where there is a children's residential activity centre. It is thought that some of the buildings in this area were built from the masonry of an early castle, now completely dismantled. A suspension bridge links the hamlet to Foy Church, on the opposite bank, which dates mainly from the 11th century and is worth the short diversion.

FAMOUS PASSENGER
Once more the walk secures a position alongside the tranquil and relatively unpolluted River Wye, a favourite with fishermen in search of trout, salmon and chub. The path follows the riverbank beneath steep, wooded slopes to Kerne Bridge, which dates from 1828. Before this time there was a ferry a short distance upstream. One famous passenger was Henry IV on his way up from Monmouth. He was met at this point by a breathless messenger who had ridden hard to catch the monarch to announce the birth of his son, Harry of Monmouth, the future King Henry V. The king was so elated that he generously presented the ferry and all the revenues to be made from it to the overawed ferryman.

To the left of the bridge is the site of Flanesford Priory, the ruins having been cleverly incorporated into attractive holiday apartments adjacent to Flanesford Farm. Beyond stand the gaunt, red sandstone towers and facade of Goodrich Castle, still impressive and mighty today.

The castle is one of many fortresses peppering this area, which reflects the trouble and violence in this turbulent border zone known as the Marches.

STAGE 4
KERNE BRIDGE to ROSS-ON-WYE

To return to Ross-on-Wye, cross the suspension bridge (grid ref. SO 605 284), turn left to Foy Church and then on to Backney Common, Bridstow and Wilton Castle. It is mainly on roads. The circular walk is approximately 8 miles (13km) in all.

PLEASANT ROAD WALKING

This section of the walk offers very pleasant road-walking, with wide green verges leading down to the riverbank. The path cuts off left after 1.5 miles (2.5km), before a cattle grid, to rejoin a path through fields to the sleepy hamlet of How Caple. Bear left on the metalled road. The interesting old manor house of How Caple Court, now privately owned, lies off to the right. Turn right again after a few paces, to join a bridleway to Totnor, a small settlement gathered around a mill on a brook. The way is to the left, along a metalled road, before shortly turning left along a bridleway through rich arable farmland to Brinkley Hill and on, past Capler Lodge, to Capler Wood and the ramparts of an Iron Age hill fort of the same name. The walk then descends by Caplor Farm to join the B4224. Bear left for a short distance, then climb once again into the rich and undulating farmland of the Woolhope Dome, through Lea and Paget Woods.

The walk then continues to Common Hill by way of a green track, across a metalled road and shortly left on another series of tracks to Nupend Farm. Near by is a nature reserve and an unusual monument to son of Fownhope and one-time prize boxer, Tom Spring, who fought his way through to the English championship in the early 1820s, before retiring to become landlord of Booth Hall public house in Hereford. Just before Nupend Farm the walk meets the Fownhope–Woolhope road. Fownhope is 0.5 miles (800m) away to the left. The agricultural community here also engaged in bark stripping for tanning purposes. The bark was despatched by boat on the River Wye and several lanes lead down from the village to the riverside, where there also used to be local ferries to Ballingham.

STAGE 6

FOWNHOPE to HEREFORD

DISTANCE 7.2 miles (11.6km)
MAP OS Explorer 189
START AT GRID REFERENCE SO 577 344
START POINT Fownhope village, at the crossroads

Fownhope lies just off the Wye Valley Walk but is an excellent place for access, accommodation and refreshment. Walk the short distance from the village centre, along the road signposted to Woolhope at the crossroads near The Greenman Inn. As the road bends right, 0.5 miles (800m) along it, look for the Wye Valley Walk waymark directing the walker to the left by Nupend Farm. The path rises gently through rich farming country, in a very quiet part of the Woolhope Dome, to isolated cottages and then follows a bridleway down to the large farm at Hope Springs. Once through the farm buildings, bear left to the clustered houses of Bagpipers Tump and then go between orchards to pass by a mill in the village of Mordiford. The village was at one time a hive of local industry, with tanning and milling near by. As at Fownhope, the river was an important means of distributing goods, and research suggests that the River Lugg was also used for navigation purposes, possibly as far as Leominster, although it is difficult to see how, even when the river is full.

The Wye Valley Walk crosses the road and uses old back lanes through to the bridge at Mordiford. Those seeking refreshment should turn right to visit the Moon Inn at Mordiford and muse awhile about the legend of the Mordiford dragon, a people-eating monster who was killed by a cunning convict fighting for a pardon. He hid in a cider barrel and when the dragon came for its habitual drink, the criminal dealt it a deadly blow with an arrow through an opening. However, the dragon breathed one last revengeful blast of fire at him before expiring!

Mordiford Bridge, overlooked by the parish church, is thought to be the oldest bridge for miles around, with a part of one 14th-century arch still remaining. A mile (1.6km) from here, on slopes reaching to the Woolhopes, is the impressive Sufton Court, set in parkland landscaped by Humphrey Repton. Alongside is Old Sufton, a manor farm which illustrates additional building through the ages. There is a splendidly restored 18th-century dovecote near to it. Unfortunately, none of these buildings is open to the public on a regular basis.

From Mordiford Bridge (grid ref. SO 568 375), there is an excellent circular walk via the village of Clouds, approximately 1.5 miles (2.5km) back northeast, waymarked throughout as 'The Mordiford Loop' and offers a morning or an afternoon's exploration of the Woolhope Dome.

ⓘ PLACES TO VISIT

• MONMOUTH CASTLE AND REGIMENTAL MUSEUM
www.monmouthcastlemuseum.org.uk
☎ 01600 772175
Since the walk passes through Monmouth it is worth visiting the castle remains, behind the shops and attractive Agincourt Square. There is little left of the castle now, which was the birthplace of Henry V, so the free Castle and Regimental Museum next door offers extra interest. It tells the story of the local Royal Engineers regiment, and the Militia system from which they evolved. There is also a small medieval herb garden. Open afternoons only, daily Apr–Oct.

• SYMONDS YAT WEST
www.wyedeantourism.co.uk
While the east side of the river is tranquil, beneath the pretty viewpoint of Yat Rock itself, the west side of the river is a little louder. Take the ferry across to experience a number of tourist attractions. The Symonds Yat West Leisure Park includes a traditional fairground and amusement arcades, in addition to river cruises on the Wye (*www.symondsyatleisure.co.uk* ☎ 01600 890350; open daily all year, fair and cruises Apr–Oct only). Next door is the Amazing Hedge Puzzle (*www.mazes.co.uk* ☎ 01600 890360; open daily all year), featuring the Jubilee Maze; an octagonal hedge maze over 6.5ft (2m) high. Closer to the A40 is the Wye Valley Butterfly Zoo (*www.butterflyzoo.co.uk* ☎ 01600 890360; open daily all year), where you can walk amongst all manner of exotic butterflies.

• GOODRICH CASTLE
www.english-heritage.org.uk
☎ 01600 890538
Although ruined, this sandstone fortress still has an imposing air; high above the Wye and bounded by a dry moat. Peer through arrow slits at the view. Open daily Apr–Oct, Wed–Sun Nov–Mar.

LEFT The tomb of Elizabeth Denton, who died in childbirth, depicted with her husband Alexander and their child alongside, is one of the most memorable tombs in Hereford Cathedral

WALES & THE MARCHES • WYE VALLEY WALK

HAMPTON BISHOP

At the far end of Mordiford Bridge, the walk bears right to follow the flood levee, or embankment, to the edge of Hampton Bishop, a village with several listed half-timbered houses and a delightful church, dating mainly from the 12th and 14th centuries. The path joins a track on the left, which meets a metalled road. Turn right here and walk through the village, until a path is joined on the right to cut across a pasture to the B4224 road near the Bunch of Carrots pub. Almost opposite is another path which leads up to another levee known as the Stanx, this time protecting farms from the Wye at times of flood (although it failed to do this during the floods of 1960 and had to be reinforced). The route leaves this to follow the riverbank for a short distance before sweeping back to the main road on the outskirts of Hereford.

The Wye Valley Walk bears left along the B4224 to descend towards the city, passing by an old established pub, the Salmon Inn. Once under the railway bridge, the walk route bears left down to Hereford and on to the edge of the Castle Green. Those diverting into the centre of Hereford to take advantage of the facilities should turn right here and then shortly bear left to pass by the Castle Pool and into St Owen's Street, which leads to the commercial heart of the city. The Wye Valley Walk, however, bears left down to the Victoria suspension bridge over the Wye. Turn right on the opposite side and walk through the Bishop's Meadows to come out on to the old Wye Bridge.

HEREFORD TO HAY-ON-WYE

STAGE 7

HEREFORD to BREDWARDINE

DISTANCE 14.7 miles (23.6km)

MAPS OS Explorer OL 13, 189, 201, 202

START AT GRID REFERENCE SO 508 395

START POINT The A49 Wye Bridge in Hereford

The Wye Valley Walk sets out from Hereford unceremoniously beneath the new Wye Bridge and along a well-used riverside route towards Hunderton. Here the walk crosses a path known as Marches Way; an unofficial borderland trail between Chester and Cardiff. At the old railway bridge, climb up the steps and cross over the bridge to drop down the embankment on to the opposite side of the river. Rejoin a riverside path by playing fields and pass the distinctive brick tower of Herefordshire Waterworks Museum on the right. The path soon leads into open countryside for a walk of a mile (1.6km) to the very rural hamlet of Lower Breinton, where the National Trust now owns a moated site thought to date from the 12th century. Adjacent is Breinton Church, dating from a similar period but much restored in the mid-19th century.

For a short circular walk out of Hereford to Lower Breinton, it is possible to return from Breinton Church (grid ref. 472 395) along quiet back lanes to Broomy Hill and the city.

ROMAN TOWN

Walk through the National Trust car park and look for a path on the left that cuts through an orchard, across an access road and by a house. The walk bears left through fields to a metalled road at Upper Breinton. Go right, and then left at the junction. The Wye Valley Walk then follows a track by Manor House Farm on the left, which soon peters out into a path over fields to Breinton Common. Here, it becomes an enclosed lane again and comes out by houses and bungalows on to a metalled road.

Turn right here and follow this quiet road to the A438, where the walk bears left to pass by the former Kite's Nest Inn, now the Basmati Restaurant. Continue along this main road and at the next main junction turn right along quieter lanes, to walk through the hamlet of Kenchester, site of the Roman town Magnis. Remains of mosaic floors and other artifacts have been found and are now in the Hereford City Museum. The walk follows a Roman road through the village of Bishopstone to a crossroads, continuing ahead past farms on the Garnons estate. Once again, the parkland is the work of Humphrey Repton. The road bears left beyond Home Farm to meet the A438 once more and then turns right for a short distance before turning left into Byford, a hamlet of half-timbered cottages with a pretty church.

TOP Hereford Cathedral viewed across the River Wye
MIDDLE Stanbury Chapel inside Hereford Cathedral
ABOVE Herefordshire is known for its plentiful orchards
RIGHT Arthur's Stone in the Golden Valley
FAR RIGHT Canoeing on the River Wye

It is possible to shorten the Hereford–Bredwardine section of the route by catching a bus out to Byford or back from there, but this requires careful planning as the service is very limited. Some walkers might prefer to catch a bus to Byford and then walk through to Hay-on-Wye.

ARTHUR'S STONE

Bear right after the church to follow a bridleway through acres of cider apple orchards cultivated by the world's largest cider maker, HP Bulmer. Information boards welcome the walker and explain modern cultivation of cider apples. The bridleway leads into the churchyard of Monnington Church and Court, the latter dating mainly from the 17th century but having some remnants of 13th- and 15th-century building. It is not open to the public on a regular basis. One previous dwelling on this site is said to have been the last home of the exiled medieval Welsh Nationalist leader, Owain Glyndwr. This may have been possible, given that several of his daughters had settled in these parts but whether he lived here or not cannot be substantiated. The woodwork of the church is exceptional and is probably the craftsmanship of John Abel, King's Carpenter to Charles I. He was also a capable designer, and historians suggest that he was architect of several major half-timbered buildings in the county. He is buried in Sarnesfield churchyard, a few miles away. Locals say that his tomb bears an inscription that he carved himself, aged 90.

Follow the green swathe of path to a metalled road. Here, bear left and then right to join the 1-mile (1.6km) avenue, Monnington Walk, between specially planted Scots pine and yews, and probably the best surviving example in Britain. It ends at a metalled road at Brobury Scar. Bear left and left again at the next junction, to drop down to redbrick Bredwardine Bridge where, on the other side, a little link path cuts off left through the old castle ramparts to Bredwardine parish church. This is the resting place of famous 19th-century diarist, Reverend Francis Kilvert, who unfortunately succumbed to peritonitis on returning home from his honeymoon, at the age of 38. He described life in Victorian times at nearby Clyro and here with such skill that his diary is rated as a minor classic. Some of his diaries were destroyed by his wife as they contained references to their courtship, and most of the remainder were disposed of by a descendant who felt that some of the entries were of dubious moral standard.

The walk follows the church drive into the village centre, to pass to the right of the Red Lion Hotel. There is a strenuous circular walk from Bredwardine, climbing Merbach Hill, then bearing left for Arthur's Stone, a Neolithic burial mound, before returning on roads to Bredwardine.

STAGE 8
BREDWARDINE to HAY-ON-WYE
DISTANCE 9.1 miles (14.6km)
MAPS OS Explorer OL 13, 201
START AT GRID REFERENCE SO 331 445
START POINT The Red Lion Hotel, Bredwardine

RURAL RAILWAY

The climbing really begins at Bredwardine, for within a mile (1.6km) or you reach the highest point of the route, Merbach Hill. Standing at over 1,040ft (317m), it offers views for many miles around. The road out of Bredwardine, to the right of the Red Lion Hotel, becomes very steep. At the top of the first bank look out for an access road off to the right, the direction of the walk. Beyond the cottage, however, it climbs to the left, up to Woolla Farm beyond, to an isolated barn.

The path soon reaches a bracken-clad hillside, where the walker has to bear right and very shortly left. This clear path leads to the right of the summit of Merbach Hill, but many walkers divert to the triangulation point to pause awhile, especially on a summer's eve when the sun is setting over the Wye below.

The path drops down to a lane which bears right near Croft Farm. This leads to the main B4352 road at Clock Mills. The walk turns left and, at Clock Mills Bridge, bears right to skirt Clock Mills and Castleton Farms before joining the old track bed of the Golden Valley Railway; a very rural railway which survived until 1950, despite making chronic losses throughout its existence. At the time, however, before the advent of the bus and car, it was a lifeline to the community.

This soon brings the walker to a metalled narrow road where the walk bears left up to Priory Wood, an isolated and scattered hamlet named after a former Cluniac priory. Within 0.25 miles (400m) the walk cuts left up a path to a small common between roads. It then bears right on the higher road and, at the austere-looking chapel, cuts left across a paddock to another metalled road.

Turn left to walk a few paces down to a junction, and then walk along a narrow path adjacent to houses to pass by Priory Farm and on to another metalled road. The walk turns left, but look for a stile very shortly on the right. This leads through fields first above the Hardwicke Brook, then cross it and onwards towards Hay-on-Wye. It crosses a metalled road by a bungalow and then goes forward to reach another stile, leading to the Dulas Brook and into Wales, although the route from Bredwardine feels distinctly Welsh in its entirety. This is the heart of the Marches, where England meets Wales, and where culture and custom change quite noticeably within a few short miles.

The path dips down to a ford and then rises up to a field. The walker heads slightly left here to the left of a house. The walk dips down to a bridge and up to a narrow road leading into Hay-on-Wye by way of Heol-y-Dwr. Continue left at The Old Black Lion to Oxford Road, and right for Tourist Information and buses to Hereford and Brecon.

Hay-on-Wye, famous for its annual literary festival, held each June, has a number of local walks as well as being the meeting point of Offa's Dyke Path national trail. It is an excellent place to finish the walk.

ABOVE An open-air book sale taking place outside Hay-on-Wye Castle

Cley Mill, one of Norfolk's many windmills at Cley next the Sea

CENTRAL ENGLAND & EAST ANGLIA

Staffordshire Way

COMPLETE ROUTE MOW COP TO KINVER EDGE **92 MILES (148KM)**
SECTION COVERED MOW COP TO ABBOTS BROMLEY **44 MILES (71KM)**
MAPS OS EXPLORER OL 24, 218, 219, 242, 244, 258, 259, 268

Among the many delights of the Staffordshire Way, not least is the sheer variety of countryside it passes through, a spectrum which few of the long-distance paths can hope to match. From the tough and demanding gritstone hills in the north, affording truly magnificent views across England, the route passes through wooded valleys, by river, lake and canal, through quiet and beautiful nature reserves, across ancient pastureland and through seas of corn and plough. It is almost as though it is attempting to show the walker as many aspects of English scenery as possible along its length.

TOP Rushton Spencer, amid gently sloping hills
ABOVE The ancient Abbots Bromley Horn Dance is held annually on Wakes Monday

MOW COP TO KINGSLEY

STAGE 1

MOW COP to RUDYARD

DISTANCE 12.8 miles (20.6km)
MAPS OS Explorer 244, 258, 268
START AT GRID REFERENCE SJ 857 572
START POINT The car park at Mow Cop

The first section of the route, between Mow Cop and The Cloud, is also known as the Mow Cop Trail, and is waymarked by arrows with the letter M. It basically follows the boundary between Cheshire and Staffordshire, straying into each of the counties in turn. Mow Cop Castle is a very early example of a folly, built in 1754 by Randle Wilbraham, to be admired from nearby Rode Hall. Mow Cop is also the birthplace of the Primitive Methodist movement, founded at the beginning of the 19th century by Hugh Bourne, a carpenter, and William Clowes, a potter, who organized open-air meetings here. The local types of stone, millstone grit and whetstone, have both proved valuable in the past for a variety of industrial uses. There are magnificent all-round views from the trig. point (1099ft/335m) above the Old Man of Mow, as the pillar of rock that survived the quarrying all around it is called. Indeed this part of the Staffordshire Way is hardly short on views, demonstrated by the walk along Congleton Edge on path and road. This gritstone ridge is the western boundary of the Pennines, and on a clear day it is possible to see right over Cheshire, and as far as Merseyside and the Welsh mountains. After the viewpoint at Cheshire's Close, the road swings to the left and the route continues straight ahead along Edge Hill, through Willocks Wood, and descending to Nick i' th' Hill after 0.5 miles (800m).

A circular walk of 6 miles (9.5km) back to Mow Cop may be taken from Nick i' th' Hill. Leave the route at grid ref. SJ 876 599, taking lanes and footpaths to Gillow Heath. Follow the lane to Towerhill Farm, turn right, take the second footpath on your left, and turn right along the road for the short distance back to Mow Cop.

APPROACHING THE CLOUD

From Nick i' th' Hill, the route now descends via Whitemore Farm to the disued railway which runs parallel to the A527. The track crosses the main road after 0.75 miles (1.25km), and then crosses Reade's Lane. The path leaves the railway after another 0.25 miles (400m) and approaches The Cloud by a series of footpaths and charmingly named lanes: Brook, Weathercock, Acorn and Gosberryhole. Just before the plantation on The Cloud itself (the trees obscure the remains of an Iron Age hill fort, while a short distance to the south, at Bridestones, there is an impressive Neolithic burial chamber), bear left where the paths divide and make for the 1,125ft (343m) summit, where once again the views are superb. To the northwest can be seen the giant reflector of the Jodrell Bank radio telescope.

From The Cloud, take the southeasterly path downhill to the road to Ravensclough Farm and then down through beautiful Ravensclough Wood, over the stream and across the water meadows in the valley of the River Dane, until the path joins the southerly route of the now-dismantled Churnet Valley Railway. Past Rushton Spencer and to the right, a footpath leads to the charming little church of St Lawrence, standing by itself in the fields, with its weatherboard bell-turret. It dates from the late 17th century.

The route then leads to Rudyard Reservoir, passing it by on the west side. The lake was created in 1831 to supply the Caldon Canal to its south and has become not only a famous

Mow Cop with its ruined castle, a folly built in 1754

beauty spot but also a favourite place for sailors and water sports enthusiasts. Walkers are well catered for too, there being a 5-mile (8km) circular walk around its shores. The writer Rudyard Kipling was named after the lake, where his parents met for the first time in 1863. His father, John Lockwood Kipling, was an architectural sculptor who had a hand in designing the Wedgwood Memorial Institute in Burslem. The potter Josiah Wedgwood founded the famous firm that still bears his name (the Wedgwood Visitor Centre at Barlaston is well worth a visit) and the influence of the family is everywhere in these parts. Half-way along the lake, indeed, the path passes by Cliffe Park Hall, an interesting gothic house built for the Wedgwood family in about 1830.

At the southern end of the lake the path becomes a track giving access to various houses. Turn right into Lake Road and then turn left after 100yds (90m) at the footpath sign, down the path to the dam. Continue right, along the canal feeder, emerging on to Rudyard Road at Rudyard village.

STAGE 2

RUDYARD to KINGSLEY

DISTANCE 10.7 miles (17.2km)
MAPS OS Explorer 244, 258, 259, 268
START AT GRID REFERENCE SJ 955 578
START POINT From the more southerly of the two car parks at Rudyard, just off the B5331

The next section of the Staffordshire Way is, for the most part, very easy walking, with rises and falls at both ends, and extremely enjoyable. From the B5331 the route follows the canal feeder past delightful meadows and the twin nature reserves of Cowhay and Longsdon Woods. The path can be muddy at certain times of the year. Harracles Hall, a Georgian home of the Wedgwood family, is situated to the northeast of Cowhay Wood. Just to the east is the town of Leek. Leek is an ancient settlement which became increasingly industrialized from the 18th century onwards but has managed to remain a reasonably sized market town, enhanced by the fine country around it. The canal engineer James Brindley started out as a millwright here.

Just before the A53 the path crosses the feeder and continues up through the southern tip of Longsdon Wood, past some cottages, left along the lane, left along the A53 for a short distance, and right into Mollatts Wood Road. It then continues down past Hollinhay Wood, on to the road at Horse Bridge, across the Leek Arm canal bridge, over the railway bridge and down on to the Caldon Canal at the next bridge, turning left (east) along the towpath.

For a circular walk of some 10 miles (16km) back to Rudyard, leave the prescribed route at grid ref. SJ 964 548, continuing straight across the lane on the footpath, rather than turning left towards the A53. Turn right on to the A53 when the footpath ends, continue over the crossroads and take the footpath to your right, past the church. Continue to Bradshaw then follow the footpaths in a northeasterly direction back to the canal feeder, where you turn left back to Rudyard.

ALONG THE TOWPATH

The route itself continues along the canal, perhaps the most interesting part of the route. The Caldon Canal runs for 17.5 miles (28km) between Etruria, the site of the factory opened by Josiah Wedgwood in 1769, and Froghall. The Staffordshire Way takes in some 5 miles (8km) of this. Near Horse Bridge is the very attractive Deep Hayes Country Park, which offers circular walks.

After a mile (1.6km) along the towpath, the walker comes to Cheddleton Flint Mill, now a museum of great interest. The Red Lion public house is just across the canal in Cheddleton. From the mill, the walker passes two locks and so comes to Basford Bridge, where the Churnet Valley Railway joins the route of the canal. Various industries once existed along the canal here, all now defunct, including many limekilns in the hillside.

In another mile (1.6km), the route passes a restored, wooden drawbridge, and then the canal falls to the same level as the River Churnet at Oakmeadow Ford Lock. Beyond is the site where the iron from nearby foundries was once forged, and up to 2000 men are thought to have worked in the valley. There is a tremendous atmosphere of history here, and it is quite easy to close one's eyes and imagine the scene of activity and noise that would once have held sway. The canal, river and railway lie alongside each other at the Black Lion Inn. A good footpath crosses the valley at this point. Consall Nature Park, with its visitor centre, is near by.

The towpath continues past Consall New Lock, across a 'trickle ridge', where the water flows across the towpath, between Booth's and Hazles Woods, and so to Cherryeye Bridge. Here the Staffordshire Way at last leaves the canal, ascending the side of the valley steeply via path and steps, past a falconry to the fields above Banks Lane. The path then crosses the fields towards the village of Kingsley.

KINGSLEY TO ABBOTS BROMLEY

STAGE 3

KINGSLEY to ROCESTER
DISTANCE 9.4 miles (15.1km)
MAP OS Explorer 259
START AT GRID REFERENCE SK 014 469
START POINT The war memorial on the A52, Kingsley

From Kingsley, the route continues towards the smaller settlement of Kingsley Holt to the southwest, crossing a recreation ground and some fields and heading for the landmark of the tower of the Methodist Church. Cross the A521, turn right for a few steps, and turn through a stile on your left. The path now leads down through ancient pasture land, past Hag Wood and Lockwood Waste, to the Churnet valley.

Near here a circular walk of about 5 miles (8km) can be taken back to Kingsley. Leave the prescribed route at grid ref. SK 032 455, and double back along the footpath to cross the River Churnet at Ross Bridge, then taking the footpath and lane to Eavesford. Cross the railway and river at Winston Bridge, and follow the footpaths through Bauktop and the northern end of Kingsley Holt back to Kingsley.

NATURE RESERVE

The Staffordshire Way itself follows the Churnet for a short while and then leads over a stile and up a bank. Note the series of large stones standing in the line of hawthorn trees on the other side of the river. The route makes for a stone post near the river, through a stile beyond it and so into Hawksmoor Nature Reserve and to East Wall Farm. Avoiding going through the farm itself, and keeping to its right by two stiles, the Staffordshire Way joins the track leading to Hawksmoor, taking the right-hand fork when the track divides. The Hawksmoor Reserve's 250 acres is owned by the National Trust and has many interesting species of flora and fauna. There are several nature trails to follow.

The route passes between Hayes and Hawksmoor Woods, coming out on the road by Hawksmoor Cottage, leading left along the road for a short while and then turning off right at the footpath sign. After an uphill stretch of 100yds (90m), take the right fork and descend steeply between Sutton's and Lightoaks Woods. Oakamoor is to the northeast, at the centre of one of the most thickly and variedly forested districts in the county. It seems incredible that this area was once the site of a huge copper works, which badly polluted the area in the middle of the last century until it closed down in 1962.

At Stoney Dale, the route turns right and then left, and so continues into Ousal Dale. Dimmingsdale Youth Hostel is close at hand for those wishing to break the journey. At the far end of the pond is a disused mill. Built in the mid-18th century, it originally smelted lead ore from Ecton, and it then became a corn-grinding mill. There was once quite a little community living around it in the dale. The path comes out on the road at the Ramblers Retreat café and then runs parallel with, and then follows, the road to Alton. It eventually dives off at the footpath sign marked 'Alton 0.5 mile', climbing steeply through the wood, under a crag and so to the marvellous viewpoint of Toothill Rock. Go back through the stile and into Alton.

TOURIST ATTRACTION

Alton is a village of great interest. St Peter's Church, the Old Coffee Tavern, and the rare Italianate design by HA Hunt for the old station (North Staffordshire Railway) are all worthy of inspection. So too, of course, are Alton Castle and the Hospital of St John; the work of the great Victorian Roman Catholic architect AWN Pugin, on the site of a medieval castle. Across the river, also partly by Pugin for the Earls of Shrewsbury, is the massive shell of Alton Towers, whose pleasure ground and gardens are now one of the biggest tourist attractions in the country. As you leave Alton through the fields, the sounds of the largely unseen rides and crowds sound almost ghostly.

The Way threads through the village and then heads into the country again down Saltersford Lane. This ancient track was once part of a saltway used to bring salt to the Midlands from Cheshire by packhorse. The Staffordshire Way skirts Denstone via Quixhill Bridge, then goes south along the Churnet, over the junction of the B5031 and B5030, and into the village of Rocester.

TOP A rushing stream in Consall Nature Park
MIDDLE Consall Station on the Caldon Canal
ABOVE The Pugin-designed St Giles' Church, at Cheadle

STAGE 4
ROCESTER to ABBOTS BROMLEY

DISTANCE 12.1 miles/19.5km

MAPS OS Explorer 244, 259

START AT GRID REFERENCE SK 109 393

START POINT The car park in Rocester

Rocester was appropriated by the great Victorian lady novelist George Eliot, whose real name was Mary Anne Evans, as the setting for her novel *Adam Bede*, published in 1859. She renamed it 'Rosseter'. Rocester was originally a Roman settlement on the old Roman road of Ryknild Street, which ran from Derby to Chesterton and possibly into Lancashire. The old Roman fort lay in the area near the church.

The route runs through the town past Tutbury Mill, across the bridge over the River Dove, and then through a stile. It continues across three fields bordering the river, and through the left of two stiles in the field corner. It follows the track bordering Abbotsholme School playing fields and on past Sedsall Rough, Sedsall Farm, Eaton Dovedale Farm and so to Eaton Hall Farm.

At this point, a circular walk of some 8 miles (13km) may be taken back to Rocester. Leave the prescribed route at Eaton Hall Farm (grid ref. SK 106 363), turning right (west) along the track, which first crosses the county border back into Staffordshire and then the River Dove. Turn right at the footpath which leads to the B5030 at Brookend. Turn right on to the road and then right again along the footpath that heads back to the B5030 at the lakeside on the outskirts of Rocester.

INTO DERBYSHIRE

The stretch of the Staffordshire Way east of the Dove is firmly in Derbyshire, the river forming the county boundary. The noise of shotguns will here assail the ears, as members of the Doveridge Clay Sports Club fire at clay pigeons. Walk through the club car park, up the track, turn right along the field edge and so eventually downhill and across the water meadow to Dove Bridge. Near by is the pretty village of Doveridge, with its fine church. Dove Bridge itself dates from the 14th century and brings the walker back into Staffordshire. Cross the A50 and turn right. Go to your left after 200yds (183m) through a metal gate into a field. Pass to the left of the electricity pylon to the kissing-gate at the corner of the field, go over a stile and turn right towards the farm buildings. Go right along the farm track for a few yards and then through a stile on your left. Cross this field and the next, then cross the

disused railway line. The track to your right soon joins Brookside Road, near Uttoxeter Station.

Uttoxeter is a thriving town, complete with livestock market and racecourse, at the heart of a part of the country that has long been renowned for its dairy farming. The town has experienced two disastrous fires in the past, in 1596 and 1672. In 1642, during the English Civil War, Prince Rupert also torched the houses of certain civilians who would not join the king's cause. The tower of St Mary's Church, however, survived all these trials and tribulations. It was built by Henry Yevele, architect of the naves of Westminster Abbey and Canterbury Cathedral, and son of an Uttoxeter couple. In the market place is a monument marking the spot where Dr Johnson paid penance for his boyhood sin of refusing to help his father with his bookstall by standing for a long time bare-headed in the rain.

The Staffordshire Way now crosses the railway bridge, passes through a stile on the right, climbs the bank into Bank Close, turns left into Leighton Road and right into West Hill. It then continues straight ahead past Field Head, Knightsfield and Knightsland Farms, continuing then past Hanging Wicket Farm, across Scounslow Green and so down the track through Marlpit House Farm and into Bagot's Park.

Bagot Forest is just about all that remains of the old royal forest of Needwood, and wild fallow deer are still to be seen here. It was also, from as long ago as the 13th century, the site of furnaces for the making of glass. It is named after the ancient Staffordshire family of Bagot, still resident at nearby turreted and battlemented Blithfield Hall. The Staffordshire Way passes through the 815 acres of Bagot's Park, following for some distance the line of the Story Brook, before zig-zagging its path south towards Abbots Bromley. It enters the village by a housing estate, Swan Lane, and Schoolhouse Lane, finally ending in the town's market place.

Abbots Bromley is a splendid place to end the walk. It is famous for its annual Horn Dance, performed in September, in which villagers dance around the village bearing six sets of reindeer horns, dating from the 11th century. After collecting the horns from the church at eight o'clock in the morning, the Horn Dancers perform their dance to music at locations throughout the village and its surrounding farms and pubs. It is thought that the dance may originally have been devized to celebrate the villagers' rights in the forest of Needwood. Abbots Bromley is an attractive village with welcoming pubs and shops.

PLACES TO VISIT

• RUDYARD LAKE
www.rudyardlake.com
☎ 01538 306280
Often referred to as Rudyard Reservoir, this long straight lake presents an ideal spot for a picnic. There is a visitor centre at the damhead, and the activity centre houses a café. Boating and fishing take place on and around the lake, and there is a wealth of wildlife to spot. The Rudyard Lake Steam Railway operates narrow gauge trains on the east side of the lake. They run on most weekends Mar–Oct.

• CHEDDLETON FLINT MILL
people.exeter.ac.uk/akoutram
☎ 0161 408 5083
Beside the SW, alongside the Caldon Canal, are these listed buildings. There are actually two water mills here; one specifically built to grind flint, and one that was converted from a corn mill. The white calcined flint produced here was used by local potteries. Call for current opening times.

• CHURNET VALLEY RAILWAY
www.churnet-valley-railway.co.uk
☎ 01538 360522
Just a short walk from the canal is this restored steam railway. Trains run on most weekends in the summer and in the run up to Christmas. From the original Victorian station at Cheddleton you can ride in style to Kingsley and Froghall station, with its Victorian-style tea rooms. It is then a short walk to rejoin the SW. See website for details of operating days and times.

• ALTON TOWERS
www.altontowers.com
☎ 0871 222 3330
The Alton Towers resort is clearly audible from the SW. In addition to the theme park there is a water park, spa and hotel. Theme park open daily Mar–Oct; rest of resort open daily all year.

TOP The hexagonal 17th-century Butter Cross stands in front of the 16th-century timber-framed Goat's Head Hotel in Abbots Bromley

Limestone Way

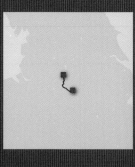

COMPLETE ROUTE ASHBOURNE TO CASTLETON **46 MILES (74KM)**
SECTION COVERED MATLOCK TO CASTLETON **26 MILES (42KM)**
MAPS OS EXPLORER OL 1, OL 24, 259

Waymarked by signs of the Derbyshire ram, the Limestone Way is a delightful walk through the Peak District National Park. Despite the hilly nature of the terrain, its 46 miles (74km) are not over-taxing, and could be accomplished in three days. The route follows the limestone plateau of Derbyshire's White Peak, with fine views and constantly changing scenery, and visits some interesting hamlets and villages on the way. There are also constant reminders of Derbyshire's lead mines of the 18th and 19th centuries, and of its agricultural past, with a criss-cross pattern of white drystone walls dominating much of the landscape.

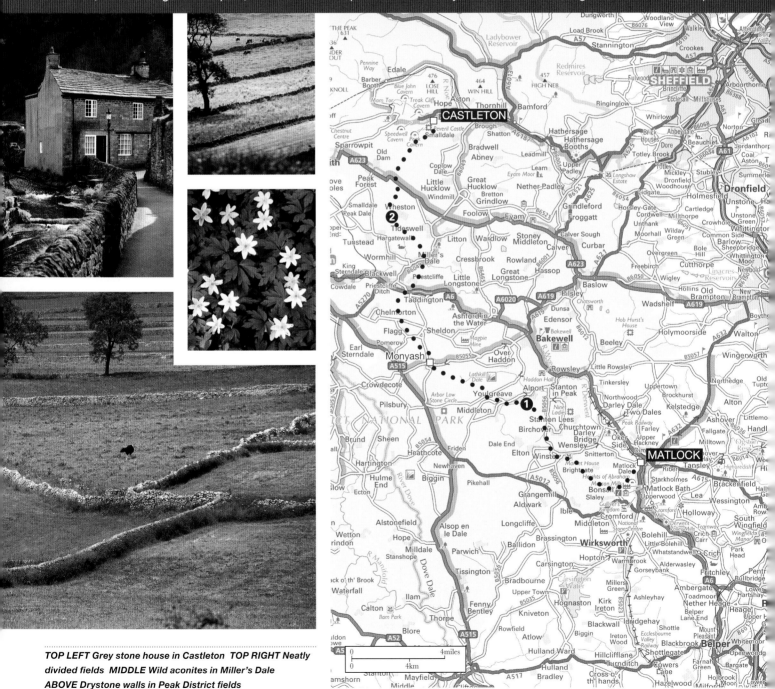

TOP LEFT Grey stone house in Castleton TOP RIGHT Neatly divided fields MIDDLE Wild aconites in Miller's Dale ABOVE Drystone walls in Peak District fields

ABOVE LEFT *Market Cross and King's Head pub in Bonsall* ABOVE RIGHT *Youlgreave near Bakewell*

MATLOCK TO CASTLETON

STAGE 1

MATLOCK to MONYASH

DISTANCE 13 miles (21km)

MAPS OS Explorer OL 24

START AT GRID REFERENCE SK 298 602

START POINT Matlock Bridge

Matlock Bath, approximately 1.5 miles (2.5km) south of Matlock along the A6, has numerous tourist attractions and, if wished, the route of the Limestone Way can be joined from there instead, by climbing directly up the Heights of Abraham and joining a footpath signposted to Bonsall.

From Matlock Bridge, the route follows the minor Snitterton road westwards, climbing steeply and bearing left on a footpath to cross fields towards Masson Lees Farm. Keeping right along field boundaries over Masson Hill, the route joins a narrow walled lane which leads down into Bonsall, the first of several delightful villages. Like many Derbyshire villages, Bonsall takes part in an annual well-dressing ceremony during the summer.

Believed to be an early Christian custom based on pagan worship of water gods, the ceremony has now become highly specialized, with well-dressings being set in large wooden frames lined with clay and using flowers, foliage, berries, mosses, bark, cones, vegetables, wool and other suitable organic materials. Nothing synthetic is used. The wells are then blessed at a special service, and remain dressed for several days.

Past Bonsall, the route follows a narrow walled track that leads up through fields to Upper Town. In some places on this part of the route the waymarks are difficult to spot, in others the walker should follow the Public Footpath sign, and in a few cases there is no obvious sign at all. This makes careful use of the map important. At Upper Town, a Limestone Way signpost shows the way back to Matlock, but does not show the way forward. In fact, the route goes straight ahead as far as Bromlea Farm, where it leaves the road to follow a Public Footpath sign diagonally across the field ahead. The footpath winds across the fields in a northwesterly direction, going gently downhill to

cross a quiet road by Blakelow Farm. The route leads over more fields across Bonsall Moor, where care is needed in looking out for both stiles and waymarks to find the correct route past Luntor Rocks. There are disused mines close by. From here, the official route leads straight on past Wyn's Tor, but a diversion down the hill through Winster is worthwhile. This quaint village is surrounded by the remains of shafts and tip-heaps and its dark gritstone cottages on the south side, now popular as holiday homes, were once the homes of lead miners. Interesting buildings include the late 17th-century Market House, open most summer weekend afternoons.

A return may be made to Matlock from Winster, by taking the footpath (grid ref. SK 242 606) northeast past Clough Wood and turning southeast to Wensley, from where a footpath leads along the side of Wensley Dale to Snitterton and the road to Matlock Bridge. It is a circular walk of approximately 9 miles (14.5km).

ROBIN HOOD'S STRIDE

To rejoin the Limestone Way, a pleasant footpath leads westwards through the churchyard towards Westhill Farm. Here the route bears north along a track, crossing the Elton road.

(i) USEFUL INFORMATION

THE ROUTE
• www.visitpeakdistrict.com/ activities/limestone-way.aspx
☎ 01629 583388
The official web page of the LW does not give much information but an official Walkers Guide can be purchased by calling the Matlock TIC on the number listed above, or visiting in person.

TOURIST INFORMATION CENTRES
• www.visitpeakdistrict.com
Crown Square, Matlock DE4 3AT;
☎ 01629 583388
• www.visitcastleton.co.uk
Buxton Road, Castleton
S33 8WN; ☎ 01629 816572

PLANNING YOUR TRIP
• www.ldwa.org.uk
The Long Distance Walkers Association has some good detail and links for the LW, including downloadable GPS route files (for members only).
• www.ramblers.org.uk
☎ 020 7339 8500
The Ramblers Association website has general information about long-distance walking and some specific help covering the LW route.
• www.yha.org.uk
☎ 0800 019 1700
The Youth Hostel Association has a number of sites near this route.

OTHER PATHS
Being in the Peak District, the LW is crossed by, and linked to, many other trails. At the end of the LW, the Staffordshire Way (pages 124–127) can be found at Rocester. For a longer adventure, the Pennine Way National Trail (pages 188–195) starts its 251 miles (404km) just a few miles away from Castleton, at the village of Edale. The White Peak Way starts and finishes in Bakewell and completes a circuit of 85 miles (137km) around many of the limestone dales and their youth hostels. It shares small sections of the LW just south of Youlgreave and on the approach to Castleton.

CENTRAL ENGLAND & EAST ANGLIA • LIMESTONE WAY

RIGHT *Opened in 1984, these cable cars over the Heights of Abraham are accessed from Matlock Bath*

Elton is 0.5 miles (800m) to the west, with even finer buildings than Winster. Its Old Hall, dated 1668 and 1715, is now luxury self-catering group accommodation. The route follows a tarmac lane downhill straight ahead, before bearing left on a track at the bottom just before the B5056. This track bears left uphill, away from Cratcliff Cottages, then climbs through the natural gap between Robin Hood's Stride, a spectacular tor of gritstone rocks, and another outcrop that includes the Hermit's Cave.

Beyond the rocks, the route crosses two fields to reach the road ahead. The direct route here is straight on, along the footpath that skirts Harthill Moor Farm, but the Limestone Way takes a prettier if slightly longer route, turning right along the road to turn left on to a woodland trail, before rounding the next hillside to resume the northwesterly direction. This leads down across fields to cross Bleakley Dike, reaching the lane ahead on the outskirts of Youlgreave, which sits on the ridge between Bradford and Lathkill Dales. This is another village well known for its well-dressings. Its 15th-century church has one of the best towers in the Peak District.

CLAPPER BRIDGE

The Limestone Way does not go into the village, but crosses the River Bradford and then turns along its north bank to follow a pretty route upstream, passing remains of 19th-century weirs. The route crosses to the south bank on a clapper-bridge. It then follows the river to an old stone bridge, where it crosses once again, climbing through the woods on a zig-zag track to join the road by Lomberdale Hall. Another footpath leads uphill across the Hall's parkland, crossing fields to eventually reach the car park and picnic site at Moor Lane.

From here the footpath leads on to the northwest, using a well-defined track that goes straight across a wide expanse of fields which are sometimes sown with cereals. Skirting a patch of woodland, the path leads around the side

of Calling Low Farm. The path then heads steeply downhill, with fine views of the countryside ahead and Lathkill Dale over to the right. At the bottom it follows steps steeply down into the wildlife reserve of Cales Dale. On the far side, a less steep path leads uphill by caves and soon reaches One Ash Grange Farm.

The route follows the side of fields and drystone-walled paths to the roadside on the outskirts of Monyash. Turn right for the picturesque village green with its solitary listed building named The Bull's Head. This simple and unpretentious village was chronicled in the Domesday Book, with its market and fair recorded in 1340. It has a pleasing collection of typical White Peak cottages, originally built for the lead-mining community. The area now depends on farming and tourism.

STAGE 2
MONYASH to CASTLETON
DISTANCE 13.1 miles (21.1km)
MAPS OS Explorer OL 1, OL 24
START AT GRID REFERENCE SK 150 666
START POINT The green at Monyash

From Monyash the character of the walk changes as the views grow more impressive. Heading out of the village on the lane that goes north, look out for a noticeboard on the left giving some interesting historical pointers about the village. Carry on past footpaths on the left into the bottom of a dry valley, where the route is clearly waymarked. Following drystone walls, the route skirts Knotlow Farm, joining a tarmac track by the hamlet of Flagg, where it meets the road.

Flagg is a quiet, unremarkable place, with the road leading to the northwest for the longest on-road section of the Limestone Way at about 2 miles (3km). There are few cars around and, once the route crosses the Bakewell–Chelmorton road, it feels as if the straight lane ahead is seldom, if ever, used by traffic. To the west, Chelmorton is famous for its pattern of narrow enclosure walls; a classic illustration of medieval farming practice.

A green lane leads northwards, and soon gives the first really fine view of the Limestone Way, over the A6 in the valley to the hills beyond. The A6 is one of only two major roads to be encountered on the 26 miles (42km) of this walk, and a track zig-

TOP Shops and houses of Matlock Bath
TOP RIGHT The fast-flowing River Wye passing through the village of Miller's Dale
MIDDLE The River Wye is crossed by this dainty bridge at Miller's Dale
ABOVE War memorial by the village green at Monyash

zags down the hillside to cross it by the Waterloo Hotel and Inn, close by a blind brow. Once past here, the route follows a pretty cart track downhill by the side of Blackwell Dale. Overgrown with wild flowers in summer, it is a reminder of the way many of our roads used to be.

OLD LIMEKILNS

At the bottom, join the B6049, going downhill into Miller's Dale, which is a charming small place carved out of bedded limestones by the side of the River Wye. The road passes under the formidable viaduct, built to carry the old railway line that has now become the Monsal Trail. Miller's Dale was famous for its lime, and the remains of 19th- and 20th-century kilns can be seen near the station.

From Miller's Dale the route goes north, forking uphill past the church and then doubling back up a steep track which zig-zags past Monksdale Farm. A walled track leads on across fields to a quiet lane near Monksdale House, where the route turns downhill to follow a path through the delightful nature reserve of Peter Dale. Past Dale Head Farm, the route continues along Hay Dale before turning uphill on a walled track, passing a sheep-wash on the way to the long, straight lane that crosses the track ahead. From here, it is just under a mile (1.6km) to the A623, where the route turns left for about 150yds (135m). It is best to walk on the grass verge for safety. The right turn is among trees by the side of Mount Dale Farm, on to a disused railway track.

Down in the next valley a minor road leads up to the Cop Farm on the hillside ahead. The route passes over a stile on the right, by the first footpath sign for Castleton. A field path joins another walled track above the forested clump of Oxlow Rake to the left; 'rake' being the common name for a large vein of lead in the Peak area. Indeed, there are many signs of disused mine-workings around here. The first is to the west, at Eldon Hill. This limestone quarry closed in 1999 and now stands unused, with vegetation starting to grow on the quarry face. Hope Valley Cement Works, to the east of Castleton, is an eyesore for tourists but an important local employer.

CAVE DALE

The camping and caravan site of Rowter Farm now comes into view on a far hillside ahead. Here, the route crosses a track, passing through two gates to emerge on to a faint path over springy turf, with upland sheep grazing peacefully on the hillsides above Castleton.

The Limestone Way path goes downhill, passing the remains of a waymark signpost, where it bears right through an old metal gate to join the path going down the side of Cave Dale. Be warned; this turn can easily be missed, taking you over the hill rather than down the dale.

Cave Dale is a water-cut limestone dale that was formed in the Ice Age, and is now completely dry. The path is sometimes steep and rocky and better suited to sheep or goats. Peveril Castle, in a fine position on the ledge ahead, is worth a visit once you reach Castleton. It was built by William Peveril, an illegitimate son of William the Conqueror, who was made Steward of the Royal Forest of the Peak, which was an important hunting area. With a curtain wall, Peveril was one of the earliest Norman stone-built castles to be built in England. It was mentioned in the Domesday Book and is sited in an almost impregnable position between Peak Cavern and Cave Dale.

Once past the castle, the path leads down to Castleton's small square, and the end of the Limestone Way. There is a good selection of pubs, tea houses and cafés to choose from in this pleasant village, with its show caves and amenities, making it an excellent place to end the walk.

From Castleton, there is a magnificent ridge walk between Mam Tor (grid ref. SK 128 835, height 1,700ft/517m) and Hollins Cross (grid ref. SK 136 845), which can be approached via footpaths that pass Blue John Cavern and Treak Cliff Cavern, returning via Dunscar Farm. The entire trip is approximately 5 miles (8km).

*BELOW LEFT **The bulk of Mam Tor above Castleton village*** *BELOW **Banks of yellow daffodils and dandelions below the grey stone church at Miller's Dale***

PLACES TO VISIT

• HEIGHTS OF ABRAHAM
www.heightsofabraham.com
☎ 01629 582365
The famous alpine-style cable cars of the Heights of Abraham take visitors up to the Hilltop Park high above the Derwent valley near Matlock Bath. The ride is just the beginning of a full day out, with two show caverns to explore, stunning views of the valley from the Prospect Tower, and two outdoor play parks. There are exhibitions and woods to wander through. Open Sat–Sun Mar, daily Feb & Apr–Oct.

• PEAK CAVERN
www.peakcavern.co.uk
☎ 01433 620285
Set in the cliffs below the ruins of Peveril Castle is the famous Peak Cavern, near Castleton. Known locally as the Devil's Arse, it has the largest natural entrance in the British Isles. In the 17th century, a whole community of rope-makers lived in the entrance, supplying rope to Castleton's thriving mining industry. There are multiple chambers within the cavern, lit by fibre-optic systems. Open daily all year.

• SPEEDWELL CAVERN
www.speedwellcavern.co.uk
☎ 01433 620512
There are a number of other caverns in this area. Near by, at the foot of Winnats Pass, is Speedwell Cavern. Here, visitors descend over 100 steps inside the cave to arrive at an underground landing stage. From there, the tour is by boat, gliding quietly through channels 650ft (200m) to the Bottomless Pit subterranean lake. Open daily all year.

Fields and drystone walls in Miller's Dale

Peddars Way & Norfolk Coast Path

COMPLETE ROUTE KNETTISHALL HEATH TO CROMER **93 MILES (150KM)**
SECTION COVERED AS ABOVE
MAPS OS EXPLORER 229, 230, 236, 237, 238, 250, 251, 252

The Peddars Way & Norfolk Coast Path begins at Knettishall Heath, passes through the fascinating Brecks of Norfolk, continues through the remote and lonely north-west of the county, and then turns east at the sea to follow the line of one of the most unspoilt and beautiful coasts in the country, justifiably famous for its harsh beauty and remoteness. It runs from the Victorian resort of Hunstanton in the west along wild stretches of marsh, beach and cliff, interspersed with a few attractive villages and small towns on or near the route, and ends at the attractive town of Cromer, famous for its crabs, pier and fishing boats.

TOP Sailboat at Burnham Overy Staithe
ABOVE The magnificent ruins of Castle Acre Priory

KNETTISHALL HEATH TO NORTH PICKENHAM

STAGE 1
KNETTISHALL HEATH to THREXTON HILL
DISTANCE 13.2 miles (21.2km)
MAPS OS Explorer 229, 230, 237
START AT GRID REFERENCE TL 943 807
START POINT Knettishall Heath Country Park

Knettishall Heath Country Park is a particularly attractive place to set off on the Peddars Way, the start of which is clearly marked by a wooden post with an acorn sign directly opposite the car park. For a short distance, until the Little Ouse River (which is the county boundary), the Peddars Way is in Suffolk. The path leads gently down for 650yds (590m) to the bridge over the river at Blackwater and into Norfolk.

A short distance to the east is Riddlesworth Hall girls' school, once attended by Diana, Princess of Wales, while to the west is the small village of Rushford, Here, in 1342, Edmund Gonville, founder of Gonville and Caius College at Cambridge, established a college for a master and five priests, which lasted until the Dissolution. Still further to the west lies the substantial town of Thetford; the power-base in Saxon times of the king of the East Angles. In 1737, it was the birthplace of the influential radical writer and politician Tom Paine, whose statue stands in the town. Despite the ravages of modern development, Thetford is still worth a visit.

After the bridge, continue along the path, skirting the wood to your right and passing a magnificent old oak tree until you come on to a straight section of Roman road leading up to the A1066. Following a line of trees to the left and a wide arable field to the right, this section is now a very charming footpath. Watch out for a peculiar, half-buried stone with 'Rs' clearly carved on its surface.

ALONG THE OLD AGGER
Cross the A1066 and, shortly afterwards, the road to East Harling. The route of the Peddars Way along the old agger, or embankment, is now clearly visible alongside the footpath. Shadwell Park estate, with its huge Victorian mansion (not open to the public) is some way away on the left, and the path borders copious woodlands to the right. A good circular walk is clearly marked along this section. The footpath then crosses an attractive meadow, turns right along the bank of the River Thet and crosses it by a wooden bridge at Droveway Ford.

As a prominent 'No Fishing' sign would suggest, the River Thet is teeming with fish, and in summer months this lovely spot is a perfect place to linger. Downstream there is an Anglo-Saxon burial ground at Brettenham and various early remains. Upstream, the nomenclature of Thorpe Woodlands embraces the sites of three abandoned medieval villages. Beyond is the location of an Iron Age riverside settlement at Micklemoor Hill.

Cross the Brettenham road past an open pig farm to the right and skirt a delightful wood. To the left, where once heathland would have been undisturbed, there is now a wide area of agricultural land. The path continues on the old, raised embankment and then leaves it to pass through a gap in an old wire fence. You are now on Brettenham Heath, a national nature reserve run by Natural England, and the view to the left gives a splendid impression of what much of the Breck landscape would have been like before the intrusion of the modern world. This is now the territory of thousands of rabbits and their predators. To the right, the forest protects the walker from the east wind and assails the nostrils with the smell of pine.

For a circular walk of about 9 miles (14.5km), leave the Peddars Way at grid ref. TL 935 864, turning right along the small road to High Bridgham. From Bridgham Church (near Hall Farm), follow footpaths to Thorpe Woodlands and Dolphin Farm, and turn left on to the A1066. Then, taking the first right, follow the lane over the Little Ouse River and so back to Knettishall Heath Country Park.

ROE DEER
The Peddars Way crosses the minor road to Bridgham and then the busy A11. This is now Bridgham Heath, where it is thought that Sweyn and the Danes defeated Ulfcytel and the Saxons at the bloody battle of Hringmara (perhaps modern Ring Mere) in 1010. A short length of metalled road leads to the Norwich–Ely railway crossing, then the path continues through the pines of Roudham Heath, past a gas pipeline service station, and alongside the dismantled Thetford–Watton railway to the village of Stonebridge, or East Wretham. Roe deer are occasionally seen here, and there is a circular walk clearly marked just before the abutments of the old railway bridge.

There is a pub, the Dog and Partridge, in the village. Turn left after the pub to continue along the Peddars Way. Much of this next section is a Ministry of Defence training area, and it

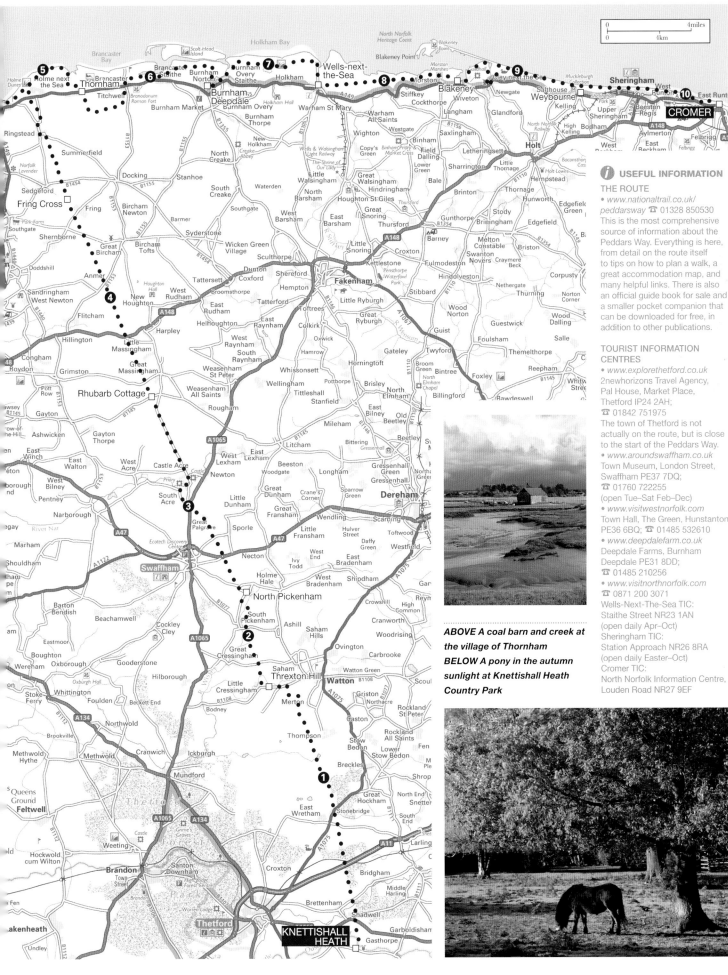

ℹ USEFUL INFORMATION

THE ROUTE

• www.nationaltrail.co.uk/peddarsway ☎ 01328 850530
This is the most comprehensive source of information about the Peddars Way. Everything is here, from detail on the route itself to tips on how to plan a walk, a great accommodation map, and many helpful links. There is also an official guide book for sale and a smaller pocket companion that can be downloaded for free, in addition to other publications.

TOURIST INFORMATION CENTRES

• www.explorethetford.co.uk
2newhorizons Travel Agency, Pal House, Market Place, Thetford IP24 2AH;
☎ 01842 751975
The town of Thetford is not actually on the route, but is close to the start of the Peddars Way.
• www.aroundswaffham.co.uk
Town Museum, London Street, Swaffham PE37 7DQ;
☎ 01760 722255
(open Tue–Sat Feb–Dec)
• www.visitwestnorfolk.com
Town Hall, The Green, Hunstanton PE36 6BQ; ☎ 01485 532610
• www.deepdalefarm.co.uk
Deepdale Farms, Burnham Deepdale PE31 8DD;
☎ 01485 210256
• www.visitnorthnorfolk.com
☎ 0871 200 3071
Wells-Next-The-Sea TIC:
Staithe Street NR23 1AN
(open daily Apr–Oct)
Sheringham TIC:
Station Approach NR26 8RA
(open daily Easter–Oct)
Cromer TIC:
North Norfolk Information Centre, Louden Road NR27 9EF

ABOVE A coal barn and creek at the village of Thornham
BELOW A pony in the autumn sunlight at Knettishall Heath Country Park

is important not to stray into the protected zones off the path. The country on both sides is heavily forested and unspoilt. Deer abound, as do small, semi-wild flocks of sheep. The names of the wooded areas have a resonant ring: Broom Covert, Woodcock Hill, Cranberry Wood, Blackrabbit Warren and, more ominously, Madhouse Plantation.

Opposite the latter is Thompson Water; a beautiful lake created in 1854 by the damming of a tributary of the River Wissey. This and the adjoining Thompson Common are now in the hands of the Norfolk Wildlife Trust and both are open to the public. The path continues through an area of wood and heath, over a crossways created by a track to the Stanford Battle Ground to the left and the road at Sparrow Hill to the right, and then continues north alongside fine woodland on the right and bordering the estate of Merton.

This property is owned by Lord Walsingham, who did much to open up this part of the Peddars Way to the public. The fine Jacobean hall, for long the home of the ancient de Grey family, was burnt out in a fire in 1956.

Edward Fitzgerald, the first translator of *The Rubaiyat of Omar Khayyam*, died at Merton Rectory in 1883. North of Home Farm the path turns left and then right, until it meets the B1108 Bodney–Watton road just to the east of Threxton Hill.

STAGE 2
THREXTON HILL to NORTH PICKENHAM
DISTANCE 6.1 miles (9.8km)
MAPS OS Explorer 229, 236, 237
START AT GRID REFERENCE TL 892 000
START POINT Junction of the Peddars Way with the B1108 Bodney–Watton road

The next section of the Peddars Way is along metalled roads. Turn left on to the B1108 to Little Cressingham, making use of the verges and the signposted path that runs along the north side of the road. In the village of Little Cressingham, turn right opposite the former White Horse pub and continue across a stream and a crossroads towards South Pickenham, through an attractive undulating landscape.

For an 'escape' route of about 6.5 miles (10.5km), turn left off the Peddars Way (grid ref. TL 866 027) at the lane to Great Cressingham. Go through the village and turn left again up the lane past Chalkhill, then take the second turn left down the lane to Little Cressingham, and so back to your starting point along the Peddars Way (B1108) to Threxton.

ROUTE USED BY PILGRIMS
Shortly before South Pickenham village you will see handsome Pickenham Hall, rebuilt in 1904, to your left and, to your right, the smaller but lovely Hall Farm. The church in the estate village contains an ornate organ case by Pugin.

Across the road the path continues at the side of the minor road for nearly a mile and then turns left across a field. Then it zig-zags across more fields, over the River Wissey, towards the village of North Pickenham and the 350ft (107m) high British Telecom relay tower beyond. It has been claimed that this was the route used for centuries by pilgrims on their way to Walsingham, and certainly there is an old feel to this part of the walk, emphasized perhaps by the pleasure of once more being away from the road. In North Pickenham, turn right on to the road and then left at the junction to continue your route. There is a pub in the village called the Blue Lion.

NORTH PICKENHAM TO FRING CROSS

STAGE 3
NORTH PICKENHAM to RHUBARB COTTAGE
DISTANCE 11.1 miles (17.9km)
MAPS OS Explorer 236, 238, 250
START AT GRID REFERENCE TF 862 066
START POINT North Pickenham village

From North Pickenham the Peddars Way runs along the road, going in a northwesterly direction until it meets the road to Swaffham. Here, it crosses over and, passing through a disused railway bridge, becomes a pleasing, broad grassy track known as Procession Way. It may have been called this after the ceremony of 'beating the bounds' that used to be practiced along it, but more likely because of the number of religious processions that are thought to have followed this part of the route on pilgrimage to Walsingham.

After a mile (1.6km), you reach a crossways of paths, the left-hand of which leads to the interesting and still largely unspoilt market town of Swaffham, with its fine Georgian houses, market cross and legend of the pedlar's dream. It is said that a pedlar, John Chapman, dreamed that if he went to London Bridge he would hear something to his advantage. There he met a shopkeeper who told him that he had dreamed that in the garden of a certain John Chapman in Swaffham were buried two pots of gold. Chapman hurried home and literally found his fortune. With some of the gold he rebuilt much of the fine parish church of St Peter and St Paul, famous for its especially magnificent double hammer-beam roof. In Georgian times, Swaffham became a social and sporting centre. On Saturdays there is an extensive open-air market and public auction that is well worth attending.

After another 100yds (90m) meet the hurly-burly of the A47. This is a good example of how, along the Peddars Way, you can lose yourself in a sort of timewarp, for much of the route has doubtless been walked by man since time immemorial, and the occasional reminders of the hustle and bustle of the late 20th century only serve to reinforce your enjoyment.

Thankfully leaving the A47 behind, now make your way down a metalled farm lane, across the old Swaffham–East Dereham railway line, then go right and left past a row of cottages, past Palgrave Hall on your left and on to the farm at Great Palgrave. Between here and Little Palgrave Hall to the north is the site of the medieval villages of Great and Little Palgrave, deserted since the terrible ravages of the Black Death. A certain melancholy atmosphere still lingers here. Near by is the particularly attractive village of Sporle.

The route now leaves the original Peddars Way and follows metalled roads across high country, down to the ancient crossroads with the A1065 at Bartholomew's Hills.

For a 12-mile (19.5km) circular walk back to North Pickenham, leave the Peddars Way route (at grid ref. TF 818 132), turning right on to the A1065 for a few yards. Turn right again along the track leading

----

TOP Poppies growing next to a barley field at North Pickenham
MIDDLE Unique combined water and windmills, built in 1821 at Little Cressingham
ABOVE Sheep with lambs rest near the ruins of Castle Acre Priory

past Little Palgrave Hall. Keeping right, turn right at the crossroads to Sporle, where you pick up a track by the church which takes you right, left and right again, across the A47 and so back to North Pickenham.

IMPRESSIVE EARTHWORKS

The Peddars Way now goes up and then down again, past South Acre to Castle Acre in the valley of the Nar, affording fine views of the priory. The original Peddars Way is likely to have continued its straight course over Hungry Hill towards Castle Acre.

Castle Acre is a charming and fascinating village, and it is well worth spending a little time here. Granted to William de Warrenne by the Conqueror, it was he who built the castle, of which the fine bailey gate still guards the entrance to the village. It was his son who founded the Cluniac priory. The earthworks of the now mainly vanished castle are considered by some to be the most impressive in the country, and are certainly some of the largest, while the magnificent remains and attachments of the priory should on no account be missed. Until the Dissolution, one of the priory's greatest treasures to attract pilgrims on the Walsingham Way was what was claimed to be the arm of St Philip. There are now various pubs, restaurants and bed-and-breakfast establishments in the village to cater for a more modern sort of sightseer.

From Castle Acre, the Peddars Way turns left out of Stocks Green and follows the road to Great Massingham. It must be said that this stretch of the route is not the most exciting, for, after a stretch of footpath behind a hedge, the walker is forced to walk on the gradually ascending road for well over 2 miles (3km). Large agricultural estates, farmed with maximum efficiency, border both sides, and it is with some relief that you continue straight on, when the road eventually bends right at Shepherd's Bush. The route descends a pleasant, broad track to the junction with the B1145 by Rhubarb Cottage and Betts Field Barn.

STAGE 4
RHUBARB COTTAGE to FRING CROSS

DISTANCE 9.9 miles (15.9km)
MAPS OS Explorer 236, 250
START AT GRID REFERENCE TF 791 210
START POINT Junction of Peddars Way and B1145, 3 miles (5km) west of Rougham

For this section of the Peddars Way the route is a wide, sometimes stony, sometimes grassy, cart-track affording easy walking and always gently rising or falling through one of the loneliest parts of Norfolk. Much of the land is arable and, except in small parts, there is little sign of the forest which would once have held sway. Yet all along the way there are fine views on both sides of distant villages, farms and churches, and there is a pleasing sense of solitude and calm. From the junction of the B1145. the track crosses, in fairly quick succession, three small roads south-west from the pretty villages of Great and Little Massingham. The former once boasted an Augustinian priory, fragments of which remain, and was the home of the late-Elizabethan physician Stephen Perse, who founded the Perse School at Cambridge. It is an attractive village, with a large pond and two greens at its heart. There was once both a market and a fair here.

The route leads downhill to cross the busy A148 at Harpley Dams. The former house of the crossing-keeper of the old railway line is now the 'Paradise Dogotel'.

For an 8.75-mile (14km) circular walk returning to Rhubarb Cottage, leave the Peddars Way at grid ref. TF 771 255 and take the lane to the right to Little Massingham (you can walk some of the way along the abandoned railway line running parallel). Turn right at the end and walk through the villages of Little and then Great Massingham. Past the second pond in Great Massingham, go straight on along the road to Castle Acre, and then branch off on the first right. Take the footpath on your left at a bend in the road. This leads you to the B1145. Turn right here and walk the short distance back to the junction with the Peddars Way at Rhubarb Cottage.

BRONZE AGE BARROWS

The Way then climbs up towards Harpley Common. Several Bronze Age barrows are clearly visible here on your right, one just before Bunker's Hill wood. There are also some fifty 18th-century marl pits on both sides of this section of the Peddars Way (marl being a fertilizer made of clay and carbonate of lime). To the east, beyond the woods, is Houghton Hall, a great Palladian house (the biggest in Norfolk) built for Sir Robert Walpole, chief minister to the first two King Georges. Built of Yorkshire stone, it was designed by Colin Campbell with a fine interior by Kent, and was completed in 1735.

The Peddars Way then crosses a small road to Anmer, a village on the 20,000-acre Sandringham Estate, beyond which is Sandringham itself; the Norfolk home of the Queen and Duke of Edinburgh. The lovely gardens and grounds are open to the public. The area of scrub to the left of the route after the crossroads is known as Anmer Minque, and after the next crossroads, with the B1153, the profile of Great Bircham Windmill can be seen to the north.

The path continues its straight course, passing between the villages of Great Bircham to the east and Shernborne, whose fine church was splendidly rebuilt by the Prince of Wales (later King Edward VII) at the turn of the century, to the west. Near Fring it crosses two roads before descending past two woods

USEFUL INFORMATION
THE ROUTE
• www.ldwa.org.uk
The Long Distance Walkers Association has some good detail and links for the PW and NCP, including the interactive map of linking trails and nearby hostels.
• www.ramblers.org.uk
☎ 020 7339 8500
The Ramblers Association website has general information about long-distance walking and specific help covering the PW and NCP, such as public transport details. There is also an accommodation list and guide to the route, by the Norfolk Ramblers group.
• www.yha.org.uk
☎ 0800 019 1700
The Youth Hostel Association has several sites close to the route.

OTHER PATHS
The PW and NCP is a long route which has many other long-distance path links. The Weavers' Way (pages 144–149) follows on from the NCP at Cromer and continues to Great Yarmouth, where it meets the Angles Way. This route then crosses back to the Peddars Way start point at Knettishall Heath, via Diss, and thus completes a circuit known as the Around Norfolk Walk. Also at Knettishall Heath, the Icknield Way is a long distance path which joins the PW to the Ridgeway National Trail (pages 74–81) at Ivinghoe Beacon. The combination of the PW, Icknield Way, Ridgeway and Essex Ridgeway is referred to as the Greater Ridgeway (which in its entirety runs from Hunstanton to Lyme Regis). Not far north of Knettishall Heath, just beyond the A11, the Hereward Way crosses the PW on its way between the nearby village of Harling and the Rutland town of Oakham.

BELOW Beautiful Castle Acre Priory is a ruined Cluniac monastery

to the footbridge and road to Sedgeford, where a beautiful torc from the Iron Age was unearthed, at Fring Cross. To the west is Snettisham, where several important Iron Age hoards have been unearthed in the last few decades, some as recently as the 1990s. This part of northwest Norfolk was evidently as rich and prosperous then as now.

FRING CROSS TO BURNHAM DEEPDALE

STAGE 5

FRING CROSS to THORNHAM

DISTANCE 9.6 miles (15.4km)

MAP OS Explorer 250

START AT GRID REFERENCE TF 727 355

START POINT Fring Cross, where the road from Fring to Sedgeford crosses the Peddars Way

From Fring Cross the Peddars Way rises to Dovehill Wood, changes to the other side of the hedge, then turns left and right and past some cottages to Littleport, at the junction with the B1454. Turn right for a few yards along this road and then left at the distinctive Sedgeford Magazine House, said to have been built by the royalist Sir Hamon Le Strange as an armoury at the time of the Civil War. Two and a half miles (4km) further on along the B1454 is Burntstalk, a huge workhouse built in 1836 and intended to house some 500 paupers.

The route continues past Magazine Farm and crosses the line of the former railway from Heacham to Wells-next-the-Sea. To the west, Heacham is the centre of the Norfolk lavender trade. Until 1941, when the Hall was destroyed by fire, it was also home to the ancient Rolfe family. It was a John Rolfe who married the celebrated and beautiful Indian princess Pocahontas in Virginia

TOP The village pond at
Great Massingham
MIDDLE Great Bircham
windmill
ABOVE The two-tone cliffs
at Hunstanton

in 1613, and she returned to live at the Hall with him until dying of the old-world disease of consumption. After turning left and right, descend towards the village of Ringstead. Just to the west, the Icknield Way ends its long journey at Ringstead Downs. Courtyard Farm, to the east, is owned by the former president of the Ramblers' Association, Lord Melchett. He encourages walkers on the estate, which has a bunkhouse, and has devoted much of it to conservation purposes. There is both a pub and a shop in Ringstead village.

For an enjoyable circular walk of a little over 7 miles (11.3km), returning to Fring Cross, leave the Peddars Way at Ringstead (at grid ref. TF 707 403) and head back due south along the lane to Sedgeford. Turn left in the village and then right at the war memorial, following the lane back to Fring Cross.

VIEWS OF THE SEA

The main route continues through the village and turns right and left towards Holme next the Sea. The sea is now visible in the distance and there is a sense of excitement that one has walked from the southern border to the north coast of one of Britain's biggest counties.

Just after Ringstead Mill, the Peddars Way turns left and right along the boundary of a field. It descends between hedges across the A149 and finally arrives at its destination, the pleasant little village of Holme next the Sea. Continue walking along Seagate, past the car park and towards the sea. Walkers who began their journey at the start of the Peddars Way long-distance path will have travelled some 46 miles (74km) to its northern end, and now make their way eastward along the Norfolk Coast Path.

Others may prefer to walk the coast path from its beginning in Hunstanton. Hunstanton (pronounced 'Hunston' locally) was developed as a seaside resort in Victorian times by Hamon Le Strange, whose family held the manor for eight centuries until 1948. Little remains of their hall at Old Hunstanton but there are fine family memorials in the church. One of the most interesting Le Stranges was the long-lived Sir Roger (1616–1704), who during the English Civil War unsuccessfully attempted to win back King's Lynn from Cromwell's forces in 1644, was sentenced to death for his troubles, eventually escaped to the Continent, returned to England at the time of the Restoration and then began a busy career as pamphleteer and writer. He is these days perhaps best remembered as the translator into English of *Aesop's Fables*.

The coast path begins at the central green near the Golden Lion Hotel and the Pier Family Entertainment (the pier itself sadly no longer exists) and follows the road towards the Garden of Rest, which is dedicated to the many East Anglians who lost their lives during World War I. On your left is the Wash, and on fine days there are wonderful views from here of the Lincolnshire coastline and the unmistakable outline of Boston Stump (the church at Boston). Ahead lies a disused lighthouse, and just before this, the few remains of St Edmund's Chapel can be made out on the right.

WILDNESS AND ISOLATION
This is St Edmund's Point, where the Saxon King of East Anglia is said to have landed after his journey across the sea from Germany. Walk through the car park on the cliffs (this is another good place from which to begin) and take a little path towards the beach at the far left. Walk through the dunes and beach huts to the lifeboat station, then cross the sandy track to continue walking through the sand dunes, at this point largely grassed over. This path eventually rejoins the Peddars Way on Holme next the Sea beach.

Pass through Holme Dunes Nature Reserve, which is a haven for all manner of flora and fauna. The reserve is managed by Norfolk Wildlife Trust, and there are hides and a nature trail. At Gore Point and beyond there is an exhilarating sense of wildness and isolation, as you leave all trace of humanity behind. Then, at Broad Water corner, the path turns inland along the sea bank and heads past Thornham Creek, with its pleasing jumble of boats, and eventually into Thornham village.

In common with most of the villages and towns along this part of the coast, Thornham is no longer a commercial port and, apart from a fishing boat or two, all the craft are now used for leisure purposes. Indeed, the last commercial vessel, the *Jessie Mary*, was sailed in by the merchant Nathaniel Woods in 1914. The village is a delightful spot and has shops, three pubs and overnight accommodation.

STAGE 6

THORNHAM to BURNHAM DEEPDALE
DISTANCE 6.4 miles (10.3km)
MAP OS Explorer 250
START AT GRID REFERENCE TF 733 434
START POINT Thornham

The coast path now makes a brief detour inland. Walk east through the village of Thornham, towards Titchwell, and turn right up the lane signposted to Choseley. You now face a steady climb of 1.25 miles (2km) until the familiar coast path sign points left off the road by a small plantation. To the west is Beacon Hill, occupied since Neolithic times and once a Roman signal station. Continue along the edge of a couple of fields and soon the path becomes a broad track.

For a circular walk of approximately 7 miles (11km), leave the Norfolk Coast Path at grid ref. TF 763 422, turning right along the southbound lane. Turn first right along the lane to Choseley Farm.

Keep right at the junction here, and so head northeast along the lane back to Thornham.

BRANODUNUM
The path continues over the crossroads and then over a second small road to Titchwell, and then itself turns left towards the coast again. Now there are skylarks singing overhead, and once more there are fine views of the sea beyond Titchwell, where the Titchwell Marsh Nature Reserve, in the safe hands of the Royal Society for the Protection of Birds, boasts many fine and rare species of bird and plant life. The path itself descends past ancient barns to Brancaster.

At Brancaster, the route crosses over the main road and then makes its way along the edge of the marsh. Conditions can be wet and muddy along this stretch. Continue towards the site of the Roman fort of Branodunum. The Dalmatian cavalry was garrisoned here in the times when the harbour was one of the main bases for Rome's British fleet. The National Trust has acquired the site, which is open to the public and can be reached from the coast path. Brancaster is also the site of a fine golf course, part of the Royal West Norfolk Golf Club, and the path to the course affords fine views of the creeks.

The next point of interest is the village and harbour of Brancaster Staithe; once the focal point of a busy trade in coal and grain before the harbour became inaccessible to big boats. It is now a highly popular centre for sailing. Mussels are still bred, sorted, riddled and cleaned here, and the path runs between fishermen's huts and past the cleansing pools.

Brancaster Staithe runs almost imperceptibly into the small village of Burnham Deepdale, the first of five (once seven) villages with the prefix Burnham. Before embarking on the next stage of the journey, you would do well to investigate the fascinating Saxon Church of St Mary's, with its superb and famous font whose carvings illustrate the months of the year by depicting life on the land.

BURNHAM DEEPDALE TO BLAKENEY

STAGE 7

BURNHAM DEEPDALE to WELLS-NEXT-THE-SEA
DISTANCE 10.5 miles (16.9km)
MAPS OS Explorer 250, 251
START AT GRID REFERENCE TF 804 445
START POINT Burnham Deepdale village

BELOW Walkers at Holme Sand Dunes National Nature Reserve

TOP *Late evening light at*
Thornham Creek
MIDDLE *High tide on*
a summer evening at
Thornham
ABOVE *View across*
Holkham Bay beach

From Burnham Deepdale, the coast path curves out on the sea bank towards Scolt Head Island and its nature reserve. Once more, you find yourself alone in a world of creek, marsh, birds, sand, sea and sky. Facing Gun Hill, the route turns inland again, bordering creeks, and winds round to the village of Burnham Overy Staithe. As it does so, it affords magnificent views of coastal villages and well-known landmarks such as Burnham Overy Mill. This is one of the prettiest sections of the whole route, and some might say that Overy Staithe is the most satisfactory of all the coastal villages.

It is off this tricky coast that Britain's greatest naval hero, Horatio Nelson, may have learned to sail. He was born in 1758 at nearby Burnham Thorpe, where his father was rector, though sadly the rectory no longer stands. It was there that he wished to be buried, though his posthumous fame after Trafalgar assured him of a grander resting place in St Paul's Cathedral. There are various memorabilia of Nelson in the church.

From Overy Staithe, the coast path follows the sea bank along Overy Marsh and Creek, and out towards Gun Hill and the dunes to its east. Cross through the dunes and emerge on to the wide expanse of Holkham Bay. This is one of the finest beaches in the country and so large is it that, despite its popularity, it never feels crowded. When the tide is out the sea can be a long way away, and it comes in and goes out at quite a rate. The walker now has a wonderfully airy 2.5 mile (4km) walk across the beach towards Holkham Gap, identified as the point where the line of pine trees dips momentarily, only to rise again eastwards. Alternatively, walk along tracks leading through the fresh-smelling pinewoods covering Holkham Meals.

COKE OF NORFOLK

Just inland is one of the great houses of Norfolk, Holkham Hall. This grand Palladian mansion was built by Thomas Coke, 1st Earl of Leicester, of local brick, and to the designs, inside and out, of the eminent architect, William Kent. Both house and grounds are open to the public. Coke's great-nephew, another Thomas Coke, inherited the estate in the 1760s. He became famous as 'Coke of Norfolk', on account of his far-sighted and far-reaching ideas for agricultural reform and improvements. Made 1st Earl of Leicester of the Second Creation by Queen Victoria, he died in 1842.

At Holkham Gap, follow the boardwalk towards Lady Anne's Road and the car park, turning left at the edge of the trees and continuing along a track bordering the woods to Wells. This leads past a lake, a caravan site and a car park and joins the beach road near the lifeboat station. This was all once part of the fishing boat harbour. Turn right here and walk along the top of the bank for a mile (1.6km) into town. In summer months, footsore walkers can take a ride on the miniature railway.

Wells-next-the-Sea is the busiest port left on the north Norfolk coast. Although its trade is by any standards only small, dealing mainly in fishing and pleasure craft, it still retains the charm and atmosphere of a thriving port. In summer this quiet little town is swelled by an influx of tourists, many from the Midlands, and it takes on a carnival atmosphere. There are no big hotels (most visitors stay in camp sites or bed-and-breakfast accommodation) and Wells avoids undue sophistication or pretentiousness.

At times of high tide, Wells is susceptible to flooding. It was particularly badly hit in the great floods of 1953, and a ship was stranded in the streets in 1978. Wells has now installed flood barriers which can be moved across the road if extreme high

📷 *For a circular walk of about 8 miles (13km), leave the route at the second of the two tracks leading inland between Wells-next-the-Sea and Stiffkey, known as Cocklestrand Drove (grid ref. TF 949 438). Walk up to and cross the A149, and descend the lane to Warham. Turn right at The Three Horseshoes pub, an excellent and old-fashioned establishment, and take the small lane at the bend in the road by the church. Cross the B1105 and then the miniature railway, and continue on to the junction at Callow Hill on the edge of Holkham Park. Turn right here, and so back to Wells and the Norfolk Coast Path.*

THE PROSTITUTES' PARSON

There is a pub at Stiffkey, to which three separate tracks give access. Part of the (private) Hall built by Sir Nathaniel Bacon at the end of the 16th century remains. He was the half-brother of the great essayist and philosopher, Francis Bacon. The author and naturalist Henry Williamson came to live in the village in the 1930s and was, indeed, briefly interned at Wells police station at the beginning of World War II, for his political views. The village also gained notoriety in the 1930s for its eccentric rector, Harold Davidson, who became known as the 'prostitutes' parson'. After eventually being unfrocked, he died after being mauled by a lion while making a living as an attraction at a Blackpool fair.

The Norfolk Coast Path continues past the Freshes Creek (a lovely spot where a few boats are moored) past Morston Quay with its fine views of Blakeney Point, and on towards Blakeney, whose tall church tower has been a reassuring landmark for much of this section of the route. Once a thriving port, Blakeney contents itself nowadays with being a focal point for holidaymakers, amateur sailors and tourists, and its bustling quay and two pretty streets leading down to it are certainly very attractive. Here, the walker will find everything required in the way of supplies.

BLAKENEY TO CROMER

STAGE 9
BLAKENEY to WEYBOURNE
DISTANCE 7.9 miles (12.7km)
MAPS OS Explorer 251, 252
START AT GRID REFERENCE TG 027 441
START POINT Blakeney quay

After the bustle of Blakeney, the coast path leads north, away from the village, towards Blakeney Point, before turning in an easterly direction along the coast. This part of the route is popular with holidaymakers staying in Blakeney, and the long-distance walker may find that he or she suddenly has lots of company. There are wonderful views of Blakeney and its neighbouring village, Cley next the Sea, with its prominent windmill.

The River Glaven has been rerouted at this point and the National Trail follows a new sea defence bank on its approach towards Cley.

📷 *For an enjoyable circular walk, leave the coast path just before Cley next the Sea (at grid ref. TG 042 438), turn right along the coast road for a short distance, and then turn left into Wiveton. From Wiveton you can either take the road directly back to Blakeney or, if you wish to walk further, take the lane towards Langham. Turn right at the first crossroads and so make your way back to Blakeney by Ruberry Hill, a distance of about 6 miles (9.5km).*

Now cut off from the sea, Cley, along with its neighbour Wiveton, whose church can be seen in the distance, was once a prosperous trading port. As you approach the village, the basin

tides ever threaten again. All in all, it is a charming little town and well worth investigating. The walker anxious to get on his way turns left at the quay, walks along it and then along the road continuing by the sea, eventually passing a few workshops and thus gaining the sea bank beyond the town.

📷 *For a circular route of about 7.5 miles (12km), leave the Norfolk Coast Path at grid ref. TF 836 438, and take the path which leads from the gate to the left of the A149. Turn left on to the main road and walk up it a short distance, almost immediately turning right up a farm track and so into a lane leading to Burnham Overy Town. Walk through the village, cross the River Burn, turn first right, then left along a path beside the school. Continue along it, over the B1355 and past Burnham Norton Church, and along the edge of a field until turning right on to the road back to Burnham Deepdale.*

STAGE 8
WELLS-NEXT-THE-SEA to BLAKENEY
DISTANCE 7.7 miles (12.3km)
MAP OS Explorer 251
START AT GRID REFERENCE TF 915 438
START POINT The quay at Wells-next-the-Sea

From Wells-next-the-Sea, the coast path runs along a lonely stretch of salt-marsh towards Stiffkey. These marshes are flooded on the occasion of really big tides, but usually the sea is only a distant glimmer beyond the marsh and, at low tide, tempting wide open areas of sand. These marshes are a haven for all sorts of birds. That great delicacy, samphire, grows in abundance in the summer, and the sands hide great profusions of cockles, known locally as 'Stewkey Blues' ('Stewkey' is an old pronunciation of Stiffkey), that used to be gathered by the women of the village. Now the only people seen out on the sands are the occasional diggers for bait worms.

Indeed, this is a very quiet and peaceful section of the walk. The marshes have a rare, mournful beauty that is enhanced in July and August by the blue of the sea lavender. At various places, a series of footbridges leads out towards the sea and the marshes can be explored by those with waterproof boots or bare feet. Care should be taken not to wander out too far and become cut off by a quickly rising tide.

ℹ️ **PLACES TO VISIT**

•**TITCHWELL MARSH RSPB RESERVE**
www.rspb.org.uk/titchwellmarsh
☎ 01485 210779
By turning left along the A149 at Thornham village, a visit to this reserve will be rewarded with sightings from the dune, reedbed and marsh habitats and hides. Marsh harriers, avocets and redshanks can all be seen here. There are three nature trails on the site, a visitor centre and a shop. Open daily all year.

• **HOLKHAM HALL AND PARK**
www.holkham.co.uk
☎ 01328 710227
A quick walk inland to Holkham village will bring you to the entrance to this impressive estate. The hall itself is a Palladian mansion full of opulent rooms and treasures; many brought from Italy or created to resemble the Italian style. There is a dramatic colonnaded marble hall, actually created from alabaster, with a ceiling modelled on that of the Pantheon. Rooms are decorated with master paintings and grand Flemish tapestries, and the kitchen gleams with copperware. Also within the estate is a serene lake, which it is possible to cruise on in the summer, a deer park, walled gardens, and the Bygones Museum, which includes exhibits ranging from farming tools to toys and vintage cars. Opening hours vary and are on the website.

• **WELLS AND WALSINGHAM LIGHT RAILWAY**
www.wellswalsinghamrailway.
co.uk
☎ 01328 711630
Travel on this narrow-gauge steam locomotive between Wells-next-the-Sea and the medieval village of Little Walsingham, which has long been a centre for pilgrimage and has multiple shrines. The journey takes 30 minutes each way and trains run at least three times a day Apr–Oct. Note: cash only.

of the old harbour, now a mass of reeds and rushes, can clearly be seen. Cley now offers other attractions in the form of a couple of good food shops and pubs.

The coast path runs parallel with the A149 for a short distance as it crosses the River Glaven, affording good views to the south along the Glaven valley. Turn left at the village for a few yards. Just past a telephone box on the right-hand side of the street, find a narrow alley on your left. Take this and turn right at the end. Now follow the path along the old quay wall, up some steps and to the windmill (open to the public at times, and offering accommodation).

The path now leads out along a sea bank towards the sea again. The car park at the end of the road is the place to set off on a rewarding exploration of Blakeney Point. Here, the path turns right and follows the coast for some miles. There is no disguising the fact that this part of the long-distance route is the hardest of all. The walker can walk most of the way to Weybourne either along the beach, on the landward side of the steep sea bank, or wherever they can find a harder surface that makes for easier walking. The beach route has obvious attractions, with the waves crashing in, the vast expanse of the North Sea, a fresh breeze, and the diversion of groups of shore fishermen with their long rods and lines. The problem is that the beach is shingle, and deep shingle at that, and the walking is extremely hard going. The landward side can be tough too, especially in wet weather, but is less so. It is a little frustrating to be so near the sea and not see it. On the other hand, you have the compensation of fine views inland.

WEYBOURNE HOPE

The route slowly passes the village of Salthouse, and there are paths to each end of it. Salthouse, too, was once a port (the main road approximately follows the old shoreline) and, as its name suggests, was for many centuries the centre of a trade in sea salt. The sea continues to cause problems, even in modern times, in that the village is susceptible to floods.

It is with some relief that you will approach hillier ground towards Weybourne, and then the beginning of the cliffs. RAF Weybourne is on the right, and the walking becomes somewhat easier. This has always been an area of the coastline that an invader might easily exploit, due to deep water inshore. This was a fear even in Elizabethan times, and it was then that this saying was coined:

He who would old England win
Must at Weybourne Hope begin.

Walkers wishing to visit the pretty village of Weybourne in search of rest and refreshment can do so by taking the access lane leading to it from this point. Those that don't want to deviate from the main route can pause at the car park and congratulate themselves on having accomplished the hardest part of the Peddars Way and Norfolk Coast Path.

TOP A walker on the Norfolk Coast Path at Cley next the Sea
MIDDLE The River Glaven flowing through Cley Marshes
BOTTOM Cley Mill is one of many windmills to be found in
the relatively flat county of Norfolk

LEFT *The sun sets over Cromer Pier*
ABOVE *Eroded cliffs at West Runton, with Cromer Pier in the distance*

STAGE 10

WEYBOURNE to CROMER

DISTANCE 8.5 miles (13.7km)

MAPS OS Explorer 252

START AT GRID REFERENCE TG 110 436

START POINT The pay-and-display car park at Weybourne beach

From Weybourne, the walking becomes easier. The coast is now one of crumbling cliffs, slowly losing their battle with a treacherous sea. There are fine views inland and in both directions along the coast. The walker, nearing the end of the 93-mile (150km) route, feels a spring in the step, aided and abetted by a fresh breeze and the wide expanse of the sea. A steam train clanks along the old Sheringham–Holt railway line. The woods and farmland eventually give way to an extensive golf course.

At Skelding Hill, climb steeply to the coastguard lookout hut at the top. Pause here. There is a certain satisfaction to be had by looking back westward along the coast. On a clear day, the lifeboat house at Wells-next-the-Sea can be discerned in the far distance, and even on a dull one, Blakeney Church, that great coastal landmark, is clearly visible. The curve and shape of a good portion of England's coastline presents itself. To the east, the bustling seaside resort of Sheringham is laid out, with Beeston Bump or 'Beeston Dump' as it is known locally, in the distance.

Descend Skelding Hill and walk into the town. Sheringham has the knack of being a jolly and friendly place in summer and winter, and there are various good pubs, shops and cafes. Originally a small fishing village, it was developed as a holiday resort at the end of the last century, but lobsters, crabs and other fish are still landed here by the handful of fishing boats still operating.

A splendid 9.75-mile (15.75km) circular walk can be taken by following the Norfolk Coast Path from Sheringham to Cromer, and then walking back along the cliffs

ROMAN CAMP

Walk along the front, past holidaymakers either basking in the sun or huddling in corners away from the sharp wind. Eventually there is a sign saying 'Beeston Hill'. Mount steps and continue past a putting green towards the summit. Here there is another spectacular view of the coast. Ahead lie the villages of West and East Runton, and, beyond them, the town of Cromer and

journey's end. Descend Beeston Hill towards a rough meadow, which in July is a dazzling blaze of poppies, reminding you that this is indeed 'poppyland'. At the end of the meadow, turn right by the entrance to a caravan site and skirt the meadow. Cross the single-track railway line, and then the coast road. Continue on the other side, soon turning right on to a track that leads past Beeston Hall preparatory school, and on and up towards some attractive woodland.

This is National Trust property, and the path leads up through the woods towards Roman Camp. Near by is the highest point in Norfolk, at 346ft (105m). Roman Camp is somewhat of a misnomer. Roman pottery has been found hereabouts, but there is no certainty that the unexcavated earthworks are, in fact, Roman. What is sure is that the many ancient pits, mainly concealed by the woods, are the remains of iron smelting carried out between the 9th and 12th centuries. Cross the clearing and take the left of the two paths ahead, then turn left down an unmade road to a camp site. Keep straight ahead here, past the entrance, and continue down a path which skirts the site. Cross the fields towards Manor Farm and then take the track which leads under the railway line, and eventually past houses, to emerge on the A148 Cromer–Holt road. From here it is a question of walking downhill and into the town of Cromer, where refreshments and accommodation abound.

CRABS AT CROMER

There was once a village called Shipden-juxta-Mare here, but it had lost its battle with the ravaging sea by 1400 and Cromer took its place. It remained a small fishing village until the early 19th century, when it began to gain a reputation as a bathing place. It became progressively more fashionable and prosperous, reaching a pinnacle in the Edwardian era. Nowadays, it is famous principally for the crabs that are caught in pots in the shallows. The pier was built in 1899 and has a theatre and, at its tip, a lifeboat house. The famous cox, Henry Blogg (1876–1954) commanded the crew for half a century and, during his courageous and distinguished career, saved the lives of some 873 people, for which he was awarded the George Cross, among other honours.

The 93-mile (150km) route from the Suffolk border is now at an end, and by traversing such a fascinating range of shifting scenery, from Brecks heath to marsh and cliffs, you will have gathered a huge amount of knowledge about the character of Norfolk, available only to those who explore on foot.

ℹ PLACES TO VISIT

• **THE MUCKLEBURGH COLLECTION**
www.muckleburgh.co.uk
☎ 01263 588210
This is the largest privately owned military museum in the country, and the real stars are the myriad tanks and armoured cars. There are many fully operational vehicles here, including the Gama Goat personnel carrier, which you can take a ride on on Sundays. There are also field guns, anti-aircraft weapons and maritime models. Open daily Apr–Oct.

• **NORTH NORFOLK RAILWAY**
www.nnrailway.co.uk
☎ 01263 820800
This steam railway runs for just over 5 miles (8km) between Sheringham and Holt. Built in 1887, the line is often referred to as the Poppy Line. There are special events on the railway and some trains even run a buffet service. At Holt station there is a museum with artefacts and photographs from the age of steam. You can pay for a lineside pass to gain closer access for those special photographs, or even book a driver experience. See website for details of operating days and times.

• **SHERINGHAM PARK**
www.nationaltrust.org.uk
☎ 01263 820550
Stop off at Weybourne station on your return journey on the North Norfolk Railway, to enjoy a walk back to Sheringham through this expansive park, or simply detour to it from the coast path. The landscaped parkland is one of the finest examples of 19th-century designer Humphrey Repton's work. It is particularly famous for its great displays of azaleas and rhododendrons, and has a gazebo viewing tower with stunning scenery. There is a visitor centre and shop. Park open daily all year.

Weavers' Way

COMPLETE ROUTE CROMER TO GREAT YARMOUTH **56 MILES (90KM)**

SECTION COVERED AS ABOVE

MAPS OS EXPLORER OL 40, 238, 252

The Weavers' Way is aptly named. Not only does it weave a genuinely circuitous route through northeast Norfolk, seldom content with a straight line when a loop or a diversion can be found, but it also passes through that area of the county which for many centuries was renowned as a centre of the weaving trade. Its 56 miles (90km), connecting two of Norfolk's larger towns, present extremely easy walking through a variety of different types of country, and take the walker past or near to many places of great interest. The clear and consistent waymarks make detailed directions unnecessary, except in a couple of cases.

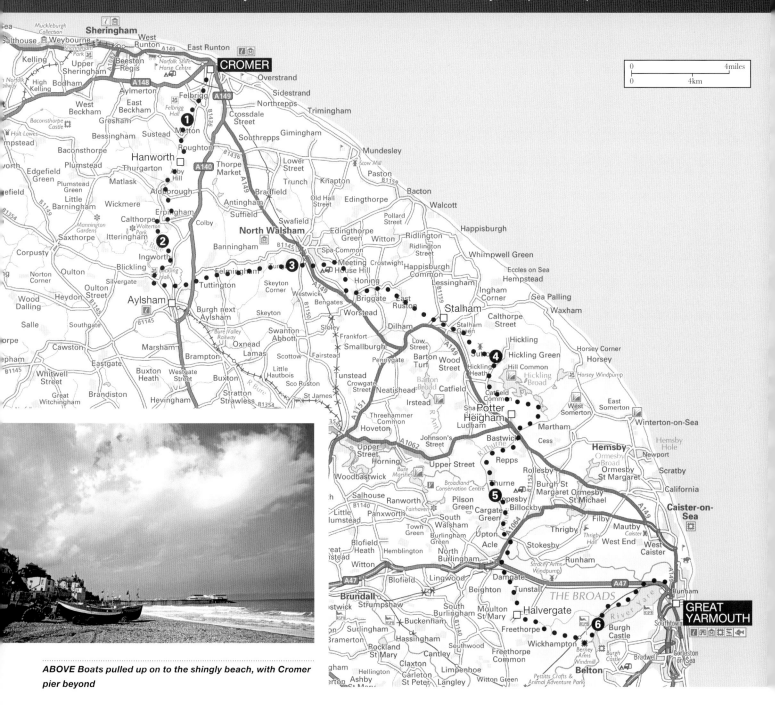

ABOVE *Boats pulled up on to the shingly beach, with Cromer pier beyond*

CROMER TO AYLSHAM

STAGE 1

CROMER to HANWORTH

DISTANCE 7.3 miles (11.7km)

MAP OS Explorer 252

START AT GRID REFERENCE TG 217 421

START POINT The car park in Cromer, near Cromer Methodist Church

The Weavers' Way begins in the car park in Cromer and heads out of town along the road past Cromer Hall before ducking off to the right, through fields and over the railway line. This branch line mercifully escaped the Beeching axe of the 1960s, and a small diesel train still plies its trade between Norwich and the coastal town of Sheringham. Do not take the track to your right after the railway, but keep straight ahead along the edge of the field. At the minor road, go right for a few yards and then left. The route comes out on the B1436 at Felbrigg, and turns left at the cross to pass by Felbrigg Hall and its park, in which there are several delightful walks.

For a circular walk of some 7.5 miles (12km), leave the Weavers' Way (at grid ref. TC 199 396) in Felbrigg Park and carry straight on, passing alongside the Hall, to the Lodge on the minor road. Turn right here, along the Lion's Mouth, cross the A148 and take the minor road leading to Beacon Hill and Roman Camp. At the crossways, near the television mast, turn right and then left along footpaths waymarked as the Norfolk Coast Path, back to Cromer.

PEACE AND SOLITUDE

Felbrigg was left to the National Trust by the writer and scholar RW Ketton-Cremer. It was built by Thomas Windham in about 1620 and enlarged later in the century, and again in the 1750s by James Paine. Equally worthy of inspection is the Church of St Margaret, easily reached down a path from the Weavers' Way. The church, which stands alone in the park (the medieval village having disappeared) is famous for its very fine collection of brasses, particularly the one to its builder, Sir Simon de Felbrigg, and his wife. The route continues past Felbrigg Hall and Felbrigg Pond, then across a minor road to pass Common Farm on the

left. Join a minor road near Lower Gresham and turn left on this lane for 300yds (275m) to find a footpath on the left. Enter the footpath and cross three fields to the church near Sunstead Old Hall. Turn left on the road through Sunstead, towards Metton. Roman pottery has been found at Metton and there is evidence of a substantial settlement at the nearby village of Cresham. The early 14th-century church has a brass to Robert Doughty and his wife (1493), and the manor is Elizabethan or Jacobean.

After 0.75 miles (1.25km), turn right on a lane (grid ref. TG 193 370) towards Little Fen Plantation. Follow this track past Glen Farm and then the footpath across fields, heading south to join Emery's Lane. Turn right and follow the road to Hanworth. There is a feeling of great peace and solitude here. The village stands around a common, where animals graze, and the very fine Hall, which dates from the early 18th century, stands away from the rest of the village facing the 14th-century church. The church at the nearby village of Roughton is also notable, particularly for its Saxon, semi-fortified round tower. There are a number of prehistoric barrows on Roughton Heath.

Across the A140 from Hanworth, standing in its own grounds of lake and woods, is another great house, Gunton Hall. For long the seat of the Harbord family, it was built in two stages by Matthew Brettingham and James Wyatt in the 18th century and became a favourite haunt of the Prince of Wales (later King Edward VII) until gutted by fire in 1882. It has recently been restored into residential apartments. The fine classical Church of St Andrew was built by Robert Adam in 1769.

STAGE 2

HANWORTH to AYLSHAM

DISTANCE 9.9 miles (15.9km)

MAPS OS Explorer 238, 252

START AT GRID REFERENCE TG 192 354

START POINT Hanworth, just off the A140 south of Roughton

The route leads southwest along Ringbank Lane, then left towards Manor Farm, where it goes right and then left into Aldborough. Bear left after Aldborough across fields and a quiet lane to Alby Hill. Just before Alby Hill, turn south across fields to the church at Thwaite House. Cross the road here and continue

ⓘ USEFUL INFORMATION

THE ROUTE
• *www.countrysideaccess.norfolk. gov.uk*
☎ 01603 222769
Norfolk County Council have few details on this site but a click on the Long Distance Paths tab will take you to downloadable maps of sections of the WW. There is a free leaflet of the WW itself, and one of 12 circular walks from it, available by calling the Environment Dept number above, or the general enquiries line on 0344 800 8020.

TOURIST INFORMATION CENTRES
• *www.visitnorthnorfolk.com*
North Norfolk Information Centre, Louden Road, Cromer NR27 9EF;
☎ 0871 200 3071
• *www.visitnorfolk.co.uk*
Bure Valley Railway Station, Norwich Road, Aylsham NR11 6BW;
☎ 01263 733903
• *www.enjoythebroads.com*
The Staithe, Bridge Road, Potter Heigham NR29 5JD;
☎ 01692 677016
• *www.great-yarmouth.co.uk*
Maritime House, 25 Marine Parade, Great Yarmouth NR30 2EN;
☎ 01493 846346

PLANNING YOUR TRIP
• *www.ldwa.org.uk*
The Long Distance Walkers Association has some detail and links for the WW, including the interactive map of linking trails.
• *www.ramblers.org.uk*
☎ 020 7339 8500
The Ramblers Association website also has general information about long-distance walking and specific help covering the WW, such as good publications and guides.

OTHER PATHS
The Wherryman's Way and Marriott's Way both connect the WW to the city of Norwich, from Great Yarmouth and Aylsham respectively. The Angles Way continues from Great Yarmouth, via Diss, to just east of Thetford. The Angles Way, the Peddars Way and Norfolk Coast Path (pages 134–143), and the WW link to form the Around Norfolk Walk.

***LEFT** Felbrigg Hall can be seen from the footpath*

south across large fields to Goose Lane Farm. Turn right on the road and shortly left across Thwaite Common, crossing a footbridge, to reach a road to the east of Erpingham. Turn right to pass through the village.

The family of Erpingham were prominent landowners hereabouts from the time of the Norman Conquest onwards and they gained royal favour by their support of John of Gaunt, whose son Bolingbroke acceded to the throne as Henry IV. Sir Thomas Erpingham commanded the archers at Agincourt. 'Lend me thy cloak, Sir Thomas,' says the King in Shakespeare's *Henry V* on the eve of the battle, and, so disguised, he mingles among his men.

Turn second left at the end of Erpingham, on School Road, and at the 'T' junction go straight across on the field path to join a track (Beech Lane). Follow Beech Lane westwards, turning left at the end to pass Ash Hill Farm. Beyond the farm, turn right on a track which then leads down to a couple of cottages. Keep on down the twisting lane, till Weavers' Way signs point down a footpath to a footbridge over the River Bure. This is a place to take your time and linger a while, before taking the lane past the beautiful mill and, after a short distance, turning left into Blickling Park. Blickling is the best known of several great houses in the area and there are various delightful walks in the grounds. The Weavers' Way emerges at the Buckinghamshire Arms and then takes you past the celebrated front aspect of the Hall itself. Ghosts are said to abound at Blickling, including that of Anne Boleyn, the second of Henry VIII's six wives, who met her end at the hand of the executioner. Blickling belonged to her family for a time, and the headless queen can apparently be seen approaching the Hall, in a carriage driven by a headless coachman and drawn by a headless horse.

WORSTED STOCKINGS

Other great houses near by include Wolterton Hall, the home of the Walpole family, and the moated and beautiful Mannington Hall. The latter is also owned by the Walpole family and is a fascinating house, dating from 1640 and open by appointment. It was substantially altered by the Earl of Orford in 1864. His eccentric inscriptions can still be seen. 'A tiger is something worse than a snake,' reads one of them, 'a demon than a tiger, a woman than a demon, and nothing worse than a woman.' The grounds of both houses are delightful and open throughout the year. There are fine rose gardens and several countryside walks and trails.

From Blickling, the Weavers' Way leads to the hamlet of Silvergate, along the edges of fields, down a broad green avenue towards the very fine Aylsham Old Hall, and then, by means of a dismantled railway line and minor roads, crosses the River Bure again and skirts the north side of Aylsham. This charming town is well worth a visit, if time allows. In the Middle Ages it relied mostly on linen-weaving for its prosperity. Then, in 1372 the manor came into the hands of John of Gaunt, Duke of Lancaster, and the town began to concentrate on the weaving of woollens and, in particular, the making of worsted stockings, waistcoats and breeches; an industry which kept it prosperous until the great industrial changes of the late 18th century.

Everywhere in the town are examples of this Georgian wealth and the wide Market Place is as attractive as any in the county. Markets and auctions are held Monday and Friday, bringing an added zest to the town. The Church of St Michael is sizeable and handsome, and dates from the 14th century. It is said to have been refounded by John of Gaunt. In the graveyard is the tomb of the great landscape gardener Humphrey Repton, who had many connections with the locality and had a hand in the design of the grounds of several big Norfolk houses. His self-composed epitaph reads:

> Not like Egyptian tyrants consecrate,
> Unmixed with others shall my dust remain;
> But mold'ring, blending, melting into Earth,
> Mine shall give form and colour to the Rose
> And while its vivid blossoms cheer Mankind,
> Its perfumed odours shall ascend to Heaven.

It is pleasant to note that his rose-covered grave is carefully tended by the Aylsham Society. He died in 1818.

AYLSHAM TO POTTER HEIGHAM

STAGE 3
AYLSHAM to STALHAM
DISTANCE 14.2 miles (22.8km)
MAPS OS Explorer OL 40, 238, 252
START AT GRID REFERENCE TG 192 276
START POINT Where the Weavers' Way crosses the Ingworth–Aylsham road

From the start point, the Weavers' Way makes use of minor roads (well waymarked) in order to skirt the north side of Aylsham and cross the A140, after which it settles down for a spell along the dismantled railway line which used to run between King's Lynn and Great Yarmouth (opened in 1883 and closed in 1959). This is easy walking, if not the most exciting part of the route, and many different varieties of plants, shrubs and trees can be seen along here. The cutting before the road leading to Felmingham is a butterfly nature reserve and it is quite likely, too, that there may be an adder or two basking in the sun here (they are quite harmless unless interfered with). This whole section of the route can become extremely hot in fine summer weather.

For a circular walk of some 11 miles (17.5km) back to Aylsham, leave the Weavers' Way at the junction with the Felmingham road (at grid ref. TG 252 286), taking minor roads to Tuttington and then following a small road back to Aylsham.

ADMIRAL NELSON

Not long after the Felmingham road, the Weavers' Way divides, and you have the choice of going into North Walsham or avoiding the town by keeping to its south via Stone Cross, Scarborough Hill, and White Horse Common. Both routes have their advantages, both are well waymarked and there is little difference in terms of distance.

North Walsham is well worth a visit for those with a little time to spare. For many centuries it was a centre of the weaving and worsted trades, and it still remains a prosperous community, with a market on Thursdays. The ruined tower of the church was once the highest in Norfolk, at 147ft (45m), while the attractive market cross was rebuilt after a fire in 1602. In 1606 Sir William Paston, of the great Norfolk family, founded a grammar school to instruct the young to 'become good and profitable members in the Church and commonwealth'. The Paston School moved to its present site in 1765 and, among several famous pupils passing through its portals over the centuries, none was more so than the future admiral, Horatio Viscount Nelson. He was a Norfolk lad born and bred, who studied here between 1768 and 1771 and is said to have scrambled down into the headmaster's garden one night, by means of knotted sheets, to steal pears.

A sailboat on the tranquil waters of Hickling Broad

The route leaves town by the old Yarmouth road, follows the pavement and turns left into Thirlby Road. At the end of the houses it goes straight ahead across the field to join Field Lane. Turn left on Field Lane and continue to Happisburg Road, then turn right into Holgate Road in the hamlet of White Horse Common. Continue south, passing Meeting House Hill and on to meet the A149, where the route takes again to the disused railway line. To the south is Worstead, which gave its name to the famous cloth, with its huge 'wool' church, St Mary's, whose 109ft (33m) tower is a local landmark.

The Weavers' Way continues across the disused North Walsham and Dilham Canal, never a great success and now peculiarly melancholy, to the village of Honing; a quiet backwater with an 18th-century Hall, whose grounds were laid out by Humphrey Repton. After Honing, the landscape and atmosphere of the countryside becomes more and more that of the Broads, especially around Brumstead Common, and the route eventually leads to Stalham; a bustling little town which supplies the many holidaymakers making use of Barton and Sutton Broads, and the River Ant. Note Stalham Hall towards the east end of the High Street. It is a delightful and much admired house of the late 18th century.

STAGE 4

STALHAM to POTTER HEIGHAM

DISTANCE 10.5 miles (16.9km)

MAPS OS Explorer OL 40, 252

START AT GRID REFERENCE TG 372 251

START POINT From outside Stalham Hall, in Stalham High Street

The Weavers' Way heads east out of Stalham from the Hall along the road towards Hickling. It eventually turns right and then left, past Sutton Hall, and then takes the footpath to the right that leads to Sutton Mill.

For a circular walk of some 8 miles (13km), instead of turning right down the footpath to Sutton Mill (at grid ref. TG 395 242), continue along the minor road, past a junction to the right, and take the footpath on the left to Whinmere Farm. Take the road to Calthorpe Street and on to Ingham Church. Take the minor road south, past the mill, to the junction with the road back to Stalham.

THE NORFOLK BROADS

The Weavers' Way now continues along minor roads through Hickling Green and Hickling Heath, until finally leading round to the south side of Hickling Broad and becoming footpath again. Apart from Breydon Water, Hickling Broad represents the largest area of water in the Broads. Swallowtail butterflies can be seen here in some abundance, but the once common marsh harriers and bitterns are now sighted extremely rarely. There is, however, still a huge variety of birds to be spotted: warblers, tits, flycatchers, reed buntings, redshanks, snipe, sandpipers, kestrels, and any number and type of ducks and geese. Much of Hickling Broad, and the Broads in general, is a nature reserve. As so often is the case, it is the walker who is able to get to the more remote areas, and who is able to experience, more than his fellow man, the essence and true nature of a place. Certainly walking the Weavers' Way along the edge of Hickling Broad and Heigham Sound, or for that matter along any of the numerous paths and nature trails hereabouts, down paths through the reeds, with the occasional glimpse of sail and water, and with the songs and the cries of the birds in one's ears, is an experience not to be missed.

From Heigham Sound, the route takes a straight track southwest, almost parallel to the River Thurne. It crosses the A149 and turns left on to the minor road that leads into the bustle of shops and boatyards that surround the lovely old bridge at Potter Heigham, which probably dates from the late 14th century. Potter Heigham is a centre of the huge holiday industry that now threatens to engulf the Broads, and a good many of the 100,000 or so people who have their own boats keep or

PLACES TO VISIT

• FELBRIGG HALL
www.nationaltrust.org.uk
☎ 01263 837444
The Felbrigg Estate is passed on the WW. It sits within an estate of over 1,760 acres (700 ha), which includes the Great Wood and its many waymarked trails. The house is a fine example of Jacobean style, and is filled with Grand Tour treasures. There are formal gardens in addition to the parkland, and a dovecote in the walled kitchen garden that supplies the brasserie and tea rooms. Park open daily all year; house open Sat–Wed Mar–Oct.

• WOLTERTON PARK
www.manningtongardens.co.uk
☎ 01263 768444
The Wolterton Estate is owned by the historic Walpole family, who also own the nearby Mannington Estate. The hall is Georgian, built in the 1720s. However, the main draw is the park, which has lovely walks, an orienteering course and an adventure playground. Park open daily all year; hall open Fri afternoons only May–Oct.

• BLICKLING HALL
www.nationaltrust.org.uk
☎ 01263 738030
One of the finest Jacobean houses in the country, with a spectacular Long Gallery. The gardens include a dry moat, parterre, orangery, secret garden, and a wilderness garden. There is a second-hand bookshop, a restaurant and café. Park open daily all year; house open Wed–Sun Mar–Oct; garden open daily Mar–Oct, Thu–Sun Nov–Feb.

bring them here. Some 200,000 more people hire boats on the Broads for holiday cruises. The village itself was, since Roman times, the home of potters making beakers and urns from the local deposits of clay.

POTTER HEIGHAM TO GREAT YARMOUTH

STAGE 5

POTTER HEIGHAM to HALVERGATE

DISTANCE 10.3 miles (16.6km)
MAP OS Explorer OL 40
START AT GRID REFERENCE TG 419 184
START POINT The bridge at Potter Heigham

The Weavers' Way crosses the ancient bridge at Potter Heigham and sets off on the south bank of the Thurne River in the direction of Thurne itself. For some time, the path runs behind an extraordinary assortment of holiday huts, chalets and cottages, many with boats moored alongside, that are crammed together along both banks of the river. Some are quite unsightly, some rather charming and some are plain eccentric. All along this stretch of the river, proud boat owners, with jaunty yachting caps on heads, perhaps paintbrushes in hands and pipes in mouths, move slowly and contentedly around their crafts. Meanwhile, the river itself is host to all sorts of vessels, from large and expensive cruisers to tiny sailing dinghies, all jostling for their fair share of the water. The most attractive to look at are the flat-bottomed, wooden Broads sailing boats, often with galley and three or four berths, that are a feature of these waters. Many were built earlier this century and, maroon or white sails aloft, still afford a great deal of fun and excitement to their crews. It is not uncommon to see sailing races in progress, with many boats of similar build straining into the wind, tacking from one reed-lined bank to the other.

As the walker leaves Potter Heigham behind, the chalets die out and the path becomes increasingly lonely, and the landscape increasingly beautiful. To the left, cattle graze contentedly in the low-lying meadows and the twin windmills of Thurne are visible around the bend in the river. Eventually you approach the village. A few boats are moored up alongside the banks of the river, and the pub is probably doing good business, but Thurne is a wonderfully unspoilt place, cut off as it is and only approachable by car on small roads.

To the west, across the river, are the remains of St Benet's Abbey. This was an early foundation and was endowed with three manors by King Canute in 1020. It withstood attack by John Litester's rebel peasants in 1381 and prospered until the Dissolution when it fell into ruins. An 18th-century windmill was built inside the gatehouse, and now little remains. The Bishop of Norwich, who also retains the title of Abbot of St Benet's, arrives by boat at the Abbey once a year to conduct an open-air service amongst the ruins.

Now make your way through a farm, across a couple of fields, past the 14th-century church and so across country and back to the river. The river has now become the Bure; the Bure having met the Thurne just south of the village.

🔲 *For a circular walk of some 7.5 miles (12km), leave the Weavers' Way at Thurne Church (at grid ref. TG 405 156) and instead of crossing over the minor road, turn left along it. Take the first proper turning left again along the road past Ashby Hall and on into the village of Repps. Turn left in the village and right along the River Thurne, back to Potter Heigham Bridge.*

BLACK DEATH GRAFFITI

The path along the east bank is delightful, and once again one feels that there can be no better way of getting to know the countryside than by walking it. At Acle Bridge, cross the A1064

and then take the path along the other side of the river for a while, before turning right by a boatyard towards Acle. Acle is a busy little town, standing as it does at the junction of two main roads and including a railway station. The church of St Edmund is well worth visiting. It contains graffiti thought to date from the time of the Black Death, referring to the 'brute beast plague that rages hour by hour'. The Weavers' Way does not go into Acle, however, but turns south, crosses the A47 and then the railway line to Yarmouth, before setting off on a thoroughly enjoyable stretch by woods and pastureland to the hamlet of Tunstall, and from there to Halvergate.

STAGE 6

HALVERGATE to GREAT YARMOUTH

DISTANCE 8.6 miles (13.8km)
MAP OS Explorer OL 40
START AT GRID REFERENCE TG 420 069
START POINT Where the Weavers Way meets the road in the centre of Halvergate

From Halvergate the route strikes east, following the minor road out of the village and taking the track at the sharp bend in the road. This is now marsh country, intersected with hundreds of ditches and sparsely populated. The rich pastures between the Rivers Yare and Waveney were once famous for their cattle. Daniel Defoe, the author of *Robinson Crusoe*, visited the district in the 1720s and reported that the preferred Scottish-bred cattle were doing well. 'These Scots runts, so they call them,' he wrote, 'coming out of the cold and barren mountains of the Highlands in Scotland, feed so eagerly on the rich pasture in these marshes, that they thrive in an unusual manner, and grow monstrously fat.'

It has to be said that there is a desolate atmosphere about these parts, especially in the winter when the winds blow from east and north. The Weavers' Way now becomes footpath again. Take the footpath which leads southeast, crosses the railway line at Berney Arms Station and takes you to Berney Arms Mill. Built in the mid-19th century, it was originally designed to grind cement but soon became a pumping mill. There is a pub and shop near by.

A few hundred yards downstream, the River Yare and the River Waveney, which forms the border with Suffolk for much of its length, meet in Breydon Water, which is effectively their estuary, though a landlocked one.

For a circular walk of around 11 miles (17.5km) you can take the northern alternative of the Weavers' Way (where the footpaths divide at grid ref. TG 435 066) as far as the railway crossing at Breydon Water

and then return to Halvergate by the southern alternative via Berney Arms Mill.

THE BLACKPOOL OF THE EAST COAST

The path runs along the north side of Breydon Water. Great Yarmouth is visible in the distance, looking not so much like a popular English coastal resort as part of some sprawling industrial American town. To the southwest is Burgh Castle, nowadays a Mecca for campers and caravanners, but once the proud Roman fort of Gariannonum; an area of six acres surrounded by an impregnable wall 15–20ft (4.5-6m) high and 9ft (2.75m) thick, built in the 3rd century AD to keep out the Saxon raiders. Much of it still exists.

After the departure of the Romans there was a monastery here, founded in about AD635 by St Fursa, the Irish missionary, but this too fell foul of the changing circumstances of history and was destroyed after only 250 years, probably by Danish invaders towards the end of the 9th century. Indeed, this whole area was settled by the Danes.

The Weavers' Way continues along the lonely north shore of Breydon Water. Much of it is a nature reserve and a haven for birds. Eventually it meets the A47 and together they journey the short distance towards Great Yarmouth. To the north is the resort of Caister-on-Sea.

Though now mainly a holiday suburb of Yarmouth, Caister has two glorious links with the past. As its name suggests, it was originally a Roman settlement, probably begun in the 1st century AD and then developed over the years. It may have become a Roman town for retired seamen. English Heritage now looks after the Roman remains. The Saxons made use of the massive defences in later centuries. Many 'boat burials' have been discovered outside the walls and a number of Saxon huts inside. Caister's other fascinating site is the 15th-century castle.

The Weavers' Way's final destination, Great Yarmouth, suffers from its modern reputation as the Blackpool of the east coast, and it is true that much of the modern development in pursuit of the holiday trade has done the town no favours. However, Yarmouth has a long and proud history, and for many centuries was an extremely important port, trading in everything from cloth to coal, but above all in herrings.

At the start of the 20th century, the herring industry was at its peak, and fisher-girls from Scotland would flock to the town in the autumn to clean and gut the herrings at the rate of a cran (1,200–1,500 fish) an hour. Yet as early as the 18th century, Yarmouth was a fashionable resort, and the Victorians capitalized upon this. Now, in the 21st century, it is the holidaymaker, not the herring, that provides the town's prosperity.

ⓘ PLACES TO VISIT

● **BURE VALLEY RAILWAY**
www.bvrw.co.uk
☎ 01263 733858
The former trackbed of the Great Eastern Railway has been re-used to carry this narrow gauge steam and diesel service. Trains travel for 9 miles (14.5km) between Aylsham and Wroxham, famed as the unofficial capital of the Norfolk Broads. There is a footpath beside the line, so you can take the train out and, if you have the time, can then walk back to Aylsham. Alternatively, the railway have teamed up with a local boat company that are a short walk from the Wroxham station, to provide a cruise around the Broads for 90 minutes before your return train. See website for details of operating days and times; boat trains run daily Apr–Oct.

● **GREAT YARMOUTH**
www.great-yarmouth.co.uk
☎ 01493 846346
The seaside town of Great Yarmouth provides all manner of entertainment at the end of your walk. The wide promenade of Marine Parade allows you to wander between many of the main attractions, such as the bright and lively Britannia Pier, the bowling alley at Wellington Pier and the more genteel Jetty. There are miles of sandy beaches to enjoy, or perhaps the thrill of the Pleasure Beach rides could make a fine contrast to days of peaceful countryside walking. The Sea Life Centre allows you to get close to a wide variety of sea creatures, from starfish to turtles, and there is an underwater tunnel through a shark tank (www.sealifeeurope. com ☎ 0871 423 2110; open daily all year). For a look at the history of the area, visit Time and Tide, a museum set in a Victorian herring smokehouse, with interactive displays and a courtyard café (www.museums. norfolk.gov.uk ☎ 01493 743930; open daily all year).

TOP LEFT Berney Arms Mill stands beside the River Yare
TOP RIGHT People on the merry-go-round at Great Yarmouth Pleasure Beach

Sunset across Derwent Water

The North Country

Ribble Way

COMPLETE ROUTE LONGTON TO GAVEL GAP **72 MILES (115KM)**

SECTION COVERED AS ABOVE

MAPS OS EXPLORER OL 2, OL 21, OL 41, 286, 287

Footpaths have ever laced the lovely Ribble valley, but not until 1 June 1985 was a middle-distance way opened that extended rom the salt flats at the Ribble's mouth to its lonely source on the slopes of Gayle Moor. The walk sews up a number of local paths, many of which have been upgraded, and some existing rights of way have been diverted, thus establishing harmony between walkers and those whose livelihood comes from the land. The Ramblers' Association first proposed it and Lancashire County Council, North Yorkshire County Council and the Yorkshire Dales National Park Authority maintain it.

TOP *View across fields to Ribblehead at dawn*
ABOVE *Neo-classical style at the Harris Museum and Art Gallery in Preston*

LONGTON TO RIBCHESTER

STAGE 1

LONGTON to A6 PRESTON

DISTANCE 8.3 miles (13.4km)

MAP OS Explorer 286

START AT GRID REFERENCE SD 458 254

START POINT The Dolphin Inn, Marsh Lane, Longton

From the Dolphin Inn, turn west along Marsh Lane and right along the tidal embankment overlooking Longton Marshes. Longton Marshes form a small part of the Ribble Marshes National Nature Reserve, 5,689 acres of saltmarsh and intertidal flats on the south side of the River Ribble. It protects the habitat of waders, ducks, geese, gulls and terns. It is a staging point for Arctic migrants, and oystercatchers, grey plover and redshank winter there.

At Longton Brook the path bends sharply to the right, leaving the track by a stile in the hedge to the right. Continue along the waymarked path, crossing a series of stiles, and Longton Brook. Follow the path around a field boundary, northwards and, after crossing a lane and another field, rejoin the embankment.

The path turns right, to follow the south bank of the River Ribble for 3.5 miles (5.5km) to Preston. After a while it goes downhill and crosses a beck. Continue over a stile to the left of a padlocked gate to rejoin the embankment. Follow the path past Higher Penwortham golf course and the site of the former Penwortham Power Station into Holme Road. Continue along it to the Liverpool Road (A59). Cross the road and follow a riverside footpath directly opposite. Turn left on to Leyland road (A582) and left again to cross Penwortham Bridge. Descend steps at its northern end, turn right into Riverside and follow a tree-lined, riverside avenue in Miller and Avenham Parks.

PRESTON'S PAST

This district of Preston, the area south of Fishergate dominated by Winckley Square, where Georgian streets run into landscaped Miller and Avenham Parks, is the towns's visual pride and joy. The many fine 19th-century buildings include the Harris Museum and Art Gallery, deservedly known as 'The Jewel in the Town'. The building is one of the most notable examples of the Greek Revival in the country. It dominates the town centre and its 'Story of Preston' gallery attracts thousands of visitors. Preston's past is Roman and medieval. It was granted its first charter in 1179. The lowest crossing of the River Ribble was at Preston and this aided its development. Spinning and weaving began there in the 16th century. Arkwright, a Preston man, born in 1732, developed a spinning or water frame. The first cotton mill was started in 1777. Every 20 years a local festival, 'Preston Guild', re-enacts the town's history with processions and many associated events.

Pass the end of the horse-drawn tramway bridge. Climb slightly, curving right, along a tree-lined avenue adjacent to the riverbank and continue along the Boulevard. Across the river is the confluence of the Ribble and Darwen at Walton Flats.

STAGE 2

A6, PRESTON to RIBCHESTER

DISTANCE 9.7 miles (15.6km)

MAPS OS Explorer 286, 287

START AT GRID REFERENCE SD 552 287

START POINT The London Road, A6, where it crosses the Ribble

Cross London Road (A6) and follow a track between the bridge parapet and the Shawes Arms. Soon, just beyond a small bridge, leave the track by a stile on the right, go back to the river and keep close to it around a long loop. Mete House and its associated farm buildings are seen on the left. On reaching the entrance to Melling's Wood, which climbs an escarpment, descend some riverside steps, continue through the wood and turn right at its end, edging a golf course to rejoin the river bank and follow it to Brockholes Bridge.

Cuerdale Hall is seen near the south bank of the River Ribble. There, in 1840, workmen discovered 10,000 early silver coins and some silver ingots, believed to have belonged to an invading Scandinavian army. The coins were minted between AD815 and 930. Most of the Cuerdale Hoard is now on display in the British Museum.

In pre-turnpike days, travellers between Blackburn and Preston crossed the River Ribble at Brockholes on an ancient ferry. A temporary structure, built in 1826, superseded the ferry and had a halfpenny toll. Today, slightly upriver, the M6 motorway spans both the A39 and the River Ribble near a ford that, centuries ago, brought history to this part of the valley. Cross Brockholes Brow (A59) and follow a farm track immediately opposite, bearing right, along a fenced track on the approach to Lower Brockholes, edging the river and going under the motorway.

ABOVE *Tidal innundation on the Ribble Marshes*

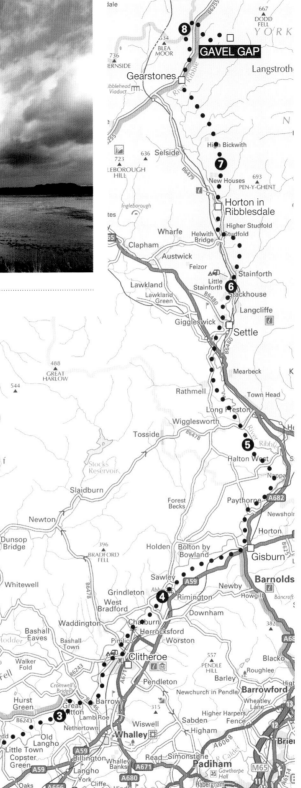

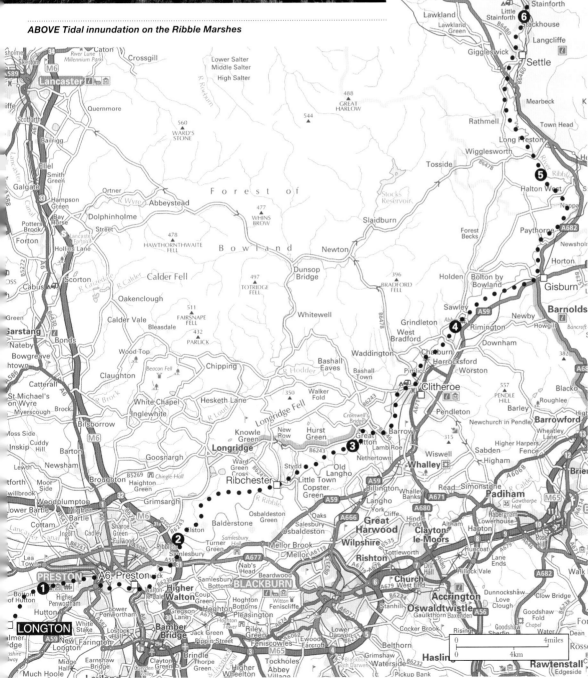

USEFUL INFORMATION

THE ROUTE

• www.visitribblevalley.co.uk/
downloads
There is a downloadable file
showing the RW on extracts
of OS mapping available on a
few sites, but it is difficult to
find. The easiest way is to go
to the address above, scroll to
the bottom of the page, and
find a link to The Ribble Way in
the list of frequently requested
downloads. The Lancashire
County Council look after the
RW but do not produce an
official guide.

TOURIST INFORMATION
CENTRES

• www.visitpreston.com
The Guildhall, Lancaster Road,
Preston PR1 1HT;
☎ 01772 253731
• www.visitribblevalley.co.uk
Ribble Valley Borough Council,
Church Walk, Clitheroe BB7 2RA;
☎ 01200 425566
• www.settle.org.uk
Town Hall, Cheapside, Settle
BD24 9EJ;
☎ 01729 825192
• www.yorkshiredales.org.uk
Pen-y-ghent Café, Horton-in-
Ribblesdale BD24 0HE;
☎ 01729 860333

PLANNING YOUR TRIP

• www.ldwa.org.uk
The Long Distance Walkers
Association has some information
on the RW, such as the interactive
map of linking trails.
• www.ramblers.org.uk
☎ 020 7339 8500
The Ramblers Association
website has general information
about long-distance walking and
a little help on the RW.
• www.visitlancashire.com
This official tourist website lists
accommodation that specifically
welcomes walkers and cyclists.

OTHER PATHS

The Pennine Way National Trail
(pages 188–195) passes close to
the northern end of the RW, at
Gayle Moor. They link officially at
Horton-in-Ribblesdale. The Dales
Way (pages 160–167) crosses the
RW north of there, at Gearstones.

TOP Samlesbury Hall is a restored Tudor mansion dating from 1325
ABOVE The west tower of the Church of Saint Wilfrid, Ribchester

On the river's south bank, slightly to the east, lies 14th-century Samlesbury Hall. It was extensively altered in Tudor times to a moated manor house, and much of the existing building dates from that period. Now National Trust property, it houses collections of antiques and paintings. Exhibitions are held there throughout the year.

FOOD FOR THOUGHT

The track turns sharp left and then veers northeast, crossing meadows, to the site of Higher Brockholes. Here, cross a stile and turn left along a field boundary to enter Red Scar Wood along a well-defined, climbing path. Where the path forks at the hilltop, turn right, along the back of a wood, and cross a field. At the end go right, through woodland, to join another path. Continue along it round the back of Red Scar Wood. Follow the fenced track to the edge of the woodland and, where it veers off in a northerly direction, cross a stile on the right and then cross three fields on a clear path, keeping roughly parallel to the wood on your right. The path cuts across the corner of the fourth field to enter Tun Brook Wood. Go down steps to cross Tun Brook. Climb steeply up the other side, out of the wood, cross a meadow and turn left on to a metalled lane. After a short distance turn left, into Elston Lane, follow it for 0.5 miles (800m) and turn right, on to a track which passes Marsh House. Cross a stile at the end of the track and continue alongside a hedge. Cross a large field to join Alston Lane on the north side of Alston Hall Cottages.

Turn left on to the road and take the footpath almost opposite, signposted to Hothersall Lane. The path crosses meadows and several small streams before descending to the bottom southeast corner of King Wood, where it crosses a bridge and leaves the wood, going uphill over a meadow alongside the wood. Continue northeasterly, following field boundaries, and turn right into Hothersall Lane. Just beyond Hothersall Hall, leave by a stile on the right. Continue along the top of Red Bank Wood and descend to a gate to reach a riverside track leading into Ribchester. Here, in the churchyard, a motto carved on a sundial gives food for thought:

I am a shadow, so art thou;
I mark time, dost thou?

From Ribchester there is a bus service back to Preston.

RIBCHESTER TO GISBURN

STAGE 3
RIBCHESTER to CLITHEROE
DISTANCE 10.1 miles (16.3km)
MAPS OS Explorer OL 41, 287
START AT GRID REFERENCE SO 650 350
START POINT Anchor Holme, on the riverside, near Ribchester

Ribchester, 'the walled town by the Ribble', was a major Middle Bronze Age settlement that was occupied through the Iron Age. The Romans recognized its importance and established the cavalry fort of Bremetennacum there, at the hub of five great roads. It remained an active cavalry fort on Julius Agricola's military highway linking Chester and Manchester with Hadrian's Wall. Roman pillars, intended for temples, now hold up the porch of the White Bull Hotel. From Anchor Holme, follow the riverside path along the Ribble, turn left along Huddle Brook to Greenside, then turn right, on to the Blackburn road. Follow this road to the point at which it turns sharp right across Ribchester Bridge and continue straight on along the west bank of the river to Dewhurst House.

From Dewhurst House farmyard, turn right towards the river, cross a small meadow and turn left, along the riverbank, to Haugh Wood. Follow the path round the bend of the river and, on leaving the wood, turn left and continue around a field boundary. When close to the bottom left-hand corner of the field go left, uphill, to the top left-hand corner of the next field, between Hey Hurst and a country house. Cross a farm track, continue round another field boundary alongside Clough Bank Wood and cross Starling Brook. Continue eastwards, alongside field boundaries to a fenced track. Follow this to Trough House farmyard, then along Lambing Clough Lane to Hurst Green. Trough House takes its name from Trows Ferry; resembling a pair of troughs lashed together, it was dragged by ropes across the Ribble between Dinckley and Hurst Green.

Anyone wishing to return to Ribchester from Hurst Green may do so by taking the Longridge road (grid ref. SD 684 379) to St John's Church. Turn left along a farm track to Merrick's Hall, thence over field paths to Bailey Hall, continuing via rights of way past Dutton Hall and Low Dutton to Ribchester Bridge.

WHITE LADY
From Trough House follow the riverside path for 1.4 miles (2.25km) to Jumbles Farm, passing it and Hacking Ferry boathouse. A tablet on the side of the front door of Jumbles Farm dates the house to 1723. Built in the late Stuart style, it takes its name from Jumbles Rocks; an ancient ford that links the two Bronze Age sites of Winckley Lane and Brockhall Eases. The two large mounds near Hacking Ferry boathouse are man-made. The one beside a barn, excavated in 1894, contained a cinerary urn of circa 1250BC, with a cremated body and the skulls of a young man, a boy and a child. The burial was one of an important person, probably a local chieftain. The larger mound, known as Loe Hill, is also man-made. It is thought that it was built after the Battle of Billington in AD798, at a time when the Anglo-British kingdom of Northumbria was fraught with internal conflict. A third mound once stood across the river at Brockhall Eases. During the summer of 1836 the farmer at Brockhall, while leveling the earth mound, discovered a stone-lined cist. It was said to have contained human bones and the rusty remains of some iron spearheads. All crumbled to dust when exposed to the air.

Hacking Hall, on the Ribble's eastern bank near the confluence of the River Calder, is a magnificent Jacobean mansion with a five-gabled, many-mullioned frontage. Follow the riverbank to where the River Hodder joins the Ribble as the latter turns sharp east. Continue up the Hodder, through a gate, along a road past Winckley Hall Farm and through the wooded grounds of Winckley Hall. The Hall's most notable occupant was Dorothy Winckley, the ghostly 'White Lady' who walks the lanes around the Great Hall at Samlesbury.

THE BATTLE OF PRESTON
When the drive curves left around Winckley Hall, go through a kissing-gate on the right and continue walking along a field path, parallel to Spring Wood, aiming for the right of Stonyhurst College, which is seen ahead. On reaching the Longridge–

PLACES TO VISIT

• RIBBLE STEAM RAILWAY
www.ribblesteam.org.uk
☎ 01772 728800
The Ribble Steam Railway runs on the opposite bank of the river to the RW, and has been open to visitors since 2005. About 2 miles (3km) from the centre of Preston, it runs locomotives along the Preston dockside of the Ribble for a round trip of almost 3 miles (5km), which takes around 35 minutes. The line passes over the Preston Marina entrance via a swing bridge. On-site there is also a workshop, where you can watch the engineers work on the trains, a museum, and a small tea room. The entrance fee allows unlimited rides on the railway all day. See website for details of operating days and times. Note: cash only.

• HARRIS MUSEUM AND ART GALLERY
www.harrismuseum.org.uk
☎ 01772 258248
The Harris Museum is located right in the centre of Preston, in the market square. It is located in the same building as the library and contains collections of fine art, photography, and decorative art items such as perfume bottles. There is also an exhibition on the Story of Preston, and regular changes to the temporary exhibition spaces. Local artists are encouraged to submit work for display. The museum has a program of family activities and workshops, and is free to enter. Open Mon–Sat all year, except bank holidays.

ABOVE Cromwell's Bridge over the River Hodder

Clitheroe road at a junction, turn right along it, using the footpath, and cross Lower Hodder Bridge, which is slightly upstream of Cromwell's Bridge. This medieval bridge with three segmental arches, one of the prettiest over the Hodder, is so named because it was there, in 1648, that Oliver Cromwell decided to advance westwards, along the Ribble to cut off the Scots. The Battle of Preston was the result.

Continue along the roadside, now using the verge, for 0.5 miles (800m) and turn right to Great Mitton. Cross Mitton Bridge and, just beyond the Aspinal Arms, turn left over a stile. Follow a path along the line of the river, joining a track near where a pipe-bridge crosses the Ribble. Follow the track to Henthorn Road. Take this, edging a wood on the left. Opposite 'Langdales' turn left along a track for 30yds (27m). Turn right and in a few yards cross a stile and follow the boundary of the field ahead to its far corner. Turn right, following a riverside path past a caravan site and picnic area to reach Edisford Bridge, on the outskirts of the town of Clitheroe.

Clitheroe lies at the heart of the Ribble Valley. A bustling market town, it is dominated by a huge limestone rock crowned with the Norman keep of Clitheroe Castle. This proud town has accommodation, a range of shops and plenty of character.

STAGE 4

CLITHEROE to GISBURN

DISTANCE 10 miles (16km)
MAPS OS Explorer OL 21, OL 41
START AT GRID REFERENCE SD 726 414
START POINT Edisford Bridge, Clitheroe

From Edisford Bridge turn right along Edisford Road, then left along a metalled path, passing the right side of the Ribbleside Pool, continuing to a riverside path. Turn right along it, soon to curve right away from the river to go between houses into Low Moor, Clitheroe.

Bear left into High Street, which turns right and, just past Union Street on your right, bear right, past a former Wesleyan School. Follow a fenced track and go over a field to cross a stile. Follow a fence on your right and continue to the edge of Boy Bank Wood. Descend through it and follow the riverside to Brungerley Bridge. Turn right, along Waddington Road, and left, as signposted, into Brungerley Park. Follow a wooded riverside path, leaving the park where the river bears left to follow it to the Bradford Bridge. Cross the Bradford road and follow the riverbank to a wooded escarpment, Bond Hurst, and continue above it into a field. Cross this and climb two stiles into Ribble Lane. Turn left, along it, to Grindleton Bridge, which you cross. Follow the riverside path signposted 'Rathmell Sike' and after the first field continue along a flood bank. When the river curves right, leave it over a ladder-stile in a wall to your left and climb two meadows to a road at Foxley Bank (SD 768 460).

Turn right to Sawley and, where a meadow lies between road and river, follow a footpath diagonally right across it to Sawley Bridge. Cross and go into Sawley. The village is known mainly for its ruined Cistercian abbey. Turn left, along the river bank at the Spread Eagle Hotel, continue through the gates of Sawley Lodge and along a metalled drive to another set of gates. Continue to follow this track, bearing right past the Lodge and onto and across Skinners Syke. The track continues to Dockber. When you have passed Dockber continue heading northeast across the fields to Huggan Ing. Through Huggan Ing, the track bears right through Gisburn Cotes Cottages and over the railway then turn left to Gisburn Cotes Farm and then left again back over the railway. The path then goes through Long Holme Row and down to Steep Wood to rejoin the River Ribble. Turn right and follow the riverside path. On reaching the upstream end of Steep Wood, follow a clear uphill track (SD 803 485), climbing the embankment and keeping above the woods.

The path bears right, following two sides of a field and crossing a stile on the right. Turn right along a field boundary east of Wheatley Farm and continue on a farm track towards Higher Laithe. Just before it, go left, over a stile, descend to cross Wheatley Beck and continue through a shallow wood and across a field to a farm road left of Coppice Cottages, with Coppice House on your left. Turn right, into Mill Lane, follow it to the A59 on the edge of Gisburn and turn left into the village.

GISBURN TO HORTON IN RIBBLESDALE

STAGE 5

GISBURN to SETTLE

DISTANCE 11.9 miles (19.1km)
MAPS OS Explorer OL 2, OL 21, OL 41
START AT GRID REFERENCE SD 828 488
START POINT The village store, Gisburn

Gisburn, which sits astride the busy A59, is very old and possesses many attractive buildings, including the former Ribblesdale Arms, dated 1635, now apartments. The village is the venue for a weekly auction and an annual steeplechase. Parts of Gisburn Church date from Norman times.

From Gisburn Post Office (closed), follow the A59 through the village and turn left along the Settle road at the churchyard. Follow it for 1.5 miles (2.5km) and, as the road bends right, turn left, as signposted. Continue diagonally right, to the top right-hand corner of the field. Pass through a fenced enclosure to the right of Castle Haugh, continue alongside a fence and down a path through Bridge Wood. Turn left, over Paythorne Bridge, and follow the road uphill to Paythorne village.

Annually, on the Sunday nearest 20 November, spectators congregate on and around Paythorne Bridge, hoping to watch salmon spawning on the sandy gravel river bed. This is one of the two main spawning areas for Ribble salmon, the other being at Nappa Flatts. When opposite the Buck Inn, turn right into Bow Hill Lane, signposted 'To Nappa', and, just before Broach Laithe, turn left as signposted, along a track. Continue along the edge of a field and turn right along the raised right-hand side of an ancient way, Ings Lane. At its end, enter Paythorne Moor over a stile and continue across the left-hand side of the next field, as signposted, to another stile. Keep in the same direction, signposted at regular intervals, and cross a slab-bridge to a step-stile. Now cross to the top left-hand corner of the next field to a stile alongside a hawthorn. Turn left up the field to a gate.

The boundary between Lancashire and North Yorkshire crosses the Ribble Way at the eastern end of Paythorne Moor. Keep ahead to a road, turn right along it to Halton West and, just before Town Head Farm, turn left along a broad track

signposted 'To Deep Dale'. On reaching Low Scale farmyard, skirt the farm, going left then right, and continue ahead, passing a barn and crossing two stiles. Turn right over a third stile and go left towards the left-hand end of a wood. Follow metalled Todmanlaw Lane to the B6478, where you turn right, briefly, then turn left over a stile before Cow Bridge.

An 'escape' can be made from Cow Bridge (grid ref. SD 570 827), by crossing the Ribble and following the B6478 for 1.5 miles (2.5km) to Long Preston, which is on a bus route between Settle and Skipton.

HAVEN OF PEACE

Follow the right-hand bank of a drain and continue along the left-hand side of Wigglesworth Beck. On approaching Wigglesworth Hall go right, in front of a house, cross a bridge and turn left, away from the Hall.

Wigglesworth Hall, a haven of peace, overlooks an area of uncultivated wetland where the Ribble performs a succession of ox-bows that overflow every winter. This forms an important habitat for a variety of birds including grey heron, curlew, lapwing, redshank, oystercatcher and pied wagtail.

Hereabouts the Hammerton family reigned supreme over many centuries. One of their seats was Hammerton Hall, above Slaidburn, and much of the River Hodder was theirs. They also lived at 14th-century Wigglesworth Hall, with its own chapel. To protect their dependants when raiding Scots swept through the Aire Gap, they built a pele tower at Hellifield. They worshipped in Long Preston Church, where the hammer heads of their family crest are carved on their tombs. The Hammertons were a bold family with a proud boast: 'From Bowland to the Plains of York we ride over our own ground'. Their good fortune, however, came to an end when Sir Stephen Hammerton joined the ill-fated Pilgrimage of Grace and was executed for his pains. It is said that his son, on hearing of his father's death, died of a broken heart. Until destroyed by fire in the 1950s, the tithe barn at Wigglesworth Hall was one of the largest in England.

Cross over a cattle grid, bear right over a footbridge and climb to a large ash at the right end of some trees. Continue in the same direction over a series of stiles, to eventually join a track leading from farm buildings. Where it bends sharp left, continue on rising ground, to the right of a ruined barn, guided by a post ahead to a stile.

Turn left alongside a wall on your left, and bear right to a wood. Just before it, turn right downhill, cross Hollow Gill Beck and skirt a large enclosure to follow a farm track to a road. Turn right towards Rathmell.

CELTIC RATHMELL

Celtic Rathmell, with its windbreak of sycamore and ash trees, sits on a hillside because the valley bottom was once a vast uninhabitable swamp. It is an unpretentious village of closely gathered stone-built cottages and farmhouses, all of which share fine views that embrace long, blue fells, the flat 'Ings' of the valley floor and the towering scars and mountains at the dale's head. A Rathmell farmer, so the story goes, climbed on to a haystack to sleep, following a heavy drinking session. While he slept a storm broke at the dale's head and the rising waters of the Ribble lifted the haystack, which was floated downstream for some considerable distance before being deposited on the river bank. The following morning the farmer woke to find himself surrounded by enquiring strangers in what was to him unknown country. When asked where he had come from the farmer shouted, 'I come fra Rothmell – Ra'mell in England'.

Dr Richard Frankland's Non-Conformist Academy, one of the earliest Congregational centres, was founded at Rathmell in 1670.

After 150yds (135m), turn left to Far Cappleside Farm. Continue past the farmhouse and, on approaching woodland, cross a stile on your right and continue left to a signposted stile. Cross a field towards a cricket pitch and go over the road, edging it at its left-hand corner. Continue along an unsurfaced lane to meet the wood on your right at a tangent. Descend, through it, to cross Rathmell Beck and turn right, along a walled lane. Where it turns right, continue ahead, following arrows. Within 30yds (27m) turn right, along a smaller track to a stile marked RW. Continue close to a wall on the right and where it ends keep ahead to a facing wall-stile, with Rathmell over on your right. Keep ahead, using a large sycamore tree as a guide. A stile beneath it leads to a road entering Rathmell. Turn left, as signposted, and turn right at a signposted stile near the road's summit. Cross a lawned paddock and keep straight ahead to a large barn. Pass it and, in a field corner on your right, near some dwellings, go through a gap-stile. Turn right, along an unsurfaced track, past some buildings and through two gates into a field. Continue diagonally left, downhill, to a stile near its bottom corner. Cross a stile and continue between buildings. Turn right, along a track towards the river, then left at a metalled road for 60yds (55m) and right over a stile signposted 'To Settle'. Continue northwards, cross a bridge and a stile, and join the river bank. Follow it upstream to Brigholme Barn, passing beneath the A65.

After 220yds (200m) beyond the farm buildings, veer left as the river curves right. Go over a field to a road. Cross and continue along a narrow passage between bungalows. Cross part of a housing estate, as signposted, to return to the riverside. Follow it upstream to Settle Bridge.

To the left is Giggleswick; a delightful village with a gurgling beck, the Terns, cawing rooks, a quiet green, delightful cottages and lots of back lanes and paths. The name Giggleswick could have had a double derivation; Norse Farmer Ghikel had a farm, or wick, and it was sited near a bubbling or gugglian, spring. To the right is Settle, which has a station and several places to stay, as well as many buildings of interest.

STAGE 6

SETTLE to HORTON IN RIBBLESDALE

DISTANCE 7.5 miles (12.1km)

MAPS OS Explorer OL 2, 0L 41
START AT GRID REFERENCE SD 816 640
START POINT Settle Bridge, on the western side of Settle

Settle, which received its market charter in 1249, is surrounded on three sides by impressive limestone uplands. Located where stock-rearing, uplands farming meets the mixed farming of the south, it has prospered from both. Later, 18th-century development reduced the town's reliance on farming and today tourism plays an important part in its economy.

Impressive Giggleswick Scar, which lies on a major fracture in the earth's crust, the South Craven Fault, is just west of Settle. It forms the edge of the limestone upland of the Yorkshire Dales National Park, through which the Ribble Way passes.

Follow the riverside path, signposted 'Stackhouse', past a sports ground and over fields to Stackhouse Lane. Continue right along it, and turn right into a lane at a white house. At the river turn left, along a clear stiled path, and past Stainforth Force to Stainforth Bridge. Cross the bridge, continue along the lane and turn right on to the B6479, then left into Stainforth, passing the church. Pass the war memorial, turn left beyond Stainforth House along a short lane, cross a field diagonally left to a stile and, ignoring the obvious path, go diagonally right, uphill, to a field corner stile. Continue uphill, with a wall on your left, cross a ladder-stile and continue uphill, gradually bearing right, to a facing ladder-stile on the horizon. Follow the clear, stiled path ahead to Moor Head Lane and turn left along it. Descend steeply to the B6479. Turn left on to it briefly, and right at the junction. Cross Helwith Bridge, the inn car park and field. Turn right into a narrow road and, where it bears left, go through a gate, under the railway line and along a walled lane. Follow the riverbank to the New Inn Bridge, Horton in Ribblesdale.

HORTON IN RIBBLESDALE TO GAVEL GAP

STAGE 7

HORTON IN RIBBLESDALE to GEARSTONES

DISTANCE 5.8 miles (9.3km)
MAP OS Explorer OL 2
START AT GRID REFERENCE SD 807 726
START POINT New Inn Bridge, Horton in Ribblesdale

From New Inn Bridge, Horton in Ribblesdale, go through the Crown Hotel car park to join the Pennine Way and follow its route along Harbor Scar Lane.

PLACES TO VISIT

• RIBCHESTER

The village of Ribchester has a few notable buildings to visit. St Wilfred's church, dating from the 8th century, is one of the most attractive in the Ribble valley, both inside and out. The church stands in what was the centre of Ribchester's famous Roman fort, Bremetenacum Veteranorum. The fort is believed to have been occupied for 400 years, and there are a few exposed remains of the granaries close to the church. The columns of the portico at the local White Bull Inn are said to have originated from the Roman site. The main attraction, though, is the Ribcester Roman Museum (www.ribchesterromanmuseum. org ☎ 01254 878261; open daily all year). It has been extended with lottery funding and displays original artefacts and replicas of finds from the site, many of which were sold to the British Museum in London.

• CLITHEROE CASTLE KEEP AND MUSEUM
www.lancashire.gov.uk/museums
☎ 01200 424568
The Norman keep of Clitheroe Castle is said to be the second smallest in England, but the museum which is attached to it has much to offer. There are exhibits, sound stations and hands-on displays which explain not only the castle's history but that of the surrounding area, from geology to folklore. There are fossils, a period kitchen, and historical costumes that you can try on. The museum also has its own Atrium café and terrace. The complex is set in parkland, which is also home to formal gardens, a labyrinth, adventure playground, bowling green, bandstand and café. Open daily all year.

BELOW Stepping stones leading over the rushing river at Stainforth

ABOVE Stainforth village, hemmed in by fields and drystone walls
RIGHT Boardwalk leading to the summit of Pen-y-Ghent
FAR RIGHT Ribblehead Viaduct never fails to impress

At Horton in Ribblesdale, the lush valley that takes the mature Ribble to the sea is far behind. Horton in Ribblesdale, as its name implies, is not in the Ribble valley; it is in Ribblesdale, where the mountains of West Yorkshire cradle the infant river. The Ribble valley and Ribblesdale may be synonymous but there are many differences.

Historically, the Ribble has been a natural boundary between Celtic Cumbria and Scottish Strathclyde. South of Swanside Beck and east of the Ribble, walkers encounter brooks, cloughs, moors and barns. North of Swanside Beck, Anglican and Danish names are left behind and their Scandinavian and Norse equivalents, ghyll or gill, foss or force, fell and field, become the new language.

The lead on the roof of the Norman church at Horton in Ribblesdale pre-dates the warring years of the Reformation and the Civil War. Thanks to its out-of-the-way situation, the church escaped the roof-stripping that happened to other churches on main travel routes.

A strange story lies behind a mysterious inscription on a brass plate brought in from the churchyard to protect it from the weather. It reads:

Sacred to the memory of Richard Thornton, a short time ago schoolmaster here for the district, an honest man, fleeing from the Law, anxious to prove his innocence, and also Elizabeth, his wife. Catherine, their only daughter, erected these tombstones at her own expense as a token of appreciation of the life of her dead parents. Died 29th August, 1744, 57 years.

Nobody knows why the honest teacher was fleeing from the Law. The enigma remains to tantalize.

Close to Horton in Ribblesdale lie famous Alum Pot, Long Churn Cave, Hull Pot, Pen-y-Ghent Hole and Ginger Pot; names honoured by caving people and reminders that this area is singularly rich in potholes and caves. Alum Pot is 130ft (40m) long by 40ft (12m) wide and Alum Pot Beck hurls into its depth of 292ft (89m), dropping sheer for over 200ft (61m). Just 150yds away is Long Churn Cave from where a stream and a passage enter Alum Pot's main shaft. Pen-y-Ghent Pot, which does not look impressive at ground level, is a frightening 500ft (152m) deep, making it one of the deepest pots in Yorkshire. Hull Pot

is 300ft (91m) long and as deep as it is wide, some 60ft (18m). Horton is a starting point for people attempting the famous circular Three Peaks challenge over Pen-y-Ghent, Whernside and Ingleborough. Pennine Way and other long-distance walkers use it as a base, as do cavers and pot-holers. The Three Peaks are the best-known of the Yorkshire Dales and their shapes are perhaps the best-loved of all the Dales mountains. Whernside, to the northwest, is the highest at 2418ft (737m); westwards Ingleborough rises to 2,373ft (723m), eastwards and just 100ft (30m) lower, is Pen-y-Ghent at 2,273ft (693m).

LIMESTONE OUTCROPS

In 1887, two Giggleswick schoolteachers, Canon J R Wynne-Edwards and D R Smith, walked over Ingleborough to have tea at the Hill Inn, Chapel-le-Dale. Whernside beckoned and they decided to tackle it. From its summit, Pen-y-ghent lured them on, to complete the three. So the golden age of peak bagging in the Dales began and the Yorkshire Ramblers was born. In 1897, four of its members started and finished the Three Peaks in 10.5 hours from Gearstones. Today, 12 hours is considered a reasonable time in which to 'do' them, clocking in and out at the Pen-y-ghent Café in Horton in Ribblesdale. Because of erosion the present route has been extended to 25 miles (40km) with 5,000ft (1,524m) of ascent. Just past Sell Gill Holes (SD 812 744) turn left, away from the Pennine Way. Go through a small gate and behind a barn. Continue over stiled fields and, at the far end of a long field, pass through a gate below a disused limekiln. Pass to the left of a water-tank and enter another long field, soon to cross a deep valley. Climb through a series of limestone outcrops to join a track which passes over Birkwith Cave. Continue along the track and turn left at the first junction. Turn right at the second junction, signposted 'Nether Lodge'.

The walk can be shortened by taking a farm lane south from High Birkwith (grid ref. SD 800 768), through New Houses, back to Horton.

AMONG THE DRUMLINS

To continue on the Ribble Way, where the track turns right, up the hillside, leave it and follow the wall on the left to God's Bridge over Brow Gill Beck (SD 798 776). The grassy path bears left and becomes a clearly defined track as it descends to Nether Lodge. Just past some buildings, turn left to Gearstones, as signposted. Continue along the bottom of the hill on your right and cross a ladder-stile in a fence that soon comes into view. Keep forward to Back Hools Barn, which soon appears between drumlins. There are many drumlins along this section of the Ribble Way. Deposited by retreating ice sheets, these mixtures of broken rock debris, called boulder clay, are clearly identified, rounded hills, frequently shaped like half an egg that has been sliced lengthways. The more pointed tail ends of the drumlins point in the direction of the moving ice.

Continue past Back Hools Barn and alongside a wall on your right, to Thorns; a cluster of isolated farm buildings. This is home to the Swaledale sheep and its variant, the Dalesbred. Other breeds are the Rough Fell and the Wensleydale.

Turn right into a walled lane and at its far end follow the wall round to the left and over the hill to Thorns Gill. Cross a footbridge and bear left along a faint track to the Ingleton–Hawes road (B6255) at Gearstones.

STAGE 8
GEARSTONES to GAVEL GAP

DISTANCE 4.9 miles (7.8km)
MAP OS Explorer OL 2
START AT GRID REFERENCE SD 779 799
START POINT Gearstones, on the B6255 Ingleton–Hawes road

Two centuries ago, thousands of head of cattle were gathered annually on Newby Moor and Gearstones, where the autumn sales were held. In the 1870s, the solitude of the wilderness around Batty Moss was shattered, by gangs of tough navvies building the Settle–Carlisle railway through this wild, inhospitable countryside. An incident in May 1873 shook Gearstones Inn, a roadside hostelry near Ribblehead, to its foundations.

A railway labourer drinking there threw a compression cap on to the fire. A loud explosion followed and the oven and the fireplace grate were dislodged. A clock, part of a window frame and 15 panes of glass were broken. Otherwise damage to the inn was less severe than expected. The labourer was committed to the Assizes and the Gearstones Inn entered local folklore.

Turn right along the road and, soon after it bends to the right, turn left, along a track signposted 'to Denthead'. Here, the Dales Way is joined. Continue past Winshaw, climb steeply alongside a wall and swing right, contouring to the top side of the fell wall. On reaching a footpath sign (SD 785 817) bear left along a more obvious track, climbing slightly, and ignoring a track branching off to the right. Continue ahead, following a clear track and cross into Cumbria at a fence. Cross some duck-boarding and follow the bottom of Blea Moor Hill. Turn right on to the road to Newby Head, leaving the Dales Way. When the Ingleton–Hawes road is reached turn left, along it, for about 110yds (100m), and turn right on to a moorland footpath signposted 'to Gavel Gap'.

Go southwards, past a derelict circular sheepfold, and continue up past a small building. Descend slightly and continue up Long Gill, with the beck on your right. Cross it at a junction of streams and follow the right-hand one, Jam Sike, passing a small cairn. Soon the path reaches a wall which once marked the boundary between the old West Riding and North Riding counties. This is Gavel Gap (SD 813 83) and the concrete block seen in the wall at this lonely spot marks the end, or the beginning, of the Ribble Way.

As there is no right of way between Gavel Gap and Cam High Road (the route of both the Pennine Way and the Dales Way, about 0.5 miles (800m) away to the southeast) steps must be retraced for 1.5 miles (2.5km) to the Ingleton–Hawes road at Newby Head, an ideal support-party pick-up point.

PLACES TO VISIT

• **SETTLE**
www.settle.co.uk
☎ 01729 825192
The town of Settle is a charming place to stop for refreshment. It has a market each Tuesday in the central Market Place, which is backed by an interesting building known as The Shambles. Dating from the 18th century, it is on four storeys, the lower two of which are colonnaded and contain shops. Just up the road is The Folly; an interesting Tudor-style house built in the 17th century, now the Museum of North Craven Life (*www.ncbpt.org.uk/folly* ☎ 01729 822361; open Tues, Sat–Sun & bank holidays Apr–Oct). Settle is, however, best known as the terminus of the Settle–Carlisle railway line, built in the 1870s.

• **STAINFORTH FORCE**
The route crosses the pretty stone packhorse bridge at Stainforth. Just below the bridge is the small waterfall of Stainforth Force. It is really a series of minor cascades over limestone steps but when the river is in spate its force can be heard from some distance. Since waterfalls are rare in limestone landscapes (they tend to disappear underground), this is a welcome scene and a popular picnic spot.

• **RIBBLEHEAD VIADUCT**
There are 17 viaducts on the Settle–Carlisle line, the longest and most impressive of which is that at Ribblehead, originally known as the Batty Moss viaduct. It has 24 elegant arches and is almost twice as long as the next longest on the line. So many men were killed in the building of the structure that the railway paid for an extension to the local graveyard at Chapel-le-Dale.

Dales Way

COMPLETE ROUTE ILKLEY TO BOWNESS-ON-WINDERMERE **80 MILES (130KM)**

SECTION COVERED AS ABOVE

MAPS OS EXPLORER OL 2, OL 7, OL 19, OL 21, OL 30, 297, 298

The Dales Way is one of Britain's longest established and most popular recreational long-distance footpaths, created to allow a continuous riverside walk along three of the most beautiful rivers in the Yorkshire Dales, the Wharfe, the Dee and the Lune.

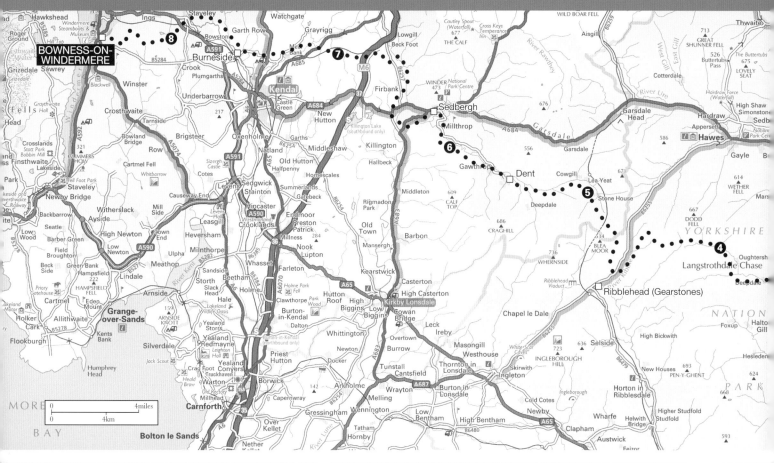

ABOVE Dr Manning's Yard, Kendal

RIGHT The panoramic view from Ilkley Moor

ILKLEY TO GRASSINGTON

STAGE 1

ILKLEY to BARDEN BRIDGE

DISTANCE 9.1 miles (14.6km)
MAPS OS Explorer OL 2, OL 21, 297
START AT GRID REFERENCE SE 112 480
START POINT Old Bridge, Ilkley

The official start of the Dales Way is at Ilkley Bridge. Not the Edwardian Middleton Bridge carrying the road across the River Wharfe, but the narrow, hump-backed, 17th-century stone structure about 400yds (365m) upstream. For many years, this was the only bridge across the Wharfe between Otley and Bolton Bridge; a distance of some 12 miles (19.25km).

Ilkley was originally a Celtic settlement, Llecan, within the kingdom of Brigantia. After the Roman Conquest it became a small military camp, Olicana, guarding the river crossing and a junction of important campaigning roads. Warriors of a later age anglicized Olicana's name to Ilkley and left behind three magnificently carved Anglo-Viking crosses, probably grave-markers, which are kept inside the church. For centuries Ilkley was a quiet village. Then, the discovery of the healing properties of its moorland springs (on Ilkley Moor, of 'Baht 'At' fame) led to its growth during the Railway Age as the Heather Spa, famed for its hydropathic cures, bracing air, and elegant shopping parades, which have survived into the 21st century.

A signpost by Ilkley Bridge confirms the start of the Dales Way. The route follows a riverside track behind gardens to a driveway to a sports centre. A kissing-gate on the left leads to a path across low-lying fields, heading to the riverside and squeezing between gardens and river before crossing more pastureland and emerging on the old road to Addingham.

The Dales Way follows the riverside to a lane, right, which leads into Addingham Low Mill; an interesting adaptation of a former textile mill and early Industrial Revolution cottages. A stile leads out of the cul-de-sac lane into another tarmac lane, just beyond which a narrow path, through a stile on the left, leads over a tiny hump-backed bridge to Addingham's fine medieval church. Its size reflects the importance of this early industrial settlement from the Middle Ages onwards. The route crosses to another footbridge and by cottages to the road, Bark Lane. Just 200yds (183m) to the right, just by the suspension bridge over the Wharfe, the riverside path begins again.

PRINCE RUPERT

A popular Dales Way diversion which takes in some splendid views is reached directly through the village past Highfield and Haw Pike to Bolton Bridge, but most Dales Way walkers keep to the riverside path past High Addingham Mill (another former watermill converted for residential use). The path curves towards the B6160 road but stays by the riverside to reach a lovely stretch of riverside path, which is dominated by the view of Beamsley Beacon.

The path reaches the road at Paradise Lathe and then crosses the road and passes the ancient Quaker Meeting House, and onto the track towards Lobwood House. A stone stile is found almost immediately on the right leading into the fields. The path is then followed northwest, with the wall and road on the right, for 0.5 miles (800m) and over two stiles, to reach the road at GR SE 071 523. Reach the road at a stile, turn left and 300yds on the right, past the layby, a stile leads over a footbridge to a path alongside the stream, which emerges at Bolton Bridge on the A59. Steps at the far side of the bridge lead to a path close to the riverside. The large expanse of pasture on the right is reputed to be the cornfield where Prince Rupert spent the night before his defeat at the hands of Cromwell's Ironsides in the Battle of Marston Moor, near York, in 1042.

For the next few miles path-finding is easy. Bolton Priory is soon reached (Bolton Abbey is the name of the village, where

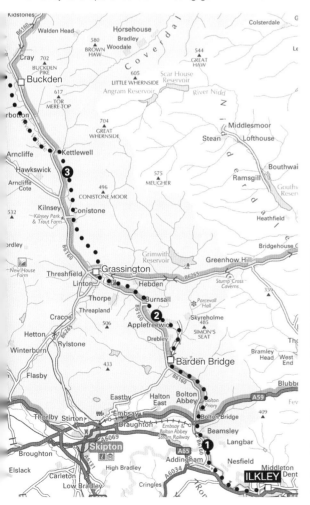

i **USEFUL INFORMATION**

THE ROUTE
• www.dalesway.org.uk
The DW runs through many administrative areas, so this excellent website (The Dales Way Association) is the best place to find information about every aspect of walking the route. There are detailed lists of facilities available at every point along the route, accommodation, and travel options. It also gives updates on diversions in place on the route and lists all relevant maps and guides, including their own inexpensive but thorough *Dales Way Handbook*. There are brief summaries of the three extension links to the DW start, from Leeds, Bradford and Harrogate.

TOURIST INFORMATION CENTRES
• www.visitilkley.com
Station Road, Ilkley LS29 8HA;
☎ 01943 602319
• www.yorkshiredales.org.uk
National Park Centre, Hebden Road, Grassington BD23 5LB;
☎ 01756 751690 (open daily Apr–Oct, Fri–Sun Nov–Mar)
• www.sedbergh.org.uk
The Dales and Lakes Book Centre, 72 Main Street, Sedbergh LA10 5AD;
☎ 015396 20125
• www.golakes.co.uk
Glebe Road, Bowness-on-Windermere LA23 3HJ;
☎ 015394 42895
• www.southlakeland.gov.uk/tourism
Town Hall, Highgate, Kendal LA9 4DL;
☎ 01539 797516
Although the DW does not go into the town of Kendal, it does pass close to it and this TIC and website may be useful.

LEFT The graveyard and ruins of Bolton Abbey, founded in 1154

there is a tea shop). The Dales Way crosses the Wharfe by a footbridge (stepping stones can be used if the river is low) and takes the path up the steps that leads through the woods, with magnificent views back to the priory.

🏠 *From the footbridge (grid ref. SE 014 542) a return to Ilkley can be made along paths and minor roads on the east side of the river. This is approximately 5 miles (8km).*

ROMANTICALLY BEAUTIFUL

The path eventually joins a lane where, soon after a ford over Pickles Gill, the Dales Way heads for the riverside. A path leads over the wooden bridge to Cavendish Pavilion, a welcoming café and restaurant, open most days of the year.

Now follows one of the most romantically beautiful parts of the Dales Way, through Strid Woods, a magnificent riverside walk rich in natural history. The woods are mainly beech and the area is noted for its variety of lichen, fern and fungi, as well as birdlife. The well-waymarked nature trails provide interesting variations to the main path. The paths converge at the terrifying Strid; a narrow sandstone chasm through which the entire force of the River Wharfe plunges, carving out deep underwater caverns. The name 'Strid' is derived from 'stride': many of those who have attempted the deceptively difficult leap have paid with their lives, the most famous of these being the Boy of Egremond, heir to the great de Romille Estates in the 12th century.

The riverside path climbs rather thrillingly between crags (some care is needed), to descend to the path leading past the Edwardian aqueduct that carries waters of the Upper Nidderdale Reservoir to Bradford, before reaching the lovely, traditional stone bridge at Barden.

TOP Mountain views above Burnsall village
MIDDLE Close up, Burnsall is a typical Yorkshire village of sheep and grey stone
ABOVE Kettlewell nestles in a dale, surrounded by fields of livestock

Another wooded section of route follows, the path traversing the gnarled roots of trees by the water's edge before crossing to Woodhouse Farm, and open pasture to Burnsall.

Burnsall is a jewel; a village in an almost perfect setting, within a great fold of heather-covered fells. There is a superb 17th-century bridge, a medieval church with Viking 'hog-backed' gravestones, and a pub with rose-covered walls.

🏠 *Burnsall is served by a bus service, useful for an escape back to the start of the walk.*

LOUP SCAR

The route to Grassington starts at the riverside between the Red Lion and the bridge, and soon passes a dramatic geological feature, Loup Scar, a limestone cliff above rocky rapids. This is the result of the great Craven Fault which crosses Wharfedale at this point. From Ilkley the predominant rock has been acid millstone grit; north of Burnsall is the Carboniferous limestone country of the Dales, creating a softer, gentler, landscape with more fertile pastures, more wild flowers, and drystone walls which gleam grey white in sunlight, or moonlight.

The Dales Way crosses a low, limestone headland before returning to the riverside along a newly reconstructed stretch of path. At Hebden, the river is crossed by an elegant little suspension bridge. The path now follows a gentle section of riverside, along a fine avenue of chestnut trees, going over stiles to another great curve of the river where, on the far bank, the long, low profile of Linton Church will be seen. This handsome church, sometimes called the Cathedral of the Dales, dates from the 12th century, and can be reached, when the river is low, by an ancient parishioners' way across worn stepping-stones.

Otherwise, the Dales Way turns right through a gate along Mill Lane, past Grassington's old manorial corn mill (now a trout farm), the powerful spring clearly visible in the fish ponds.

A stile on the right, some 50yds (45m) above the mill, gives access once more to the riverside path, which leads to Linton Falls; a series of spectacular rapids and waterfalls over water-carved limestone, and another manifestation of the Craven Fault. The footbridge over the river at this point provides a fine viewing platform for the falls. Dippers are usually to be seen in and out of the water. A narrow, enclosed path to the right, known as Snake Walk, leads to the main Grassington car park and National Park Centre.

GRASSINGTON TO RIBBLEHEAD

STAGE 2
BARDEN BRIDGE to GRASSINGTON
DISTANCE 6.8 miles (10.9km)
MAPS OS Explorer OL 2, 297, 298
START AT GRID REFERENCE SE 052 574
START POINT Barden Bridge

Barden Tower was originally a hunting lodge built for the Cliffords, Lords of Craven.

Between Barden and Grassington the Dales Way is easy to follow, along the north side of the river, from Barden Bridge. Pass Drebley Stepping Stones, curving into the lane at Howgill Bridge and then returning to the riverside path through a wooded gorge, past a series of white-water rapids. Soon the path passes camp sites by Appletreewick, a village once known for its onion fairs. It has some charming 17th-century cottages and two pubs.

STAGE 3
GRASSINGTON to BUCKDEN
DISTANCE 10.6 miles (17km)
MAPS OS Explorer OL 2, OL 30
START AT GRID REFERENCE SB 003 637
START POINT Grassington National Park Centre, Hebden Road

The Dales Way leaves the pretty village of Grassington along its main street, turning left in front of the town hall along Chapel Street. After 300yds (275m), the route turns right off Chapel Street into an enclosed lane but shortly turns left through a gate. The wood on the left is Grass Wood, an exceptionally fine nature reserve, nationally known for its orchids.

The main line of the Dales Way now crosses upland pasture, the path marked by stiles. There are some superb exposed limestone beds in the crags above Dib Scar. In spring, the wild flowers include yellow mountain pansies and the lovely pink and yellow bird's eye primrose; an alpine plant remarkably common on the limestone pastures of the Yorkshire Dales.

The path crosses broad fields, the line of route marked by stiles, soon approaching more scars. This time it is the top of Conistone Dib, a deep limestone ravine. The Dales Way goes along the top of the scar, crossing an ancient monastic track known as Scot Gate, or Bycliffe Road. This is one of its most spectacular sections — superb, high-level walking, past ancient enclosures and medieval ridge-ploughing terraces or lynchets. There are magnificent views into and across the valley below, past the confluence of the River Wharfe and its tributary the Skirfare which forms Littondale. A notable landmark to the south is Kilnsey Crag.

As the Dales Way reaches an area of woodland just before Scargill House, it bears down a crossing track to join the lane to Kettlewell. Scargill House is a former Anglican study retreat, and the tall, Scandinavian-style roof of its chapel makes a notable landmark. Past Scargill House on the quiet lane, a narrow path on the right marked by stiles crosses fields into Kettlewell.

Kettlewell, a compact village of grey stone houses and cottages in a dramatic setting of green fields, takes its name from a Norse invader, Ketel. It is another popular tourist and walkers' centre, with a choice of pubs, shops and cafés.

🏠 *Anyone wanting to return to Grassington or Ilkley can do so by catching a bus.*

From Kettlewell, the Dales Way is once again a riverside path, the route starting from the far side of the bridge over the Wharfe. The path follows a narrow ledge along the riverbank, eventually leading to a broader, partially enclosed path never far from the river, and along a valley whose sides become ever steeper. It is a classic U-shaped glaciated valley with a flat bottom, which is often, after heavy rain or melting snows, flooded to form a series of shallow lakes. The next village is Starbotton, reached from the Dales Way across a footbridge. This is another compact Dales village with a traditional pub.

The Dales Way heads north-westwards, again on an easy-to-follow route. It soon leaves the river and follows another narrow enclosed way, before joining an estate track through handsome, ornamental woodlands. Just after the point where the river comes close to this track, the Dales Way bears to the right, to join and follow the river floodbank to Buckden Bridge. Two hundred and fifty yards (227m) along the lane to the right is Buckden village.

🏠 *Buckden is also served by buses, for a return to Grassington.*

STAGE 4

BUCKDEN to RIBBLEHEAD (GEARSTONES)

DISTANCE 12.1 miles (19.5km)
MAPS OS Explorer OL 2, OL 30
START AT GRID REFERENCE SD 939 772
START POINT Buckden Bridge

Buckden is the site of a former hunting lodge in the medieval reserve of Langstrothdale Chase. Its name is literally derived from the hunt and the forest of the buck or deer. As the last village in Wharfedale, it still has the feeling of an outstation, with an attractive village green, tea rooms in the summer, and the last shop until Dentdale. This is yet another former lead-mining community with lead mines deep into Buckden Pike, the hillside which climbs steeply above the village. It is also the terminus of the upper Wharfedale bus, which returns to Ilkley.

From Buckden Bridge, the Dales Way continues along the west bank of the river via a field gate on the right, again crossing to the river and following it as it loops round to re-emerge in the lane below Hubberholme. This is about the point where upper Wharfedale changes its name to Langstrothdale, a name with strong Viking associations, like other hamlet names along this valley, indicating the settlement pattern of the Vikings who came to northern England via Ireland in the 10th century. The first of such communities is Hubberholme, with its sturdy church, like many in the Dales, built to give some degree of protection against marauding Scots in the 13th century. It is also one of the few churches in England to have a rood loft; a pre-Reformation screen above the altar, said to have survived because Oliver Cromwell's men never reached remote Langstrothdale during the bloody battles of the English Civil War. The ashes of the great Yorkshire novelist, playwright and broadcaster, J B Priestley, lie scattered in the vicinity. Hubberholme was one of Priestley's favourite places.

ℹ️ **PLACES TO VISIT**

PLANNING YOUR TRIP
• www.sherpavan.com
☎ 0871 520 0124
The Sherpa Van Project serves a number of long-distance paths with a luggage and lodgings service. They also give details of the route, maps and trailplanners to buy, and an accommodation booking service. Once on the Dales Way pages, use the 'About the Walk' link at the bottom of the screen to see some handy FAQs.
• www.ramblers.org.uk
☎ 020 7339 8500 and www.ldwa.org.uk
Although the Dales Way Association gives all the help you will need, you could find some general information on long-distance walking useful. The Ramblers Association and Long Distance Walkers Association both have good websites, with a downloadable description and map of the Bradford–Shipley link.
• www.yha.org.uk
☎ 0800 019 1700
The Youth Hostel Association has a number of sites along, or close to, the DW.

OTHER PATHS
A fine cross-Yorkshire route can be made by starting the DW at Windermere, then taking the Ebor Way (pages 168–173) from Ilkley to York and onto Helmsley in the North York Moors. From there, the Cleveland Way National Trail skirts the moors to reach the coast at Saltburn-by-the-Sea and heads south on the coast path to Filey. As you would expect, there are numerous trails throughout the Yorkshire Dales and many of them meet the DW. The Pennine Way National Trail (pages 188–195) crosses the DW at the Cam End cairn, on Gayle Moor. The Ribble Way (pages 152–159) crosses the DW close to Ribblehead Viaduct, at Gearstones. Between Ilkley and Buckden, the Three Dales Way follows the same route as the DW, before crossing over to Richmond via Wensleydale and Swaledale.

LEFT Mist rising towards the arches of handsome Ribblehead Viaduct

TOP Sweeping views over the green fields of Dentdale
ABOVE Swaledale sheep are a hardy breed

The Dales Way continues behind the church, soon following the riverside once again. In Langstrothdale the Wharfe is now little more than a turbulent stream. As you pass the hamlet of Yockenthwaite, with its handsome bridge, it runs in a rocky gorge. Not far beyond Yockenthwaite, on the right, are the remains of a Bronze Age stone circle. Its purpose and origin are unknown, but it was quite possibly a place of worship on an existing cross-Pennine trade route.

WATERSHED OF ALL ENGLAND

Beyond Deepdale Farm, with its series of stiles, the path crosses to the other side of the river, which is now a number of shallow waterfalls between grassy banks, and a popular picnic place on summer afternoons. Beckermonds is soon reached, and for a time the Dales Way has to join the Hawes road, which can be busy in summer, climbing the narrow gorge past a little roadside spring before descending again into Oughtershaw itself. The former school building on the right was originally designed, in Venetian style, by John Ruskin.

The Dales Way now bears off to the left along a lonely farm track. Ahead is Nethergill and, beyond, Swarthgill Farm, a remote sheep farm with its scatter of trees looking like the end of the world. But the route continues to climb slowly upwards, over rough pasture, towards Breadpiece Barn ahead. The tiny stream to the left, now known as Oughtershaw Beck, is in fact the source of the River Wharfe, and on the hillside opposite, on Oughtershaw Moss, is the moorland spring where this great river emerges, little more than a narrow sike. Only a few yards to the west lies the source of Cam Beck, a tributary of the River Ribble. This flows into the Irish Sea, whereas the Wharfe flows into the North Sea. This is the watershed of all England.

Breadpiece Barn owes its name to its curious shape, like a loaf. The route climbs past it over bleak gritstone moorland, but the ascent is soon rewarded, in clear weather, by views of all three of Yorkshire's famous peaks, Ingleborough, Pen-y-ghent and Whernside, in magnificent profile.

At one of the highest farms in the Dales, Cam Houses, walkers can sometimes find welcoming refreshment and, by prior arrangement, bed-and-breakfast accommodation. From Cam Houses, the route climbs up through a forestry plantation, eventually reaching a track on the summit of the ridge of Cam Fell, at a cairn. This is part of the old Roman Road between Ribchester and Bainbridge, built by Julius Agricola in the 1st century AD to tame the warlike Brigantes. It also carries the 256-mile (412km) Pennine Way between Derbyshire and Scotland.

The views from the Cam Fell High Road are breathtaking, and include not only a splendid panorama of the Three Peaks but also the great multi-arched Ribblehead Viaduct on the Settle–Carlisle railway. It is a magnificent engineering feat on a scale that matches the epic grandeur of the landscape.

The Dales Way follows the Cam Fell High Road to Cam End, a cairn where the Pennine Way bears off to the left, and then continues steeply down to Gayle Beck. Here, a ford and footbridge crosses the beck, leading to a track up to the main Ingleton road. Turn left along the road for Gearstones and Ribblehead, where there is a railway station and pub.

RIBBLEHEAD (GEARSTONES) TO SEDBURGH

STAGE 5
RIBBLEHEAD (GEARSTONES) to DENT
DISTANCE 9.5 miles (15.3km)
MAP OS Explorer OL 2
START AT GRID REFERENCE SD 783 802
START POINT Gearstones, on the B6255 Ingleton–Hawes Road

The scattered communities between Ribblehead and Gearstones can hardly be said to constitute even a hamlet. In both the 18th and the 19th centuries, however, the situation was very different. At Gearstones there was an inn, part of which still survives as a roadside farmhouse offering bed-and-breakfast and camping facilities. This was one of the most important drovers' inns in the north of England, where Scottish drovers would spend the night while bringing down huge herds of cattle on foot along the drove roads from the Scottish uplands (mainly Galloway and Ayrshire) to the cattle markets of the English Midlands. Many were too poor to afford a room in the inn, but would sleep rough, wrapped in their great tartan plaids, entertaining themselves in the evenings around camp-fires with eating, drinking and dancing. The trade ceased abruptly when the Settle–Carlisle railway was opened in the 1870s, though the inn lingered on until World War II.

Activity of a very different kind was seen on Batty Moss, around what is now Ribblehead Viaduct, about a mile (1.6km) down the valley, when, in the 1870s, the mighty Midland Railway was pushing its main line northwards to Scotland. Here developed a series of shanty villages, housing a vast army of navvies to build the great 24-arch, 165ft (150m) high viaduct and the adjacent Blea Moor Tunnel. Many of the workers were Irish but others came from Devon, Scotland and the already-declining Dales lead-mining communities. Traces of the villages, which had Wild West, biblical or military names (such as Jericho and Sebastopol), can still be seen on the moor, together with the tramways used in building the viaduct. Over 1,000 lives were lost, in one of the last major railway schemes in Britain to be built almost entirely by manual labour.

MARBLE WORKS

One fine variation of the Dales Way at this point is the old Craven Way, a medieval packhorse route from Ribblehead Viaduct, which climbs the shoulder of Whernside to run along a narrow, limestone shelf before descending into Deepdale towards Dent. Another popular variation for railway enthusiasts is to follow the line of Blea Moor Tunnel, the path marked by great spoil-tips and brick ventilation shafts, across the empty moor.

The main Dales Way route, however, starts from a lay-by just at the unenclosed section of the main road. It follows a track past Holme Hill and goes up around the outside of enclosed land above Winshaw and High Gayle Farms along the edge of Blea Moor, before crossing Gayle Moor to join the road from Newby Head, where it turns left down the lane under Dent Head Viaduct, just beyond the mouth of Blea Moor Tunnel. This impressive viaduct is built of 'black' limestone (which is ordinary carboniferous limestone with a high carbon content), is 100ft (90m) high and has ten arches along its 197ft (60m) length. The lane is a favourite vantage point for photographers taking shots of the occasional Steam Special, as well as the modern blue and grey Super Sprinter trains, crossing the viaduct.

The Dales Way follows the lane alongside the little River Dee into Dentdale. Walking on tarmac (the road is usually quiet) is here amply compensated by the intimate beauty of the valley, with river, trees and quiet farms sharing the narrow gorge, the railway high above along the fellside. Just above the junction with the path from Artengill (the old track from Widdale and Hawes), is another fine piece of railway architecture, crossing a narrow gill. Also built of black marble, Artengill Viaduct has 11 arches and is 117ft (36m) high.

Just below the Artengill Viaduct is the site of a long-vanished water-powered marble works. Dentdale black marble was highly prized in the 19th century as an ornamental stone for use on table-tops and fireplaces, its many fossils gleaming a pale grey when polished. A young Tyneside engineer known as William Armstrong came on a walking holiday to Dentdale with his wife in the 1830s and, fascinated with the waterwheel, conceived the idea of creating a more efficient form of harnessing that power; the turbine. Armstrong went on to found the great Newcastle engineering and shipbuilding dynasty that bore his name, the turbine principle perhaps being one of the most significant engineering discoveries of all time.

The Dales Way continues past the 18th-century Sportsman's Inn (which sells locally brewed real ales).

....

At Lea Yeat (grid ref. SD 761 868), where in former times there was a Quaker Meeting House, a lane to the right zig-zags up a 1-in-4 hill to Dent Station. This is England's highest mainline railway station, at 1,150ft (350m) above sea level, and a useful starting or finishing point for anyone walking the Dales Way in stages.

ADMINISTRATIVE ERROR

The main path takes the stile to the left of the little bridge, and follows a rocky, narrow path on the south side of the river. Much of the river here and further along the valley runs dry in the summer, or after a period without rain. The stream follows subterranean passageways and cave systems through the water-carved limestone, only to re-emerge with spectacular energy after heavy rainfall.

The chapel with a small bell-tower across the river, by the trees, is Cowgill Chapel, the cause of a curious dispute in the 1860s. Professor Adam Sedgwick (1785–1873), the great Victorian geologist who was born in Dent, wrote a booklet known as *The Memorial by the Trustees of Cowgill Chapel,* which claimed that through an administrative error the chapel had been wrongly named Kirkthwaite. Queen Victoria, a close personal friend of Professor Sedgwick from the time when Sedgwick had worked with Prince Albert on university reforms, intervened in the dispute and an Act of Parliament was passed to restore the ancient name of Cowgill.

Sedgwick wrote a subsequent pamphlet, like its predecessor, filled with notes on local geology and history, and personal anecdote. Together, the two pamphlets constitute a remarkable record of a Yorkshire dale as it was in Sedgwick's

boyhood at the end of the 18th century; a time when new factories in the West Riding were destroying the cottage hand-knitting industry and the 'terrible' (i.e. fast and furious) knitters of Dent were soon to be no more.

The Dales Way rejoins the lane at Ewegales Bridge before once again taking a lovely, meandering footpath across pasture past Rivling Farm, through a conifer plantation to Little Town and on past scattered farms (some now converted to second homes) at Coat Faw, Clint and High Laithe. Being an old Viking settlement, Dentdale was originally divided in a democratic Norse fashion into long, narrow farms, each containing its share of good bottom meadow land and higher poor pasture. Hence, there are few villages or hamlets, but isolated 'statesman's' or yeoman farmsteads.

Beyond High Laithe, the Dales Way leads back to the lane before crossing to the riverside at Nelly Bridge; a footbridge across a rocky gorge of the Dee, where there are fantastic limestone formations to be seen. It then follows the riverside to Tommy Bridge (who Nelly and Tommy were is lost in history), before crossing the pasture to Mill Bridge. At the farm here, in the early 19th century, there was a 'knitting school', where local children learnt the techniques of hand-knitting. Both men and women knitted the rough but hardwearing local wool from Swaledale or Herdwick sheep, when tending flocks or undertaking housework, or on winter evenings around the peat or fell coal fire, supplementing otherwise meagre incomes. Most of the vast quantity of woollen gloves, hats and stockings were sold at Kendal market, sometimes supplying the military with winter gloves.

The riverside path continues from Mill Bridge, along flood banks above Deepdale Beck, to its confluence with the River Dee, then alongside the Dee itself to Church Bridge below Dent. Dent is well supplied with cafés, two pubs, and shops, in addition to the heritage centre.

STAGE 6
DENT to SEDBERGH
DISTANCE 5.4 miles (8.7km)
MAPS OS Explorer OL 2, OL 19
START AT GRID REFERENCE SD 707 871
START POINT Church Bridge, Dent

The Dales Way leaves Dent by the riverside. The path follows the flood embankment, rejoining the road for a few yards before again following the riverside to Barth Bridge. The route continues along the same side of the river, across stiles and a footbridge, the River Dee here being more sluggish, lined with willows.

The Dent Fault crosses the valley about here, the typical carboniferous limestones and sandstones of the Yorkshire Dales yielding to the older, harder silurian slates and shales of the Lake District, a difference which is soon apparent in building style and drystone walls. The colour, form and even vegetation of the landscape change noticeably as you pass the line of the fault. A certain instability on the hillside, including landslips, is caused by the fault line, roughly marked by the road from Barbon and by Helms Knott, the round hill to the north.

The riverside path eventually emerges in the narrow lane at Ellers, and the Dales Way follows this farm road up past Rottenbutts Wood to Brackensgill, to cross the river. The route then crosses the main Sedbergh road, climbing up to a grassy track across the edge of Long Rigg where there is a spectacular panoramic view of the town of Sedbergh. The track winds down the hillside, through the hamlet of Millthrop and into Sedbergh.

For a less steep route to Sedbergh, stay on the south side of the river at Brackensgill, and go via Cat Holes and Birks Mill.

ⓘ PLACES TO VISIT
- **BOLTON ABBEY ESTATE**
www.boltonabbey.com
☎ 01756 718009
The DW enters the Bolton Abbey Estate, which belongs to the Cavendish family, who also own Chatsworth House in Derbyshire. The Duke and Duchess of Devonshire have made the area a very popular tourist attraction. Entrance on foot is free and gives you access to the ruins of the Augustinian priory (there is still a parish church in the nave), and the fields and woodland beside the River Wharfe. There are cafés and shops at both the Cavendish Pavilion and Dusty Bluebells, at the Strid car park. It is tempting to try and jump across the narrowing of the river that is known as The Strid, but lives have been lost in failing the challenge, even in recent times. Open daily all year.

- **GRASSINGTON**
www.grassington.uk.com
☎ 01756 751690
This small Dales town is a picture-postcard sight, which is very popular with walkers, cyclists and day trippers. It centres around a cobbled market square, where there are a number of cafés and interesting shops. Also here is the small but excellent Folk Museum (www.grassingtonfolkmuseum. org.uk ☎ 01756 752469; open Tue–Sun afternoons Apr–Sep, Sat–Sun afternoons Oct)

- **DENT VILLAGE HERITAGE CENTRE**
www.dentvillageheritagecentre. co.uk ☎ 015396 25800
This beautiful stone building in the charming village of Dent has been restored to include a wealth of information and exhibits on local life and history, including a working model of the Settle–Carlisle railway line approaching the local Artengill Viaduct. There is a nature trail, and tea and cakes are available, too. Open daily Mar–Oct; call ahead in winter.

SEDBERGH TO BOWNESS

STAGE 7

SEDBERGH to BURNESIDE

DISTANCE 15.9 miles (25.6km)
MAPS OS Explorer OL 7, OL 19
START AT GRID REFERENCE SD 657 921
START POINT Sedburgh town centre

Sedbergh enjoys a magnificent position immediately below the southern ramparts of the Howgill Fells, with one particular hill, Winder, dominating the town. Though most of the town is relatively modern, some old parts remain, notably the Tudor shops and courtyards off the Main Street, where, down quiet alleyways, weavers' galleries are still to be seen.

That the town once had a strategic importance is revealed by the fact that a grassy mound immediately behind the town is the site of a Norman motte-and-bailey castle, which guarded what was an important pass across the Pennines, now followed by the A684 between Kendal and Richmond. The little National Park Centre in Sedbergh (open daily in summer) occupies a former wool shop which, according to a reputable source, was patronized by playwright George Bernard Shaw because it was the only shop he knew in England that would supply odd socks, one to fit his left foot and one his right.

It was to Sedbergh that George Fox, son of a Leicestershire weaver, made his way in 1652 after his great vision on Pendle Hill, Lancashire. Soon afterwards, Fox preached an inspirational sermon to over 1,000 'Seekers' on nearby Firbank Fell, standing on a rock still marked as Fox's Pulpit. These Seekers were told to spread the word far and wide, and it was from this moment that the Quaker Movement, or Society of Friends, as it came to be known, was established. Despite much suffering and persecution, the Quaker faith became strongly established in both Britain and the United States and has an enormous, still continuing influence. Sedbergh is also celebrated for its Sedbergh School, the village grammar school that expanded during the 18th and 19th centuries to become a major public school. The buildings and playing fields now dominate much of the town.

The Dales Way winds out of Sedbergh, past the school grounds along a path that leads down towards Birks. It continues along the narrow riverside path past Birks Mill and bridge, and a beautiful stretch where the Rivers Dee and Rawthey meet at a point not far short of where they both join forces with the Lune.

An interesting variation can be made by taking the field path that leaves the riverside before Birks, and crosses to Brigflatts, an unusual early Quaker Meeting House dating from 1675 — a time when the Friends were suffering persecution and, being too poor to fit a ceiling, lined the roof with moss for warmth. The gallery was added in 1711.

The main Dales Way follows the A683 for a short distance before taking a field path across to High Oaks Farm, and then a narrow, grassy track past Luneside Farm, eventually meeting the A684 at Lincoln's Inn Bridge. There now follows a lovely section of Lunesdale. The route passes the remains of the Lune Viaduct, on the long-vanished and much lamented Ingleton–Tebay railway, before taking a series of linking farm and field paths up the valley below Firbank Fell, Low Branthwaite, Bramaskew, Nether Bainbridge, Hole House, Ellergill and Crook of Lune.

THE FOOTHILLS OF THE LAKE DISTRICT

Ahead is the Crook of Lune Bridge, the narrow, stone bridge that once marked the most northwesterly point of the old West Riding of Yorkshire, at its boundary with Westmorland (now part of Cumbria). The Dales Way goes under the fine, disused brick viaduct of the Tebay line, to Beck Foot, where a grassy track and field paths lead to a farm bridge across the roaring M6 motorway to Lambrigg Head. A field path crosses a series of stiles past Holme Park, a fine country house. The route now cuts in front of Morsedale Hall to a lane at Hardrigg. Turn left here and right at Thatchmoor Head, to cross over the high-speed electrified West Coast main railway by a road bridge. Turn left alongside the railway into a field. The Dales Way is now entering the foothills of the Lake District, with the route bearing right across pasture to Green Head and Grayrigg Foot on the A685, before taking a meandering path across the River Mint to Shaw End.

The route continues past Biglands Farm across fields, marked by stiles, heading past little Black Moss Tarn, to reach a good farm lane. Keep walking straight ahead, past some farms, with Skelsmergh Tarn visible on the right. The route now crosses the A6 and passes through Burton House Farm, and over a little stream, before crossing more fields by way of stiles, to bear right past Oak Bank Cottages. It continues to the banks of the little River Sprint and the lane at Sprint Bridge, then on into Burneside village.

Burneside is notable for its fine pele tower, Burneside Hall. It is one of several such fortified houses in Cumbria, dating from the 14th century and built as defence against raids by marauding Scots. There is limited bed-and-breakfast accommodation in Burneside, which also has good rail and bus services into Kendal for a wider choice of accommodation.

STAGE 8

BURNESIDE to BOWNESS-ON-WINDERMERE

DISTANCE 9.5 miles (15.3km)
MAP OS Explorer OL 7
START AT GRID REFERENCE SD 508 959
START POINT Burneside

Between Burneside and Staveley, the Dales Way is easy to follow. It starts to the right of Burneside Mill, around by a tall fence, goes to reach the River Kent and continues upstream past the weir to Bowston. It then turns right along the main road past bungalows. Next it picks up the line of the old industrial railway between bungalow gardens and on to Cowen Head, the former paper mill having been converted into apartments. It then goes past some mill cottages with another weir, the path continues along a pretty stretch of riverside.

This is another good area for birdlife, with mallard and swans usually to be seen. Past Hagg Foot Bridge, the Dales Way eases its way below Cockshoot Woods and soon after crosses the boundary of the Lake District National Park. This stretch of riverside path makes its way on narrow and awkwardly sloping stones, but the attractive views and wooded areas more than compensate for the tricky features of the path. Soon, past the trees, the path once again comes along narrow fields into the village of Staveley. Though not really a tourist centre, Staveley has several shops, an inn, accommodation, a café, and transport links.

🏠 *A return can easily be made from Staveley to Burneside or Kendal by rail or bus.*

IMPRESSIVE BEAUTY

A popular and quite spectacular alternative to the Dales Way from Staveley is to take the lane to Kentmere. Past the mill reservoirs, a track leads into Kentmere village, 4 miles (6.5km). From here, a superb ancient track, the Garbun Pass, crosses

over to Troutbeck, between Windermere and Ambleside, with footpath links that will take you into Windermere town.

From Staveley, the Dales Way uses a combination of quiet farm tracks and roads, and linking field paths, through countryside of impressive beauty. The hills get increasingly steep and more craggy approaching Windermere. A track past Field Close Farm leads to the tarmac track by New Hall, to Waingap; a name evoking old farm wagons lumbering through a narrow pass between the hills. A short way to the right on this lane, and the route once again plunges along a green lane, now taking a twisting route past a wood and over a lovely area of gorse before climbing to Crag House Farm. From here, the Dales Way winds past cottages known as Outrun Nook and an isolated farm, Hagg End, on the shoulder of Grandsire Hill. There is accommodation and a seasonal tea room here.

Now follows a gentle climb to a low saddle between the hills, where there is a sudden, magnificent view; a vast panorama of Lakeland fells unfolding around you. Directly ahead is the long, dark tree-covered valley that contains Windermere.

The last few miles have a feeling of pleasant anticipation as the Dales Way descends along School Knott, bearing left along the track to the B5284 near Cleabarrow, then along the drive towards Low House Farm, before bearing left along a lovely footpath across parkland by Matson Ground. The well-waymarked path passes mature trees, crosses a farm drive, and bears left by woods and across pasture on the side of the Brant Fell before bearing right to where there is a magnificent view across Windermere itself, usually white with sails, the wooded backcloth of hills shimmering in the water. Ahead is a fine slate seat, bearing a plaque with the words: 'For Those Who Walk the Dales Way'.

This is the official end of the Dales Way, although most people are likely to continue down through the kissing-gate ahead, on down Brantfell Road into the centre of Bowness and across to the shores of Windermere, England's largest natural lake. Though Bowness is a busy tourist metropolis, it has its older and more interesting side, with a fascinating medieval church, Britain's only steam launch museum, some really old pubs, and some excellent shops and cafés. Minibuses link the town centre with Windermere Railway Station, while lake steamers run to Ambleside and Lakeside. The ferry to the western shore leads to Hawkshead and the link path to the Cumbria Way for Carlisle.

ℹ️ **PLACES TO VISIT**

• **KENDAL MUSEUMS**
Home of the walkers' favourite, Kendal Mint Cake, the fine town of Kendal is often overlooked by visitors to the area, who speed by on their way to Windermere. Those on foot could detour just 2 miles (3km) south of the DW at Burneside. The town has ruins of two castles, fine shops, and a wide variety of architecture. The parish church on the riverside dates from the 18th century and is both large and ornate, with five aisles. The town's two museums are worthy of a visit. Abbot Hall's Museum of Lakeland Life is beside the church (www.lakelandmuseum.org.uk ☎ 01539 722464; open Mon–Sat all year). This fine museum has recreated period rooms to show local life before the advent of tourism, and items associated with the famous local author, Arthur Ransome. The Kendal Museum sits opposite the station (www.kendalmuseum.org.uk ☎ 01539 815597; open Thu–Sat all year). Its collections are primarily of natural history, and both local and international archaeology. There is also a recreation of the office of Alfred Wainwright, the Cumbrian fellwalker and writer.

• **BROCKHOLE**
www.lakedistrict.gov.uk
☎ 015394 46601
Just beyond the route, 2 miles (3km) north of Bowness-on-Windermere, is the Lake District National Park Visitor Centre at Brockhole. There are exhibitions and displays in the main house, formal and wildflower gardens with amazing views beyond, a croquet lawn, woodland walks, and an adventure playground. During the summer months, water activities are on offer at weekends and a boat cruise runs around the north end of Windermere lake, between Brockhole, High Wray and Waterhead, near Ambleside. Open daily all year.

Ebor Way

COMPLETE ROUTE HELMSLEY TO ILKLEY **70 MILES (112KM)**

SECTION COVERED AS ABOVE

MAPS OS EXPLORER OL 25, 289, 290, 297, 300

The Ebor Way was created to provide a linking route between the Cleveland Way at Helmsley and the Dales Way at Ilkley. The route chosen for the Ebor Way was not the most direct path but it does pass through some interesting countryside. From Helmsley it heads south, crossing the Howardian Hills to Sheriff Hutton, and on along the banks of the River Foss into York. The route along the city's ancient walls gives good views of York Minster and passes three of the four main gateways. The final 15 miles (24km) is through parkland and along the Chevin, with extensive views. Ilkley Moor is crossed before descending to finish in Ilkley.

ABOVE Castle Howard is considered to be among the most beautiful stately homes in Britain
ABOVE RIGHT Castle gate and All Saints Church in Helmsley

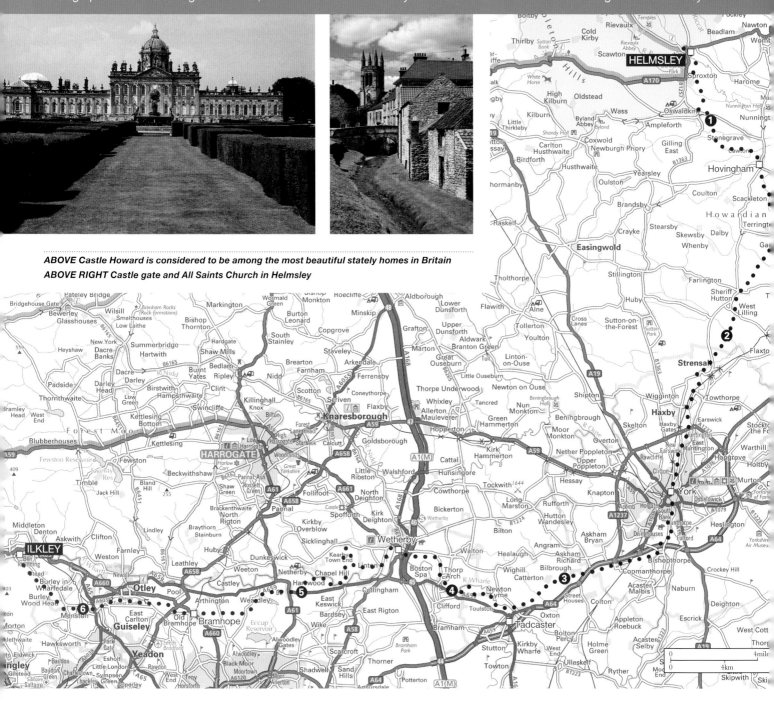

HELMSLEY TO YORK

STAGE 1

HELMSLEY to HOVINGHAM

DISTANCE 9 miles (14.5km)
MAPS OS Explorer OL 25, 300
START AT GRID REFERENCE SE 612 838
START POINT The old market cross, Helmsley Market Place

The small market town of Helmsley stands near the River Rye under the southern edge of the North York Moors. Stone buildings surround the Market Place and close by is the castle.

From the Market Place, walk down Bridge Street and just before the bridge turn right along Ryegate. After 100yds (90m), turn right again into Sawmill Lane. At the end the track turns right. At the next junction, turn right and then left on a broad track that becomes a riverside path. Eventually it bears left towards a gate, passing some yellow flag irises in a bog. Bear right beside the river, then turn right over a footbridge. Cross the field, then turn left. A stile and two gates lead to a climb, passing Low Parks Farm. The farm access road crosses a wooded valley to a track just east of Sproxton.

For a 4.5-mile (7.25km) circular walk, continue straight ahead from here (grid ref. SE 620 814) into Sproxton village. Turn right along the road back into Helmsley.

VIEWS ACROSS RYE DALE

The Ebor Way turns sharp back left towards Throstle Nest. Pass through a wood and then turn right to follow the edges of the fields. Cross a footbridge, climb to a tarmac farm road and turn right. Climb towards Oswaldkirk Bank Top, with a wide view opening up behind across Rye Dale.

At the road turn left for 0.5 miles (800m) and just beyond Laysthorpe turn right. There was once a village at Laysthorpe but it had diminished in size even by the time of the Norman conquest. Pass through the yard to a gate on the right. The Ebor Way descends and then crosses the valley to the Cawton–Gilling East road. Turn left, pass through Cawton, a hamlet of stone-built farms and cottages, and carry on along the track to Spa Villar, a large stone house set amongst trees. The spa was commercialized in the 19th century.

Continue along the track, heading for Hovingham's church tower. Cross the second bridge over a stream in Hovingham and turn right past the church and the entrance to Hovingham Hall.

LEFT Thirteenth-century Rievaulx Abbey is set among glorious countryside near Helmsley

STAGE 2

HOVINGHAM to YORK

DISTANCE 20 miles (32km)
MAPS OS Explorer 290, 300
START AT GRID REFERENCE SE 667 755
START POINT The centre of the village, on the B1257 Helmsley-to-Malton road

Hovingham nestles under the edge of the Howardian Hills. The church retains a Saxon tower with walls 3ft (1m) thick. There is an 8th-century stone altar frontal used as a reredos, and parts of a 9th-century stone cross. Near by is Hovingham Hall, built by Thomas Worsley, a friend of George III, in the middle of the 18th century. Occasionally the gardens are open to the public. The hall was the home of Katherine Worsley, the present Duchess of Kent, before her marriage.

Leave the village on the road to Malton and just after the sharp bend turn right on to the road to York. After 200yds turn left up a lane which in summer supports a mixture of wild flowers. The lane leads into South Wood and soon joins the Centenary Way, an 83-mile (134km) walk from York Minster to Filey Brigg opened in 1989 to celebrate the centenary of Yorkshire County Council. Bear left in the wood, follow 3ft-high (1m) marker posts for 0.5 miles (800m) to a gate. Continue to a bridge, turn left through a gate and follow waymarkers. Turn right to go past Howthorpe Farm and along its access road. Cross over the hill and at the bottom, turn right through a gate. Cross a footbridge and continue over the fields to Terrington. Bear right, then left round a walled garden, passing a sports ground with views back over the Howardian Hills. Turn left into the village, passing All Saints' Church, whose herringbone stonework is typical of the Saxon period from which the church dates.

A return can be made to Hovingham by taking the road opposite the church. Turn right along a lane at grid ref. SE 668 707. Pass Rose Cottage Farm and go through a wood. At the far corner of the wood bear left to meet a road. Turn right, back into Hovingham, a circular walk of about 4 miles (6.5m).

GOLD SOVEREIGNS

The Ebor Way continues into the village of Terrington, to the road junction where there is a village pump opposite. The attractive houses stand back from the road. In 1896 one lucky householder found a tin of 100 gold sovereigns while repairing his roof. Turn right, then left along Mowthorpe Lane, continuing past the cemetery to a stile on the right. As you cross the stile there is a distant view of the stark ruins of Sheriff Hutton Castle on the skyline.

Cross the field at the third stile and turn right downhill, past the former Primrose Farm. Cross the stream at a bridge and continue on the path, crossing two more bridges. Bear right, across a racehorse gallop, before turning right and later left on to a lane that leads to a road. Turn right, then left on to a field route to Sheriff Hutton Church. Before reaching the church, turn right through a yard and along the village street. Look out for a pair of stocks on the spacious green near the Castle Inn.

Down the entrance to Castle Farm there is a path that turns right along the side of the castle ruins. Ralph Neville, Earl of Westmorland, rebuilt and enlarged the castle in the early 15th century. In 1471 the castle passed to Richard of Gloucester, later Richard III, who had married Warwick's daughter, Ann. The castle then became politically important. Edward, Earl of Warwick and Elizabeth of York, niece of Richard III and later Queen of Henry

USEFUL INFORMATION

THE ROUTE
• The only detailed guide still in print for this route is a pack of walking cards and maps produced by a member of the former Yorkshire Footpath Trust, which is now disbanded. There may still be a few copies available from the Helmsley TIC, or direct from the author, Ken Piggin (☎ 01904 412917). It may be best to walk this route in spring or autumn, when facilities are still open but the vegetation is less overgrown.

TOURIST INFORMATION CENTRES
• www.northyorkmoors.org.uk
Helmsley Castle, Castlegate, Helmsley YO62 5AB;
☎ 01439 770442 (open Thu–Mon Mar–Oct, Fri–Sun Nov–Feb)
• www.visityork.org
1 Museum Street, York YO1 7DT;
☎ 01904 550099
• www.wetherby.co.uk
17 Westgate, Wetherby LS22 6LL;
☎ 01937 582151
• www.visitilkley.com
Station Road, Ilkley LS29 8HA;
☎ 01943 602319

PLANNING YOUR TRIP
• www.ramblefest.com
The Ramblers Association give little detail on the EW, but this independent site has much to offer, particularly accommodation and facilities listings.
• www.ldwa.org.uk
The Long Distance Walkers Association has some detail on the EW, such as their interactive map of linking routes.
• www.yha.org.uk
☎ 0800 019 1700
The Youth Hostel Association has sites at both Helmsley and York.

OTHER PATHS
The EW joins the Cleveland Way National Trail, which terminates at Helmsley, with the Dales Way (pages 160–167), which starts at Ilkley, thus creating a fine cross-Yorkshire route. As you would expect, there are numerous trails throughout Yorkshire, many of which link with the EW. The Yoredale Way joins York with Kirkby Stephen, in Cumbria, and the Minster Way runs from York to Beverly, north of Kingston upon Hull.

THE NORTH COUNTRY • EBOR WAY

TOP Dome and roof statues
at Castle Howard
TOP RIGHT Gardens at the
Treasurer's House, York
MIDDLE The exterior of
the wondrous York Minster
ABOVE Micklegate Bar in
York was built in the 13th
century, as the main city
gate on the London road

VII, both stayed here in safe keeping from the Lancastrians. It achieved great importance during the reign of Henry VIII, who sent his illegitimate son Henry, Duke of Richmond, to live in it as Lieutenant-General of the North in 1530. The castle later declined and was in ruins by the reign of Charles I.

The Ebor Way continues to the road junction. Turn left. After 100yds (90m) turn left before the village hall, to join a path to West Lilling. Turn left at the village street, then turn right along a quiet unsigned tarmac lane out of West Lilling.

FOSS NAVIGATION

The lane crosses a road and continues as a broad track to Lilling Green. A tubular bridge takes the path over the River Foss. Continue, turning right through a nature reserve and alongside the lane beside the railway into Strensall.

Before the level-crossing, turn right through the village. Turn right along the road just before the Ship Inn, cross the bridge over the Foss and turn left along the river bank. The riverside path leads to Strensall New Bridge; the last surviving bridge built by the Foss Navigation Company in 1796. The creation of the Foss Navigation from York meant improved communications for the villages of Huntington, Strensall and Sheriff Hutton.

The route continues beside the river, going under a railway bridge to Towthorpe Bridge. The path now bears right across the field to a road, where the route turns left into Haxby. Just after the sharp bend in the road, turn down Landing Lane. After passing some old railway trucks, turn left on a waymarked path and turn right along the riverbank. Pass Lock House, a delightful place with water lilies growing on the site of the lock. Cross at a footbridge and return to the west bank at the next footbridge.

Pass under the York outer ring road and continue beside the river to Huntington Church. The church was built in 1874 but contains a fine Jacobean pulpit. Robert de Skitherby, an Augustinian friar, collected tolls from travellers at Huntington to be used for making a safe way through the Forest of Galtres. Continue beside the river until you join a road at Lock House, New Earswick and then bear left after a short distance, when the river veers away from the road. Your nose indicates the next point of interest: as you pass close to the Nestle Rowntree factory you will notice the sweet, pleasant smell of chocolate. The path turns right to join a road near traffic lights. The route

now goes across the road, and down steps to continue beside the river and then on for a short distance beside the road to reach Monkgate Roundabout. Cross the road at the roundabout and proceed along Monkgate to Monk Bar.

YORK TO WETHERBY

STAGE 3
YORK to TADCASTER
DISTANCE 12.6 miles (20.3km)
MAP OS Explorer 290
START AT GRID REFERENCE SE 608 524
START POINT Monk Bridge roundabout, York, on the A1036

From the roundabout walk along Monkgate to Monk Bar, one of the four main gateways into the city of York in medieval times. Go under the bar, turn left and left again up the steps to join the bar walls. There are excellent views of the Minster and the Treasurer's House as you walk to Bootham Bar and descend into Exhibition Square. Walk on past the Theatre Royal and turn right along Museum Street to cross Lendal Bridge. Immediately after crossing the river, turn right, back on to the walls, to walk to Micklegate Bar. In medieval times it was on this bar that the barbaric custom of sticking the heads of traitors and other criminals on poles was practised. Sir Henry Percy, known as Hotspur, and the Lancastrian leaders captured at the Battle of Towton, met this fate. The last victims were Jacobites from the 1745 Rebellion.

Continue on the city walls over Victoria Bar, an opening cut in the walls in 1838. When the opening was cut, a former gateway from medieval times was discovered. This part of the walk ends when you descend to the road below Baile Hill. This hill was the site of one of William the Conqueror's early castles which defended the River Ouse. Turn right and cross over the busy road at the pedestrian crossing, and turn left down to the river beside Skeldergate Bridge.

The Ebor Way turns right along the western bank of the Ouse. There is a camping ground about 200yds (183m) further on. On the opposite bank is the Minster Way, a 50-mile (80km)

PLACES TO VISIT

• HELMSLEY CASTLE
www.english-heritage.org.uk
☎ 01439 770442
Helmsley Castle has sat above the small market town for 900 years. It is an impressive ruin now, with extensive earthworks all around the site. The keep is striking, even though only half survived the Civil War, and a Tudor mansion house added to the castle houses an exhibition. There is also an audio tour available. Open daily Apr–Sep, Thu–Mon Oct–Mar.

• HELMSLEY WALLED GARDEN
www.helmsleywalledgarden.co.uk
☎ 01439 771427
This lovely walled garden sits next to Helmsley castle. Originally built to feed the nearby Duncombe Park estate, it has been rescued by volunteers to provide a tranquil area for horticultural therapy and learning. It contains a wide variety of plants; the walls alone support over 250 varieties of clematis and fruit trees. There is a plant shop and a vegetarian café in the glass vinehouse. Open daily Apr–Oct.

• CASTLE HOWARD
www.castlehoward.co.uk
☎ 01653 648333
Although a 3 mile (5km) diversion from the EW at Terrington, this estate is stunning. The house took most of the 18th century to build, its signature silhouette created by the central dome which creates the dramatic and ornate Great Hall. A major tourist attraction, there are formal gardens, parkland walks, a large adventure playground, boat trips on the lake and various cafés. House open daily Mar–Oct, rest of the estate open daily all year.

• SHERIFF HUTTON
This historic village has ruins of a 14th-century castle, and mounds that indicate the site of a former Norman castle. The pretty parish church is 900 years old and houses what is thought to be the tomb of Edward, the son of Richard III.

footpath linking York and Beverley Minsters. The Ebor Way follows the riverbank, passing under the York bypass. As the path approaches Bishopthorpe, the palace comes into sight beside the river. At one time there was a custom whereby vessels passing the palace gave a salute, and a can full of ale was lowered to the deck for the crew. The palace was originally built in the 13th century by Walter de Grey, as a residence for the Archbishops of York. Shortly before Bishopthorpe, the path turns right to reach the road.

To walk back into York turn right on entering Bishopthorpe from the river (grid ref. SB 596 478), cross over the bypass and skirt the Knavesmire, a large open space used for York's horse-racing. When you reach the A1036 turn right to pass through Bootham Bar into the city, a circular route of about 6 miles (9.5km).

On reaching Bishopthorpe, the Ebor Way turns left, passing the palace grounds near to the gatehouse. The gardens are occasionally open to the public. Turn right beyond the palace and walk through the village, passing three inns. At the junction, bear to the right of the school along Copmanthorpe Lane and at the end of the road continue straight on to a small footbridge. Turn right, then left along the edge of the fields, following a line of poles. This leads to the main railway line. Warning of approaching trains is given by red and green lights beside the track.

Cross the railway with care, turn left beside the line and take the third street on the right, Sawyers Crescent, then the second street on the left off Farmers Way; a short street that soon turns into a stoney path. After a gate, fork left, join a road, then eventually turn right past the shops to the Royal Oak on the corner. Turn right, then left along School Lane, then right on Manor Heath and finally left on Colton Lane to leave Copmanthorpe.

The Ebor Way is now running along the line of an old Roman road. After about a mile (1.6km) the road turns sharp left. The Ebor Way follows the old Roman road straight ahead, through a small gate and beside a hedge, eventually passing behind a main road. Cross carefully to the other side of the dual carriageway. Turn left, passing the Little Chef restaurant and bear right down a lane. This leads to a minor road on the outskirts of Tadcaster. Turn left, then right, to walk into the centre of a town noted for brewing ale.

STAGE 4
TADCASTER to WETHERBY

DISTANCE 8.4 miles (13.5km)
MAPS OS Explorer 289, 290
START AT GRID REFERENCE SE 487 434
START POINT The bridge over the Wharfe in Tadcaster

Cross over the bridge coming from York and turn right beside the River Wharfe. It was to the centre of Tadcaster Bridge that kings were escorted by the mayor and bailiffs of York, this being the limit of their control.

Tadcaster saw the remnants of the Lancastrian forces pass by after their defeat at the Wars of the Roses Battle of Towton Moor in 1461; the bloodiest battle fought in Britain, with between 28,000 and 38,000 men killed out of some 76,000 on the field.

The walk beside the river passes Tadcaster Church on the left. The church was taken down and reconstructed in 1877 to reduce the risk of flooding from the nearby river. Inside are some interesting Art Nouveau furnishings which were made locally. It is a pleasant riverside walk for the next 2 miles (3km).

The route to Wetherby coincides with the 44-mile (71km) Bounds of Ainsty Walk, beside the Rivers Nidd, Wharfe and Ouse. When the riverside path approaches Newton Kyme, the Ebor Way turns left, away from the river and around the boundary of Newton Kyme Hall, to reach a road. On the way there are good views of both the church and Newton Kyme Hall. Turn left down the road, passing the pretty stone cottages, and further on pass the old tithe barn.

When you reach the A659 (grid ref. SE 455 447), for a 3-mile (5km) walk back to Tadcaster, cross straight over the road, pass under a bridge and turn left along Rudgate, an ancient trackway. After 0.75 miles (1.25km) turn left along a bridleway, past Smaws Farm, to a road. Take the path opposite to the riverbank and turn right to return to Tadcaster.

BOSTON SPA

For the Ebor Way, turn right for 0.25 miles (400m) along the A659, then turn right again along a signposted path to the river, where the Ebor Way turns left. At this point there is an ancient crossing over the River Wharfe. On the Newton Kyme side of the lane is the site of a small Roman fort and the prehistoric Rudgate trackway leads down to it.

ABOVE River Wharfe and St Mary's Church, Tadcaster

Follow the riverside path, one of the finest stretches on the walk, until it passes along the edge of Boston Spa and reaches the bridge into Thorp Arch. On the approach to the bridge, pass the spa which gave the town its name; it was discovered in 1744 and the saline spring was believed to be beneficial in treating rheumatism.

Turn right on to the narrow bridge over the River Wharfe, into Thorp Arch. The Ebor Way continues through the pleasant village of Thorp Arch, which is mentioned in the Domesday Book as Torp. All Saints' Church was rebuilt in 1871 by the noted architect GE Street, and it retains its Norman south doorway. The walk passes the Pax Inn, an unusual name probably taken from the racehorse that won the Ebor Handicap at York in 1860. Continue along the road for 0.5 miles (800m) beyond the village, then turn left along a signposted track. Turn right to pass along the top edge of a wood and bear left to Flintmill Grange Farm. The flint mill used to be on the other bank of the river and flint powder was used as a whitening agent by the pottery trade in the 18th century. The walk continues between the farm buildings and across the fields to the A1(M) road. Turn right and cross over the road bridges into Wetherby.

WETHERBY TO ILKLEY

STAGE 5

WETHERBY to BRAMHOPE

DISTANCE 14.8 miles (23.8km)
MAPS OS Explorer 289, 297
START AT GRID REFERENCE SE 404 480
START POINT The bridge over the River Wharfe in Wetherby

Cross the bridge over the River Wharfe and turn right to the swimming pool car park. Turn right to the riverside path, then turn left and walk round to the footbridge. Cross this and turn right, then left. Cross the park to a stile and go over the golf course to the road. Turn left into Linton, a pretty village set above the River Wharfe. Just before you reach the Windmill Inn, turn right along a tarmac road, signposted to Woodall. The minor road climbs, and there are extensive views across the valley to Collingham and Bardsey. The village of Bardsey on the ridge-top has the site of the oldest

inn in Britain. There are records of ale being brewed on the site of the Bingley Arms in the 10th century. Known at that time as the Priest's Inn, it also served as the local court in the 11th century. Bardsey is the birthplace of Restoration playwright, William Congreve.

The tarmac road leads to a small wood, where you turn right, following field boundaries to Sicklinghall House.

ⓘ *For a 6-mile (9.5km) circular route, turn right at Sicklinghall House (grid ref. SE 367 474). Continue along the road into Sicklinghall village, then turn right along the road back to Wetherby.*

CASTLE RUINS

To continue along the Ebor Way from Sicklinghall House, turn left to pass the Wood Hall Hotel. Signs indicate the route to the right and then the left, down a grassy path to the iron bridge over the River Wharfe. The path turns right, then left to reach the A659 road, where you turn right.

Take care walking along this busy road and take a right turn (north), opposite the next (south) turn to East Keswick. The signposted path follows first the hedge, then a green lane down to the River Wharfe, where you turn left along the riverbank. After about 2 miles (3km) Harewood Castle can be seen on the hilltop. The castle may date back to the middle of the 12th century. The bulk of the castle ruins that can be seen today were built for Sir William Aldburgh. In the time of Edward II the Scots marauded this area, the castle being the only place to withstand the invaders.

From the banks of the River Wharfe climb up a track to join the road into Harewood; an interesting estate village worth exploring. From Harewood, turn right on the road marked with a public bridleway sign, and before the Harewood Arms Hotel. Carry straight on along the private road. The road passes through a wood which may well be alive with birds and animals early in the morning. On the left of the road a track leads to Harewood Church, 15th-century in origin. The medieval alabaster monuments inside include one to Sir William Gascoigne, a Lord Chief Justice.

After the cattle grid an extensive view opens out across the River Wharfe to Armscliffe Crag on the skyline. Further ahead you can see the Chevin above Otley, still some 8 miles (13km) of walking away. At the junction of tracks, take the road to the left.

A short circular walk back to Harewood can be made by turning right at the junction of tracks (grid ref. SE 506 451). Eventually cross the A659 to reach the riverside path near the road bridge and turn right, continuing for nearly a mile (1.6km), before climbing back up to Harewood on the broad track used by the Ebor Way.

DISAPPEARING VILLAGES

To continue on the main route, from the junction of tracks where you turned left on to the tarmac road, cross a cattle grid and pass the buildings of Home Farm. Note how the windows are set upright while the building is on a steep slope, looking altogether rather odd. Continue along the road, passing over a stream, then climb steeply before descending to go through two gates across the road. Turn right on the track which climbs up to a house. Look back for a view of Harewood House and the fish pond over the tree-tops.

When the estate was created, four former villages disappeared; Stockton, Tonehouse and Stubhouse, which were already only very small hamlets, and Lofthouse, which stood to the west of the Leeds–Harrogate road, near the entrance to the present estate. The new Harewood village was built in the 1760s and the inhabitants of the four hamlets probably moved into it. Pass to the right of the house and continue on the track into the woods. Turn right twice on the broad track that passes through the wood and joins the road from Eccup to Weardley. Eccup reservoir, to the south, is popular with birdwatchers in winter. Turn left up the road and at the first junction turn right, before reaching Burden Head Farm. Descend Bedlam Lane and take the second turn left at a public bridleway sign. The track passes Bank Side Farm and Bank Top Farm before reaching a road, where you continue straight ahead. On the outskirts of Bramhope look out for a stile on the right. Cross the stile and turn left along the road into the village. At the junction with the A660 there are old milestones at each side of the road, on which the distances to local places are given in miles and furlongs.

STAGE 6

BRAMHOPE to ILKLEY

DISTANCE 11.6 miles (18.7km)
MAPS OS Explorer 289, 297
START AT GRID REFERENCE SE 255 430
START POINT On the A660 Leeds–Otley road, at Bramhope crossroads

Walk into the centre of Bramhope, where there is a former market cross that now acts as both a lamp-post and a signpost. The road to the right leads down to the Puritan Chapel, but the Ebor Way continues straight ahead. At the end of the village, turn right on a signposted footpath to Pool Bank. Cross straight over the road at Pool Bank. The signposted path passes through a squeeze-stile beside a gate and the track leads into a wood. Keep the wall on the left until the path meets a broad track. Turn right. There are several routes through the wood but the third track on the left leads through the Chevin Forest Park to a car park. Another lower route gives extensive views over Wharfedale, then climbs back to the same car park beside the Otley–Cookridge road.

Just before the car park, bear right down a path, with the road over the hedge on your left, to exit opposite Danefield House. Cross the road and take the track opposite signposted Public Byway, Miller Lane. The broad track climbs on to the top of The Chevin, a ridge offering an exhilarating walk and some superb views. Set below is Otley, where Thomas Chippendale, the master furniture-maker and designer, was born in 1718. The Ebor Way reaches a wood. Keep the wood to the right, then turn left down to Yorkgate. Turn right down the road, turning left and then right to reach the Chevin Inn.

Walk into the car park and bear left, passing a barn on the right, and descend to a track. Turn left and after 200yds (183m) turn right. Keep the hedge to the right, then turn right beside the railway to cross a bridge into Menston. Go straight ahead along Station Road and turn left up Cleasby Road, opposite the railway station. Turn right along Main Street. Pass the Menston Arms and continue on until the road turns sharp left. Turn right on Bleach Mill Lane, signposted 'Public Footpath, Burley Woodhead'. Sweep left past the houses and follow the track to reach the entrance to a former Bleach Mill.

COW AND CALF ROCKS

Take the path to the left of the entrance. The route is nearly straight, passing close to the right of Hag Farm and through several stiles to reach a drive. At the top of this drive is the Hermit Inn, named after Job Senior, who used to frequent the local inns. He became known for his remarkable range of songs, often singing to earn a drink, and used to appear in local theatres. He married his wife when she was 80, much to her relatives' disapproval. Indeed, when she died, they pulled down their house in anger. From then on, he lived the life of a recluse in the ruins of the house and became a popular sight for travellers.

The Ebor Way carries straight on at the foot of the road, across the fields through more stiles, to turn left up the next drive. At the top turn right down the road, then left on a track that climbs to Barks Crag.

The next section of the walk, along the edge of the moor and over the famous Ilkley Moor, is magnificent and heads for the large outcrops called the Cow and Calf Rocks. There are extensive views over Wharfedale, with Ilkley now in sight. From the rocks, head over the moor to the trees, where a footbridge leads to the outskirts of Ilkley. Walk down into the town, crossing straight over the main road to reach the River Wharfe. Turn left through a park and walk along the riverside to the old packhorse bridge. This is the end of the Ebor Way and the start of the Dales Way.

FAR LEFT Walking along the beck at Linton
LEFT Cow & Calf Rocks, on Ilkley Moor
BELOW Lower Wharfedale

View across Lower Wharfedale from Caley Crags in Chevin Forest Park

Yorkshire Wolds Way

COMPLETE ROUTE HESSLE TO FILEY BRIGG **79 MILES (127KM)**

SECTION COVERED AS ABOVE

MAPS OS EXPLORER 281, 291, 292, 293, 294, 300, 301

The Yorkshire Wolds form an arc of chalk uplands swinging north and east across from the River Humber and ending abruptly on the coast between Filey and Bridlington. It is an area unknown to many walkers outside the former East Riding of Yorkshire, although it offers some delightful walking. Even on Bank Holidays it is possible to walk on the Wolds without meeting crowds of people. Typical features of the Wolds are the dry valleys without rivers or streams, making firm walking conditions which would be the answer to a walker's prayer on the Pennine Way.

HESSLE TO GOODMANHAM

STAGE 1

HESSLE to SOUTH CAVE

DISTANCE 12.7 miles (20.4km)

MAPS OS Explorer 293

START AT GRID REFERENCE TA 032 256

START POINT San Luca Restaurant, Hessle Haven, 4 miles 96.5km) west of Hull

The Yorkshire Wolds Way National Trail starts at Hessle Haven, one of a number of places from which ferry boats used to cross to the southern side of the Humber. Across the creek which forms Hessle Haven there is still shipbuilding, which has gone on here for over 400 years. On 30 March 1693, John Frame launched the 80-gun warship *Humber* at Hessle.

Cross over the road from the San Luca Restaurant and take the gravel path. This turns right along the riverbank and heads towards the Humber Bridge. The towers which support the suspension wires are 533ft (162m) high and the span between the towers was, at 4,626ft (1,410m), the longest in the world when it was built. After passing under the bridge look for an old whiting mill on the right, in the Humber Bridge Country Park. It was built in the early 19th century to replace a horse-powered mill and was wind-powered until 1925, when a gas engine was used. Chalk was quarried near by, crushed at the mill and passed through settling pits. The resultant whiting was used in the manufacture of paints and putty.

Continue for 2.5 miles (4km) beside the River Humber, whose mudflats are a rich feeding ground for wildfowl and waders in winter, and for birds in passage in spring and autumn. On the approach to North Ferriby, pass a former brickyard pond that is now a conservation area attracting tufted duck, sedge warbler, reed warbler, reed bunting and shelduck. There is also an interesting variety of plants. At North Ferriby a set of steps leads to a car park, where instructions are given for an alternative route through the town if the next section of the walk is impassable due to exceptionally high tides. Otherwise, continue on to another set of steps, which gives access into Long Plantation. Continue through the plantation to the busy A63 road. Be careful crossing at this busy intersection and use the road bridge to the left to continue opposite.

The route continues through Terrace Plantation to a road where you bear right to a metal gate near quarry buildings.

Pass to the south of the large quarry, with views over the River Humber. When you reach a lane, turn left and descend into Welton, an attractive village with a duck pond. The infamous Dick Turpin was captured here, at the Green Dragon Inn. Most of Turpin's crimes were committed in the London area, where he had been a cattle thief, smuggler and robber. With a price on his head, he headed north, changed his name and took up horse dealing. He was apprehended after threatening to shoot someone. Eventually his identity was discovered and he was hanged at Tyburn, York in 1739.

Descend Chapel Hill, taking the first turn right up Dale Road that leads into Welton Dale, the first of many attractive Wolds valleys. After 1.75 miles (2.75km) the path emerges from a wood. Cross the concrete road and turn right along the field side, turning left to Wauldby Manor Farm. This is the site of a deserted village, one of a number on the Wolds, but only the farm and church remain. The path continues, turning right to join a lane, where you turn left to a road.

Continue straight ahead along the road opposite and when it turns left, carry on along a green lane, which eventually becomes a surfaced road. Approaching Brantingham village there are extensive views over the plain and the River Humber.

For a 6.5-mile (00km) circular walk back to Welton, or the main road, take a path to the left at grid ref. SE 941 298, through a plantation, which leads into Elloughton Dale, where you can turn right down to the outskirts of Elloughton and then left along the minor road to Welton.

NORMAN DOORWAY

For the Yorkshire Wolds Way, watch for a fingerpost that indicates a right turn and descend the field to Brantingham Church. The church is picturesquely set at the foot of conifer-clad Brantingham Dale. There is a Norman doorway and font, but the church was one of a number restored by G E Street for Sir Tatton Sykes.

Walk up the dale for nearly 0.5 miles (800m), then turn left up a track into the wood. Descend a lane and then turn right above Woodale Farm. Climb to Mount Airy Farm and take the access lane down to the road, where you turn left towards South Cave. The Yorkshire Wolds Way turns right 100yds (90m) down the road.

STAGE 2

SOUTH CAVE to GOODMANHAM

DISTANCE 11.5 miles (18.5km)

TOP Humber Bridge

MIDDLE Brantingham Church

ABOVE Hessle foreshore

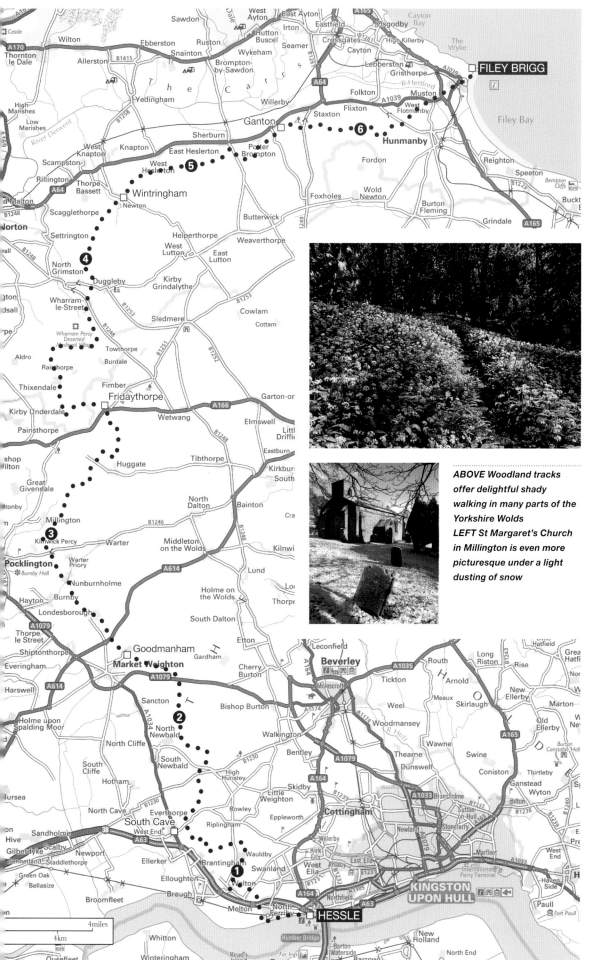

ABOVE Woodland tracks offer delightful shady walking in many parts of the Yorkshire Wolds
LEFT St Margaret's Church in Millington is even more picturesque under a light dusting of snow

USEFUL INFORMATION

THE ROUTE
• www.nationaltrail.co.uk
☎ 01439 770657
This is the most comprehensive source of information about the YWW. Everything is here, from detail on the route itself to the link onto Google Maps, which shows the route clearly over their satellite imagery. There are GPS data files for accommodation sites, in addition to the official route guide and a downloadable leaflet and accommodation list.

TOURIST INFORMATION CENTRES
• www.realyorkshire.co.uk
Humber Bridge North Bank Viewing Area, Ferriby Road, Hessle HU13 OLN;
☎ 01482 640852
• www.yorkshiremoorsandcoast.com
Evron Centre, John Street, Filey YO14 9DW;
☎ 01723 518000

PLANNING YOUR TRIP
• www.walkingtheriding.co.uk
This website covers many walks within Yorkshire's East Riding and includes several sections of the YWW, between Hessle and Huggate. There is good detail here, including downloads of the route marked on OS map extracts.
• www.ramblers.org.uk
☎ 020 7339 8500 and www.ldwa.org.uk
The National Trail website gives all the help you will need but both the Ramblers Association and Long Distance Walkers Association have good websites with some detail on the YWW.

OTHER PATHS
From Filey, the YWW connects with the Cleveland Way National Trail, which continues north up the coast. Southwards, the Headland Walk hugs the coast to round Flamborough Head and arrive at Bridlington. At Hessle, it is possible to cross the Humber Bridge and pick up the Viking Way at Barton-upon-Humber, which runs for 147 miles (237km) to Oakham, in Rutland.

TOP Locally bred Shire horses are known to be excellent workers
MIDDLE View from the gatehouse at Cave Castle
ABOVE The village of Huggate, set in the rolling landscape of the Wolds

MAPS OS Explorer 292, 294
START AT GRID REFERENCE SE 923 312
START POINT South Cave

Walk up the road from South Cave and turn left along the signposted Yorkshire Wolds Way path. This path climbs to a lane. Turn right along the edge of Little Wold Plantation. There are extensive views to the south and east over South Cave, which stands on the line of the Roman road from York to Lincoln. All Saints' Church at South Cave was restored in the 17th century after a fire.

At the top, turn right along the track until the Yorkshire Wolds Way turns left into Comber Dale. After 500yds (455m) turn right and cross the disused railway track in Weedley Dale. This railway line between Hull and Barnsley was built to break the monopoly of the North-East Railway Company in carrying coal to Hull for shipment from the docks. The construction of the line, which was opened on 20 July 1885, required 4900 workers. The biggest project was the 1.25-mile (2km) long Drewton Tunnel, driven through the chalk wolds from the end of this cutting to Little Weighton. The last train ran on the line in 1959.

The Yorkshire Wolds Way turns right, running parallel to the old railway line, then left into the mixed woodland of West Hill Plantation. Bear left up East Dale and, on emerging from the wood, continue to the B1230 North Cave–Beverley road. Turn right and, after 200yds (183m), take a path on the left to a minor road. Turn right, pass over a crossroads and then turn left. The route descends and turns left into Swin Dale, leading to a road 0.75 miles (1.25km) east of North Newbald.

North Newbald has two inns. The church is the most complete example of a Norman church in East Yorkshire, the central tower being raised in the 13th century.

🏠 *Those wishing to return to South Cave can pass through South Newbald and along the A1034 Roman road to South Cave.*

The Yorkshire Wolds Way turns right along the road and left just beyond a farm, up a broad track that rises to another road. Turn right for 200yds (183km), then turn left up another wide track. The broad track leads eventually to a road, continues ahead passed Hessleskew and over a crossroads, then bears left along a track to Arras. This area is noted for its 5th-century cemetery, which has yielded information on what has become known as the Arras culture. There are estimated to be up to 200 small barrows surrounded by small ditches in the area. The burials can be compared with similar ones in northern France, indicating that there was probably an influx of people from that area at this time.

The path crosses fields to reach a road junction. Go ahead, passing a disused railway track which offers an easy route into Market Weighton, where there are inns and other services. The Yorkshire Wolds Way continues along the road into Goodmanham, where there is another inn, below the church.

GOODMANHAM TO WINTRINGHAM

STAGE 3
GOODMANHAM to FRIDAYTHORPE
DISTANCE 16 miles (25.8km)
MAP OS Explorer 294
START AT GRID REFERENCE SE 890
START POINT Goodmanham Church, 1.5 miles (2.5km) northeast of Market Weighton

All Saints' Church, Goodmanham, probably built on the site of a pagan temple, has Norman work with later additions, and an ornate carved font. The pagan temple was destroyed by Coifi, the high priest, after King Edwin of Northumbria was victorious in battle; the king had promised his queen he would become a Christian if he was successful and, true to his word, on Easter Day AD 627 he was baptized in York, on the site of the present York Minster.

The Yorkshire Wolds Way passes the top side of the church and continues under the former Driffield–Market Weighton railway. The path then climbs to the A163 Bridlington–Selby road at Towthorpe Corner, where there is a large car park and picnic site. Just over 2 miles (3km) to the east is the racecourse on which the Kipling Cotes Derby is run. Dating back to the 16th century, this is believed to be the oldest horse race in the world. It is always run on the third Thursday in March and one year, 1947, the Wolds were still covered in snow from the harsh winter. The only entrant was a local, Fred Stephenson. The Clerk of the Course read the rules and away Fred went on Londesboro Lad. He made detours around the worst snowdrifts, but even so, had to dismount at one point and lead the horse through a 4ft (1.25m) drift. It took him an hour and 20 minutes to complete the 4-mile (6.5km) race, the slowest ever.

Cross the road and continue through the parkland of Londesborough Hall. A castellated building was built about 1589 by Francis, Lord Clifford. It was enlarged in about 1670 by Richard Boyle, 1st Earl of Burlington. The estate passed to the Duke of Devonshire, who pulled the house down in 1818 to build farmhouses. In 1845 the estate was bought by George Hudson, the 'Railway King'. A more modest Londesborough Hall, built in brick, is seen as you pass through the parkland into the village.

🏠 *A waymarked path leads from Londesborough to Market Weighton. This offers a 7.5-mile (12km) circular route back to Goodmanham when coupled with Hudson Way, a walk on a disused railway line named after the 'Railway King'.*

ENIGMATIC EARTHWORKS
The Yorkshire Wolds Way turns left in the village, then right after the church. It turns left at Warrendale Farm and goes straight on at the crossroads. After a mile (1.6km), at the T-junction, turn right, then left through Partridge Hall. Pass above a wood and eventually turn left to descend into Nunburnholme, which takes its name from a vanished Benedictine nunnery. The church is partly Norman and contains the shaft of an Anglo-Saxon cross. The rector from 1854 to 1893 was Reverend F O Morris, who is famous for writing a six-volume book on British birds.

Turn left past the church, then right around a field to the road, where you turn left. Fork right up a steep track through Bratt Wood to Wold Farm, cross the Warter–Pocklington road (B1246) and continue with Kilnwick Percy below to the left. Pass Warrendale House Farm and eventually turn right up a track beside Warrendale Plantation, and along the wold top above Millington. The path crosses two valleys before climbing out above Pasture Dale.

For a short while the Yorkshire Wolds Way coincides with the Minster Way, a 51-mile (82km) walk between York and Beverley Minsters. It then continues over the Wolds to a point north of Huggate, where you turn left on the road towards Northfield House. On the roads in the vicinity are some curious quasi-Roman milestones and markers bearing pseudo-Latin inscriptions that were erected during the last century.

The Yorkshire Wolds Way continues over the fields to reach an earthwork running along the top of the valley. These earthworks are something of an enigma: they may have been built to mark boundaries in prehistoric times, and here, set at the top of the valley, they would make a defensive mound (especially with a palisade).

Descend into Horse Dale and bear left into Holm Dale, the name being all that is left of the vanished village of Holme Archiepiscopi, the seat of a York prebend. In 1295 there was a manor house, chapel and nine tenants and the outline of the row of houses with their garths can be seen on aerial photographs of the fields.

The path continues into Fridaythorpe, a village set on the A166 York–Bridlington road. It was the home of a man called Wellburn; an expert at making the dewponds that were used to water animals all over the riverless Wolds.

STAGE 4

FRIDAYTHORPE to WINTRINGHAM

DISTANCE 16 miles (25.7km)

MAPS OS Explorer 294, 300

START AT GRID REFERENCE SE 875 590

START POINT The centre of Fridaythorpe on the A166 York–Bridlington road

The route out of the village is along the Thixendale road, which turns left off the main road at the Farmers Arms. After 400yds (365m) bear left on the signposted path. This leads to another path that descends into West Dale, then climbs more gradually to Gill's Farm. At the road turn right, then left after 100yds (90m) to the top of a valley. The path swings left down the hillside, then right towards Thixendale.

At this point the Yorkshire Wolds Way coincides with the North Wolds Way, a 20-mile (32km) circular walk covering the high wolds and valleys. Turn left on the road through Thixendale. Set in these remote valleys, the village is easily blocked off by winter snowfalls. The church, like the former school, was designed by GE Street at the expense of Sir Tatton Sykes.

The Yorkshire Wolds Way leaves Thixendale up a broad track on the right at the end of the village. Cross over Cow Wold and descend into a valley with an earthwork along the bottom. Climb out along another earthwork and turn right, passing North Plantation to reach a minor road from Wharram le Street to Thixendale. At this point you are on the same route as the Centenary Way. This 80-mile (129km) walk from York to Filey Brigg was opened in 1989 to celebrate the centenary of the founding of Yorkshire County Council. As well as Yorkshire Wolds Way signs there are Centenary Way signs and yellow waymarkers with CW. In a few places the Centenary Way route to Filey Brigg varies from the Yorkshire Wolds Way route.

MISSIONARY

The path drops left to Wharram Percy, a deserted village set in the valley bottom. Close to Wharram Percy is Burdale Tunnel, where the Malton–Driffield railway cut through the Wolds. The 200 navvies who built the tunnel lived a hard and rough life in temporary lodgings, much of their wages being spent on beer. In 1849, to improve their spiritual life, it was decided to employ a missionary for six months, at a cost of £39 6s 8d.

The Yorkshire Wolds Way climbs out of the valley and turns left at the car park. It passes Bella Farm and eventually continues over the fields into Wharram le Street, where you turn right to the road then left through the village. Just beyond the end of the village, when the road bears left, carry straight on up a track to join the North Grimston-to-Duggleby road (B1253). There is a superb view from here as the Wolds drop away towards Malton, the Derwent valley and the Vale of Pickering.

Cross straight over the road along a track then turn left down to Wood House Farm. A climb past High Bellmanear

ⓘ PLACES TO VISIT

• HUMBER BRIDGE COUNTRY PARK
www.humberbridgecountrypark. co.uk ☎ 01482 640852
The YWW starts very close to, and passes by, this lovely Local Nature Reserve. The site of an old chalk quarry, its wooded terraces offer dramatic views of the Humber Bridge. It features a number of short trails around woodlands and ponds, including a sculpture trail. There is a bird feeding station, with living willow screens and a viewing tunnel from which to watch the wildlife. The reserve is particularly well known for its butterflies, recording over 20 species each year. There is a café and the Humber Bridge TIC is in the car park. Open daily all year.

• BURNBY HALL GARDENS AND MUSEUM
www.burnbyhallgardens.com
☎ 01759 307125
The village of Pocklington is just a short diversion to the west of the YWW. It is home to a 12th-century church, and to the lovely Burnby Hall Gardens. The gardens feature an internationally important collection of hardy water lillies, which float upon two lakes surrounded by various gardens and walks. Visitors can even feed the fish in the lakes. There is a visitor centre with a tea room, and a play area. Entrance to the gardens includes admission to the Stewart Museum, named for Major Stewart, whose collections are housed within. Former owner of the Burnby Hall Estate, he made eight world voyages in the early part of the 20th century and returned with many cultural and religious artefacts. Open daily Apr–Sep.

ABOVE Scarlet poppies add their colour to a rape field near Thixendale

TOP The abandoned village of Wharram Percy
ABOVE Part of the Yorkshire Wolds Way near East Heslerton

leads to Settrington High Street, probably a prehistoric ridge route. Near by is the site of Settrington Beacon, which was established to warn local people of the threat of the Napoleonic invasion.

Slightly to the right, the Way continues on a path through the trees to turn right, and then left, to descend off the northern edge of the Wolds. The route continues straight ahead for a mile (1.6km) before turning right over the fields to cross a footbridge and enter Wintringham.

Just over a mile (1.6km) down the road, to the left, is the A64 Malton–Scarborough road, along which there is a good bus service into Malton (where there is accommodation).

The Yorkshire Wolds Way bypasses the village of Wintringham, but both the village and its church are worth exploring if you have the time for a short detour. The Yorkshire Wolds Way turns left at the road then sharp right to head over the fields towards Wintringham Church, where there is a car park.

WINTRINGHAM TO FILEY BRIGG

STAGE 5

WINTRINGHAM to GANTON
DISTANCE 9.4 miles (15.1km)
MAP OS Explorer 300
START AT GRID REFERENCE SE 887 731
START POINT The car park near Wintringham Church

From the car park, facing the church, turn right and walk towards the bend in the road. Turn left, then right at the Yorkshire Wolds Way signpost. Cross the field and begin climbing steeply through the wood. From the top there are views northwards across the Vale of Pickering to the North Yorks Moors. An earthwork leads to a lane, where you turn right past West Farm. Then turn left and right above Knapton Wood.

Rising out of the wood is a chalk hill named Staple Howe. In the early 1950s, the noted local archaeologist Tony Brewster became aware of prehistoric pottery on the site and subsequent excavations revealed an Iron Age settlement of three buildings, and a wooden palisade defending the hilltop. The Yorkshire Wolds Way continues on the ridge-top until a right turn leads to a road above West Heslerton.

For a 6-mile/9.5km circular walk you can turn right along this quiet road (grid ref. SE 911 748) over West Heslerton Wold to grid ref. SE 916 726, where you turn right down a track to a road in the valley. Turn right, back to Wintringham.

To continue on the Yorkshire Wolds Way, walk along the track opposite and turn left at the end of the wood. A right turn leads back on to the plateau top. As the path climbs, the view opens out, down to East and West Heslerton. Between the two villages, an extensive archaeological dig has been undertaken on an Anglo-Saxon site.

Continuing eastwards, the walk passes above East Heslerton, whose prominent church was another designed by GE Street and built in 1877 at the expense of Sir Tatton Sykes. Walk eastwards, until a right turn leads to a minor road at the top of Sherburn Brow. Turn left down the road for a mile (1.6km), then either follow the Yorkshire Wolds Way by turning right at the signpost or continue the short distance into Sherburn, where there is one inn and a frequent bus service to Malton and Scarborough.

For those who wish to break the journey and return to Wintringham, there is the option of taking the Malton bus from Sherburn (grid ref. SE 958 767). Alight at Wintringham Lane End and walk back into the village.

BENEATH THE WOLDS
To continue on the Yorkshire Wolds Way, follow the signposted path to the Sherburn–Weaverthorpe road and turn right. In front of you as you reach the road is High Mill Farm. High Mill ground corn, and a dam on East Beck retained the water to power the wheel. A little further downstream was Low Mill which was also used for grinding corn.

When the road forks, bear left up the Foxholes road. At the end of the first field turn left on a signposted path which leads into Brow Plantation, then descend and turn right into the hamlet of Potter Brompton. Take a right turn along the road, then left over the fields into Ganton. The route is now running beneath the Wolds, which rise to your right. When you reach the road, turn left and walk the short distance down to the main road, where there is the Ganton Greyhound Inn and a regular bus service to both Malton and Scarborough.

STAGE 6

GANTON to FILEY BRIGG
DISTANCE 12.7 miles (20.4km)
MAPS OS Explorer 300, 301
START AT GRID REFERENCE SE 987 776
START POINT The crossroads in Ganton, on the A64 Malton–Scarborough road

Walk up the road towards Foxholes and turn left along Main Street. Continue over the stream and along the track, passing the church on your left. The route continues straight ahead, then turns right just beyond a plantation and climbs back on to the Wolds. A series of left and right turns crosses the familiar open countryside to reach the B1249 Scarborough–Driffield road. Four hundred yards (365km) to the left is the picnic site at Staxton Brow which offers an excellent viewpoint.

Take the road opposite which leads to RAF Staxton, a radar defence station which first opened in 1939. The track eventually turns right over Staxton Wold, then left above Cotton Dale.

Earlier this century the Wolds had a large group of itinerant workers called the Wolds' Rangers. They were always available to farmers during the busy periods, such as harvesting. At other times some may have moved on to another district, but many stayed on the Wolds all the year round. Most were hard-working

TOP *Rock formations at Filey Brigg*
LEFT *Aerial view of the headland at Filey Brigg*

and appreciated by the farmers. A few were not adverse to a bit of stealing; usually of game or other food. A custom prevailed with the farmers of never refusing to help them and barns were left open to provide shelter. Sir Tatton Sykes had a bell fitted to the back door of Sledmere House and any ranger who rang the bell received a meat sandwich and a cup of tea. Many had unusual names: Cut Lip Sam was an excellent worker, there was Bungey Twist and Horse Hair Jack. Well Well carried his belongings around with him in a cart, and Cloggie Sam sold trinkets to the farmers' wives.

COASTAL VIEWS

Cross two valleys to reach the minor road from Flixton to Fordon, turn right for 400yds (365m) then left on a track to pass above Raven Dale on your right. Cross Camp Dale and climb the small dale opposite. The route then turns right, descending back into grassy Camp Dale and swinging left to a valley junction. At this point, the Centenary Way turns right to find a different route to Filey, while the Yorkshire Wolds Way turns left up Stocking Dale. At Long Plantation the path turns right, passing Stockendale

Farm to reach the Flixton–Hunmanby road. Continue straight ahead on a route with extensive views along the coast. The end of the walk is now in sight. After about 0.5 miles (800m) the Yorkshire Wolds Way turns right, crossing over the fields to reach the A1039 Staxton–Filey road, on the outskirts of Muston. Its claim to fame is that, in 1886, a wooden Wesleyan chapel was moved bodily from South Cliff, Scarborough, and set up in Muston. It was placed on a special carriage and hauled the 9 miles (14.5km) by traction engine.

Pass through the village and just after the road takes a sharp left turn, bear left below a triangular green (the path is indicated at the right end of the terrace of houses in front of you). Follow the path over fields to the busy A165 Scarborough–Bridlington road. Cross straight over and walk through the long field to a footbridge, where you turn right to the main road into Filey.

Turn left and walk down the road and over the railway crossing to a roundabout. The most pleasant way to reach Filey Brigg is to turn left at the roundabout and bear slightly right at the next junction along Church Street. In Queen Street, to the right, is the Filey local history museum, housed in a 17th-century cottage. Over one of the doorways is an interesting carved stone, probably erected when the house was built.

The route to Filey Brigg continues down Church Street and crosses a ravine on a footbridge. Ahead is the church where Reverend Arthur Neville Cooper, known as the 'Walking Parson', was vicar for 55 years. Reverend Cooper walked the length and breadth of Yorkshire, as well as from Filey to Rome and from Filey to Venice. He wrote books about his walking trips, and died aged 93 years.

Turn right on the path alongside the churchyard wall, to keep the wooded ravine on your right. Follow the top path and swing left along the cliff-top. Steps lead across the small valley, which is a popular place for birdwatchers to shelter, hoping to spot rare migrants. The Filey North Cliff Country Park is to the left as the cliff-top path follows round to reach the dramatic promontory of Filey Brigg. Here you will find a stone sculpture, carved with the National Trail symbol of an acorn. It marks the end of the superb Yorkshire Wolds Way and also the Cleveland Way National Trail.

PLACES TO VISIT

• WHARRAM PERCY
www.english-heritage.co.uk
The YWW passes close to the deserted medieval village of Wharram Percy. Although it is not the only such village in Yorkshire, it is undoubtedly the most well known, due to the lengthy investigations carried out there every summer for the 40 years following 1950. The village was most likely the victim of a change from crop farming to sheep rearing; the villagers evicted by the landlord to make way for pasture. There are significant remains of St Martin's church and many other earthworks that signify further village buildings.

• WOLDS WAY LAVENDER
www.woldswaylavender.com
☎ 01944 758641
Less than 0.6 miles (1km) from the YWW, at Wintringham, is this large lavender farm. They have their own narrow gauge railway to collect the harvest and take it to an on-site distillery for production of the essential oil that is used in so many items stocked in the gift shop. The tea room even serves lavender scones. There is also a living willow maze, which contains giant games and a labyrinth, and an enormous bee hive, which of course produces lavender honey. A nature trail around the grounds is another treat, full of wildflowers. Open daily Apr–Aug, Sun–Thu Sep–Oct.

• FILEY
www.yorkshiremoorsandcoast. com ☎ 01723 518000
The seaside resort of Filey has, besides miles of sandy beach and a range of formal parks, a few tourist attractions to offer. Visit the Filey Bird Garden and Animal Park (*www.fileybirdgarden.com* ☎ 01723 514439; open daily Apr–Oct), Filey Museum (*www. fileymuseum.co.uk* ☎ 01723 515013; open daily Apr–Oct), or enjoy rockpooling on the promontory reserve of Filey Brigg.

Cumbria Way

COMPLETE ROUTE ULVERSTON TO CARLISLE **76 MILES (122KM)**

SECTION COVERED AS ABOVE

MAPS OS EXPLORER OL 4, OL 5, OL 6, OL 7, 315

Journeys are explorations, and the Cumbria Way is unsurpassed in the rewards it offers discerning walkers. It begins quietly enough in the unpretentious town of Ulverston. The sea is virtually on its doorstep and from the swelling uplands on its outskirts there are breathtaking all-round views. The vast expanse of Morecambe Bay lies to the south. Westwards is the Duddon estuary, with Black Combe beyond. The Pennines spread along the distant, eastern horizon. Coniston Old Man and its attendant fells soon loom large to the north, a stunning background to the long, lovely reach of Coniston Water, lying almost due north to south.

ABOVE Hoad Monument, Ulverston

BELOW Sculpture marks the start of the long-distance path in The Gill, Ulverston

ULVERSTON TO CONISTON

STAGE 1

ULVERSTON to BLAWITH
DISTANCE 8.3 miles (13.4km)
MAP OS Explorer OL 6
START AT GRID REFERENCE SD 285 785
START POINT Ulverston, town centre

Beyond the ring of small towns circling Lakeland is an outer ring of larger ones, where contact is made between the dales and the farming and industrial lands. Ulverston is one such town which, while becoming industrialized in the final decade of the 18th century, still carried out its function as a market town.

When Rennie built a canal connecting it with the sea, Ulverston became a port for the Furness iron industry. The town thrived and by 1840 its population numbered over 5,000. The advent of the railway in 1850, however, and the discovery of the famous Park iron ore deposits, led to the rapid expansion of nearby Barrow, while Ulverston's industry declined. Ulverston's once-important blast furnaces were demolished and replaced by a penicillin factory, and today this grey and white town remains astonishingly unsullied, having about it the gentility of a minor spa town.

From the town centre, follow the beck westwards which, when Ulverston was a textile centre, provided the water power. After about 0.25 mile (400m), cross the beck and climb a walled lane. At its end turn right along a field track, signposted to Old Hall Farm. Cross the farmyard, pass the farmhouse and immediately cross a stile on your left. Just beyond the farmhouse garden, cross another stile on your left and go diagonally right, past the corner of a wood on your left and continue uphill to cross a corner step-stile. Turn right, then left uphill, to a gap-stile in a wall corner. The prominent monument seen on Hoad Hill, overlooking Ulverston, is a 100ft (30.5m) replica of the Eddystone Lighthouse, erected in 1850 to commemorate Ulverston-born John Barrow; writer, traveller, Arctic explorer and, for 40 years, Secretary of the Admiralty. He was born in 1764.

Contour a hillock, cross a depression and then a field to Higher Lath Farm. Continue right, along the road to Windy Ash, and follow a Cumbria Way signpost along a short, grassy track to Newbiggin, to go through the farmyard and along a surfaced road. When the road turns right, leave it through a gate and head across fields.

GREY HERON

Keep to the right of Stony Crag Farm and do not enter the farmyard. Instead, turn left through a gate and immediately turn right behind the farm, following a wall on the right and continue alongside a beck to Hollowmire. Turn right, through the farmyard, follow a farm road to a junction and turn left for 200yds (183m), then right through a kissing-gate. Take the field path past the church ahead and turn right, along a road to Broughton Beck.

Scafell and Scafell Pike can now be seen to the northwest, while closer to hand buttercups, oxeye daisies and a constant splurge of wild roses brighten lush hedgerows. Leave the village along a track and, on reaching a beck, turn left into a field. Head left across it, to a not-very-obvious step-stile mid-way along the wall section of a mix of wall and hedgerow. Veer left across the next field, bridging the beck in its middle, and go upstream, using a series of stiles, to an unsurfaced road.

The distinctive-looking grey heron fishes these parts and may be seen, sometimes in flight (its long neck tucked against its body and its legs stretched far beyond the tip of its tail), sometimes standing motionless at the beck's edge, waiting to pierce an incautious fish or frog.

Just past Knapperthaw, turn right at a Y-junction and left at the next one to follow the track to Keldray. Pass to the left of it and climb to a wall-stile near an electricity pole. Continue ahead, past Keldray, and cross the A5092 to Gawthwaite village.

The A5092 is the southern boundary of the Lake District National Park, which, at 866 square miles (2,242 sq km), is the largest of the National Parks. Climb sharply out of the village along a road that soon levels out. At the third gate, turn right along a gravel road to High Stennerley. Turn left here, around the back of the buildings, on to a minor road. Turn right along it for 35yds (32m) and then enter a field on the left. At a minor road, go left along it for 0.5 miles (800m). The Cumbria Way leaves the road at a sharp bend (grid ref. SD 277 871) for Kiln Bank, but anyone wishing to break the journey here can do so by continuing along the road for a further mile to Blawith, on the A5084, where church, pub and roadside parking are available.

STAGE 2

BLAWITH to CONISTON
DISTANCE 7.9 miles (12.7km)
MAPS OS Explorer OL 6, OL 7
START AT GRID REFERENCE SD 288 883
START POINT Blawith

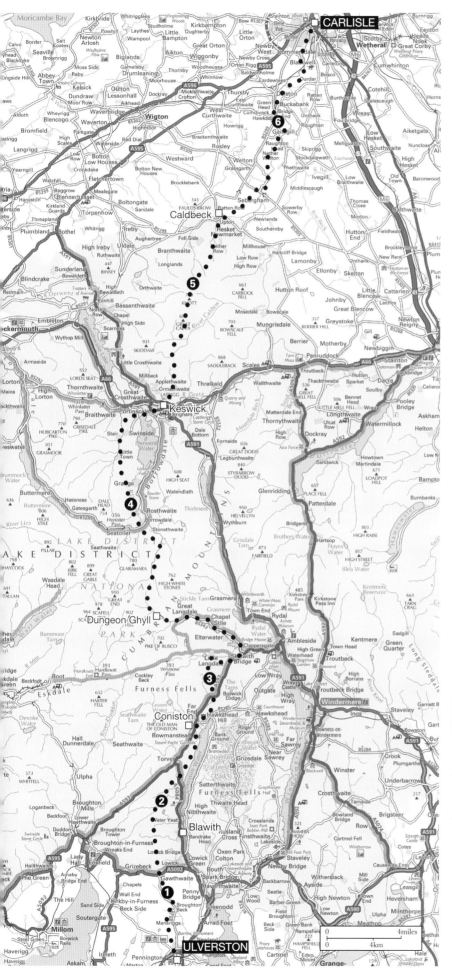

USEFUL INFORMATION

THE ROUTE
• www.thecumbriaway.info
The official guide to the CW is produced by the Lake District Ramblers Association group, and although the Ramblers' website has useful information, they also endorse this far more informative source. Put together by a CW enthusiast, it covers preparation for a trip, accommodation, service providers, publications, useful links and a gallery of photos. Also visit www.keswick. org/walking-routes to download a series of six basic leaflets on the CW sections.

TOURIST INFORMATION CENTRES
• www.golakes.co.uk
Coronation Hall, County Square, Ulverston LA12 7LZ;
☎ 01229 587120
• www.conistontic.org
Ruskin Avenue, Coniston LA21 8EH;
☎ 015394 41533
• www.keswick.org
Market Square, Keswick CA12 5JR;
☎ 017687 72645
• www.historic-carlisle.org.uk
Old Town Hall, Green Market, Carlisle CA3 8JE;
☎ 01228 625600

PLANNING YOUR TRIP
• www.ldwa.org.uk
The Long Distance Walkers Association gives help on the CW, including a link to a preview of the complete Cicerone CW guide.
• www.ramblers.org.uk
☎ 020 7339 8500
The Ramblers Association website has advice about long-distance walking and a page on the CW itself.
• www.yha.org.uk
☎ 0800 019 1700
The Youth Hostel Association has sites along the CW.

OTHER PATHS
The Cumbria Coastal Way follows almost the entire Cumbrian coast, from Silverdale on the east side of Morecambe Bay, to the River Esk, north of Carlisle. It passes through Carlisle and could be used as a return route to Ulverston.

TOP TO BOTTOM Cumbrian sheep, River Caldbeck flowing past cottages, Tarn Hows, Little Langdale, sunset over Derwent Water

From Blawith, the Cumbria Way may be re-joined at Beacon Tarn by going left at the north end of the village, along a lane to Pitchall, continuing along a path to Greenholme Farm and turning left along a lane, at the end of which a path leads to Beacon Tarn. The Cumbria Way itself continues from Kiln Bank (grid ref. SD 274 873). Where the track splits, just beyond the farm, take the right-hand, higher route to a surfaced road (grid ref. SD 272 880). Go left towards Tottlebank.

From March to October, annually, migrating wheatears are much in evidence around this climbing road, the white rumps of both sexes a complete give-away. Once served up as delicacies on Victorian dinner tables, today's delightful wheatears are definitely not for human consumption.

At a Cumbria Way sign marked on slate, turn right along a rising green track through bracken. It is a joy to walk, the views are terrific, and it soon descends to Cockenskell. Pass to the left of it, bridge a beck and climb the fellside ahead along a clear, meandering track to lonely Beacon Tarn. Follow its western shore, crossing some marshy areas, and climb a spur of Blawith Fells, to descend steeply to a marshy area.

This is glorious walking, through rough grass, bracken and rocky outcrops, with the mountains beginning to loom ahead at the entrance to this empty valley. It's a great feeling. The track is typical of lakeland fells country; sometimes smooth and grassy, sometimes rough and rocky.

The route curves eastwards, skirting Stable Harvey Moss, to join a minor road at a bend. Turn left along it, uphill, for 125yds (115m) to a point where a bridleway leads westwards. After 0.5 miles (800m), it crosses a beck on the left and bears right, goes over another beck and follows a clear track along the western side of the valley to cross first a footbridge and then the A5084.

Anyone wishing to terminate this section can do so by turning left at grid ref. SD 288 921, along the A5084 for 1 mile (1.6km) to Torver, where there is an inn. Do so only as a last resort because the thrilling climax of this section lies ahead and is highly recommended.

LAKESIDE PATH

The Cumbria Way continues along the track signposted 'Coniston via Lakeshore', which leads to the lake and then goes along the shoreline on a path, partly wooded, that is one of the most pleasant in Lakeland. Brantwood, home of John Ruskin from 1872 to 1900, can be seen on the other side of the lake. The route then passes Coniston Hall, with its splendid chimneys, and leads nicely along a well-used track into Coniston.

CONISTON TO KESWICK

STAGE 3

CONISTON to DUNGEON GHYLL

DISTANCE 11 miles (17.7km)

MAPS OS Explorer OL 6, OL 7

START AT GRID REFERENCE SD 302 975

START POINT Coniston

Coniston has a strong industrial background that goes back to Roman times, but it was not until the 16th century that miners from the Mines Royal at Keswick were brought to work the

copper mines here. The region is rich in copper and iron and was once an important charcoal-producing area. When the mining industry declined, its place in the local economy was taken by slate quarrying.

Leave Coniston along Tilberthwaite Avenue, turn left along a road signposted to Ambleside and, opposite Coniston AFC ground, cross a beck on your right and follow a footpath signposted to High Yewdale. Pass a ruined byre with a castle-like front and climb to a wood. From here, the retrospective views of Coniston Water are excellent.

Leave the wood by a stile and, after 300yds (275m), veer left through a gateway. Cross the field ahead and take a track towards Low Yewdale Farm but do not cross the stone bridge over Yewdale Beck. Instead, cross a stile on the right and follow a path parallel to the beck, to a wood. Continue along an uphill track through the wood, coming out at Tarn Hows Cottage and turning right on a track that leads to the Tarn Hows Road. Turn left, soon to reach this Lakeland jewel.

SKELWITH FORCE

The tarn is well worth circling, so, having done that, leave along its left-hand side and descend to a marshy area with some facing fir trees. Here turn left, crossing the marsh on a clear path which leads over a stile to a rough road. Turn left along it to the A593 Coniston–Ambleside road and turn right along that for 0.25 miles (400m), turning left along a road signposted to High Park Farm. From here, follow a waymarked route to a wood and descend through it to the Little Langdale road at Colwith Bridge. Do not cross the bridge but instead turn right along the road and soon cross a stile in the wall on the left to follow a clear, woodland path to the A593 Coniston–Ambleside road. Turn left along it again, briefly, and cross Skelwith Bridge. A path leads left, between slate workshops, and then continues as a wide track squashed between the River Brathay and the main road, passing impressive Skelwith Force.

The riverside route continues through fields where two exciting things happen: the Langdale Pikes loom ahead and the river swells into Elterwater Lake. At Elterwater village cross the bridge and continue upstream for 0.25 miles (400m), along a surfaced road. At a sign, follow a riverside path to a footbridge. Cross to a road and go left along it for 50yds (45m), passing the

Wainwright Inn, to a rough track on the left. Follow this track past Thrang Farm, bridge the Brathay, and take a riverside path to the former farm of Oak Howe. Contour and then descend to Side House Farm and beyond here re-cross Great Langdale Beck to the main road. Turn right to the New Dungeon Ghyll Hotel and follow the rough path, left, behind the hotel and above an intake wall. Take a fairly level route to the Old Dungeon Ghyll Hotel which, mid-way on this section, is an ideal stopping place, with its Hikers Bar.

Should the weather be adverse, end the walk here (grid ref. NY 284 062), for the next section is tough and should not be attempted in bad weather. There is an infrequent bus service to Ambleside. Alternatively, a return can be made to Skelwith Bridge by walking along the minor road that leads south and east from here through Little Langdale.

WATERFALLS

The waterfall behind the new hotel is well worth a visit and an obvious path leads along Stickle Gill, which has two waterfalls.

STAGE 4

DUNGEON GHYLL to KESWICK

DISTANCE 15.7 miles (25.3km)
MAPS OS Explorer OL 4, OL 6
START AT GRID REFERENCE NY 284 061
START POINT Old Dungeon Ghyll Hotel, off the B5343

The route west from the Old Dungeon Ghyll Hotel is along the wide, flat bottom of Mickleden, skirting a wall of rock nearly 2,000ft (610m) high, which is topped with Pike O' Stickle fell.

At the head of the valley, where the path forks at a marking stone, turn right and zig-zag up the very steep, glaciated valley side. At the top, cross an upland hollow full of glacial moraines. From the 'hause', or pass, descend the deep trough of Langstrath, edging Stake Gill and zig-zagging down 500ft (150m) in less than 0.25 miles (400m). At the bottom, take the level but rough track with Langstrath Beck on the left. After about 2 miles (3km) the beck turns sharp left as Greenup Gill joins it. At this point bridge Greenup Gill and turn left for another 1.75 miles (2.75km). Pass Stonethwaite Bridge after a mile and, after another 0.75 miles (1.25km) or so, cross a second bridge to reach Rosthwaite.

ABOVE LEFT The attractive conifer-covered shoreline of Tarn Hows
ABOVE RIGHT Langdale Pikes, seen from Great Langdale

At grid ref. NY 263 138 an escape may be made from the route to Borrowdale Youth Hostel, about 1 mile (1.6km) northwest, by crossing Stonethwaite Bridge, turning right in the hamlet, following a lane to a junction and then taking a short permissive path to the hostel and public transport.

Leave Rosthwaite along a road opposite the Post Office that leads to the River Derwent. Either bank can be followed to New Bridge. Beyond New Bridge go right, keeping close to the river, and then soon go left, around a knoll, to return to the river and enter High Hows Wood. Where the path forks, go left, through an old slate quarry, to turn right at a T-junction and descend to the river at the entrance to the famous Jaws of Borrowdale. At a junction with a bridleway, turn right along what soon becomes a rough track. At the end of the wood turn left towards Hollows Farm, beyond which a stony track leads north through fields. The Jaws of Borrowdale, where Grange Fell on the east and Scawdel (Castle Crag) on the west almost meet, mark Borrowdale's northern end. The Bowder Stone lies in the Jaws like a hazel in a nutcracker.

On reaching a conifer plantation turn left, up the skirt of Cat Bells, and where the track splits, take the right-hand path, contouring for 1.5 miles (2.5km) and descending to a minor road, which the route crosses. Follow a road downhill, continue along a lane (passing close to Hawes End outdoor education centre), and turn right at a signposted junction to Portinscale.

In the village, turn right by the Derwentwater Hotel, cross the Derwent on a suspension bridge, and after 100yds (90m) go right on a path through fields to Keswick.

KESWICK TO CARLISLE

STAGE 5
KESWICK to CALDBECK
DISTANCE 15 miles (24.1km)
MAPS OS Explorer OL 4, OL 5
START AT GRID REFERENCE NY 264 235
START POINT Keswick

Keswick, the busiest town in Lakeland, claims to be the metropolis of the lakes. An ancient place, it was granted a market charter in the 13th century and in the 16th century became a trading centre for the wool produced in Borrowdale. In 1565 Goldscope copper mine was opened in the Newlands valley and 50 German miners were brought over for their expertise (Goldscope is a corruption of the German name for the mine, 'God's gift'). Within two years of the mine opening, Keswick became a thriving industrial town and within the next 150 years huge tracts of woodland were felled to provide charcoal for the furnaces. In the l8th century, the romantic age of tourism began and Keswick became a popular resort. Today, climbers, walkers and tourists rub shoulders in its narrow streets.

Leave Keswick along Station Road, crossing the River Greta and turning sharp right to pass under a railway bridge. Turn left and continue on Brundholme Road. After 500yds (455m), turn right up Spooneygreen Lane; a rough track that soon bridges the Keswick bypass (grid ref. NY 269 243). The track now curves left, gently climbing Latrigg. After a mile (1.6km), meet a metalled road and turn right. Almost immediately, turn left

PLACES TO VISIT

• CALDBECK
www.caldbeckvillage.co.uk
This lovely village has two main sites of interest. St Kentigern's Church dates from the 12th century and is the burial place of famous local huntsman, John Peel. The churchyard also houses the Roughton Stone; a tribute to the local miners of Roughton Gill. The other local attraction is Priests Mill, tucked away beside the river. It is an old corn-grinding mill, which still has its waterwheel, though it no longer turns. There is, however, an attractive café and a few craft workshops. Open daily Feb–Dec, variable in Jan.

• CARLISLE
www.historic-carlisle.org.uk
☎ 01228 625600
England's most northerly city has the lowest population of any in the land, but the largest area. It was a garrison fort along the Roman Hadrian's Wall, and there is certainly much history to be explored here. The castle is still largely intact, the earliest parts dating from the 12th century. There are exhibitions here, in addition to the King's Own Royal Border Regiment Museum and the Carlisle Roman Dig (*www.english-heritage.co.uk* ☎ 01228 591922; open daily all year). The nearby cathedral has stood for almost 900 years and is noted for its vaulted painted ceiling, stained glass and finely carved altarpiece and choir stalls (*www.carlislecathedral.org.uk* ☎ 01228 548151; open daily all year). Between the two lies the Tullie House Museum and Art Gallery (*www.tulliehouse.co.uk* ☎ 01228 618718; open daily all year). The house itself is a grade I listed Jacobean mansion in attractive gardens. Today, it houses fine collections that cover the subjects of History, Nature and Art, with hands-on displays. Also worth a visit are the Citadel, Guildhall Museum and the city's many fine shops.

TOP Rowing boats moored on Derwent Water
ABOVE LEFT Clouds over Keswick church
ABOVE MIDDLE View of Catbells and Derwent Water from Keswick
ABOVE RIGHT Carlisle Cathedral

along a fenced path. Below the monument, fork right along a descending path to Whit Beck. The path now contours Lonscale Fell for 0.5 miles (800m), giving good views ahead and to the south, before turning left along the narrow valley of Glenderaterra Beck, contouring mid-way up its steep side. At the head of this lonely valley, where a watershed is passed, cross Salehow Beck to reach solitary Skiddaw House. Set within a vast expanse of open moorland and protected by conifers, Skiddaw House was originally built for use by shepherds. It is now open as a youth hostel, having been renovated, and is a welcome sight for fell wanderers, especially at the onset of bad weather.

From here (grid ref. NY 287 291) an escape route goes westward past Dash Falls to Bassenthwaite. This is also an alternative bad weather route to Caldbeck, joining roads near Bassenthwaite.

HIGH PIKE

Past the front of Skiddaw House turn right along a spongy track, cross the infant Caldew and follow the track close to the river for about 3 miles (5km) to the point it becomes surfaced and Grainsgill Beck is bridged. Once over the bridge turn left, pass Wolfram mine buildings and continue up Grainsgill Beck, climbing. There is no really clear track but a hut on the skyline is your immediate destination. At the head of the valley turn right, away from the beck, over boggy ground to the hut (grid ref. NY 312 336), a welcome shelter in bad weather. From here a clear track leads past Great Lingy Hill towards High Pike, but not to its summit. However, 1 mile (1.6km) from the hut, leave the track and follow a clear path to the summit, which, at 2,159ft (658m), is the most northerly fell over 2,000ft (610m) high in the Lake District. From its flat top the view towards Carlisle and the Pennines is panoramic and, just as important, it boasts a seat!

The correct way down High Pike is to retrace your steps to the track and following it, curving anti-clockwise, descending the fellside. In practice, the easy way is down the slope ahead until the original track is regained. It leads to an enclosed lane as the Cumbria Way approaches Nether Row. Continue north from Nether Row, directly over crossroads and right, after 200yds (183m), across fields and a footbridge on to a path that leads to a road. From here the middle of Caldbeck is in view.

STAGE 6

CALDBECK to CARLISLE

DISTANCE 15.3 miles (24.6km)
MAPS OS Explorer OL 5, 315

START AT GRID REFERENCE NY 324 397
START POINT Caldbeck

Caldbeck was an agricultural settlement until the discovery of minerals in the Caldbeck Fells during the 18th century brought about a gradual change of character. Riverside mills were built to provide water power, corn was ground, wool spun and paper manufactured. Lead, copper and coal were mined, limestone was quarried and, with such prosperity, pubs were built. By 1829 there were six in the village. Two famous people lie in the churchyard: Mary Robinson, the Maid of Buttermere; and John Peel, born in 1777, who lived in Caldbeck, was Master of the local hunt, died in 1854 and was immortalized in the song 'D'ye ken John Peel?'.

Leave the village along a walled path, passing the church on your right. Cross Parkend Beck, turn right, pass a sewage farm and go through Parson's Park Wood. Where the path splits, go left, uphill and then levelling out for a mile (1.6km) or so, about 100ft (30m) above the Beck. Where the forest ends, maintain height, across open pasture for 0.5 miles (800m), there being no clear track. Enter the woodland ahead at the top left-hand corner and then follow posted directions where a vast landslide has swept away the original path. Continue through the forest, contouring along a broad ridge which crosses the top of the slip. Just past it, where the ridge curves left, continue ahead, following a descending path through conifers. Cross a field, continue uphill and turn left through a gate alongside a garage. The clear track leads to a lane from the vicarage to the church. Opposite the church turn left, along a lane, keeping to the right of the Hall grounds, and descend to a road at Bell Bridge.

Cross the bridge and turn right to follow the riverbank past Bog Bridge and Rose Bridge, until the river swings right. Keep straight ahead, on rising ground and through a kissing-gate, to a track near Holm Hill on the right. Turn left, cross a tarmac road, go through a kissing-gate and along a track. At a gate, turn right to Georgian Hawksdale Hall. Turn right and follow a track northwards, through fields, to reach the B5299 and Bridge End. Cross the bridge into Buckabank. Where the road divides, turn right, curve left past a mill, keep forward at a crossroads to go alongside a millstream and through a mill, before crossing White Bridge and following the road to Dalston Green.

Once clear of Dalston the way ahead follows a railway line, passing under it when it bridges the Caldew. It then crosses the river on a footbridge, reaching Carlisle along the other bank. This superb walk ends in the city centre.

Pennine Way

COMPLETE ROUTE EDALE TO KIRK YETHOLM **256 MILES (412KM)**
SECTION COVERED ALSTON TO KIRK YETHOLM **78 MILES (125KM)**
MAPS OS EXPLORER OL 1, OL 2, OL 16, OL 19, OL 21, OL 30, OL 31, OL 41, OL 42, OL 43, 288

The Pennine Way follows an uncompromising line, seeking out the most dramatic ridges and sweeps of moorland, beginning at Edale in Derbyshire and ending across the Scottish border at Kirk Yetholm. At just over 250 miles (400km) long, the complete trail is a perfect introduction to remote scenery and a major challenge to any walker. Many Pennine Way novices fall by the wayside long before they have reached the Yorkshire–Cumbria border. The section described here receives only a fraction of the pressures associated with the corresponding southern third of the route.

ABOVE *Blackface sheep in the 'inbye' fields watch energetic walkers pass by*
ABOVE RIGHT *A wooden ladder stile in a stone wall*
RIGHT *Ferns growing along the Pennine Way, from Widdy Bank Farm to Cauldron Snout*
BELOW *Signposts marking the Pennine Way and the England–Scotland border*

ALSTON TO GREENHEAD

STAGE 1
ALSTON to SLAGGYFORD
DISTANCE 5.5 miles (8.9km)
MAPS OS Explorer OL 31, OL 43
START AT GRID REFERENCE NY 716 461
START POINT A signposted track beside the bridge of the A686, over River South Tyne at the southern edge of Alston

Prosperity for the little cross-Pennine town of Alston came and went with lead-mining. Alston had been at the hub of a rural community for centuries and had a sort of heyday when it was in the possession of the Radcliffe family. Unfortunately the Radcliffes chose the wrong side in the Jacobite rebellions and it took another century after their demise, and the arrival of the London Lead Company, to wake the town up. After a period of rapid expansion, the mining industry collapsed and Alston was back serving farmers and wagoners and waiting for better times. Tourism has taken over, but the character of the place remains as it ever was, solid with a hint of eccentricity.

Alston makes a good starting point for a walk, self-contained and with all essential services. The Pennine Way crosses the bridge at the southern edge of the town, having completed the long descent from Cross Fell. From the bridge, the route turns right, off the A686 and along the A689 for a few yards, then right along a track and through a gate beside a white house. There are good views east, over the river towards the town as the path heads north to Harbut Lodge. The route is signposted to the left of the house, then around the edge of the pasture to a stile on to a track. The 'inbye' fields are full of sheep in the spring, gathered off the hills to lamb on the better pasture around the farms. The usual breed these days is the Swaledale, but there are still some Blackface about, as well as a sprinkling of blue-faced Leicester and Suffolk for breeding purposes.

After crossing the A689 the path heads westwards, past a byre and uphill over rough pasture. Elaborate ladder-stiles then mark the route northwest across marshy ground, inhabited by snipe and redshank, to a little footbridge over a burn. After crossing the burn, the path climbs up to the shoulders of the open fell, bearing to the left of the knoll encircled by shallow grassy ridges. This is Whitley Castle, the site of a Roman fort which once protected an important link-road known as the

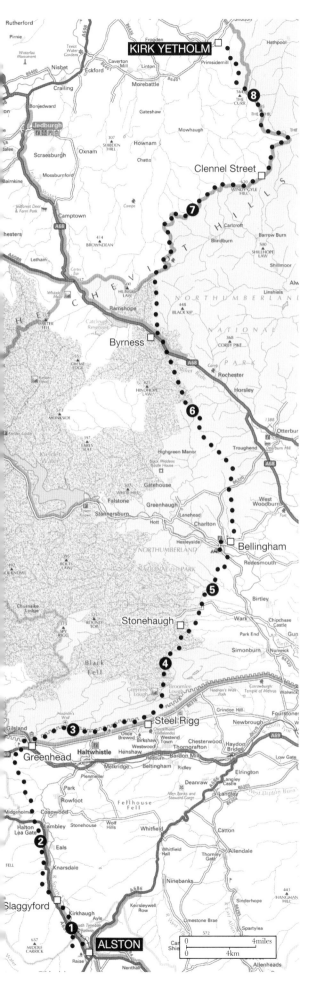

Maiden Way. The Pennine Way descends to a farm called Castle Nook and crosses the A689 again, then bears to the right around Dyke House and follows the South Tyne valley, through Kirkhaugh and parallel with the old railway line. On the far bank of the river is Barhaugh Park and Barhaugh Hall, a field studies and holiday centre. Below Lintley Farm, the route turns right to follow a burn beneath a five-arched viaduct, then arcs around a pasture and drops down to the banks of the South Tyne. The river is shallow and stony, and the home of dippers and grey wagtails. Wych elms once shadowed the riverside path but any woodland is now hazel, ash, oak and sycamore. The path meets the road close to a footbridge, and the Pennine Way continues along the verge and into the village of Slaggyford.

On weekdays, infrequent buses run from Slaggyford back to Alston.

STAGE 2

SLAGGYFORD to GREENHEAD

DISTANCE 10.8 miles (17.4km)

MAP OS Explorer OL 43

START AT GRID REFERENCE NY 678 524

START POINT Slaggyford village, on the A689, 4.5 miles (7.25km) north of Alston

Slaggyford is a bright little cluster of houses spread loosely around a green and penfold. The Pennine Way turns left off the A689 on a side road, then bears right of the old Methodist chapel (now a bed-and-breakfast) and heads along a marshy lane beside damp fields of marsh marigolds. The old South Tyne Railway line, which closed in 1976, is down to the left. The route descends through some attractive woodland, awash in their season with wild flowers such as primrose, wood anemone, early purple orchid and wood cranesbill. After crossing a footbridge, the path goes under the railway embankment, and across a field to Merry Knowe. The route is confusing here, as is so often the case around working farms. Go through the gate and between the buildings, then out of a gate and right to a stile in the wall. This brings you out again on to pasture and, although there is no clear path to follow, route-finding is quite easy, across a stile to a tumbled-down wall and towards the viaduct at Burnstones.

Just before the viaduct, drop down to the Thinhope Burn and go under the first arch of the viaduct and out on to the road. Go along the road to beyond the viaduct then, just past the drive to the big house, turn left, diagonally up a field and on to the shoulder of a wide expanse of open moorland.

The dome of the moorland to the left is Glendue Fell, part of Geltsdale and one piece in a giant jigsaw of sandstone blocks at the edge of the North Pennines. High rainfall and poor drainage has encouraged the formation of peat, which is usually wet and acidic, and stops most vegetation from growing. The result is a whole panorama of heather, cotton-grass and sphagnum moss and a specialized collection of birds and insects. Red grouse and curlew are the commonest of the larger breeding birds, but there are a few pairs of short-eared owls and merlins. The green hairstreak butterfly is on the wing here in spring. After following the shoulder of the moor for a mile (1.6km), the path drops down to cross the pretty Glendue Burn, then climbs again to contour the side of another dome of dark moorland at the edge of Hartleyburn Common. The route shadows the Maiden Way and the distant views are excellent; east over the wooded South Tyne Valley to Ashholme Common and Whitfield Moor, and south to the plateau summit of Cross Fell, which is the highest ground in England. The A689 is crossed just west of the village of Lambley, the path turning left on the descent to the road

ⓘ USEFUL INFORMATION

THE ROUTE
• www.nationaltrail.co.uk
☎ 01924 334500
This is by far the most detailed source of information about the Pennine Way. There is a plethora of sites that you could refer to, and most of them have links from here. Everything is covered, from the usual accommodation help (including GPS data) to public transport options, details of charity walks and guided walks, and even times of Roman Catholic church services near the route. The official guide to the route, with 1:25,000 OS map extracts, is split into two books, for the northern and southern halves. The single volume published by Cicerone has been updated more recently, though it uses less detailed maps.

TOURIST INFORMATION CENTRES
• www.eden.gov.uk
Town Hall, Alston CA9 3RF;
☎ 01434 382244
• www.visitnorthumberland.com
The Heritage Centre, Hillside, Bellingham NE48 2GR;
☎ 01434 220616
• www.visitnortheastengland.com
Haltwhistle Station, Haltwhistle NE49 9HN;
☎ 01434 322002
Although not directly on the route, Haltwhistle is close to the Hadrian's Wall section.
The following official tourism websites may also prove useful:
• www.visitpeakdistrict.com
• www.yorkshiredales.org.uk
• www.northumberlandnationalpark. org.uk

to cut off the corner and minimize road-walking. However, by turning right along the road and taking a footpath north of the village it is possible to get down to the river and see Lambley Viaduct; an elegant nine-arch span built to carry the old South Tyne Railway.

From grid ref. NY 666 586, a return may be made to Slaggyford by dropping down into Lambley and either taking the bus (Mondays to Saturdays) or using lanes and footpaths that follow the east bank of the River South Tyne.

OPEN COUNTRY

The Pennine Way crosses the road and heads north-west over boggy ground with no obvious path, past old mine workings and seeking the higher ground via hummocks and ridges to a derelict barn at High House. Hartley Burn is then crossed at a footbridge and, after following the burn as it angles left, a grassy path climbs out of the valley and leads through green pastures to Batey Shield. Further on, across a footbridge and a road, the route passes to the left of Greenriggs, then begins a long steady climb culminating in a stile and a sudden view over the north side of Hartleyburn Common.

TOP The Lambley Railway Viaduct, built in 1852
ABOVE A mass of purple heather growing by the wayside
ABOVE RIGHT Heather growing around an ancient-looking boulder

Having only clipped the sides of the big moors so far, it is a surprise to come on this vast expanse of open country. The route is vague, sometimes clear on the ground and sometimes quite invisible. It is a good idea to use a compass and head northwest, making for the left side of Round Hill, then continue in the same direction for a mile (1.6km) over Blenkinsopp Common. Few people would describe this country as pretty, but it is undoubtedly impressive. You will probably be the only human for miles around; even sheep are few and far between. At first the rolling plateau has no landmarks, but a triangulation column comes into view at Blade Hill and the path makes for the right of this. There is at last a real view to the north, over the Tyne Gap with the busy A69 road below. To avoid road-walking again, the route zig-zags downhill, through old mine workings, along old tracks at Todholes ('tod' means fox; this is still fox country) and under electricity pylons. The Carlisle–Newcastle

corridor is a major cross-country link, not only for road and rail but also for power and communication. Down on the A69, the contrast after the open moorland is startling as cars and lorries hurtle past. If you intend completing the day at Greenhead then go up the embankment and turn right down the old road into the village. The Pennine Way follows a different course, crossing the road and climbing the embankment the other side, then heading northeast over fields and by the golf course. It drops down to meet the B6318 just north of the village.

GREENHEAD TO STONEHAUGH

STAGE 3
GREENHEAD to STEEL RIGG
DISTANCE 7 miles (11.3km)
MAP OS Explorer OL 43
START AT GRID REFERENCE NY 650 654
START POINT Greenhead village, off the A69, 3 miles (5km) west of Haltwhistle

Greenhead used to be a very noisy little place but the bypass has transformed it, and it is now worth more than a passing glance. Most of the buildings are built from attractive honey-coloured sandstone. There is comfortable accommodation at The Greensand Hotel, and outside St Cuthbert's Church there is a war memorial and an old ornamental fountain planted up with flowers. On the west side of the village is the B6318 Blanchland road and by walking along this to a terrace of redbrick cottages, the Pennine Way is reached.

The route leaves the road at a gate beside the cottages, crosses the Newcastle–Carlisle railway line and a footbridge over a little burn, then follows an old hedge-line beside the Tipalt Burn. The stream is attractive, lined with sallows and sycamore beneath which grow primroses, anemones and butterbur. The pasture to the left is usually inhabited by an assortment of sheep breeds, including local specialties such as the Border Leicester. Hadrian's Wall crossed the gap of the Tipalt Burn at this point but nothing is visible; most of the stone was used in medieval

times in the construction of nearby Thirwall Castle. The route meets a track and turns right at Duffenfoot, over a footbridge. Once across the Tipalt and climbing the winding walled track on the other side, it is possible to look back for a romantic view of the ruins of Thirlwall Castle. It was in its prime in the reign of Edward I, who stayed here on one of his campaigns against the Scots in 1306.

At the top of the track, with a line of beech trees on the left, the route crosses a stile by a gate and heads uphill beside a deep grassy ditch. This is the ditch excavated by the Romans on the north side of Hadrian's Wall to hamper any attack by the Caledonian tribes. The wall itself has again been dismantled; an ordinary drystone wall marks its course.

HADRIAN'S WALL

At the top of the hill it is time to stop to orientate yourself by the views. If the air is fresh it should be possible to see Blenkinsopp Common and Cross Fell (the radio transmitting station in Great Dun Fell is distinctive; beside it is Little Dun Fell, then the more extensive low dome of Cross Fell at 2,930ft (893m). Looking eastwards, it should now be possible to see the dark grey cliff-face of the Great Whin Sill. Hadrian's Wall follows the crest of this famous igneous intrusion for several miles, making the most of its daunting scarp slope. Beyond the field on the right, as the route continues eastwards, is the Museum of the Roman Army and the remains of one of Agricola's forts, called Carvoran. This was built to protect the east–west road known as the Stanegate but was later employed as a garrison fort for the wall. The route meets a road and turns left along this, then left around the outside of the extensive Walltown Quarry. What was once a dreadful eyesore, extracting dolerite for roadstone and slicing away a section of the Whin Sill and any Roman remains, is now a picnic site.

Beyond the quarry the path meets a road, with some attractive marshy woodland on the right where roe deer and woodcock hide and wait for dusk to fall. After following the road over a cattle grid, the route at last bears left, uphill, to the crest of the Sill, to follow a particularly impressive section of Hadrian's Wall. In places the remains of the wall stand at head height, but even here there is only a hint of how daunting the military barrier must have been, as when it was built the wall would have been three times taller.

The rock is cut by deep gaps, created by meltwater at the end of the Ice Age, and the wall switchbacks and snakes along the best line of defence. The going is firm but never easy because of the undulating nature of the ridge. Jackdaws and wheatears nest among the columns of dolerite and among the sandstone boulders of the levelled turrets and milecastles. After Great Chesters Farm, and the grass-covered ruins of the cavalry fort of Aesica, the route drops down, crosses a road and passes another little quarry picnic site at Cawfields.

A return to Greenhead may be made from Cawfields (grid ref. NY 713 667): between Easter and October a National Park coach service runs along the route of the all. Otherwise, follow roads or paths approx. 2 miles (3km) to Haltwhistle for a bus service to Greenhead.

THE VALLUM

The Pennine Way then rises again for Cawfield Crags, where the wall is especially fine and the Vallum (the system of ridges and trenches which marked the Roman military zone) is easily visible to the south.

After Caw Gap, the Whin Sill rises to its highest point at 1,132ft (345m), with views west across the Solway to the Galloway hills. It then descends again to Steel Rigg, where there is a car park. A right turn along the road soon leads down to Once Brewed, where there is a visitor centre and youth hostel. Nearby is the Twice Brewed Inn, which has accommodation.

STAGE 4

STEEL RIGG to STONEHAUGH

DISTANCE 7 miles (11.3km)
MAP OS Explorer OL 43
START AT GRID REFERENCE NY 750 675
START POINT Steel Rigg, National Park car park, 0.5 miles (800m) north of the B6318

The view of the Whin Sill is excellent from the car park; in the distance, at the foot of the cliff, is Crag Lough, one of the shallow lakes scooped out by moving ice during the Ice Age and now being filled in slowly by reeds and silt. From the car park the route actually follows a path along the top of Hadrian's Wall for a short distance, then drops down beside it. There is then a sequence of gaps and crags, rising eventually to Highshield Crags above

ⓘ USEFUL INFORMATION
PLANNING YOUR TRIP
• www.penninewayassociation.
co.uk
The Pennine Way Association website has all the detail that you would expect, from a regularly updated accommodation guide that can be downloaded, to path updates on diversions.
• www.sherpavan.com
☎ 0871 520 0124
The Sherpa Van Project serves long-distance paths with a luggage and lodgings service. They give details of the route, maps and trailplanners to buy, and an accommodation booking service. They do not operate their luggage service south of Malham.
• www.ldwa.org.uk
The Long Distance Walkers Association has some good detail and links for the PW, including digital map suppliers and their own downloadable GPS route files (for members only).
• www.ramblers.org.uk
☎ 020 7339 8500
The Ramblers Association website offers mail order supply of the free Pennine Way Accommodation and Public Transport Guide, and many other publications and maps.
• www.yha.org.uk
☎ 0800 019 1700
The Youth Hostel Association has several sites close to the route.

OTHER PATHS
Between Greenhead and Housesteads, the PW coincides with the Hadrian's Wall Path, another National Trail. It follows the wall from Bowness-on-Solway on the west coast, to Wallsend on Tyne. The PW links with myriad other paths, such as the Ribble Way (pages 152–159) and the Dales Way (pages 160–167).

ABOVE LEFT AND RIGHT
Hadrian's Wall crosses the
Pennine Way

TOP Housesteads Fort, Hadrian's Wall
ABOVE A section of Hadrian's Wall seen from Highshield Crags

Crag Lough. The wall, and its associated turrets and milecastle, are in good condition on this most famous stretch of the monument. Further on, the route climbs again quite steeply past Hotbank farm. From Hotbank Crags, four loughs are visible and ahead lies the familiar picture-postcard view of Cuddy's Crags.

The Pennine Way leaves Hadrian's Wall at Rapishaw Gap, just before Housesteads (Vercovicium) Roman Fort. The excavated ruins, almost too neat and tidy, are worth a special visit as, of course, are the other forts and features on Hadrian's Wall.

🏠 *A return may be made to Greenhead from Housesteads (grid ref. NY 790 688) by taking tracks and lanes south to Bardon Mill to pick up a bus back to Greenhead. Between Easter and October a National Park coach may be taken from Housesteads back to Greenhead.*

WIDER VIEWS

The route turns north and heads out over marshy pasture inhabited by black Galloway cattle, then follows an indistinct path through rolling heather country with the air full of the cries of curlews and the songs of skylarks. To the left is Greenlee Lough, bought by the National Park as a wildlife refuge. To the right, in the distance, are King's Crags. Ahead lies the forest.

The path rises to the right of Stonefolds, then drops down to meet a track and enter Wark Forest. This is Forestry Commission land, part of the Border Forest Park. The paths and rides are more open, there are wider views, and deciduous trees have been planted along the watercourses. The Pennine Way stays on the main track for a while, then turns off to the right along a path. A wide sweep of moorland comes as a refreshing change as the path clips the corner of Haughton Common. It makes for an isolated sheepfold, in which stand a few stunted pines and birches. The views south and east, over miles of purple moor-grass, are memorable for anyone who had hoped to get away from civilization. However, this is just an interlude and the path is soon back in forest, descending to a road a mile east of Stonehaugh at Ladyhill.

STONEHAUGH TO BYRNESS

STAGE 5
STONEHAUGH to BELLINGHAM
DISTANCE 8.5 miles (13.6km)
MAPS OS Explorer OL 42, OL 43
START AT GRID REFERENCE NY 792 761
START POINT Stonehaugh, 5 miles (8km) west of Wark

From the little Forestry Commission village of Stonehaugh, the Pennine Way is met either by returning to the road at Ladyhill or by walking along a forest drive eastwards for just under a mile (1.6km). From the road the route turns north opposite Ladyhill and soon crosses two forest drives from Stonehaugh.

The forest ends at another block of moorland; the side of Broadpool Common. The path is indistinct but follows the flank of a burn, past a pretty waterfall and downhill, then up beside

a wall and over the brow into the valley of the Warks Burn. The route descends by an old hedge, then turns right, through a gate and past a hay barn, before dropping down between rocky clefts to cross the attractive Warks Burn.

The character of the land begins to change now, to less open moorland and more green pasture, as the route climbs through damp woodland and across a field to Horneystead, then from field to field and farm to farm. Behind the farmhouse at Horneystead stand the ruins of a 'bastle', a fortified farmhouse with massively thick walls, built at the time of border troubles in the 16th century. Past The Ash and Leadgate and across a side-road, the Way leads to Lowstead, which incorporates two bastles into its structure. The route then follows an access track above the Blacka Burn opposite Linacres Farm, then keeps to a quiet side-road with a block of marshy woodland on the left. Snipe and woodcock abound in such places.

At a junction, the route turns left and passes a small grassed-over quarry and an outstanding example of cord-rigging (narrow ridge-and-furrow ploughing) over the pasture on the left. There was a Romano-British settlement here; the ruins are thinly covered and are easy to make out and the fields were intensively cultivated. The farm produce, probably barley, was sent to feed the occupying Roman army.

HEATHER MOORLAND

At the next road junction the route crosses a stile straight ahead and follows the edges of the fields over the hill and down to the Houxty Burn. Over the footbridge close to Esp Mill, the route then heads up a track to the farm at Shitlington Hall, then down a track on the left before turning right to follow the field-edge again all the way up to Shitlington Crags. The sandstone outcrop is easy to climb via a short flight of rough-stone slabs; the path is clear once you have spotted it from the track just below. The views, all the way down to Hadrian's Wall and beyond, are very fine if the light is with you. From here the route is clear, uphill again over moorland, making for the wall at the very top of the ridge, to the left of the radar mast. Again, the views are excellent.

After crossing a stile in the wall, the route turns right, along a track and past the radar mast. To the left is Ealingham Rigg; a ridge of heather moorland where emperor moths fly and adders sun themselves. The route crosses a stile by a gate, then continues along the track for a short distance before turning left across the moorland and heading for a marker post. There is no visible path now but the orientation is easy; northeast and down into the North Tyne Valley to a road, then left off the road at a stile and downhill to meet the B6320. The route turns left to follow the road, over the North Tyne and into the town of Bellingham.

🏠 *An infrequent bus runs from Bellingham, south to Wark, from where lanes and paths may be followed westwards to the Pennine Way near Stonehaugh.*

STAGE 6
BELLINGHAM to BYRNESS
DISTANCE 15.3 miles (24.6km)
MAPS OS Explorer OL 16, OL 42
START AT GRID REFERENCE NY 839 833
START POINT Bellingham town centre. The market town lies on the B6320, 13 miles (21km) north of Hexham. Ample car parking

After making the most of the shops and services in the town, follow the West Woodburn Road, below the old Border Counties Railway line, and on for 0.5 miles (800m), then turn left along a track to Blakelaw Farm. The grass-covered mounds by the

TOP LEFT Sunset over Hadrian's Wall TOP RIGHT Pennine Way signpost ABOVE An attractive wooden bridge over a stream at Hareshaw Dene

road are old spoil-heaps from the Hareshaw iron works. The iron produced here was used in the building of the famous High Level Bridge in Newcastle. From the farm, the Pennine Way climbs up an open pasture, following posts, and eventually makes for a ruin to the right of a block of pines. Through the gate by the ruined barn, the route is soon on to open moorland below Callerhues Crag. The original Pennine Way made for the higher ground but a much better path is now signposted and can be followed northwards above the Hareshaw Burn, and below Hareshaw House. The ground is usually marshy and there are old coal workings littered around the hillsides. The route continues for 2 miles (3km) to cross the B6320, after which it rises through heather moorland, making for the stone cairn on the top of the distant hill called Deer Play. There is a strong sense of wilderness about the heather country, enhanced by the wide views and the occasional lack of a clear path. From the stone post on the brow of Deer Play, the route drops down over boggy ground and past some shake holes to make for the top of Whitley Pike; a fine-featured hill to the northwest. It then drops down to a minor road.

A wire fence makes the next few miles of the route easy to find, past Grey Mare rock and up to the ridge of Padon Hill. Its bell-shaped monument, to the right of the fence, is visible for miles. The monument commemorates Alexander Padon, an 18th-century Scottish Covenanter, who held services here.

ENGLAND'S LONGEST PLACENAMES

After Padon Hill, and still following the fence, the path heads northwest, then northeast, to the next open hilltop of Brownrigg Head. There are fine views of Redesdale and the Cheviot Hills, and of Otterburn, where one of the most famous border battles was fought in 1388. Turning left, northwest again, the route now enters forest plantations and a long walk begins through dull conifer country. Eventually, the track descends into Redesdale. Past the Forestry Commission settlement at Blakehopeburnhaugh, the route turns left along the east bank of the River Rede and meanders with it past picnic places and sallow groves to Cottonshopeburnfoot. These are the longest placenames in England! After crossing to the west bank of the river, the route follows a forest drive, then drops down to the right, across the river again and past tiny Holy Trinity Church.

The village of Byrness, built by the Forestry Commission for its workers in the days before mechanized harvesting, lies a few hundred yards along the A68, reached by turning left after the church. The road is fast and busy, leading up to Carter Bar and the border. Byrness village is the last provisioning point before

PLACES TO VISIT

• NENTHEAD MINES HERITAGE CENTRE
www.npht.com/nentheadmines
☎ 01434 382726
If you have time and transport, it is well worth a quick detour east from Alston along the A689 to Nenthead. This museum and mining site explains the long and important history of lead mining in the northern Pennines. They have bunkhouse accommodation, too. Open daily during most of the summer, all year for pre-booked groups. See website for details.

• ALSTON
www.eden.gov.uk
☎ 01434 382244
Alston prides itself on the claim of being the highest market town in England. It is an attractive spot, with steep cobbled streets and 17th-century stone buildings. There are a number of pleasant cafés, craft galleries and quaint shops hidden down alleyways.

• SOUTH TYNEDALE RAILWAY
www.strps.org.uk
☎ 01434 381696
The trackbed of the old Alston–Haltwhistle branch line has been re-laid up to Kirkhaugh with a narrow gauge track, and now runs steam- and diesel-hauled trains on a journey of 15 minutes in each direction. The original Newcastle and Carlisle Railway station building at Alston is the ticket office and shop. Work is afoot to extend the track to Lintley, and then to Slaggyford, either of which can give access to the PW, as does Kirkhaugh. If trains are not in service, the South Tyne Trail runs beside the track. It could be taken to Kirkhaugh or Slaggyford, before continuing on the PW. The Hub Museum is in the old goods shed at Alston, and has displays on local history, which includes many vehicles, and tools of all kinds (www.alston-hub.org.uk ☎ 01434 381609; open daily Jun–Sep, Sat–Sun Apr–May & Oct–Dec). See website for details of operating days and times.

the border ridge; there are no shops between here and Kirk Yetholm, 27 miles (43.5km) away. There is a youth hostel and bed-and-breakfast accommodation.

🚌 *A bus runs through Byrness (grid ref. 764 028) to Otterburn, where another bus can be caught back to Bellingham and Hexham.*

BYRNESS TO KIRK YETHOLM

STAGE 7

BYRNESS to CLENNEL STREET

DISTANCE 14 miles (22.5km)

MAP OS Explorer OL 16

START AT GRID REFERENCE NY 764 028

START POINT Byrness village, on the A68

TOP *The Pennine Way ladder stile, marking the line of the England-Scotland border near the Schil*

ABOVE *Hareshaw Linn, or waterfall, north of Bellingham*

This last section, from Byrness to Kirk Yetholm, is a long hard walk, with escape points being few and far between. From the village centre, walk along the A68 for a short distance and turn left off it, close to Holy Trinity Church, up a tarmac track and through a gate beside Byrness Cottage. A path then climbs steeply up to Byrness Hill, from where there are impressive views over Redesdale. The path is now on to open hilltops and never again goes through forest. The route heads north, from Saughy Crag to Houx Hill, then above Windy Crag to Ravens Knowe. The land to the east is owned by the Ministry of Defence, part of the 'dry training area'. Views are far-reaching and exciting.

From Ravens Knowe the route makes for Ogre Hill and follows a clear but often boggy path downhill alongside a forest plantation to a fence and stile at the headwaters of the River Coquet. This rather undramatic feature marks the Scottish border and it is very satisfying to climb over the ladder-stile and set foot on Scottish peat. The path sets out north, straight out uphill as if heading for the Highlands, but in fact the route is simply avoiding the worst of the mires of the Coquet watershed and it soon turns right to follow the valley eastwards, descending gradually to a wicket-gate beside the gathering stream.

A scatter of grass-covered earthworks, extensive and difficult to interpret, lies beyond the gate on the rising ground. This is Chew Green, a Roman marching camp, used for centuries as a stop-over en route to the wild north. A road runs just the other side of the Coquet and there is a small car park. It is a long drive anywhere from here; left heads along Coquetdale to Alwinton, right is an MoD road leading to Redesdale (it is only open at certain times or by special arrangement). From Chew Green, the Way follows the grassy course of Dere Street up to the border ridge, to the right of Brownhart Law. Continuing north, Dere Street soon disappears beyond Gaisty Law towards Woden Law, where the Romans practised battle and siege tactics. The route heads north or northeast, following a path away from the border fence, linking cairns on the hilltops. The ground is peaty and often boggy but there are some bridges or boardwalks over the worst sections. Vegetation on these exposed hills is thin, usually mat-grass with some heather and drifts of purple moor-grass, which bleaches white in the winter and spring. After about a mile (1.6km) the route bears right and heads eastwards at the head of the Rennies Burn.

Past the Grassy Loughs, the route meets up again with the border fence and keeps with this for many miles, so that route-finding is no longer a problem. It is easy to become disorientated in the Cheviots. The views seem to go on forever. After a sharp turn left in the border fence, the route leads to one of the wooden Pennine Way shelters at Yearning Saddle. Although far from comfortable, the shelter offers a respite if the weather has closed in. Lamb Hill is the next summit, then Beefstand, then

Mozie Law. They are all excellent vantage points and the route links them like pearls on a necklace. To the north, the distinctive hills in the middle distance are the Eildon Hills, close to Melrose. On the descent the eye is caught by a very obvious path off to the right, following a grassy ridge. The path is called the Street, an ancient border crossing once used as a drove road.

🏠 *It is possible to follow the Street (grid ref. NT 835 150) down into Coquetdale as an escape route or in an emergency; there are a few scattered farms in the valley but nothing else. It is also possible to make this part of the route a circular walk out of Coquetdale, by parking at Barrow Burn (grid ref. NT 867 108).*

RUSSELL'S CAIRN

The Pennine Way heads eastwards, brushing the border fence at Plea Knowe at the head of the Street, then cutting the corner at Foul Step. Ahead now rises Windy Gyle, and the path leaves the border fence to climb to its summit. Windy Gyle is certainly one of the finest features on the whole Pennine Way and from the top the panorama is breathtaking. At 2,030ft (619m), there is a view over most of the Cheviot massif. The big hills to the left of Kidland Forest are Bloodybush Edge, with Cushat Law behind. To the north-east are the even higher summits of The Cheviot and Hedgehope.

The massive pile of boulders on the top of Windy Gyle is a Bronze Age burial mound. It was such an obvious landmark that it became a meeting place for the Wardens of the Marches during the unsettled and lawless centuries of the border troubles. In 1585 Lord Francis Russell was killed here after being double-crossed at a Wardens' Meet and ever since the pile of stones has been called Russell's Cairn.

For a little while, the route descends northeastwards on the Scottish side of the fence but it soon crosses back and heads down the ridge to meet another cross-border drove road called Clennel Street.

🏠 *There are escape routes either way (from grid ref. NT 872 161), northwest down to Cocklawfoot and southeast to Alwinton. Cocklawfoot is closer but is nothing more than a farm. Alwinton makes a good start point for a strenuous walk.*

STAGE 8

CLENNEL STREET to KIRK YETHOLM

DISTANCE 11.4 miles (18.3km)

MAP OS Explorer OL 16

START AT GRID REFERENCE NT 871 161

START POINT Access along the border ridge is impossible by car; there are no roads. Clennel Street and the crossing point, Border Gate, mark the more convenient break in the route but require a stiff 7-mile (11.25km) climb from Alwinton, which is the nearest village

The cleft of the border crossing place is often shrouded in mist. The route follows the border fence along a broad ridge called Butt Roads, then rises to King's Seat, where there is nothing but a triangulation point and wide acres of windswept heather. The ridge on the English side drops away to Usway Burn (pronounced Oozy or Uzzy). Several small streams drain the ridge eastwards, including Murder Cleugh and the Inner Hare Cleugh, where Black Rory the Highlander established one of his illicit stills 200 years ago.

Above King's Seat there is a long pull northeastwards, by Green Gair and Cockersike Head, and although the ground is boggy the route is mainly by stone flagged path. As the route climbs even more steeply towards Cairn Hill there is a tumble of rocks on the brow to the right called the Hanging Stone; another

place of ill-repute which marked the boundary between the Middle and East Marches. The top of the hill is peaty and gives a foretaste of The Cheviot; an optional detour leads off to the right over Cairn Hill to the summit of The Cheviot which, at 2,674ft (815m), sounds impressive but has poor views. A stone flagged path leads to the summit. The main route heads sharp left, at a stile and over boardwalks across very wet ground to Auchope. There is then a descent, past another wooden refuge hut, at a strategic place where conditions can be treacherous and there is no easy escape route. In good light the views are excellent; in the foreground to the right is the Hen Hole, a hanging valley by which the College Burn leaps and rushes down through the andesite and heads north to join the River Glen at Kirknewton. The hills are the haunt of wild goats and peregrines.

The Schil is a shapely summit and one of the most beautiful links along the whole chain of border hills. The views are breathtaking, as is the climb. On its northern side there are several rocky tors; tors of baked andesite are small but important features of the inner Cheviots.

An exhilarating descent along the border fence from the Schil leads to a dip, with the next hill, Black Hag, ahead.

🏠 *There are escape routes here (grid ref. NT 863 233), left by a lowland path to Kirk Yetholm via Burnhead, and right into the College valley to Mounthooly, where there is a YHA Bunkhouse. Either path can form part of a circular walk; the Mounthooly circuit, via Dunsdale and the Bizzle or Goldscleugh and Bellyside, offers one of the best options for an ascent of The Cheviot.*

MAGNIFICENT WHITE LAW

The Pennine Way crosses into Scotland but follows the border for a little while longer. There is one more memorable stretch after Black Hag, as the path rises to Steerig Knowe and then sweeps along the crest of Steer Rig, with the basin of the Trowhope Burn to the right and the twin-peaked summit of Coldsmouth Hill ahead. White Law is magnificent, offering the last panorama, across to the Tweed and to Flodden where the Scots were finally defeated in 1513, and into the Cheviot foothills.

North of Whitelaw Nick, the route turns left and quits the border ridge, following a track at first towards the dome of Green Humbleton, then left to follow the Shielknowe Burn. After crossing Halter Burn, the Pennine Way turns right along a quiet road. The last mile (1.6km) into Kirk Yetholm gives you a chance to come to terms with reaching the end of the walk. The village has all the necessary services, including accommodation at a youth hostel and the Border Hotel.

ℹ️ **PLACES TO VISIT**

• **ROMAN ARMY MUSEUM**
www.vindolanda.com
☎ 01434 344277
Administered by the Vindolanda Trust, the museum at the wall fort of Carvoran is the only Roman site that lies adjacent to the PW. It houses real and replica artefacts, including replica armour, weapons and chariots. There are two films; the first gives a reconstructed eagle's eye view of Hadrian's Wall between the Carvoran and Vindolanda forts, the other shows a Centurion briefing new recruits on every aspect of Roman army life. Open daily Mar–Oct.

• **VINDOLANDA**
www.vindolanda.com
☎ 01434 344277
At Steel Rigg, the Roman fort of Vindolanda is approximately 1.5 miles (2.5km) southeast of the PW. The earliest fort here is thought to pre-date the wall by around 40 years. Excavations go down as deep as 13ft (4m) and the site is so large and well preserved that it is thought investigations could go on here for another 150 years. Among the many precious leather, wooden and metal artefacts that are on display in the museum are even more valuable items; intact and legible letters and documents. Open daily Mar–Oct.

HOUSESTEADS ROMAN FORT
www.english-heritage.org.uk
☎ 01434 344363
The Roman fort of Vercovicium is to be found 0.5 miles (800m) east of the PW at Housesteads. It is the most complete Roman fort in Britain and is thought to have housed 800 men almost 2,000 years ago. The remains of the barracks, granaries and even a communal latrine are clearly visible. The escarpment location means that the views alone are impressive. Open daily all year.

BELOW A rainbow above the Schil, on the border

Loch Lomond seen from Conic Hill

Scotland

West Highland Way

COMPLETE ROUTE GLASGOW (MILNGAVIE) TO FORT WILLIAM **95 MILES (153KM)**

SECTION COVERED AS ABOVE

MAPS OS EXPLORER 342, 347, 348, 363, 364, 377, 384, 385, 391, 392, 399

The West Highland Way takes the walker from the northern suburbs of Glasgow through some of the most splendid loch and mountain scenery in Scotland to its finish in Fort William. Along the way you walk much of the eastern shore of Loch Lomond, cross the western fringe of Rannoch Moor and pass through Glencoe. The route uses ancient military roads, drove routes and lochside paths in its varied progress. The scenery grows steadily more splendid and wild as you make your way northwards, until the final crescendo delivers you through the magnificence of Glencoe and the Mamores to the foot of Ben Nevis.

TOP Garadhban Forest at the foot of Conic Hill
ABOVE People climbing Conic Hill, Balmaha, on the banks of Loch Lomond

MILNGAVIE TO ROWARDENNAN

STAGE 1
MILNGAVIE to BALMAHA
DISTANCE 18.6 miles (30km)
MAPS OS Explorer 342, 347, 348
START AT GRID REFERENCE NS 553 743
START POINT Main Street, Milngavie, north of Glasgow

The starting point of the West Highland Way is Main Street, Milngavie, north of Glasgow and not far from the railway station. It is an appropriate place for several reasons: within a very short distance, you are into pleasant countryside; the train link to Glasgow is excellent; and Milngavie is associated with the great outdoor movement of the depression years in the 1930s, when hundreds of unemployed men journeyed into the countryside to find solace in walking and climbing.

A word about the name: it traps the unwary, for the pronunciation is 'mull-guy', and indeed it appears on some old maps as Milguy. Its origin may be the Gaelic *muileann-gaoithe*, 'a windmill'. You will come across many names with Gaelic origins on this walk, and even the briefest study of them will yield a rich harvest of understanding which will add immeasurably to your appreciation of the land and its history.

From Main Street, where you will find shops, banks and cafes, follow waymarks over the Allander Water and along to an attractive tree-lined lane, on the line of a former railway serving one of the long-defunct mills in the area. The Allander Water is rejoined for 0.25 miles (400m) or so before a right turn, uphill, takes you on to the birch and gorse moorland of Allander Park.

From here to Loch Lomondside the route passes through the ancient lands of Lennox. The Earldom of Lennox was created by King Malcolm IV in 1153, and by the late 14th century the lands of Lennox extended to the north end of Loch Lomond.

MUGDOCK WOOD

Southwards is Glasgow, westward the Kilpatrick Hills, and north the Campsies and the approach to Loch Lomond. Most of the area is set on the Clyde plateau lavas, laid down 350 million years ago during the Lower Carboniferous period. The walk continues along the former drive of Craigallian House to enter Mugdock Wood, with a fine variety of trees and many lovely wild flowers

in spring and summer. Mugdock was gifted to the people of Glasgow in 1980 by Sir Hugh Fraser, and is now run by the local authorities as one of the 40 country parks in Scotland, providing many thousands of people with an invaluable recreational lung.

Leaving Mugdock, the West Highland Way follows a track beside the Allander Water to reach Craigallian Loch, which is a favourite weekending place for generations of Glaswegians. Some of the holiday huts built decades ago, and lovingly cared for ever since, can be seen in this area. From Craigallian you can see Dumgoyne, the stubby hill at the western end of the Campsies, which dominates this part of the walk and is itself a splendid viewpoint and an easy climb.

The path continues, entering the Tinker's Loan, an old track, and crossing the low watershed dividing the Glasgow basin from the Loch Lomond lands; it too is a fine viewpoint, with Ben Lomond prominent, urging you forward. For the next few miles the route follows an old railway line through Strathblane, passing Dumgoyne (and its distillery, which can be visited). As you walk the old railway, Glasgow's water is flowing under your feet, along a 60-inch pipe from Loch Lomond to the city.

The Way passes within a mile (1.6km) of Killearn and finally the route leaves it to take to quiet lanes, crossing the River Endrick (a fine salmon stream, where herons are commonly seen) near Gartness. It climbs, with more fine views, to approach Drymen. It does not pass through the village, but a short diversion will take you there.

🏠 *Drymen ('little ridge' in Gaelic) has shops, cafes and hotels, and bus services back to Glasgow. It also has the last bank on the route before Kinlochleven, so ensure your wallet is fed here as well as your stomach. Leave the West Highland Way at grid ref. NS 482 885 to reach it.*

SHARP CLIMB

The route itself passes east of Drymen into the Garadhban Forest, owned by the Forestry Commission, and home to many woodland birds including finches, siskins and crossbills. At the forest edge a stile is crossed to an open moor, a great contrast with the enclosed woodland. To your left is Loch Lomond and ahead is the bulk of Conic Hill, which the path climbs. Here you truly pass into the Highlands, for the hill is on the line of a great geological fault that crosses Scotland from west coast to east.

Take care crossing the moorland: the waymarks can become almost buried in bracken in high summer, though the path itself is generally clear enough. It crosses two burns; the

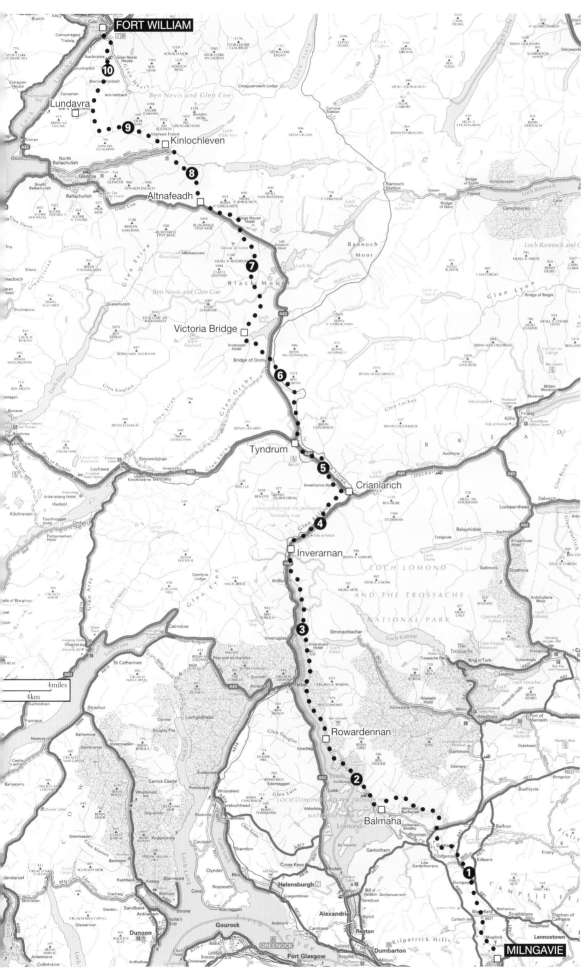

FORT WILLIAM

10

Lundavra

9

Kinlochleven

8

Altnafeadh

7

Victoria Bridge

Bridge of Orchy

6

Tyndrum

5

Crianlarich

4

Inverarnan

3

Rowardennan

2

Balmaha

1

MILNGAVIE

4 miles
4 km

ℹ **USEFUL INFORMATION**

THE ROUTE
• www.west-highland-way.co.uk
☎ 01389 722600
The official website of the WHW
has all that you would expect for
such a popular and well-used
route. There are route summaries,
accommodation and baggage
services, public transport details
and all manner of queries
answered here. There is even
an online shop, selling not only
the official guide and the Pocket
Companion but clothing, midge
nets and souvenirs, the profits
from which are used to help fund
projects along the route.

**VISITOR INFORMATION
CENTRES**
• www.lochlomond-trossachs.org
National Park Centre, Balmaha
G63 0JQ;
☎ 01389 722100 (open Thu–Mon
Easter–Sep, Sat–Sun Oct–Easter)
• www.visitscottishheartlands.com
Main Street, Tyndrum FK20 8RY;
☎ 01838 400246 (open daily
Apr–Oct)
• www.visithighlands.com
15 High Street, Fort William
PH33 6DH;
☎ 0845 225 5121 (open Sun–Fri
Apr–May, daily Jun–Nov, Sat–Sun
Dec–Mar)
• www.highland.gov.uk
Glen Nevis Visitor Centre, Glen
Nevis, Fort William PH33 6PF;
☎ 01397 705922 (open daily
all year)
• www.seeglasgow.com
11 George Square, Glasgow
G2 1DY;
☎ 0141 204 4400 (open daily
Easter–Sep, Mon–Sat Oct–Easter)
Although not actually on the
route, this central Glasgow office
may be a useful source of local
information if you are staying
over in the city before you begin
the walk.

SCOTLAND • WEST HIGHLAND WAY

WEST HIGHLAND WAY **199**

splendidly named Kilandan Blandan and the Burn of Mar, where dippers may be seen. The top of Conic Hill is some 700ft (213m) above, and a sharp climb it is too. The reward is a superb panoramic view of loch, hills and islands. Although Conic Hill is roughly conical, the name probably comes from the Gaelic *A'Coinneach*, meaning 'moss' or 'bog', so it is the hill above the bog. The hill is a steep-sided ridge of conglomerate rock, with some erratic boulders deposited by glaciation near its top.

From Conic Hill there is a sharp descent to the car park at Balmaha, a busy place in summer with its marina and cafes, and the start of the long traverse along the east bank of Loch Lomond.

STAGE 2
BALMAHA to ROWARDENNAN
DISTANCE 7.2 miles (11.6km)
MAPS OS Explorer 347, 364
START AT GRID REFERENCE NS 420908
START POINT Balmaha (infrequent bus service to Drymen from where there are more frequent services to Glasgow

Loch Lomond is the largest sheet of inland water in Britain. It is 23 miles (37km) long, has a maximum depth of over 600ft (183m), and covers over 20 square miles (52 square km). Facts cannot convey its beauty: that has to be seen, and walking its banks is the best way to do it. The West Highland Way follows the loch for nearly 20 miles (32km) of fine woodland and superb mountain scenes.

The loch alters its character markedly as you travel north. This southern section is broad, relatively shallow, and has numerous islands, well seen from Conic Hill. The north end is narrower, more confined by mountains, and also much wetter. The botanical interest is remarkable; some 25 per cent of all known British flowering plants and ferns can be found here.

Little wonder that the loch has found such fame. Ask any visitor to Scotland to name three places in the country and Loch Lomond is likely to be one of them. It is a major tourist attraction, with peak summer weekends drawing perhaps 40,000 visitors. It was designated a Regional Park in 1988, and in 2002 became part of the Loch Lomond and Trossachs National Park.

The route wanders along beside the loch. Its path from Rowardennan to Inversnaid is more demanding, and those in a hurry have been known to use a forest road option higher up. That would be a pity, for it winds in and out of attractive woods, down to little bays, round small promontories and through plantations. Above Balmaha, pass the cairn marking the official opening of the Way in 1980, on a 'dreich' autumn day. The car park at Milarrochy Bay is passed and at this point the path enters the Queen Elizabeth Forest Park, which covers much of the Trossachs.

At Cashel, where there is an excellent camp site, the road is joined for a short way before it is left again for the oakwoods of Sallochy. These woods once provided timber for housing and also charcoal for iron smelting, carried out on a small scale at 'bloomeries' in the woods. The route goes past a field centre at Ross and climbs steeply into Ross Woods, before further

meanderings end on the road just south of the Rowardennan Hotel. Here there is a large car park. The favourite place to start the climb of Ben Lomond is at the pier for the loch steamer and water taxis. A little further on, there is a youth hostel.

ROWARDENNAN TO CRIANLARICH

STAGE 3
ROWARDENNAN to INVERARNAN
DISTANCE 13.7 miles (22km)
MAP OS Explorer 364
START AT GRID REFERENCE NS 360 983
START POINT Rowardennan pier

The east bank of Loch Lomond can provide a glorious traverse through splendid oakwoods with a wide variety of birds, plants, mammals and other trees to delight the eye, plus the changing vistas across the water; or it can be a tortuous struggle through what the Scots aptly call 'glaur'. This part of the walk is undoubtedly best done in dry conditions, for here the path is at its most fragile and considerable erosion has occurred. During or after wet weather (a not unknown phenomenon in these parts) it can be unpleasantly muddy and slippery. Unless you are very fortunate or have infinite time to spare, you will have to take it as you find it; even in adversity there is pleasure in thinking ahead to the better going once Glen Falloch is gained.

Do not be put off by these words of warning, rather be prepared. If you are ready for the worst, anything better will be a pleasant surprise, and if you catch the fickle Scottish climate at its best, you will enjoy a memorable walk in unparalleled scenery. First you have to break clear of the crowds and their cars at Rowardennan. This is achieved in only a few hundred yards; most people are either picnicking by the lochside or climbing Ben Lomond, and once past the excellent youth hostel you will meet few. You may encounter mountainbikers, who on much of the route are not a problem, given the firm nature of the path. Some consider that the section to Inverarnan is simply unsuitable for them, but they are determined characters and there may be some struggling along here.

Opposite the youth hostel, on the right of the track, is the site of a large bloomery, now occupied by a number of chalets. The track continues for 0.5 miles (800m) or so to Ptarmigan Lodge, named from the shapely outlier of Ben Lomond high above, itself named after that most distinctive bird of the high tops, which with luck can still be seen (and more often, heard) on these hills. Just after Ptarmigan Lodge, a choice of routes presents itself. Either continue on the broad track or descend steps to a lochside path, which is slower going but gives much better views. About a mile (1.6km) further on is a crag known as Rob Roy's Prison, where it is said the outlaw kept hostages in a natural rock cell. The facts are difficult to unearth, but he certainly operated in these parts.

INVERSNAID
From here northwards you can see across the loch, through the Tarbet gap, the hills affectionately known to climbers as the Arrochar Alps. The distinctive overhanging crags of The Cobbler stand out among them. The pass from Tarbet to Arrochar was used by the Viking King Haakon in 1263, to drag boats through in order to mount a surprise attack on the Lennoxes. Tarbet means 'isthmus' in Gaelic. The next building on the path is Rowchoish

TOP *A family enjoys a walk on the West Highland Way, with the Hills of Crianlarich in the background*
ABOVE *Adult male Ptarmigan in late winter plumage*

USEFUL INFORMATION

PLANNING YOUR TRIP
• www.walkinginscotland.org
Although essentially an account of a trip along the WHW, this site also has some helpful sections on planning your trip.
• www.ldwa.org.uk
The Long Distance Walkers Association has some detail on the WHW, such as a map showing accommodation close to the path, and good advice on long-distance walking in general.
• www.ramblers.org.uk
☎ 020 7339 8500
The Ramblers Association website also gives advice about long-distance walking in Britain and a page specifically on the WHW, including a number of holiday and luggage companies, and many useful maps and publications.
• www.syha.org.uk
☎ 0845 293 7373
The Scottish Youth Hostel Association has several sites close to the WHW.

OTHER PATHS
It is possible to link central Glasgow with the WHW by following the Kelvin Walkway. At Easter Carbeth, where the WHW crosses the B821, the Central Scottish Way starts its route of 146 miles (235km). Crossing via Falkirk and Edinburgh, it then turns south via Melrose, to cross the border and join the Pennine Way National Trail (pages 188–195) at Low Byrness, Northumberland. To the north, you may wish to extend your journey from Fort William to Inverness, via the Great Glen Way. Alternatively, the East Highland Way provides a link between the WHW, at Fort William, and the Speyside Way (pages 210–215), at Aviemore.

ABOVE Boats moored on Loch Lomond

Bothy, restored as a memorial to William Ferris, who worked tirelessly for walkers for much of his life through the Scottish Youth Hostels Association, the Scottish Ramblers' Federation and the Scottish Rights of Way Society. You may well have the bothy to yourself if you stay overnight here; 200 years ago there were nine families at Rowchoish, a typical example of the way the Highlands have been depopulated.

After Rowchoish, the two routes combine into a lovely woodland path to the farm cottage at Cailness. The footbridge here is occasionally washed away by sudden spates down the steep burn. Woodland birds likely to be found on this stretch include jays and woodpeckers, and perhaps the little treecreeper looking for insects in the tree bark. The path continues to Inversnaid, celebrated in verse by Wordsworth and especially the Jesuit poet Gerard Manley Hopkins, whose poem 'Inversnaid' has become famous as a plea for keeping wild places wild:

This darksome burn, horseback brown,
His rollrock highroad roaring down,
In coop and in comb the fleece of his foam
Flutes and low to the lake falls home.

What would the world be, once bereft
Of wet and of wildness? Let them be left,
O let them be left, wildness and wet;
Long live the weeds and the wilderness yet.

At Inversnaid there is an elegant and unexpectedly large hotel, dating from Victorian times, a ferry pier, and the end of the road from Aberfoyle. And of course the falls, crashing down under the bridge. Inversnaid was a garrison for a time in the 18th century, and some of the buildings are still there, up on the hill. Down here, once away from the hotel, all is peaceful by the loch: as well to take a break here and gird the loins, for the next few miles are among the roughest on the whole walk. The hillslopes fall steep and broken straight into the loch and are heavily wooded, and the path has to fight a way through, with a fair amount of up-and-down and scrambling over rocks and tree-roots.

Normal time allowances go out of the window on this stretch. The really fainthearted can catch the ferry from the hotel across the loch to Inveruglas, and walk up the road on the west side to rejoin the West Highland Way at Inverarnan.

As the Way crosses the Allt Rostan it passes from Strathclyde to Central Region; shortly after this a very steep slab is crossed by a rather precarious bridge, where a certain amount of care is always needed. But in another 0.25 miles (400m) or so you emerge at the bay south of Doune, and difficulties are over. Doune is also a bothy. The path continues past the lovely little Dubh Lochan (*dubh* meaning 'dark') and at last the north end of the loch, companion for so long, is reached. The path enters Glen Falloch, and in a further mile (1.6km) a diversion can be, and often is, made along the short distance to the old Drovers Inn at Inverarnan for a well-earned refreshment.

From Inverarnan (grid ref. 318 185) an 'escape' may be made back to Glasgow by walking the 2 miles (3km) along the A82 to Ardlui, where there is a station on the Oban/Fort William–Glasgow line.

STAGE 4
INVERARNAN to CRIANLARICH

DISTANCE 6.4 miles (10.3km)
MAPS OS Explorer 363, 377
START AT GRID REFERENCE NN 317 184
START POINT Drovers Inn on A82
Buses to Glasgow and Fort William/Oban; British Rail station at Ardlui, 2 miles (3km) south

TOP A view from the West
Highland Way to Stob
Ghabhar
ABOVE Rob Roy MacGregor
cave by the banks of Loch
Lomond

From the Inverarnan Inn there is a superb view of the splendid Beinnglas Falls, crashing down the hillside above Beinn Glas Farm. It is an easy walk up to the falls from the farm and one well worth taking; after heavy rain the noise is terrific and the force of the water is exceptional.

The West Highland Way now runs up Glen Falloch, a much more pastoral scene than hitherto, following the east bank of the River Falloch for 3 miles (5km) to Derrydaroch. (From the Drovers Inn, walk up the A82 for a short distamce and cross the river by the bridge to Beinn Glas Farm to rejoin the route.) The Falloch tumbles over a succession of rapids, small falls and waterslides, maintaining interest all the way. Geologists have suggested that the river originally flowed north to Crianlarich and is still adjusting to its 'new' course after a mere 10,000 years.

You pass through several fine groups of trees, including oak, alder and birch on this stretch, and although the road is never far away, it is surprisingly secluded down here. The railway from Glasgow to Oban and Fort William is just the other side of the road. On the same slope is the Clach-na-Briton, said to mark the ancient boundary between Brythonic, Scots and Pictish territories.

Derrydaroch means 'the oak grove', though these trees are less numerous nowadays and there are as many pines. The river is crossed here and the path takes the other bank for 0.5 miles (800m) before passing under the railway through a 'cattle creep' in which it is best to take your pack off and carry it low down. The A82 road is crossed (take care) and the path strikes uphill to join the line of the old military road, built in 1752–53 after the Jacobite Risings as part of the London government's plans to quell the rebellious Highlanders.

There are fine views along this stretch of hills to either side; the Cruach Ardrain group to the east, outliers of Ben Lui above you, and Strath Fillan hills ahead. The path passes Keilator Farm, whose name may mean 'the nook on the slope', and enters a delightful small glen called Bogle Glen; a bogle is a Scots word for a ghost or ghoul.

You are now above Crianlarich, at roughly the half-way point of the full walk. The path passes west of the village, but most people elect to stop here, as there is a choice of accommodation including a hotel, several bed-and-breakfast places and an excellent youth hostel.

Crianlarich (grid ref. 385 250) has a station and is on a bus route from Glasgow.

CRIANLARICH TO VICTORIA BRIDGE

STAGE 5
CRIANLARICH to TYNDRUM
DISTANCE 6.3 miles (10.1km)
MAPS OS Explorer 363, 377
START AT GRID REFERENCE NN 384 251
START POINT Crianlarich railway station (Glasgow–Oban/ Fort William line), daily buses on same route

From Crianlarich to Tyndrum the West Highland Way follows a much more meandering course than the A82 road, which shakes itself out of Crianlarich in a dog's tail of bends and then zooms uphill, arrow-straight, as if in a hurry to pass through this lovely valley. Hurry is inexcusable here: not only is the valley itself full of interest, the hills to either side repay, in orders of magnitude, whatever time is spared to gaze upon them.

Climbing them is even better, if there is the time to spare and the energy and enthusiasm available. But these are not hills to be taken lightly, even in summer. The area is ringed with Munros of high quality, including Ben More and Stobinian, highest hills of the Southern Highlands at over 3,800ft (1,158m), and Ben Lin, felt by many to be among the most shapeliest of Scotland's mountains.

But back to the route itself. Pick it up just west of Crianlarich, or from the railway station, from where it is waymarked as it dives into the new forest. This plantation and the West Highland Way arrived here more or less together, so the path was created as the planting took place. There is a good variety of tree species and enough breaks to enjoy the views.

The path crosses the Herive Burn and joins a forest road to run down to the railway line (the Oban branch), passing a lively waterfall. The A82 is crossed (again, take care) and a path squeezed in beside the road leads to the bridge over the Kirkton Burn and the lane to Kirkton Farm; one of two farms operated as experimental units by the West of Scotland College of Agriculture. Walkers are especially requested not to use this section if they have a dog with them, keeping to the road until the path recrosses it past Auchtertyre Farm.

Kirkton is notable for the remains of St Fillan's Chapel, which is almost hidden in the trees. Fillan came from Ireland. He is said to have been the son of St Kentigern, who died on Inchcailloch Island on Loch Lomond in 734 and (as St Mungo) became the patron saint of the City of Glasgow. Fillan himself was engaged on missionary work in the area you are walking through. The chapel was a monastic establishment, probably established in the 12th century. It was raised to the status of a priory by Robert the Bruce, who is said to have received a message or sign of support from St Fillan on the eve of the Battle of Bannockburn in 1314.

From here, walk along to Auchtertyre, the other experimental farm, and back to the A82. Having safely crossed it, meander along the west side of the road through more forestry plantings towards Tyndrum.

GOLD IN THEM THAR HILLS...

The area where the path crosses the road is called Dalrigh ('the king's field'), marking this time a defeat for the Bruce, in 1306 at the hands of the MacDougalls of Lorne. From here you have an excellent view of Beinn Dubhcraig and Ben Lui. The bare patch of ground by the river just before Tyndrum is a remnant of the former lead mining industry, which was started here by Sir Robert Clifton in 1741 and continued to 1862. Over that period about 5,000 tons of ore were extracted. Tyndrum was again the focus of an exploration for riches in more recent times; in this case it was gold, a source of which was found on Beinn Chuirn, above Cononish Farm. In the 1980s and 90s, Ennex International spent over £250,000 doing test drillings and were hopeful that the mine would be very productive. A condition of their being granted rights to mine here was that they restored the land as far as possible, once mining had ceased.

Part of Tyndrum is still called Clifton, after the man who set up the mine and the workers' village here. Today, Tyndrum exists largely to service tourists, standing as it does at the junction where the roads to Oban and Fort William divide. There is accommodation here, and several cafes, and Tyndrum must

be the smallest place in Britain to have two railway stations: the lower serves Oban and the upper, 0.25 miles (400m) or so away, is on the Fort William line. Tyndrum means 'the houses on the ridge', and Scotland's main watershed is a little west of the village. It was on one of the main droving routes in former times, so it is used to catering for travellers of all kinds. Queen Victoria called it 'wild and desolate' which, especially in winter, it certainly can be — but it has a fairer face too.

From Tyndrum (grid ref. NN 328 306), a return may be made by rail to Glasgow, or an intermediate station.

STAGE 6
TYNDRUM to VICTORIA BRIDGE

DISTANCE 9.4 miles (15km)
MAPS OS Explorer 364, 377
START AT GRID REFERENCE NN 327 301
START POINT Tyndrum village. Cafes, shops, parking. Trains and buses to Glasgow, Oban, and Fort William

The West Highland Way marches up the hill out of Tyndrum as if eager to see what lies ahead and indeed another mountain treat is in store. The line of the route here follows the old military road again. Originally constructed by troops under Major Caulfeild, successor to the better-known General Wade, in 1750–2, it was later used as a motor road until the latter route was redesigned in the 1930s. Now it is again the province of the walker (and mountainbiker). The track is clear, broad and easy as it climbs past Tyndrum's water treatment plant. As it reaches the top of the rise, Beinn Dorain comes into view ahead. From this angle, Beinn Dorain looks like every child's picture of a mountain; an almost perfect cone, rising steep-flanked to a pointed summit. In fact, like so many similar hills, what you are seeing is the end of a ridge, but it is no less fine for that.

Beinn Dorain is associated with the great Gaelic poet Duncan Ban Macintyre (1724–1812) who lived for most of his life in this area and composed many verses and songs about it. They were written down by others, as Duncan himself was illiterate. The Way tracks the railway line as far as Auch Farm, where the latter swings right to cross the Allt Kinglass by a fine viaduct.

PLACES TO VISIT

• **MUGDOCK COUNTRY PARK**
www.mugdock-country-park.org.uk
☎ 0141 956 6100
The WHW passes through the Mugdock Country Park, and a pleasant walk of 1.5 miles (2.5km) through the woods and past Mugdock Castle will bring you to the visitor centre, walled garden, shops and tea room. Near by are also the park's BBQ shelters for hire and an adventure play area for children. There are walking trails and orienteering courses throughout the park. Open daily all year.

• **GLENGOYNE DISTILLERY**
www.glengoyne.com
☎ 01360 550254
The Glengoyne Distillery lies just south of the junction of the A81 and A875, between Strathblane and Dumgoyne. It is a short diversion from the WHW and offers a wide range of tours. There is no need to book for the more standard tours, but there are some very special experiences on offer here if you plan ahead. After a dram and tour there is the opportunity to blend your own bottle to take away or, if you have more time, the 5-hour Masterclass Tour is billed as the most in-depth distillery tour in the country. Open daily all year.

• **BALMAHA**
www.lochlomond-trossachs.org
☎ 01389 722100
The village of Balmaha, on the east bank of Loch Lomond, has become a bustling centre for walkers and sight-seers. The National Park Visitor Centre is here, with its interactive exhibition on the local area, in addition to local shops and cafés. The local boatyard run a ferry on-demand to the pretty island of Inchcailloch. It is possible to complete a nature trail around the island, or visit its 14th-century castle ruins, small beach and picnic sites. The views of the loch from the island's summit are simply stunning.

LEFT Dramatic countryside around Crianlarich

There is an excellent view up Auch Glen to Beinn Mhanach ('hill of the monk'); a Munro detached from the main group here and for that reason a splendid viewpoint itself. The railway is recrossed and the broad path followed to the station at Bridge of Orchy, where trains pause for breath before starting the long climb across Rannoch Moor to the remote halt at Corrour. This is a journey every rail enthusiast should take. The hotel at Bridge of Orchy has a bunkhouse.

Bridge of Orchy railway station (grid ref. NN 300 394) provides an escape route by rail.

PEAK OF GOATS

The next short section offers a choice of routes: after walking down the road to cross the rushing Orchy by a fine old bridge, the path disappears into the woods over Mam Carraigh. The climb does allow excellent views, but the path is often very muddy and the road walk round to the Inveroran Hotel is not at all unpleasant, passing the pines of Doire Darach and walking beside lovely Loch Tulla. Those who take the hill path are rewarded with a fine panorama of the Blackmount Hills ahead, Stob Ghabhar ('peak of goats') prominent among them, while eastwards the vast expanse of Rannoch Moor stretches away to the horizon.

There has been an inn at Inveroran for over 200 years. William and Dorothy Wordsworth had breakfast here in 1803. Those who stop here today are most unlikely to be served, as they apparently were, with 'butter not eatable, the barley cakes fusty, the oat bread so hard I could not chew it, and there were only four eggs in the house which they had boiled as hard as stones', in Dorothy's words. The present building dates from about 1830 and was for long a droving inn, until the 'stance' was moved to Bridge of Orchy on the insistence of Lord Breadalbane, who took his case all the way to the House of Lords in 1844, so that he could keep the land for stalking.

In more recent years, Inveroran has become popular with walkers, climbers and anglers, and remains so today. It provides the last hostelry before you tackle the section leading over to Glencoe. The true start of this is a mile (1.6km) or so further on, at Victoria Bridge.

TOP Young red deer stag
ABOVE Blackrock Cottage
on Rannoch Moor
ABOVE RIGHT The steep
valley of Glencoe beyond
the waters of Loch Leven

VICTORIA BRIDGE TO KINLOCHLEVEN

STAGE 7

VICTORIA BRIDGE to ALTNAFEADH

DISTANCE 11.7 miles (18.9km)
MAPS OS Explorer 377, 384, 385
START AT GRID REFERENCE NN 270 422
START POINT Victoria Bridge. No facilities or public transport

The next section of the route continues to follow either the old military road or the first motor road over to Glencoe. The track is excellent all the way, but for 8 miles (13km) there is no shelter of any kind, and the track reaches well over 1,000ft (300m).

In poor weather conditions it is a considerable test: and the average annual rainfall here is around 120 inches. There are no escape routes, so once you have started you must either press on or turn back. That said, in good weather conditions this is a magnificent walk, to be relished for the superb scenery, the sense of wildness, and the abundance of history around you and under your feet.

If climbing the stile by Forest Lodge seems like starting an adventure, it is a feeling that has been shared by others – among them the Marchioness of Breadalbane. Her book, *The High Tops of Black Mount*, written nearly 100 years ago, is well worth reading for the vivid descriptions of long days in the hills. She became the first honorary president of the Ladies Scottish Climbing Club when it was formed in 1908.

There is a long, steady pull up from Forest Lodge to the top of the rise between Beinn Toaig, on the west, and the smaller Meall Beag to the east. Here you pass into Highland Region for the rest of the walk. You cross a watershed: the waters ahead of you flow east into the Tay system, rather than west.

As the path continues, a large corrie opens up on the west (left). This is Corrie Ba ('corrie of the cattle'), and magnificent it is, especially when viewed against the vast expanse of Rannoch Moor to the east. On a good day there can be few finer places than Ba Bridge to stop for a rest and a brew-up. To the west is the corrie, with the Blackmount Hills soaring above it, and to the east the river gurgles down towards Loch Ba in the heart of the moor. The colouring is subtle and the sense of wilderness glorious. Odd to reflect then that this was the route of the motor road up to the mid-1930s.

VIEW DOWN GLENCOE

In the autumn here, the awesome and thrilling sound of red deer stags at the rut can be heard. Their deep and powerful roar carries for long distances and prickles the hair on the neck. The path continues past Ba Cottage, once a drovers' stance but long since abandoned, to the summit of this section at 1,450ft (442m). Above the track is a memorial to Peter Fleming, former owner of the estate and himself a great traveller, adventurer and writer, who died of a heart attack here in 1971. He is less well-known than his brother Ian, creator of James Bond, but his books are minor classics of travel literature.

It is all downhill now, round the flanks of Meall a'Bhuiridh ('hill of roaring' — another reference to the stags) to the neat whitewashed Blackrock Cottage, a climbers' hut. Meall

a'Bhuiridh has been developed for piste skiing, and the summit area is consequently spoiled, but it is a fine hill none the less, with a truly splendid rocky ridge on its west linking it with Creise, another fine Munro. The walk continues down the road serving the skiing car park to cross the A82, last seen at Bridge of Orchy, and over to the Kings House Hotel.

The Kings House was once just that; a changehouse set up by the Crown for travellers. The inn now offers every modern comfort, and has rooms for walkers and climbers. It seems things were not always thus, for here we again encounter Dorothy Wordsworth complaining that she never saw 'such a miserable, wretched place'. She cannot have been talking of the landscape, which is dominated by the craggy splendour of Buachaille Etive Mor; the great herdsman of Etive, one of Scotland's premier rock and ice climbing mountains, and irresistible to any photographer.

If there is the time and energy, a scramble up behind Kings House to the summit of Beinn a'Chrulaiste will give the best view of 'the Buachaille', as the hill is affectionately known. Beinn a'Chrulaiste (simply 'the rocky hill') stands apart from the other Glencoe hills and thus provides a superb view of them, especially the Buachaille. It can be climbed without difficulty from either Kings House or Altnafeadh, which is where the path is now heading.

There are some alternative routes there. Either walk on the route of the old military road, under the hill, or go down by the River Coupall. Each way has its attractions. The riverside walk gives a closer view of the Buachaille, and climbers may be seen on one of the classic routes, such as the Crowberry Tower or Great Gully.

Either way, arrive at Altnafeadh, where a modern house replaces the older building burned down years ago. From here there is a view down much of Glencoe, a glen redolent in history and rich in wild scenery. The story of the infamous Glencoe Massacre, its 300th anniversary marked in 1992, need not be detailed here: it is amply documented. Glencoe itself is in the care of the National Trust for Scotland.

STAGE 8
ALTNAFEADH to KINLOCHLEVEN
DISTANCE 5.9 miles (9.5km)
MAPS OS Explorer 384, 392
START AT GRID REFERENCE NN 220 563
START POINT Altnafeadh. No facilities. The daily Glasgow–Fort William bus will stop here on request

Leaving Altnafeadh, you face the long haul over the Devil's Staircase, built by Caulfeild's troops in 1750. The zig-zags are still there; please walk them and do not take short cuts, so that this fine old route will be preserved.

Take your time on the ascent: the views back across and down Glencoe are superb, the Three Sisters rising into full view and the two Buachailles, Mor and Beag, dominant either side of the deep trench of the Lairig Gartan. In early May each year (since 1907), the Scottish Six Days Trial is held in the area around Fort William and Kinlochleven. This is a noisy affair, with 270 scrambler motorbikes competing for various trophies. The event draws many hundreds of bikers and enthusiasts into the area, and the local economy benefits as a result.

At the summit of the pass (and of the whole walk, at 1,800ft/549m) there is a cairn. A short climb to the west on to Stob Mhic Mhartuin gives an even better prospect of the area, especially the whole new aspect to the north, with the glorious serrated peaks of the Mamores framing the unmistakable hunchback shape of Ben Nevis itself. Your final target is within sight.

Below, to the east, is Blackwater Reservoir, built early this century by 3,000 navvies. Tales of those days relate of hard living and hard drinking, of death and disappearance, of ten-hour drilling shifts; a different world. The reservoir feeds the aluminium works in Kinlochleven, which itself dramatically transformed a tiny Highland village into a town. Blackwater is nearly 8 miles (13km) long and its dam is over 80ft (24m) high.

The feeder pipes accompany the walker down towards Kinlochleven, with Garbh Bheinn (appropriately, 'rough hill') to the west. It too is a fine climb with a magnificent panorama, but not to be undertaken lightly. All this country was used by Robert Louis Stevenson in *Kidnapped*, and a finer setting for an escape would be hard to find.

The path passes through birchwood to meet the great pipes and runs down with them into Kinlochleven. Since the loss of jobs caused when the aluminium smelter closed down in 1996, the attraction of the West Highland Way for walkers has provided a welcome boost to the local economy. Despite the splendour of its surroundings, no one would pretend that Kinlochleven itself is very attractive, but it does provide a chance to shop, eat (it has one of the best fish and chip shops in the West Highlands), and perhaps stay overnight before tackling the final stage of the journey.

KINLOCHLEVEN TO FORT WILLIAM

STAGE 9
KINLOCHLEVEN to LUNDAVRA
DISTANCE 7.5 miles (12km)
MAPS OS Explorer 384, 391, 392
START AT GRID REFERENCE NN 187 619
START POINT Bridge in Kinlochleven (weekday bus service to Glencoe Village or Fort William, shops, bank)

(i) PLACES TO VISIT
• RSPB INVERSNAID
www.rspb.org.uk
The WHW runs through the full length of this wildlife reserve, on the eastern shore of Loch Lomond. There are no visitor facilities except toilets, but there is a nature trail starting roughly 0.6 miles (1km) north of the Inversnaid Hotel. The reserve includes oak woodland and open moorland, and is working to encourage biodiversity, including the rare black grouse. You may also see red deer, pine martens, woodpeckers, buzzards, pied flycatchers and hen harriers.

• GLENCOE MOUNTAIN RESORT
www.glencoemountain.co.uk
☎ 01855 851226
The WHW passes close to the base station of the Glencoe Mountain Resort, which offers activities all year round, not just during the ski season. There is a chairlift which takes visitors from the valley floor up to 2,200ft (670m) in around 12 minutes. The views from the top are stunning, and an ideal place for a picnic if the weather is good. There is a café at the base station, and one at the summit during peak summer months. Mountain bikes are available for hire, and there are trails for all abilities, either in the valley or downhill from the top of the chairlift. Perhaps book an archery lesson if cycling seems too frantic. In the winter, of course, this is prime skiing, snow boarding and sledging territory. Base café open daily all year; chairlift open daily Jan–Oct; see website for operating days and times of other activities.

TOP *Hillwalker looking west down Glen Coe from Beinn a Chrulaiste*
ABOVE *Purple Highland heather*

On leaving Kinlochleven, there is a definite feeling of entering the last lap of a long journey. If you are using the official guide, you are on the last map section. You are also entering Lochaber; one of the old provinces of Scotland (the name is still used in local government) like Lennox, where you started. Lochaber is a region of long lochs cutting deep into the interior, and of dramatic hills rising steeply, almost from the waterside. There are only 14.5 miles (23.5km) left, but there is still much to savour.

From Kinlochleven, the path climbs steadily through shady birchwoods, crossing the road up to Mamore Lodge. From here to Lundavra the route is still on the line of the old military road, and of a long-established right of way, the Lairigmor, which means 'the big pass'. For the fit and ambitious, there are temptations either side which are not easily ignored. To the right is the magnificent Mamore range, containing 11 Munros. Two or three of them can be savoured as a high-level alternative.

The hills to the west should not be discounted just because they are of lower height. Their position apart from the main hill groups makes Beinn na Caillich ('hill of the old woman') and Man na Gualainn ('pass of the shoulder') particularly fine viewpoints, looking not just north to the great Lochaber hills but also west, out towards the sea, and across Loch Leven to its Pap (*Sgorr na Ciche* in Gaelic).

These are for a fine day (but not during the main autumn stalking season). Access is by stalking tracks, which you will find on many Scottish hills. Superbly engineered for ponies as well as people, they always take the best line and if you can find one, use it. The track reaches about 800ft (245m) and then levels off to carry on through the broad glen. This can be a dreich place indeed in rain or mist.

THE WATER HORSE

Just over the summit you pass Tigh-na-Sleubhaich ('the house by the gully'). By turning right and climbing steeply (though always on grass) here, the Mamore ridge can be gained at a point where the rock-type changes literally in a step, from grey schist to pinkish granite, and by continuing over the easy Munro Mullach nan Coirean ('summit of the corries'), the West Highland Way can be picked up again lower down. The path over the Lairigmor passes the eponymous ruin, where the right of way to Callert on Loch Levenside diverts left, and drops down into a forestry plantation. Beyond it lies Lochan Lunn-da-Bhra. The meaning of this name is obscure, but it is one of those lochs said to hold the *each uisge*, 'the water-horse', which came out of the water, tempted young men on to its back, and then galloped under the waves with them.

Emerge from the trees at Blar a'Chaorainn ('field of rowans'), where there is a small car park, and face a choice. The path goes right, climbing up and over the extension of the Mamore ridge to drop into Glen Nevis; this is the actual route of the West Highland Way. In poor weather, an alternative is simply to continue along the switchback road which leads you straight into Fort William. Either way, you are now faced with the very last section of the walk.

STAGE 10
LUNDAVRA to FORT WILLIAM
DISTANCE 7.2 miles (11.6km)
MAPS OS Explorer 384, 392, 399
START AT GRID REFERENCE NN 100 665
START POINT Blar a'Chaorainn car park. No other facilities or public transport

Whether on the road or the path, in clear conditions there is a superb view of Ben Nevis, and of the many other fine hills surrounding it. From Blar a'Chaorainn, the path climbs to the right under a power line, partly following the line of a dyke (wall) which would formerly have marked the boundary between the better ground lower down and the rough grazing on the upper slopes.

As the path climbs, more of Ben Nevis comes into view: impressive more for its vast bulk than for any beauty of form. It hunches its shoulders way above the surrounding hills, rising to a rough plateau at 4,406ft (1,343m), the highest point in Britain.

The path enters forestry once more, contouring round to pass the site of Dun Deardail; an ancient fortified site possibly dating back to the Iron Age. It is one of many such sites in Scotland, and if you take the trees away in your mind's eye you

i PLACES TO VISIT

• THE ICE FACTOR
www.ice-factor.co.uk
☎ 01855 831100
The village of Kinlochleven was centred around the industry of its aluminium smelter for most of the 20th century, before its closure in 1996. In recent years the area has reinvented itself as an outdoor activity hub, and shelter for walkers of the WHW. If you have energy to spare, head to this centre, housed in the former carbon bunkers of the alumimium works, and make use of the largest articulated climbing wall in the UK. There are lessons for those with experience and for complete beginners, even those as young as 4 years. For competent climbers, the centre has an ice wall that is five times larger than any other indoor ice wall. Outdoors, the adventurous scale cargo nets to a height of 49ft (15m) and join the fixed rail adventure course; tackling tight ropes, rickety bridges and other obstacles while attached by a harness to a rail above. There is a large indoor play area for younger visitors, and adults can relax in the sauna and steam room, the bistro bar or the café. Open daily all year.

will realize that it commands an excellent position above Glen Nevis, which was for long an important through-route on foot between the west coast and the hinterland. The name Deardail might mean 'fort on the stormy hill', which would be appropriate in view of the high rainfall levels experienced hereabouts.

Not long past the fort, the path joins a forest road which gives easy walking down to the glen. Partway down, a branch to the right leads to the excellent youth hostel and other facilities in the glen itself. The main path continues to meet the Glen Nevis road about a mile (1.6km) from Fort William, which is the largest settlement since Milngavie.

Fort William was established in the 17th century, and named after King William III. Its Gaelic name, An Gearasdan, is linked, meaning the garrison. The original fort has disappeared, but the importance the town assumed with its strategic location has remained. It is the local administration and shopping centre, a tourist centre, and a rail and bus terminus (or more properly junction, since the separate rail line to Mallaig, one of the finest journeys in Britain, starts from here). As you would expect, there is a wide range of accommodation.

BEN NEVIS

For those going on to climb Ben Nevis, a word on the ascent may be in order here. The usual route is from Achintee, accessed from the large car park in lower Glen Nevis (grid ref. NN 125 729). A branch path from the youth hostel joins the main path partway up. The Ben Nevis path is well defined all the way to the top, for it was made when the summit observatory was constructed in the late 19th century (at that time, walking up cost you sixpence; today it is free). The path rounds the shoulder of Meall an t-Suidhe to cross the Red Burn and starts up the notorious zig-zags before reaching the summit plateau, where you will find the ruins of the observatory, a variety of cairns, and an emergency shelter. It is not a prepossessing place, but it is the roof of Britain.

The ascent needs preparation at any time of year. It is a long way and a rough one, and many underestimate it simply because there is a path. In mist (very frequent) the summit can be confusing, and it is all too possible to lose the path. There are cliffs on the north and east. Snow comes early and lingers late. The peak is busy all year round, but one notable date is the first Saturday in September, when 400 or so hardy souls tackle the Ben Nevis race to the summit and back (the record, believe it or not, is just under 90 minutes for the round trip). The descent is far worse than the climb.

The West Highland Way has now been extended into the town centre at Gordon's Square, where a sculpture has been erected to celebrate reaching the end of the walk.

TOP Ben Nevis, highest mountain in UK, rises above Fort William at the head of Loch Linnhe
LEFT The summit cairn at the top of Ben Nevis

The River Ba, looking towards the Black Mount, Rannoch Moor

Speyside Way

COMPLETE ROUTE BUCKIE TO AVIEMORE **84 MILES (135KM)**
SECTION COVERED SPEY BAY TO BALLINDALLOCH **30 MILES (48.3KM)**
& TOMINTOUL SPUR **15 MILES (24.1KM)**
MAPS OS EXPLORER 403, 404, 418, 419, 424

The Speyside Way links the Moray coast with the edge of the Grampian Mountains, generally following the valley of the River Spey. There is also a spur of 5 miles (8km) to Dufftown, which can be walked as part of a circular walk. There is a particular attraction in riverside paths, and the concept of a walk linking the foothills of the Cairngorms with the coast, largely following the course of the Spey, Scotland's second longest river, was an enticing one. Due to some access problems when the route was established, the route also follows pleasant hillside and forestry trails. The Speyside Way is in whisky country for most of its length.

SPEY BAY TO CRAIGELLACHIE

STAGE 1
SPEY BAY to BOAT O'BRIG
DISTANCE 8.9 miles (14.3km)
MAP OS Explorer 424
START AT GRID REFERENCE NJ 348 653
START POINT Tugnet Ice House

This section of the Speyside Way starts at the mouth of the river, at a car park beside the Tugnet Ice House, which is well worth a visit. It was built at a time when the best way to store perishable foodstuffs was to pack them in layers of ice inside thick stone walls. The Tugnet Ice House dates from 1830 and is now part of the Whale and Dolphin Conservation Society exhibition.

Across the river is Kingston, named after the home town of two entrepreneurs from Kingston-upon-Hull. They leased the large Glenmore Forest, between Aviemore and Grantown, from the Duke of Gordon in the 18th century, and floated timber in rafts down the Spey to this point. Some of the timber was used for boatbuilding, and at one time there were seven shipyards between Kingston and Garmouth. The industry declined with the coming of iron-clad vessels, and no trace remains today.

Beyond Kingston is The Lein, a Scottish Wildlife Trust reserve. The shingle system at the mouth of the Spey is the largest in Scotland and is second only to Chesil Beach, Dorset, in the whole of Britain. Its habitats range from marsh to heathland, supporting many orchids and other interesting plants. The birdlife is excellent too, with a good variety of waders and seabirds to be spotted at most times of the year.

The path turns away from the river for a short distance before taking a track leading south to a point quite close to the Garmouth Viaduct; a vast construction dominating the landscape. The viaduct, which carried the Great North of Scotland Railway branch line from Elgin to Portgordon, was designed by Patrick Barnett and opened in 1886. Its great length and size were necessary because of the power of the river in flood, and its frequently shifting flow pattern through sandbanks. The viaduct has ornate castellated portals and is supported by huge piers which actually drop to 52ft (16m) below the river bed, showing how the engineers respected the force of the Spey, as one of Scotland's fastest-flowing rivers. A path from the Speyside Way diverts across the viaduct to Garmouth.

TELFORD'S BRIDGE
The route itself continues, partly through woodland, sometimes veering away from the river, sometimes close to it, until it joins the B9104 for a mile (1.6km) to the outskirts of Fochabers. On the left here are the policies (estate) of Gordon Castle, former home of the Dukes of Richmond and Gordon, now luxury accommodation. Across the Spey here is the Baxters Highland Village. The route passes under the A96 road into a pleasant riverside path.

Fochabers is a planned town, one of many in Scotland. In 1776, the 4th Duke of Gordon wished to enlarge his policies and castle. The village of Fochabers was in his way, so he engaged the architect John Baxter to lay out a new town on the present site. As is commonly the case, the basic street pattern is a grid-iron and there is a handsome central square, which holds the fine Bellie Church. The history of the town is very well told in the Folk Museum on the High Street. The Speyside Way does not actually pass through Fochabers, but it would be a pity to miss visiting the town, and a short diversion around it, including the Folk Museum, can easily be taken. Fochabers town has a good range of shops.

From the riverside park, the two bridges crossing the Spey here can clearly be seen. The older bridge is based on a design by the famous engineer Thomas Telford. Built in 1806, it was a victim of the great flood of 1829, when the river flooded the whole of the surrounding area. An eyewitness account dramatically describes the bridge falling 'with the cloud-like appearance of an avalanche' and the river 'rushing onwards, its thunderous roar proclaiming its victory, and not a vestige of the fallen fragments to be seen'. The bridge was rebuilt in the 1850s, but has now been supplanted by the modern road bridge alongside it.

The Speyside Way again turns away from the river to follow the Fochabers Burn and leaves the village by passing Milne's High School. From here to Boat o'Brig, it follows a minor road, providing very easy walking. There is rarely much in the way of traffic to trouble the walker.

TOP The shore of Spey Bay
ABOVE Wild salmon thrive in the clear waters of the Spey
BELOW Tugnet Ice House at Spey Bay

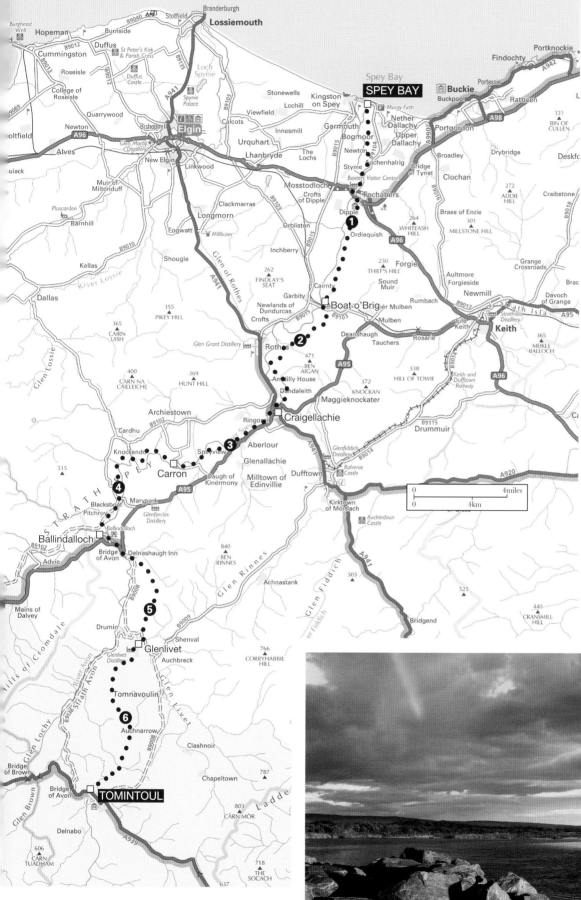

USEFUL INFORMATION

THE ROUTE
• www.speysideway.org.uk
☎ 01340 881266
The official website of the SW is hosted by Moray Council and provides a good range of detailed information, including an online guide to route sections, diversion updates, public transport routes, an accommodation list and much more. Updates are dated, which is useful, and there are helpful links, including one to the Moray Council online shop, where you can purchase guides and maps.

TOURIST INFORMATION CENTRES
• www.moray.gov.uk
Speyside Way Visitor Centre, Old Station Building, Aberlour AB38 9QP;
☎ 01340 881266
• www.visitscotland.com
Tomintoul Museum, The Square, Tomintoul AB37 9ET;
☎ 01807 580285
(open Mon–Sat Apr–Oct)

PLANNING YOUR TRIP
• www.ldwa.org.uk
The Long Distance Walkers Association has some detail on the SW, and good advice on long-distance walking in general.
• www.ramblers.org.uk
☎ 020 7339 8500
The Ramblers Association website also gives advice about long-distance walking in Britain and a page of information specifically on the SW.

OTHER PATHS
At Grantown-on-Spey, the Dava Way begins and takes a route north to the town of Forres, mostly via the old Highland Railway trackbed. There are many walks along the Moray Firth coast, forming part of the Moray Firth Trail (www.morayfirth.org). These include the Moray Coast Trail, between Forres and Cullen, which links with the SW at Spey Bay. It is hoped that this trail will eventually form part of the European-wide North Sea Trail (www.northseatrail.co.uk).

RIGHT A rainbow brightens the evening sky as the sun sets over Spey Bay, at the mouth of the River Spey

RED STREAM

At Aultderg (meaning 'red stream') a Forestry Commission car park has a path leading to a good viewpoint above the river, but for most of this section the Spey is out of sight as the road winds either through or alongside forest, high above the river plain. After a junction is passed, the road drops, gradually at first and then more steeply around a zig-zag of bends, to reach Delfur Lodge and Boat o'Brig, where there is a small Speyside Way car park beside the river.

The river is spanned here by road and rail bridges. The former carries the B9103 which leads east to Keith and west to Rothes. The railway bridge was designed by another great Victorian engineer, Joseph Mitchell. His 1858 approach arches are still there, but the river is now crossed by a later steel truss, erected in 1906. It would be nice to think that in time ScotRail might be persuaded to provide a halt for walkers at Boat o'Brig. The name Boat o'Brig is said to have derived from the fact that there was originally a bridge here. When it collapsed, a ferry was provided; the 'boat of the bridge'. The curious small building with the Doric columns was a toll house.

Roads lead from Boat o'Brig to Keith, where buses can be caught to Fochabers.

STAGE 2
BOAT O'BRIG to CRAIGELLACHIE
DISTANCE 7.8 miles (12.6km)
MAP OS Explorer 424
START AT GRID REFERENCE NJ 318 517
START POINT Boat o'Brig car park on the B9103

The Speyside Way climbs up behind the toll house to join a track leading to Bridgeton Farm. It swings left, and then sharply right, to enter the forest on the western slopes of Ben Aigan.

The path passes close to the Speyside Gun Club's range: firing is taking place if red flags are flying. The path itself is quite safe, which is something of a relief. The next section of path is along the forest edge, giving good views, before entering the forest and climbing steadily to join a broad track around the deep side valley of the Allt Daley.

Two further, smaller side valleys are rounded. Between them a short diversion leads to a seat at a viewpoint giving a magnificent and somehow unexpected panorama of the whole of the lower river valley and the coast. It is a lovely scene with a mixture of farmland and woods, the Spey winding through and the sea beyond. In very clear conditions you can pick out the mountains of Sutherland and Caithness.

In time, the track heads steadily downhill to join a minor road, which is followed for nearly 3 miles (5km) to Craigellachie. This is part of the Arndilly Estate which was noted for its splendid trees, both conifer and broadleaved. Arndilly House is passed, with a double row of neat stone toadstools lining the drive. The house was built in the 1830s by David McDowal Grant, one of the great land 'improvers' of the time.

The Spey is regularly seen but not approached on this section, which ends by crossing the River Fiddich at the Fiddichside Inn, to enter Fiddich Park. A small camp site for walkers is provided here, and toilets from Easter to October. The main path swings right under a bridge to reach Craigellachie; a popular centre for fishermen.

CRAIGELLACHIE TO BALLINDALLOCH

STAGE 3
CRAIGELLACHIE to CARRON

DISTANCE 5.8 miles (9.3km)

MAPS OS Explorer 419, 424

START AT GRID REFERENCE NJ 292 451

START POINT Fiddich Park, Craigellachie.
Buses from Elgin, Keith and Dufftown

Craigellachie should not be left without making the short diversion to see Telford's bridge over the Spey. This is the oldest surviving iron bridge in Scotland. Built in 1814, it is the work of a genius, for Telford was using a new material and allowed his imagination full rein in taking every advantage of the lightness and airiness possible in an iron bridge. The result is a graceful, elegant structure, its appearance enhanced by the frowning cliff above it on the west bank of the river (Craig Ailichidh, the original spelling, means 'strong rock'). The iron was cast in Wales by Telford's favourite ironmaster, William Hazledine, and the bridge, which cost £8,200, has castellated towers at each end.

The bridge inspired the noted local fiddler, William Marshall, to write a Strathspey dance called Craigellachie Brig. Mention of this brings us to the vexed question of what to call the river valley the Speyside Way passes along. Local usage refers to the valley as Speyside from Grantown to the sea, and Strathspey from that town to the source.

From here to Ballindalloch, the Speyside Way follows the track bed of the former Strathspey Railway (illustrating the point!). Between Craigellachie and Aberlour the path goes through the only tunnel on the line. It is a short affair some 150yds (135m) long with clear visibility and continues more or less beside the river, with the A95 close by to the left, to enter Aberlour. The

village (Charlestown of Aberlour, to give its full name) is another planned settlement, established here by Charles Grant of Wester Elchies in 1812. It has a broad, handsome main street and a small square holding the church, which has an unusual castellated tower. Aberlour is a noted salmon fishing centre. Its distillery, on the southern edge of the town, can be visited. The village shop, in the High Street, has been maintained partly in 19th-century style.

The route passes behind houses close to the river, to reach the former station, now the Speyside Way Visitor Centre and Ranger base. It has been extended and preserved, with part of the building open as a cafe in summer, selling excellent local produce at very reasonable prices. The cafe is manned on a voluntary basis by the ladies of the village, all the proceeds going to charity, so it is well worth patronizing. The station is now part of the attractive Alice Littler Park, named for the wife of Sydney Littler, a noted local benefactor. A graceful suspension footbridge crosses the river here, and the banks are favoured by anglers.

From Aberlour, the Speyside Way continues on the old railway. The plentiful tree cover and frequent cuttings mean that views are somewhat limited on this stretch, but it is easy walking. The path joins a minor road for a short distance, to cross the Spey on a bridge which gives good views not only along the river but down into it! This was in fact the last cast-iron bridge made in Scotland. It dates from 1863 and features a lattice construction. It is worth going down to the river to look up at the bridge and appreciate its lightness.

The path runs alongside the road into the small village of Carron, passing the entrance to the Imperial Distillery, home of the famous Black Bottle Whisky.

From Carron a minor road leads back to the A95 and infrequent buses to Aberlour or Grantown.

STAGE 4

CARRON to BALLINDALLOCH

DISTANCE 6.7 miles (10.8km)

MAP OS Explorer 419

START AT GRID REFERENCE NJ 221 412

START POINT Car park, Carron village. Infrequent public transport

PLACES TO VISIT

• **WILDLIFE CENTRE**
www.wdcs.org.uk
☎ 01343 820339
The wildlife centre at Spey Bay is run by the Whale and Dolphin Conservation Society. The haven is home to ospreys, otters and seals, among other wildlife. Here you can listen to live sounds transmitted from beneath the Firth waters via the 'sonobuoy', or visit the Underwater World exhibition in the Tugnet Ice House. This is the largest ice house in Scotland, originally used to store river ice for use in the salmon industry. You may even be able to spot dolphins, using the telescopes on site. Open daily Apr–Oct, Sat–Sun Nov & Feb–Mar.

• **BAXTERS HIGHLAND VILLAGE**
www.baxters.com
☎ 01343 820666
At the Baxters food factory, just a short walk from Fochabers village, is this interesting site. There is a reconstruction of the original shop opened in 1868, and more modern cookware, clothing, gift and food shops to enjoy. Sample the Baxter products and other foods in the restaurant or café before you leave. Open daily all year.

• **FOCHABERS FOLK MUSEUM**
www.fochabers-heritage.org.uk
☎ 01343 821204
Housed in a former church, this museum offers an insight into the local history of this charming village. There are photographs, various everyday artefacts, and a collection of gigs and carriages. Open Tue–Sun Easter–Sep.

• **TOMINTOUL MUSEUM**
☎ 01807 580285
Housed in the old Spalding Bakery, this museum of local life includes reconstructions of an old smithy and a farmhouse kitchen. There are displays on local peat cutting and the main exhibits tell more about local history and wildlife. Open Mon–Sat Apr–Oct, plus Sun Jul–Aug.

*TOP **Craigellachie Bridge** over the River Spey*
*ABOVE LEFT **Barrel-making** inside Speyside Cooperage*

Leaving one distillery, the route heads firmly off towards two others, still on the old railway line, elevated above the river but with little in the way of distant views.

The river curves in slow loops here and the path largely follows it towards Knockando, 3 miles (5km) from Carron. The route passes directly behind Knockando Distillery, the aroma either overpowering or inspiring, according to taste. The distillery was founded in 1898 and has attractive stone facing with a smart carved sign and a visitor centre.

Tamdhu Distillery (not open to the public) was built here in 1896, partly because of the railway line and partly because of the pure waters of the Knockando Burn. A road had to be built to serve it. The Cardhu Distillery, 1.5 miles (2.5km) away off the B9102, is open to visitors, and has great views from its picnic tables.

From Tamdhu the path runs close to the Spey most of the way to Ballindalloch. There is generous tree cover and rabbits and pheasants are almost certain to be seen on this stretch, and maybe even roe deer. These lovely small animals bound gracefully along in a way humans can only envy; they are often sighted by a flash of white rump.

Just 2 miles (3km) from Tamdhu, the path reaches Blacksboat, where the station building survives as a private house and the former goods shed as the Speyside Way workshops. The bridge over the river was extensively refurbished in 1991. The name is thought to have come from two brothers, John and James Black, who farmed here and operated a ferry in the 18th century (or alternatively, after a negro servant from Ballindalloch Castle, who operated the ferry!)

Another easy 2 miles (3km) in pleasant surroundings leads to the fine viaduct spanning the river at Ballindalloch. The engineer, G McFarlane of Dundee, proudly gives his name at each end, and why not, for this sturdy bridge, built in 1863, is a fine piece of work, as strong today as when it was first opened. The viaduct leads to the former station at Ballindalloch, now a private house. From the station, carrying straight on leads in 0.25 miles (400m) to the Cragganmore Distillery, open to visitors April to October. The route, however, goes left on the B9137, possibly one of the shortest B roads in Britain. In 0.5 miles (800m) it leads to the A95, the Avon and the start of the Tomintoul Spur.

TOMINTOUL SPUR

STAGE 5

BALLINDALLOCH to GLENLIVET
DISTANCE 6.5 miles (10.5km)

MAP OS Explorer 419
START AT GRID REFERENCE NJ 167 365
START POINT Speyside Way car park, Ballindaloch Station

From Ballindalloch Station, the Speyside Way heads up the B9137 road to join the A95. A tempting sign informs you that the Delnashaugh Inn is ahead, but don't be fooled: it is a good 0.25 miles (400m), up a steep brae, with only a narrow footpath.

It crosses the River Avon and a short diversion leads down to the old bridge, below and somewhat dwarfed by the bulky road bridge above it. On the far side is the ornate gate to Ballindalloch Castle, the seat of the MacPherson-Grant family since 1546. The Avon is here at the end of its turbulent journey from Loch Avon, deep in the Cairngorm Mountains below Ben Macdui.

The Delnashaugh Hotel and Restaurant, the only hostelry on this stretch of the walk, is an elegantly furnished hotel catering for sportsmen and general tourists. Walkers are made welcome and excellent bar meals are served.

Leaving the inn, pass the war memorial at the road junction and turn right on to the B9008 above the Avon. The road curves round, giving tempting views southward, before the route leaves it, in about 0.5 miles (800m) to take the track past the farm of Auldich. The track continues beyond the farm, surfaced for a further 0.25 miles (400m) to reach a rubbish dump and a small car park with an information board.

There is a definite feeling here of a change of mood. The Spey has been left behind. To the left, Ben Rinnes, the area's highest hill, rises to 2,760ft (840m) and the whole atmosphere is wilder and, to the mountain lover, more alluring. The track leads enticingly ahead, rising steadily. It can be seen crossing the shallow valley leftwards; the route to Tomintoul, however, leaves it a mile (1.6km) beyond Auldich to go right on a moorland path, still quite clear and with waymarks at intervals.

As the brow of the hill is reached, the view southwards opens out to reveal Glen Livet and Strath Avon, with the Hills of Cromdale away to the right. The variations in light and shade can be quite stunning, enhanced by the patchwork nature of the landscape; many darker forestry plantations alternating with lighter-coloured farmland and the rich hues of the heather moor. It is a particularly fine scene in spring, with the last of the snow

on the distant tops, and in autumn, when the heather is at its best. Red grouse are very likely to be seen – and heard – on this stretch, urging you to 'go back, go back'.

From here to Glenlivet the Speyside Way passes Deskie Farm and then goes onto the B9008 road, where you turn left for a short distance and then turn right up a lane to join the distillery road. If you have time, the rightward diversion to see the Old Bridge of Livet, a triple-span that is now grassed over, is worth taking.

 From Glenlivet, buses can be caught back to Ballindalloch.

STAGE 6

GLENLIVET to TOMINTOUL

DISTANCE 9.1 miles (14.7km)
MAPS OS Explorer 404, 419
START AT GRID REFERENCE NJ 200297
START POINT Glenlivet Village Hall

WHISKY GALORE

For whisky-lovers, one of the high points of the walk is now in sight: The Glenlivet Distillery, visible throughout the descent to the valley. This was the first distillery to be licensed after the laws were changed in 1823 to stamp out illicit whisky production and smuggling. The distillery tour takes an hour, is free, and is well worth the stop.

Fortified by the free dram, continue up the lane past Glenlivet House, to turn off on a track leading past old farmhouses. Above them a path has been made at the edge of a forestry plantation. At its top gate a much better, broader path is joined, rising to a pass below Carn Liath (grey hill) and contouring round the hill on a wonderfully well-graded track giving excellent walking. Carn Daimh, the highest point of the walk, is now clearly visible ahead.

For the whole of this section there are superb views back to Ben Rinnes, a notable landmark with its rock tors, or scurrs, prominent. It is a superb climb if you have time to spare either during or after the walk; but for the moment the target is Carn Daimh (pronounced 'cairn dye' and meaning 'hill of stags'). Just before the final climb there is a three-way signpost indicating a path down to Tomnavoulin (and yet another distillery).

Cairn Daimh commands a splendid panorama. To the west are the Hills of Cromdale, topped by Creagan a 'Chaise. South is Strathavon, leading the eye further on into the Cairngorms, up to Ben Avon itself, topped by rocky tors like Ben Rinnes. As you look back, Rinnes dominates the northeast sector, while a little further west, if conditions are right, the distant sea, left behind two days or more ago, is visible.

It is a place to savour, but it can be wild and windy too, and the last lap lies ahead. From Carn Daimh the route descends easily to enter forestry on Carn Ellick. This is another new stretch of path, and being based on peat, it can be good, though not in wet conditions. After a rather tedious trudge through the trees, the trail emerges to face a fine vista of moorland and woods.
The long descent across the peats of Feithmusach demands care in bad weather. The path is not well defined but there are regular waymarks and a bearing just west of south keeps you on course. The extensive peatmoss here is commercially worked at its eastern edge, by the B9008 road, where a display explains the process.

The Speyside Way wriggles tortuously in, around and through small plantations before descending (more metal squeeze-stiles) to a lane which is followed for 0.25 miles (400m). The Conglass Water is crossed by a fine footbridge, and a short stretch on a broad grassy track leads to the A939 at the north end of Tomintoul. This is another planned village, set up with the encouragement of the 4th Duke of Gordon. The first houses were occupied in 1780 and the village developed steadily over the following decades, with three long streets on a north–south axis, joined by short lanes.

The central square has a hotel and the Visitor Information Centre (open April to October), which includes a local history museum. The name derives from the Gaelic *Tom an t-sabhail* meaning 'barn knoll'.

It is a fine place to end a walk and to sit and reflect on the wide variety of scenery encountered since leaving Spey Bay: the walk has gone from the estuary of Scotland's second-longest river to one of its highest villages, taking in whisky, woods and wildlife. It provides an excellent introduction to the area, whetting the appetite to return and explore further the straths, glens and hills of one of Scotland's most attractive areas.

(i) **PLACES TO VISIT**
• **BALLINDALLOCH CASTLE**
www.ballindallochcastle.co.uk
☎ 01807 500205
The route passes this lovely castle. Lived in by the Macpherson-Grant family for over 450 years, it has the feel of a Victorian Highland estate, with lavish rooms, formal gardens and a tea room. There is accommodation, shooting, fishing and a golf course on offer, too. Open Sun–Fri Apr–Sep.

• **DISTILLERIES**
www.scotlandwhisky.com/ distilleries/speyside
There are many distilleries passed on the Speyside Way, as you would expect, since Speyside is home to over half of Scotland's distilleries. Start your exploration of the art of whisky-making with a visit to the galleries of Speyside Cooperage at Craigellachie (*www.speysidecooperage.co.uk* ☎ 01340 871108; open Mon–Fri all year). The cooperage is located on the road to Dufftown, and you can watch the making of the oak whisky casks that have been produced here by the same family since 1947. If you complete the full Dufftown Spur of the SW, you can visit Balvenie Distillery and the award-winning Glenfiddich Distillery, who offer a free tour in addition to their more in-depth Connoisseur Tour. Back on the main route, Aberlour Distillery is the next to be passed, where tours must be booked in advance and some even pair the whisky tasting with chocolate. Other distilleries are passed as you progress along the route, but the next one that is open to visitors is Cragganmore, at Ballindalloch. Finally, on the way to Tomintoul, the route passes the Glenlivet Distillery. HRH Prince Charles opened a new extension to the distillery in 2010, and the visitor centre includes a cafe.

TOP Barrels stacked in the snow at Speyside Cooperage
ABOVE LEFT Young robin
ABOVE RIGHT Highland cow

Fife Coastal Path

COMPLETE ROUTE TAYPORT TO NORTH QUEENSFERRY **80 MILES (129KM)**

SECTION COVERED ST ANDREWS TO INVERKEITHING **60 MILES (96KM)**

MAPS OS EXPLORER 350, 367, 370, 371, 380

This path was officially opened in June 2002 as a long-distance route running from North Queensferry to Tayport. The path is waymarked with its own brand and in 2009 came runner-up in Coast *magazine's Best UK Coastal Path contest, second only to the Pembrokeshire Coast National Trail. The coastal path is being extended to run along the entire coast of Fife from Newburgh on the Firth of Tay to Kincardine on the Firth of Forth. The path has its very own coastal centre, based in the Habourmaster's House, Dysart, where visitors can find out more information on the path.*

The section included here runs a total distance of about 60 miles (96km) from the university town of St Andrews to the railway station at Inverkeithing, in the shadow of the two great Forth Bridges. It includes superb stretches of sandy beach, wild headlands, fantastic offshore rock formations, and a considerable number of small towns and villages of great charm and character.

Fife was for many centuries a place apart: indeed, it considered itself to be a 'kingdom'. The wide Firth of Forth, crossed by ferry, separated it from Scotland's capital, and it was a journey not undertaken lightly, especially in winter. The first bridge over the Forth was 20 miles (32km) west, at Stirling. Fife developed its own industries and traded extensively with the Continent even in medieval times. Traces of those industries, notably salt and coal, will be seen on the walk.

ABOVE The ruins of the Cathedral of St Andrew, built around 1160

ABOVE LEFT Anstruther fishing village and harbour

ABOVE RIGHT A golfer pauses to assess his putt on the hallowed green at St Andrews

ST ANDREWS TO LEVEN

STAGE 1

ST ANDREWS to CRAIL

DISTANCE 13.7 miles (22km)

MAP OS Explorer 371

START AT GRID REFERENCE NO 514 167

START POINT St Andrews Cathedral

At heart, St Andrews is still a typical old Scottish burgh, with narrow wynds, courtyards and closes. The town has grown substantially and is now a major holiday and golfing centre as well as the home of Scotland's oldest university, founded in 1410 by the Augustinian priors at the cathedral. The Royal and Ancient Golf Club, founded in 1754, has its headquarters here. The West Sands stretch north for nearly 3 miles (5km) from the Old Course to Out Head on the Eden Estuary, a noted bird reserve.

The old cathedral of St Andrews is a wonderful place to start a walk. Founded in 1160, it was sacked by Presbyterian zealots, followers of John Knox, in 1559. Walk down the East Sands to the start of the coast path, climbing to the cliff-top to run along Kinkell Braes. Pass Kinkell Ness, where the rock formation known as the Rock and Spindle is very clear. There is access to the shore at this point to explore the rocks.

The path reverts to the cliff-top before dropping down again to pass the mouth of the deep, overgrown gully known as Kittock's Den. It continues along the shore, quite rough going at times, to Buddo Ness, beyond which is the eroded natural arch of Buddo Rock, which is an extraordinary formation.

Soon after Buddo Rock, turn inland towards Boarhills and turn left before the village across to Burnside Farm. Pass through the farm and then cross Kenly Water, turning left to follow the burn through a wooded area back to the coast.

The coastal path continues past an old salmon-fishing bothy on the south side of the Kinaldy Burn, to Babbet Ness and the long sandy beach of Airbow Point, before reaching the car park and picnic site at Kingsbarns. The nature of the walk is already becoming clear, with the path varying from excellent to non-existent. The scenery and birdlife more than compensate. Beyond Kingsbarns the path is more developed, as it passes through part of Cambo Estate, with a tea room a little way in from the coast. It is famous for snowdrops and has a variety of walks and accommodation. Passing one of the few plantations on this walk, the path continues to Randerston, where raised beaches can be seen, and then to Balcomie golf course.

Beyond Balcomie, Fife Ness is rounded (a real turning-point), leading from the North Sea into the broad Firth of Forth. The Dane's Dike, an ancient boundary which once ran right across the headland, is crossed, and the walk continues past the former Royal Naval air station, called HMS *Jackdaw* during World War II. It then reaches the beautiful fishing village of Crail, with its late 17th-century Customs House, Mercat Cross, and almost unbelievably picturesque harbour.

LEFT Storm clouds gather over Crail's harbour

STAGE 2

CRAIL to ST MONANS

DISTANCE 7.4 miles (11.9km)

MAP OS Explorer 371

START AT GRID REFERENCE NO 611 074

START POINT Crail harbour car park

Crail is a traditional fishing village with a 17th-century harbour. Behind the harbour and on the hill stands Crail House, built on the site of the earlier castle dating from the time of King David I in the 12th century. There is a good path all the way through this section. Leaving Crail, the path runs along the shore, with superb views of the Isle of May; a nature reserve purchased in 1989 by the Nature Conservancy Council. The reserve is managed by the Scottish Wildlife Trust, and sheep and cattle graze the area at certain times of year. It has one of the oldest lighthouses in Scotland. Summer boat trips run from Anstruther.

In a mile (1.6km) or so from Crail, the path goes through the area known as The Pans. This is one of a number of sites on the Fife coast where salt was collected; an important trade in former centuries. In a further mile (1.6km) the path reaches another set of fantastically eroded sandstone pillars and arches, called the Caiplie Caves. They can be reached only on foot. This is a place to linger, to enjoy the sea views and the birdlife, and the strange shapes carved by wind and water.

The path leads into Anstruther Easter through Cellardyke, named from cellars built here by the fisherfolk for their tackle. At Anstruther Harbour (the name is pronounced more like 'Enster' by locals) is the Scottish Fisheries Museum, full of interest and well worth a visit. The parish church of Anstruther Easter dates from 1634. Around it are narrow wynds with old buildings, including Melville's Manse, whic was built in 1590 by the minister and diarist, James Melville.

There is much to explore in the pretty town of Anstruther, but the coast beckons, and leaving through Anstruther Wester, the path passes beside another links golf course to enter Pittenweem. The name means 'place of caves'. The old kirk here dates from 1588, and in the High Street is the 16th-century Kellie Lodge.

Pittenweem is Fife's only working fishing harbour, and is the site of a cave used by St Fillan in the 7th century. It has a covered fish market and the fleet holds a gala day each summer. A further 2 miles (3km) of splendid coast-walking lead to the equally attractive village of St Monans, passing the site of the Newark Coal and Salt Company.

The route below St Monans church is tidal. At high tide walkers should follow the High Tide route signs, which follow the path inland. An information board gives details of the twin industry which flourished here from 1772 until the 1820s. There were nine salt panhouses here; production was continuous but salt could be sold only between sunrise and sunset. St Monans has been a burgh since 1621. It has fine old fishermen's cottages that have been very well restored.

Buses can be caught back to St Andrews from Anstruther, Pittenweem and St Monans.

STAGE 3

ST MONANS to LEVEN

DISTANCE 13.3 miles (21.4km)

MAPS OS Explorer 367, 370, 371

START AT GRID REFERENCE NO 526 016

START POINT St Monans harbour

SCOTLAND • FIFE COASTAL PATH

Leaving St Monans harbour, the route passes attractive cottages before crossing the burn to the superb old church, started in 1326. There is a Sailor's Loft in the north gallery and from the ceiling hangs a full-rigged model ship. The walk continues by steps cut into the rock outside the church wall and along the coast for 0.25 miles (400m) to the ruin of Newark Castle. Built by the Sandilands family in the 16th century, it was later owned by General David Leslie (the first Lord Newark), who defeated Montrose at the battle of Philiphaugh, near Selkirk, in 1645.

A good path continues to, and through, the even older ruin of Ardross Castle and on past Elie's golf course to Elie Ness and the Lady Tower, built for Lady Janet Anstruther in 1760 as a summerhouse. She often came here to bathe in the sea. Elie spreads round its rocky bay. The name may come from 'Eilean', meaning 'island'. It is worth going up to the main street of Elie to see the church, built by Sir William Scott of Ardross in 1638, with a bell-tower added a century later. Elie leads into Earlsferry, one of many places from where boats plied across the Firth. The offshore rocks are called East and West Vows.

The walk continues on the seaward side of the Earlsferry Links golf course to the foot of the cliffs at Kincraig Point. A steep climb leads to the cliff-top path, which goes over the headland. You will then reach Shell Bay, with its fine sweep of sand. Take the road and track skirting the large caravan park and cutting through plantations, to reach Cocklemill Burn Bridge. Beyond the burn is the long, lovely curve of Largo Bay. The beach may be used at low tide and can be slow-going. The high-tide route passes through Dumbarnie Links wildlife reserve, made up of calcareous dunes noted for birds, butterflies and flowers. Inland rises Largo Law; a volcanic stub reaching just under 1,000ft (300m) and a superb viewpoint.

Nearer Largo the path improves. Lower Largo, the name meaning a 'sunny slope', was the birthplace of Alexander Selkirk, the inspiration for Daniel Defoe's famous novel *Robinson Crusoe*. He ran away to sea, rebelled and was placed on the island of Juan Fernandez in the Pacific, where he remained for four years entirely alone before being rescued. There is a statue of Selkirk in Main Street. Past the Crusoe Hotel, the walk continues through Lundin Links, locally dubbed the 'Scottish Riviera', and along glorious sands towards Leven. The whole stretch between Lundin and Leven has golf greens by the shore. Continue by Leven Links and along the promenade to the River Leven, in the shadow of the power station chimney.

LEVEN TO INVERKEITHING

STAGE 4
LEVEN to KIRKCALDY
DISTANCE 9.8 miles (15.8km)
MAPS OS Explorer 367, 370, 371
START AT GRID REFERENCE NO 381 005
START POINT Leven bus station

From Leven to Buckhaven the coast is not accessible. Cross the River Leven by the A955 bridge, on the site of the former 'Bawbee Bridge', so called because of the toll (bawbee) payable. Turn left to walk through Methil past the large oil platform construction yard. Oil rigs are often anchored off shore here. Continue into Buckhaven, turning left at College Street and taking the next small road left to the shore.

Walk round a headland and continue towards East Wemyss. In a mile (1.6km) the site of the former gasworks is reached, with the first of a series of impressive caves eroded into the sandstone cliffs. Some of the caves contain wall drawings: several can be explored with care (and a torch). Just past Jonathan's Cave (named after a nailmaker who lived here for some years in the 18th century) a diversion up the cliff path leads to the ruin of Macduff Castle, the oldest part of which dates from the 13th century. In East Wemyss, a visit to the Wemyss Caves Education Centre, with its displays on the ancient pictish carvings drawn in Wemyss Caves, is an interesting feature along this shoreline and worth a detour. It opens on Sunday afternoons in the summer, in the primary school basement.

Unless the tide is out you must walk through the Michael Pit, between East and West Wemyss. There has been a great deal of coal mining in this area over the centuries. The Michael Pit closed after a tragic accident in 1967 when nine miners died in an underground fire. Continue along an old railway siding and then by woodland to reach the imposing Wemyss Castle, started in the 14th century. The name Wemyss comes from the Gaelic word *uamh*, meaning 'cave'.

The path continues past St Adrian's Church into West Wemyss, with its fine 16th-century Tolbooth. From West Wemyss, a lane and then a path leads to the 15th-century St Mary's Chapel, disused for the past 200 years. Another inland diversion is now needed around the Frances Colliery. From Blair Point steps lead up towards the pithead and thus to the A955 road. After the railway crossing, walk down through Dysart to the shore at Pan Ha; an attractive area with finely restored houses.

From Dysart harbour, the walk continues through Ravenscraig Park, with the ruin of Ravenscraig Castle, to Pathhead Sands. The road must again be taken to pass round Kirkcaldy harbour and reach the superb long sands. The famous Links Market is still held here each Easter. It lasts a week and has all sorts of stalls and fairground attractions.

🚉 *Bus and railway stations are easily reached from the shore. Trains go to Leuchars, with a bus connection back to St Andrews.*

STAGE 5
KIRKCALDY to ABERDOUR
DISTANCE 10.1 miles (16.3km)
MAPS OS Explorer 350, 367
START AT GRID REFERENCE N I 279 914
START POINT Kirkcaldy bus station

After enjoying the splendid walk along Kirkcaldy's promenade (or on the fine sands), cross the Teil Burn by the road bridge and take the lane down to Seafield Beach (past the bus garage). Ahead is the site of Seafield Colliery.

From here the walk runs parallel to the railway line for nearly 3 miles (5km) to Kinghorn, passing the ruined 15th-century Seafield Tower. Seals can often be seen on the offshore rocks on this stretch. Remains of limekilns are passed, as is a large cave (near Abden Home) which can be explored at low tide. A path leads up from the metal bridge over to the cave. Take extra care here, as there is a quite substantial drop to the rocks below. Notice Abden Home, a former poor law house, which is now converted into flats.

The path continues round a grassy bay and improves as it reaches the outskirts of Kinghorn; a name which may mean 'head of the corner'. The coast does take a swing from south to west here, round Pettycur, which was once a very important trading harbour. Another diversion is needed at Kinghorn: take the path between the caravan park and the railway line, pass under the railway viaduct and go through a playpark to the road leading back to the shore.

ABOVE Forth Road Bridge, from Queensferry
RIGHT Ravenscraig Castle, Kirkcaldy

Kinghorn has an attractive small harbour and excellent views of Inchkeith Island in the Firth. Take the road through Pettycur. From the far side of Pettycur Bay, it is best to follow the A921 into Burntisland. The shore can be walked at low tide but it is slow-going. The road walk has excellent views and you pass the tall statue of King Alexander III, killed here in 1286 when his horse stumbled in the dark and he fell over the cliff.

Burntisland gets its name from times when the land was indeed burnt, to improve its productivity. Turn down Lochies Road and then follow the promenade to the Beacon Leisure Centre. Follow the road beside the Centre, then turn down Links Place to join the High Street. Just past the post office, the road bends right to go up the hill and then down Kirkton Road. At the pedestrian crossing, turn left and follow the path beside the new housing estate. From here to Aberdour there is a good path all the way, first on the landward side of the railway past Carron Harbour and then recrossing it to the seaward side, passing the Starley Falls. The area is noted for its liverworts; flat seaweed-like plants. The path continues through woodland to Silversands Bay, a popular picnic area, then up Hawkcraig Cliffs with good views of Inchcolm, another of the Forth islands. Walk round the attractive harbour at Aberdour, cross the Dour Burn and continue to the railway station.

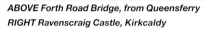 *To return to Kirkcaldy or St Andrews (via Leuchars and bus connection), take a train from Kinghorn, Burntisland and Aberdour.*

STAGE 6

ABERDOUR to INVERKEITHING

DISTANCE 5.9 miles (9.5km)
MAPS OS Explorer 350, 367
START AT GRID REFERENCE NT 191 854
START POINT Aberdour station

From Aberdour to Dalgety Bay, which is a 3-mile (5km) walk, the coast is largely out of reach, due to rocks, a golf course, and the Braefoot Bay oil terminal. From the station follow the main road round a double bend and turn left on the road leading in about a mile (1.6km) to St Colme House. The house, built in 1835 for the Commissioner of the Moray Estates, is now apartments.

Past the turning to the house, walk under the road serving the oil terminal and, in a further 300yds (275m), turn left down stone steps to walk beside a field to another minor road. Turn right towards Dalgety Bay. In 0.5 miles (800m), where the road bends right, divert to the shore to see St Bridget's Kirk, dating originally from the 13th century.

From the kirk, continue along the shore path. To the right, you will see the houses of Dalgety Bay. The path goes through Crownhill Wood. Offshore, seals may be spotted and there is a good variety of birdlife. Pass a sailing club to reach Donibristle House. Its central section was destroyed by fire in 1858, but the superb wrought-iron gateway still stands, said to have been a gift from William of Orange to the Earl of Moray, whose home this once was.

The path continues past Donibristle Chapel, and some houses, to cross Downing Point and then Hopewood Point to reach St David's Bay; once a busy port exporting coal from mines at Fordell, just inland. Seafield House, built in the mid-19th century for the Fordell Estate manager, is passed, and then a large boundary cairn.

The Forth Bridges are visible and the end of the walk is near. Go through the former Preston Quarry, which produced greenstone, and swing right into Inverkeithing. The town has a number of interesting old buildings, including the town hall of 1770. Inverkeithing Museum is in the 14th-century Friary, which has lovely gardens. The walk ends at Inverkeithing Station.

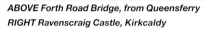 *From Inverkeithing, a return journey can be made by train to Aberdour, Burntisland, Kington, Kirkcaldy or St Andrews (via Leuchars and a bus connection).*

ⓘ **PLACES TO VISIT**

• **SCOTLAND'S SECRET BUNKER**
www.secretbunker.co.uk
☎ 01333 310301
Around 4 miles (6.5km) to the west of Crail on the B940 is this unique attraction. It is not a good road to walk, so you will need a taxi, but you will be rewarded with the exploration of the underground nuclear attack refuge that was built during the Cold War years. Blast doors hide a warren of reinforced rooms designed to house up to 300 people. Open daily Mar–Oct.

• **SCOTTISH FISHERIES MUSEUM**
www.scotfishmuseum.org
☎ 01333 310628
This award-winning museum on the harbour at Anstruther has displays on all aspects of fishing, from the earliest rafts used to a modern herring drifter. The boatbuilder's yards, forge, smokehouse, and fishmonger's are all represented here, too. Open daily all year.

• **KIRKCALDY MUSEUM AND ART GALLERY**
www.museumsgalleriesscotland.org.uk
☎ 01592 583213
Here you will find local history displays, and paintings by the Glasgow Boys and the Scottish Colourists. There are also two by Fife painter, Jack Vettriano; the only ones owned by a Scottish museum. The tea room displays local Wemyss Ware pottery. Open daily all year.

• **ABERDOUR CASTLE**
www.historic-scotland.gov.uk
☎ 01383 860519
The pretty ruins of this castle, in historic Aberdour, make a pleasant stop. There are rooms still intact, including a walled garden and tea room. Open daily Apr–Oct, Sat–Wed Nov–Mar.

Index

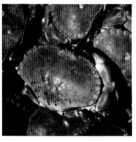

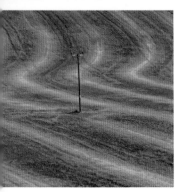

Acknowledgements

The Automobile Association would like to thank the following photographers and picture libraries for their assistance in the preparation of this book.

Abbreviations for the picture credits are as follows: (t) top; (b) bottom; (l) left; (r) right; (c) centre; (AA) AA World Travel Library.

1 AA/J Tims; 2t AA/M Busselle; 2ct AA/J Tims; 2c AA/J Miller; 2b AA/N Setchfield; 4t AA/S Day; 4tc AA/S McBride; 4tr Liquid Light/Alamy; 4cr Tom Mackie/Alamy; 4bc AA Mackie; 4b AA/J Smith; 6l AA/T Mackie; 6r AA/T Mackie; 7 AA/A Mockford & N Bonetti; 8tl AA/J Tims; 8tr Roy Childs/Alamy; 8c AA/H Williams; 8b AA/N Setchfield; 10t AA Mackie; 10c Jeff Morgan 15/Alamy; 10b AA/I Burgum; 11t AA/T Mackie; 11c David Robertson/Alamy; 11b Kevin White/Alamy; 12/13 AA/D Hall; 14 AA/M Hamblin; 15t AA Burton; 15b AA/A Burton; 16t AA/A Burton; 16c AA/A Burton; 16b AA/N Hicks; 17l AA/N Hicks; 17c Robert Convery/Alamy; 17r AA/N Hicks; 18 Richard Downer/Alamy; 19 AA Hicks; 20t AA/G Edwardes; 20b Thomas Dobner - Dartmoor Collection/Alamy; 21l AA/G Edwardes; 21r AA/G Edwardes; 22 AA/G Edwardes; 22/23 AA/G Edwardes; 23 Da Lichtneker/Alamy; 24/25 Thomas Dobner 2008/Alamy; 26l AA/P Baker; 26r Rachel Husband/Alamy; 27l Craig Joiner Photography/Alamy; 27r AA/M Moody; 28c Celtic Collect - Homer Sykes/Alamy; 28b Steven May/Alamy; 29 Antony Spencer/Alamy; 30l AA/H Palmer; 30r BlueSkyStock/Alamy; 31 AA/D Hall; 32tl Tim Graham/Alamy; 32tr AA/K Dora 32c AA/S Day; 33l AA/S Day; 33r AA/S Day; 34/35 Available Light Photography/Alamy; 36l AA/A Burton; 36c AA/A Burton; 36r AA/A Burton; 37l AA/D Forss; 37r AA/S McBri 38t AA/A Burton; 38c AA/A Burton; 38b AA/A Burton; 39l AA/S McBride; 39r AA/A Burton; 40tl AA/A Burton; 40tr AA/A Burton; 40c AA/A Burton; 41l Ian Badley/Alamy; 4 Available Light Photography/Alamy; 42t AA/J Tims; 42c AA/J Tims; 42b AA/J Tims; 43 AA/J Tims; 44t AA/J Tims; 44c AA/J Tims; 44b AA/J Tims; 45 AA/J Tims; 46t AA/J Tim 46c AA/J Tims; 47 AA/J Tims; 48l AA/M Busselle; 48c AA/J Miller; 48r John Warburton-Lee Photography/Alamy; 50tl Howard Davies/Alamy; 50tr John Warburton-L Photography/Alamy; 50c AA/J Miller; 51 AA/J Miller; 52t AA/J Miller; 52c AA/J Miller; 52b AA/J Miller; 52/53 AA/J Miller; 54c AA; 54b AA/J Miller; 55 AA/J Miller; 56/57 AA Miller; 58c Greg Balfour Evans/Alamy; 58b Martin Beddall/Alamy; 59l Seb Rogers/Alamy; 59r Linda Kennedy/Alamy; 60tl Rob Cole/Alamy; 60tr PBstock/Alamy; 60c GoSeeFo Alamy; 61 John Miller/Alamy; 62 AA/J Tims; 63 Realimage/Alamy; 64tl Christopher Holt/Alamy; 64tr AA/J Tims; 64c AA/J Tims; 65t AA/J Tims; 65b John Miller/Alamy; 66c AA Miller; 66b Ian Goodrick/Alamy; 67t Cliff Hunt/Alamy; 67tc Tony Watson/Alamy; 67c AA/J Miller; 67b AA/J Miller; 68t AA/J Miller; 68c The National Trust Photolibrary/Alamy; Tony Watson/Alamy; 69r Robert Bird/Alamy; 70t AA/J Miller; 70c AA/J Miller; 70b Tony Watson/Alamy; 70/71 AA/J Miller; 72t Ian Goodrick/Alamy; 72c still light/Alamy; 73 AA Miller; 74l AA/J Tims; 74c AA/J Tims; 74r AA/J Tims; 75 AA/J Tims; 76t AA/J Tims; 76c AA/J Tims; 76b AA/J Tims; 77l AA/J Tims; 77r AA/J Tims; 78t AA/J Tims; 78c AA/J Tim 78/79 AA/J Tims; 79t AA/J Tims; 79c AA/J Tims; 80t AA/J Tims; 80c AA/J Tims; 81 AA/J Tims; 82/83 AA/J Tims; 84bl AA/D Hall; 84bc Avico Ltd/Alamy; 84b AA/H Palmer; Cotswolds Photo Library/Alamy; 86t AA/C Jones; 86c AA/M Birkitt; 87 Tim Gainey/Alamy; 88t Anna Stowe Botanica/Alamy; 88c Tim Gainey/Alamy; 89t AA/J Tims; 89c AA Hicks; 90c AA/M Moody; 90b AA/N Setchfield; 91t AA/N Setchfield; 91b AA/N Setchfield; 92tl AA/N Setchfield; 92tr Paul Shearman/Alamy; 92c Quentin Bargate/Alamy; 9 AA/S & O Mathews; 93 Picturebank/Alamy; 94t Justin Kase zsixz/Alamy; 94c The National Trust Photolibrary/Alamy; 94b Les Polders/Alamy; 95 AA/T Mackie; 96/97 Gr Balfour Evans/Alamy; 98c AA/C Warren; 98b Rosemary Roberts/Alamy; 99 AA/C Warren; 100t Robert Conley/Alamy; 100c AA/C Warren; 100b AA/C Warren; 101t Rich Warren; 101c AA/C Warren; 102t AA/M Moody; 102c CW Images/Alamy; 102/103 CW Images/Alamy; 103t Neil McAllister/Alamy; 104c Adrian Sherratt/Alamy; 104b Richa Naude/Alamy; 105tl graham bell/Alamy; 105tr The Photolibrary Wales/Alamy; 106t Richard Naude/Alamy; 106c CW Images/Alamy; 107 AA/I Burgum; 108c Justin Kase z1C Alamy; 108b Graham Bell/Alamy; 109t Graham Bell/Alamy; 109b Graham Bell/Alamy; 110c AA/J Tims; 110b Graham Bell/Alamy; 111c AA/J Tims; 111l Jeff Morgan 12/Alamy; 1 Jeff Morgan 15/Alamy; 112/113 AA/C Jones; 114 AA/A J Hopkins; 115t Liquid Light/Alamy; 115c AA/C Jones; 115b AA/D Santillo; 116c AA/M Moody; 116b AA/H Williams; 1 AA/C Jones; 118t AA/C Jones; 118cl AA/H Williams; 118cr AA/C Jones; 118bl travelib prime/Alamy; 118br AA/C Jones; 119 AA/C Jones; 120t AA/C Jones; 120ct AA/C Jone 120c AA/C Jones; 120b AA/C Jones; 120/121 AA/D Santillo; 121 AA/D Santillo; 122/123 AA/T Mackie; 124c AA/J Welsh; 124b Jeremy Pardoe/Alamy; 125 AA/R Surman; 12 AA/C Jones; 126c AA/C Jones; 126b John Keates/Alamy; 127 AA/M Adelman; 128ll AA/T Mackie; 128lr AA/M Birkill; 128c AA/T Mackie; 128b AA/M Birkill; 129ll AA/N Coate 129tr Roy Childs/Alamy; 129b AA/T Mackie; 130tl AA/T Mackie; 130tr AA/T Mackie; 130c AA/T Mackie; 130b Realimage/Alamy; 131l AA/M Birkitt; 131r AA/T Mackie; 132/1 AA/T Mackie; 134t AA/T Mackie; 134b Mike Booth/Alamy; 135c Holmes Garden Photos/Alamy; 135b Dave Porter/Alamy; 136t Liam Grant/Alamy; 136c Robert Estall pho agency/Alamy; 136b AA/D Forss; 137 Tom Mackie/Alamy; 138t Rod Edwards/Alamy; 138c Steven Sheppardson/Alamy; 138b AA/T Mackie; 139 Dave Porter/Alamy; 140t jo gibbs/Alamy; 140c jon gibbs/Alamy; 140b AA/T Mackie; 141 AA/T Mackie; 142t AA/T Mackie; 142c AA/A J Hopkins; 142b AA/T Mackie; 143l AA/S & O Mathews; 143r AA Mackie; 144 AA/T Mackie; 145 Paul Heinrich/Alamy; 146t Tom Mackie/Alamy; 146c Karen Fuller/Alamy; 146b AA/A Baker; 147 AA/T Mackie; 148t AA/T Mackie; 148c AA Mackie; 149l AA/A Perkins; 149r AA/T Mackie; 150/151 AA/A Mockford & N Bonetti; 152c AA/T Mackie; 152b UK City Images/Alamy; 153 Dave McAleavy Images/Alamy; 15 Gary Stones/Alamy; 154c Stan Pritchard/Alamy; 155 Nigel Ollis/Alamy; 156tl David Waters/Alamy; 156tr AA/R Eames; 156c AA/J Mottershaw; 157 Andrew Crowhurst/Alam 158 David Waters/Alamy; 158/159 AA/T Mackie; 159 AA/T Mackie; 160l Julie Woodhouse/Alamy; 160r AA/T Mackie; 161 AA/T Mackie; 162t AA/J Morrison; 162c Pa Thompson Images/Alamy; 162b AA/D Tarn; 163 AA/T Mackie; 164t AA/T Mackie; 164c AA/T Mackie; 166 Peter Crighton/Alamy; 166/167 AA/A Mockford & N Bonetti; 167 AA Mackie; 168l AA/P Bennett; 168r AA/M Kipling; 169 AA/P Baker; 170tl AA/P Bennett; 170tr AA/D Clapp; 170c AA/D Clapp; 170b AA/R Newton; 171 Mark Sunderland/Alam 172 Paul White - Real Yorkshire/Alamy; 173l AA/S & O Mathews; 173c AA/T Mackie; 173r AA/J Tims; 174/175 AA/J Tims; 176t Powered by Light/Alan Spencer/Alamy; 176c Joh Bentley/Alamy; 176b Neil Holmes Freelance Digital/Alamy; 177t AA/S Day; 177c Les Gibbon/Alamy; 178t Steve Hickey/Alamy; 178c Neil Holmes Freelance Digital/Alamy; 178 Les Gibbon/Alamy; 179 Mike Kipling Photography/Alamy; 180t Mark Buckle/Alamy; 180c John Bentley/Alamy; 181t AA/D Clapp; 181c AA/D Clapp; 182t Stephen Miller/Alam 182b Michael Sayles/Alamy; 183(i) AA/T Mackie; 183(ii) AA/E A Bowness; 183(iii) AA/S Day; 183(iv) AA/T Mackie; 183(v) AA/A Mockford & N Bonetti; 184tl David Martyn Hughes Alamy; 184tr AA/A Mockford & N Bonetti; 184cl Nigel Ollis/Alamy; 185l AA/S Day; 185r AA/T Mackie; 186tl AA/A Mockford & N Bonetti; 186tr AA/E A Bowness; 186cl AA/ Mockford & N Bonetti; 186b AA/T Mackie; 187tl AA/A Mockford & N Bonetti; 187tr AA/T Mackie; 187cl AA/T Mackie; 187c AA/R Coulam; 188tl AA/R Coulam; 188tr AA/ Mockford & N Bonetti; 188c AA/R Coulam; 188b Jason Friend/Alamy; 190t Jason Friend/Alamy; 190cl AA/R Newton; 190cr AA/J Smith; 190/191 Graeme Peacock/Alamy; 19 AA/J Hunt; 192t AA/R Coulam; 192c AA/R Coulam; 193tl AA/R Coulam; 193tr AA/T Mackie; 193c AA/R Coulam; 194t Jason Friend/Alamy; 194c AA/R Coulam; 195 Jaso Friend/Alamy; 196/197 AA/S Day; 198t AA/S Day; 198b AA/S Anderson; 200t AA/D W Robertson; 200c AA/M Hamblin; 201 David Robertson/Alamy; 202t David Robertson Alamy; 202c UK City Images/Alamy; 203 Craig Roberts/Alamy; 204t drpics/Alamy; 204c colinspics/Alamy; 204/205 AA/R Weir; 206t Peter Chisholm/Alamy; 206c AA/N Hicks 207t David Lyons/Alamy; 207b Lonely Planet Images/Alamy; 208/209 AA/S Day; 210t AA/M Taylor; 210c Epicscotland/Alamy; 210b Craig Buchanan/Alamy; 211 Ma Photographics/Alamy; 212t Jim Henderson/Alamy; 212c Jim Henderson/Alamy; 213t AA/J Smith; 213c AA/S Anderson; 214t David Gowans/Alamy; 214c Holmes Garde Photos/Alamy; 214/215 David Gowans/Alamy; 215tr AA/S Anderson; 215cl AA/J Smith; 215c AA/J Smith; 216c AA/R Weir; 216bl David Gowans/Alamy; 216br AA/J Smith; 21 AA/M Taylor; 218t Stephen Finn/Alamy; 218c Phil Seale/Alamy; 218b D Hale-Sutton/Alamy; 219t John Devlin/Alamy; 219c Ian Paterson/Alamy; 220(i) AA/T Mackie; 220(ii) AA/ Mackie; 220(iii) AA/J Tims; 220(iv) AA/D Tarn; 220(v) AA/N Setchfield; 221(i) AA/J Tims; 221(ii) AA/N Setchfield; 221(iii) AA/J Tims; 221(iv) AA/D Hall; 221(v) AA/T Mackie; 222 AA/J Tims; 222(ii) AA/A Mockford & N Bonetti; 222(iii) AA/J Miller; 222(iv) AA/R Coulam; 222(v) AA/J Tims; 223(i) AA/N Setchfield; 223(ii) AA/M Haywood; 223(iii) AA/J Hun 223(iv) AA/L Noble; 223(v) AA/J Hunt; 224l AA/J Tims; 224r AA/J Tims.

Every effort has been made to trace the copyright holders, and we apologize in advance for any accidental errors. We would be happy to apply the corrections in the followin edition of this publication.